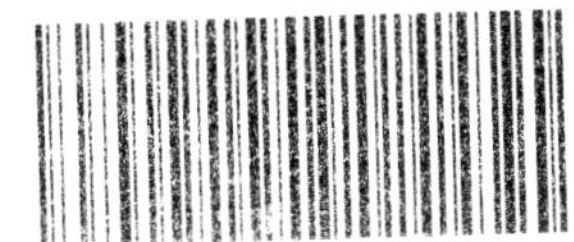

The Politics of Antisemitic Prejudice

The Politics of Antisemitic Prejudice

The Waldheim Phenomenon in Austria

Richard Mitten

Westview Press

BOULDER • SAN FRANCISCO • OXFORD

For My Mother

Published in 1992 in the United States of America by Westview Press, Inc., 5500 Central Avenue, Boulder, Colorado 80301-2877, and in the United Kingdom by Westview Press, 36 Lonsdale Road, Summertown, Oxford OX2 7EW

Library of Congress Cataloging-in-Publication Data
Mitten, Richard.
The politics of antisemitic prejudice : the Waldheim phenomenon in Austria / by Richard Mitten.
p. cm.
Includes bibliographical references.
ISBN 0-8133-7630-0
1. Austria—Politics and government—1945– 2. Waldheim, Kurt.
3. Antisemitism—Austria—History—20th century. I. Title.
DB99.2.M58 1992
943.605—dc20 92-14286
CIP

Printed and bound in the United States of America

The paper used in this publication meets the requirements of the American National Standard for Permanence of Paper for Printed Library Materials Z39.48-1984.

10 9 8 7 6 5 4 3 2

Contents

Acknowledgments

Writing acknowledgments for one's first book presents its problems. One strongly inclines to utilize the opportunity to pay tribute to any and all who might have contributed something along the meandering path leading to the book's completion. Having decided not to pay homage to the elementary school teacher who first taught me to read and write, I nonetheless hope that those since then who have been positive influences on my intellectual development, but whom I have chosen not to mention here, will forgive my somewhat arbitrary criteria of selection and not infer any ingratitude on my part for the contributions they have made. The line had to be drawn somewhere.

First of all, I would like to express my sincerest thanks to my mother, Henry Etta Mitten, to whom this book is gratefully dedicated. She has offered unstinting moral and frequent material support while I was acquiring my academic training and, later, while I was gathering the material to write this book. She has also developed an enviable ability to feign interest in arcane pieces of Waldheimiana heard for the twentieth time.

The idea for this book first began to take shape in 1986, and its initial outlines emerged from the frequent discussions I had then with Misha Glenny, at that time the *Guardian* correspondent in Vienna. I would like to pay proper acknowledgment to Misha here, since in some cases I can no longer remember who first suggested which ideas to whom. In a similar vein, it was largely Frederick Praeger's confidence in this book that provided me with the impetus needed to rework the original study, written in German, into its current form. I would like to thank him for his encouragement and especially for having suggested the book's title. I hope that in his eyes the final product has justified the faith he placed in me.

Given the way the Waldheim controversy developed, with individual items about his past surfacing from the most divergent sources, those of us trying to gain an overview of the affair were heavily dependent upon one another's assistance. My own investigation of Waldheim's wartime career began after I had completed most of the research on the election campaign itself, so I was able to benefit from the prior efforts of many. Among those to whom I owe the greatest debt for my understanding of Waldheim's wartime past, either because they provided documents or background information or indispensable points of clarification, are Hanspeter Born, Hubertus Czernin, Walter Manoschek, Hans Safrian and Hans Schafranek. My colleagues on the Thames Television–Home Box Office coproduction *Waldheim: A Commission of In-*

quiry, in particular Roland Bettschart, Ed Braman, Nick Goodrick-Clarke, Tim House, Mark Mazower, Felix Moreau and Alexandra Wiesler, were all important sources of information and offered new ways of thinking more generally about the problem of Waldheim and criminality. They were good for a great many laughs as well.

Intellectual debts of a more general kind are exceedingly difficult to pin down, but I could not in good faith avoid mentioning two. During the years I spent at Cambridge, John Dunn was not only an exemplar of rigorous critical thinking; his teachings had more influence on the way I think about history and politics than he probably realized. I hope that he will recognize in my musings here something of the wisdom he tried to impart to me. Similarly, over the past several years my discussions with Tony Judt have been the proximate occasion of virtually every important new idea I have had. The paucity of these latter, of course, ought not reflect unfavorably on the quality of his contributions. In any case, I hope he will understand just how significant these conversations were for me.

As anyone who has worked in Austrian libraries will know, the effort involved in gaining access to important sources, especially those in English, is frequently of the Sisyphean variety. I am therefore particularly grateful for the assistance I received from Elisabeth Klamper from the Dokumentationsarchiv des österreichischen Widerstandes and from Günter Anger and Eva Muhm from the Amerika Haus library in Vienna. Their assistance saved me countless hours of work and considerable expense. A vote of sincere thanks also goes to Eli Rosenbaum and Elan Steinberg, who generously provided me with essential materials related to the World Jewish Congress's involvement in the Waldheim debate.

Various parts of this book have been read and criticized by colleagues and friends. In addition to providing a great deal of expert knowledge, Walter Manoschek also read the drafts of what would eventually become Chapters 4 and 5. Though he may still despair that I could not meet more of his criticisms, I am grateful for his stimulating comments. Both Tony Judt and Quintin Hoare read an earlier version of Chapter 9, and they may take most of the credit for whatever virtues still remain. Apart from correcting some careless errors in Chapter 2, Robert Knight's keen eyes were also able to detect an embarrassing number of the indecent linguistic liberties that several years of reading, writing, speaking and thinking in German had taken with my native English. That not more stylistic and semantic infelicities survived is due principally to Carolyn Richards's very careful reading of the completed manuscript and her invariably helpful suggestions for change. I would also like to express my gratitude to the anonymous reader engaged by Westview for her or his very sensitive reading of and valuable comments on the manuscript.

In addition, several people have helped me in various ways toward the completion of this book, not all of which can be so easily specified but all of which was greatly appreciated. They will all, I trust, know what I mean: Michael Agar, Sam Beck, Neil Belton, Gerhard Botz, John Bunzl, Georg Heinrich, Patricia Hilden, Istvan Hont, Harry Kuhner, Alan Levy, Branka Magas, Nelson Mitten, Jürgen Pelikan, Christoph

Reinprecht, Robert Rotenberg, Anton Staudinger and Jonathan Steinberg.

Finally, I would like to express my gratitude to Ruth Wodak, to whom I owe the biggest debt. She has earned a place in nearly every category I have listed above and in several additional, as well. Ruth has served as a personal model to me, even though her distinguished and exacting scholarship represents a standard against which I hesitate to measure my own modest endeavor. I hope that she will find something of value in this book, for in many ways it is her book, too.

None of those who have given their time, of course, bears any responsibility for the remaining deficiencies of the book, but this study would have looked far different without their efforts.

—Richard Mitten
Vienna

1

Introduction: "*Homo austriacus*" Agonistes

Gaiety, a clear conscience, the happy deed, the confidence in the future—all these depend, for the individual as well as for a people, on there being a line that separates the forseeable, the light, from the unilluminable and the darkness; on one's knowing just when to forget, when to remember; on one's instinctively feeling when necessary to perceive historically, when unhistorically. The reader is invited to reflect on precisely this sentence: the unhistorical and the historical are equally necessary to the health of an individual, a people and a culture.

—Friedrich Nietzsche[1]

Karl Kraus, noted Viennese cultural critic in the early decades of this century, reportedly wrote in 1913, "Through its political disasters, Austria has at last caught the attention of the wider world. No one will confuse it with Australia any more." Vienna's mayor Helmut Zilk, in New York to open an exhibition of fin-de-siècle Austrian art immediately after Kurt Waldheim's election in 1986, may secretly have wished his name were Bruce and have wanted to exchange his Klimt paintings and Veltliner wine for a boomerang and a can of Foster's. To his everlasting good fortune Zilk was spared the added embarrassment of opening "Dream and Reality" (*Traum und Wirklichkeit*), the title of the exhibition's Viennese predecessor: the scaled-down American version bore the more anodyne name "Vienna 1900." Reality was definitely not for export.

If mayor Zilk was able to avoid a small degree of discomfiture, however, Austria itself has of late been spared very little. Traces of glycol alcohol were discovered in Austrian wines, millions of taxshillings were squandered in misguided oil speculation by a nationalized trading firm, and then Defense Minister Friedhelm Frischenschlager warmly welcomed home convicted war criminal Walter Reder, a man he termed "the last prisoner of war." Such scandals had served to produce an unwanted patina on the luster of Austria's international image, cultivated, as it were, to convince the world that Beethoven was an Austrian, Hitler a German.

All translations from the German have been made by the author unless cited from English-language secondary sources in which they had already been translated.

The fleeting hopes that Austria could corner the antifreeze market with its confiscated wine, with the revenue solve the debt crisis and quietly set about preparing for the Mozart bicentennial were permanently dashed by Kurt Waldheim's reappearance on the international stage. The controversy surrounding the past of Austria's favorite son and the ensuing international attention given to the inconvenient series of anniversaries (*"Anschluss," "Reichskristallnacht,"* etc.) have created a public relations disaster. Images of cherubic young boys, Lipizzaner horses and delectable Mozartkugels have been displaced by those of Wehrmacht soldiers, antisemitic slurs and cheering crowds on "Heroes' Square" (Heldenplatz). The hills of Salzburg, once alive with the sound of music, seemed to reverberate anachronistically with the pounding of jackboots. Austria's rear guard international campaign of artistic self-promotion has done little to assuage this unwanted vitiation of Austria's good name abroad. The dream of what Austria once was has given way to the reality of what under Waldheim it appeared to have become. Basking in the reflected glory of fin-de-siècle artistic brilliance could not obscure the less exalted coeval features of Austria's political past.

It is not as though Austria's public relations peripeteia has not commanded the sedulous attention of politicians great and small. Former Foreign Minister Peter Jankowitsch, whose term in office set a record for its brevity, did his best to prolong his chances of serving the Socialist-Conservative grand coalition by summoning prominent Austrian historians to a campaign against a foreign colleague whose "hair-raising theses" about Austrian history—published abroad—did little more than summarize the findings of Austria's own critical historians. Jankowitsch's appeal did not enjoy the success of Kurt Waldheim's earlier calls to close ranks against the foreign enemy, but hope apparently sprang eternal on the academic front. During Waldheim's election campaign, several prominent Austrian historians and political scientists put both their intellectual integrity and their political judgment on the line by issuing a statement disparaging ostensible interpretations of documents made by Robert Herzstein, the historian who had discovered the first substantial batch of documents related to Waldheim's past. At least one of the interpretations they ascribed to Herzstein, however, had been invented by the historians themselves. Shortly thereafter, several self-described scholars close to the Austrian People's Party (ÖVP), which had supported Waldheim in the election, offered their own modest contribution to Kurt Waldheim's domestic rehabilitation in the form of a book entitled *Die Kampagne.* Since then both the international historians' commission, established to investigate Waldheim's wartime service, and the solemn commemorations identified with the year 1988 have come and gone. Waldheim has been cleared of responsibility in the deaths of Allied commandos by the British government, but his chances of visiting the Queen have not improved. Meanwhile, attention has shifted eastwards in Europe and official Austria, more embarrassed than incensed about Waldheim's isolation but relieved that the end of his presidency was in sight, has been able to breathe a bit easier.

For his part, Waldheim, sensing an ethical desideratum in the life of the nation, devoted himself after his election to reversing the perceived decline in values among his fellow Austrians. As country after country withdrew invitations they had extended to the Austrian president when his name was Kirchschläger, Waldheim, as the West German magazine *Der Spiegel* wrote, "dug himself in." Conveniently displaying discretion in his choice of travel destinations, Waldheim instead exercised his moral authority at every local trade fair, garden show and memorial service that would have him. U.S. Attorney General Edwin Meese's "watch list" decision suggested that not everyone's memory was as short as Waldheim's own, and while the Pope's accedence to persistent demands from Waldheim's office to extend an official invitation to the self-described "practicing Catholic," Jordanian King Hussein's defiance of "Zionist" circles, or even Waldheim's spectacular "rescue mission" to Iraq after the occupation of Kuwait, may temporarily have broken President Waldheim's diplomatic isolation, he was unable officially to set foot in any Western European country during his incumbency. And if Waldheim was able to derive some personal satisfaction from his meeting during the Salzburg Festival with presidents Vaclav Havel of Czechoslovakia and Richard von Weiszäcker of Germany, two internationally recognized moral authorities, it did not portend a more promising travel schedule for the Austrian president.

Today Austria is but a rump remnant of the once expansive Hapsburg empire, its cultural pretensions correspondingly modest. If, however, the sardonic acerbity of a Karl Kraus seems directed at the rhetorical flatulence of a Kurt Waldheim, then this is perhaps no accident. What binds the age of the *Neue Freie Presse,* arguably the greatest liberal newspaper in fin-de-siècle Europe, with that of its contemporary very pale imitation and legatee *Die Presse,* is not merely the selfsame land mass. It is, rather, an abiding political culture which has survived two republics and two fascist interludes, a "political philosophy of muddling through," as novelist Robert Musil called it, which has created its own distinctive vocabulary and spawned cultural stereotypes so enduring that Kraus's wit rings instantly true even today. Although it is more, it is also the culture of Herr Karl, a fictional but deadly accurate ideal-typical Austrian "little man" immortalized by the late actor and cabaret performer Helmut Qualtinger. Avatar of a certain strain of Austrian *Gemütlichkeit,* that nearly untranslatable Germanic cultural something so inadequately captured by the English "conviviality" or "atmosphere," Herr Karl was always around: never quite close enough to be blessed with praise, but far enough away not to be tainted with guilt. This is Kurt Waldheim's Austria.

Yet the Waldheim phenomenon in Austria is not merely, and perhaps not even principally, the story of one man's cloying opportunism and his attempts to conceal or deny the more odious forms which this took. Waldheim's election campaign roused many Austrians from the slumber in which the historical fantasies of the postwar Austrian national identity had found such comfortable repose. The international attention given to Austria during and since the election has forced the architects and contemporary bearers of the country's postwar political culture to reckon with a history at odds with the official myth of Austria's collective innocence of a Nazi past. The response to criticisms from abroad was a predictably defensive one, while the idiom they employed, rebutting the impugnation of their past with a catalogue of their virtues in the present, was a familiar one. In the United States this was widely viewed as a particularly egregious moral delinquency; in the provinces of Austria as the legitimate indignation of an unjustly accused innocent, in this case both Waldheim and Austria.

The dictum of Fritz Mauthner, linguistic philosopher in Vienna at the turn of the century, "only that which you are able to express in words are you able to think," was given a manifestly Orwellian twist in the language of the Waldheim candidacy. Although voting for the office of president, Waldheim supporters understood the proper attributive adjective preceding campaign not to be electoral, but vilification. For most of the Austrian press the scandal involved in the exposure of documents casting light on Waldheim's elusive biography lay not in this past and Waldheim's somewhat labile commitment to the truth, but in the act of publication. Campaign slogans which had served as potent electoral assets before the disclosures of the gaps in Waldheim's curriculum vitae were transformed effortlessly into their opposites, and in this new form elicited an even more enthusiastic response. If, prior to March 3, 1986, the date of the first article exposing his hidden past, Waldheim received ovations as "a man who knows the world, and whom the world knows," after the disclosures concerning his years as a student in Vienna and a soldier in the Balkan theater showed that if he knew the world, the world certainly did not know and had not known him, Waldheim, newly packaged as *homo austriacus,* was cheered wildly by those prepared to declare, in a nearly xenophobic frenzy, "now more than ever," "We Austrians will vote for whom *we* want!" Using the slogan "an Austrian the world trusts," Waldheim and his campaign managers wagered that his international experience would redound to his electoral favor. After he had become an Austrian the world distrusted, this "great Austrian" became the symbol of a wounded national pride and the exponent of a rhetorical provincialism and primitive national chauvinism which belied the cool cosmopolitan image Waldheim had until then so assiduously cultivated.

The focus of the international media, as of his principal accuser, the World Jewish Congress (WJC), not surprisingly, has been Waldheim himself. What did he do and when did he do it? The apparent conundrum that Waldheim not only did not forfeit his support but actually improved his electoral chances not despite his past and his bumbling attempts to explain it away, but rather precisely because of them, has been distressing as well as incomprehensible to many inside and outside Austria. This stunned incredulity, however, masks a more profound ignorance of twentieth-century Austrian history, and not a small amount of selective moral outrage on the part of those thus perplexed. Edgar Bronfman, president of the World Jewish Congress, came to recognize, somewhat late in the game, that the problem was perhaps not Waldheim himself but Austria, and the unanimity of the hostile reactions to his remarks suggests he was on to something. Kurt Waldheim personally, however, was almost certainly never a "secret follower" of Hitler, as *New York Times* columnist William Safire representatively wrote. He was, and has remained, the quintessential opportunist, whose overriding sustaining thought throughout has been his own career. Waldheim's very boast during the campaign, that he has never carried a party card, intended to stress his independence, in fact offers an ironic clue to his strategy for advancement. Irrespective of what authority happened to be in power, Waldheim followed orders, competently, if not necessarily with the passion of the true believer: as Waldheim himself claimed, he just did his duty.

Waldheim's presidential campaign itself, moreover, encapsulated various themes of the enigmatic *"Lebenslüge"* of postwar Austrian political culture. A combination of delusion and deliberate suppression of unwanted and unpalatable facts which can be rendered insufficiently into English as a (mentally) helpful self-deception, here the term *Lebenslüge* figuratively refers to the account(s) of history which come to be seen as the national history, and the assumptions and values of a political culture which both inhere in them and which such histories "ground" by explaining these values' genesis and development. In the construction and reinforcement of this specific Alpine variety, all major Austrian political parties, assisted by the former occupying powers themselves, have been complicit. The shared presuppositions about Austrian political culture, moreover, explain both the virtual political paralysis of Waldheim's Socialist opponents as well as the profound resonance Waldheim's crude appeals found among many Austrians, particularly those of his generation.

Yet however salient the symbolism of the images chosen by Waldheim's campaign staff was, however little prominent politicians of the People's Party as well as Waldheim himself shrank from pandering to the voters' basest emotions, however grotesque Waldheim's attempt to equate the violence of the German army against the civilian population of Yugoslavia with the violence of the Partisans against the Wehrmacht might appear, it does not ineluctably follow that this symbolism and these appeals alone accounted for Waldheim's victory over his rivals. For the assumptions which underlie this view, that Austrian voters both conceived the election in precisely these ethico-political terms and that their votes reflected their respective moral choices, are difficult to sustain. It is the inability to understand this point which has led to such confused hyperbole in the discussions of the entire Waldheim affair.

That both Waldheim's supporters and his critics pressed their convictions with equal vehemence was to have been expected. Not so, perhaps, that the moral vocabulary would be identical. In Austria, insofar as moral elements were introduced into the campaign, the terms in which these were formulated emanated from the organizers of the Waldheim candidacy and were obsequiously taken up by an overwhelmingly pro-Waldheim majority of the Austrian press. Indeed, the putative ethical arguments which critics in the United States and Western Europe arrayed against Waldheim were but a mirror image of the moral fortitude which sustained his Austrian supporters. This symmetry was not accidental. Though the discourse both inside and outside the Danubian republic stressed righteousness, the assumptions which underlay it were diametrically opposed, even if clearly symbiotic. Thus whereas abroad, "the Austrians" were frequently viewed more or less collectively as morally insensate reactionaries, in Austria itself the criticisms made against Waldheim were successfully portrayed as an (often hypocritical) hostility to "Austria." If editors of the international press could metaphorically wring their hands at the Austrians' tolerance of someone whose credibility had been so clearly shattered, politicians of the People's Party wondered aloud why the U.S. government should tolerate the World Jewish Congress's "defamation" of so respected an international figure. Finally, the fact that investigations into and the critical reportage on Waldheim's past had spread to every major newspaper in Western Europe did not undermine the Waldheim camp's claim that the extensive media coverage given to the Waldheim affair reflected the immense "Jewish influence" in U.S. newspapers. On the contrary, it was seen to prove just how far the tentacles of Jewish power reached.

The Waldheim campaign appealed to the antisemitic prejudices of Austrian voters, while Waldheim himself attempted to render harmless both Nazi crimes and the role of Austrians in their commission. Moreover, it was a fortuitous windfall from which Waldheim could only stand to benefit that the debate centered on Waldheim's service in the Balkans, precisely because the prominent role that Austrians, officially the first "victims" of Hitler, played in the war against the partisans could not but beget moral ambiguities which the myths surrounding the war in the Balkans bedim. However, the problems which in Austria go by the name of "coming to terms with the past" were not the only ingredients in the Waldheim victory. To those familiar with the attempt to remake the U.S. intervention in Vietnam into a "noble cause," for example, Waldheim's claim that he, like thousands of other Austrians, only did his duty during World War II should have come as no great surprise. Nor should the response which such an idiom was able to call forth. Still, the contest for the Austrian presidency seems in the end to have been determined by issues largely independent of Waldheim's past. By examining the election campaign in a more comprehensive historical context, it should be possible to illuminate the conflicting loyalties and political motives which inured Waldheim supporters to criticisms emanating from abroad, irrespective of their content; which made it less important to register a protest against accommodations to antisemitism than to send a message to the Socialist-led coalition government; which enabled many of those who voted for Kurt Waldheim to conceive of their electoral behavior as a patriotic act; or which made the entire discussion of Kurt Waldheim's military past essentially irrelevant.

It is this indifference to the appeals to anti-Jewish resentment, however, which makes the Waldheim election of more than ephemeral significance, for it indicates that the potential for mobilizing political support on the basis of such appeals still exists in Austria more than four decades after the end of the Third Reich. The ways in which antisemitic prejudice was summoned and expressed in the Waldheim campaign forms the principal subject of this book. It makes no claim to be an exhaustive account of either Waldheim's career or the election campaign itself, but rather to show how the events themselves offered the Waldheim camp a favorable context for their propaganda efforts, which were antisemitic in substance even if the language it normally employed was coded and allusive.

Antisemitism was not brought to Austria by German tanks, but had been a constitutive feature of Austrian political culture for decades. Austria's most prominent antisemitic politician prior to the First World War, the mayor of Vienna, Karl Lueger, received fulsome praise in Hitler's *Mein Kampf*, not for his antisemitism, but for his political acumen. Though Lueger's antisemitism, as Hitler recognized, like his politics generally, was highly pragmatic, it was his Christian Social Party which made antisemitism into a popular political force. This party is the direct political ancestor of the conservative Austrian People's Party, which supported Waldheim's officially nonpartisan candidacy. The once thriving Jewish community in Austria has been reduced to a few thousand. However, although few Jews live in the country, and even fewer are in positions of prominence (Kreisky, of course, is an exception, but his is a special case), studies inside Austria itself suggest what was confirmed in a particularly repugnant experiential way during the Waldheim campaign, namely, the existence in Austria of what has been called an antisemitism without Jews and without (acknowledged) antisemites. That Bruno Kreisky, himself of Jewish background, could become a respected chancellor, is often taken as evidence of the decline in antisemitic attitudes in Austria today. Without wishing to equate contemporary attitudes with those of the 1930s, however, it appears that Kreisky's verbal expression of his own complex relationship to his Jewish origins provided a cloak of respectability to antisemitic utterances otherwise officially tabooed. This book attempts to trace in detail one example of how prejudice against Jews could be expressed and employed politically after Auschwitz. The construction, in other words, of a refurbished Jewish stereotype, a new *"Feindbild 'Jud.'"*[2]

It is important to explain how the various chapters of the book relate to this objective. In the second chapter, we survey briefly the historical context of the Waldheim election, emphasizing those elements of historical consciousness which are particularly relevant to the Waldheim campaign. Our interpretive look at the history of antisemitism is designed to demonstrate the plausibility of two propositions: that antisemitic prejudice historically was a diffuse congeries of beliefs and suspicions for the most part impervious to attempts to introduce sectarian "rigor," and that there is no reason to suspect that anti-Jewish prejudice (as opposed to discrimination) has significantly dwindled, much less disappeared, from post-World War II Austria. The point being that there exists a kind of reservoir of more or less firm beliefs about Jews which, under certain circumstances, might be tapped for political ends short of discrimination. Indeed, after Auschwitz an antisemitic politics per se is not even possible. Antisemitic prejudice does not appear as, and thus cannot easily be identified through, explicitly anti-Jewish utterances, much less discriminatory measures. This is so, I argue, precisely because of the negative sanction which in general attaches to such openly antisemitic statements and acts. The expression of anti-Jewish sentiment has thus been displaced from the overtly political arena, only to surface periodically at the level of public discourse, whenever a specific political context offers favorable circumstances and opportunities for the emergence of stereotyped anti-Jewish beliefs to "explain" a series of events whose actual causes were not known or at least not self-evident. Such discursive manifestations of prejudice are a sui generis post-Auschwitz phenomenon I have termed the politics of antisemitic prejudice.

After the historical survey in Chapter Two, we turn to the election campaign itself. During the early phase of the electoral contest, in which few outside Austria had shown any interest, certain patterns of argument emerged which helped explain (away) discomfiting disclosures—all unrelated to Waldheim's military service—by branding them "slanders" against Waldheim motivated by electoral considerations. The disclosure on 3 March 1986 by an Austrian news weekly of details of Waldheim's membership in two National Socialist organizations and his military service in the Balkans altered the political context of this debate significantly. One day later, similar items were made public by the World Jewish Congress and the *New York Times,* thus introducing an international and a "Jewish" dimension to the discussion. In this changed situation, one account of the origins and reasons for this ostensible anti-Waldheim "campaign" promoted by certain leaders of the Waldheim campaign organization and their media supporters, which could draw upon both the reservoir of anti-Jewish hostilities (our argument in Chapter Two) and the established argumentative pattern which saw only vilification in such inconvenient inquiries (our argument in Chapter Three), implied that an international Jewish conspiracy lay behind it. And this, it should be emphasized, unaccompanied by any open professions of hostility to the Jews as a whole, and frequently attended by its obverse.

However, the plausibility of the belief in an international Jewish conspiracy, the indispensable moment of this antisemitic *Feindbild,* could only be retained by neutralizing information which potentially threatened to disconfirm it. In the Waldheim election campaign, this took two basic forms. In the first place, the Waldheim camp and most sympathetic media accounts systematically distorted the actions and views of the World Jewish Congress as well as the reporting in the *New York Times* on Waldheim's political affiliations during his university days and his assignments and responsiblities as a Wehrmacht soldier in the Balkans. Secondly, closely related to the first, with few exceptions, public discourse in Austria on the Waldheim controversy either imputed or implied iniquitous motives to the World Jewish Congress, on the one hand, and the *Times* and its journalists, on the other. By reading a specific normative intent into the World Jewish Congress' persistent critical stance and the *Times'* perceived editorial recalcitrance, otherwise comprehensible gaps in the detailed knowledge of, and mistaken assumptions about, Waldheim's past could be recast as well-placed tactical thrusts in a much larger common strategic offensive.

In my view, this conspiratorial explanation of the Waldheim affair could not be constructed and maintained from disingenuous insinuations or contrived evidence alone. The irregular and frequently amateur disclosure and interpretation of documents about Waldheim's past meant that there would be unavoidable deficiencies of reliable unambiguous knowledge. Given these conceptual and informational gaps, an account which provided an explanation of both the significance of the evidence itself and the motives of those involved in its disclosure could, in the given political and cultural context, command acceptance and retain tenability among a wide section of the Austrian public. It behooves us, therefore, to examine the structural determinants and avoidable failings which led to such gaps in knowledge, in order to demonstrate how Waldheim and his supporters utilized these first to establish and later to confirm the assumptions underlying the conspiratorial explanation of the "campaign" against him. Thus, in Chapter Four we investigate the issues raised by the discussion of Waldheim's past Nazi affiliations and his military duties on the basis of the most comprehensive information currently available. This chapter is designed to provide a guide of sorts through the bulk of inconclusive and frequently contradictory evidence about Waldheim's military past, which, it is hoped, will make comprehensible the allusions that turned up in the documents, statements and reports in the course of the election campaign.

Chapter five also addresses the debate on Waldheim's possible criminality, but in a much broader framework. One of the most extensively documented areas of Waldheim's military service deals with the fate of Allied commandos at the hands of Army Group E, at a time when Waldheim served in its military intelligence department. I have chosen to examine one of these cases in depth, both to suggest why Waldheim did not incur criminal liability for the deaths of any of the commandos which have been examined to date and, more importantly, to help clarify some issues which often remained obscure in the debate on Waldheim's military career. My evaluation of Waldheim's possible complicity in the commission of war crimes in Chapter Four is based on a series of assumptions about criminal behavior in war which are expounded in more detail in this chapter, by means of a critical inquiry into allegations made against Waldheim by the historian C.M. Woodward. However, I believe that my arguments have more than mere polemical force, for they help elucidate the conceptual framework of the debate in 1986 on Kurt Waldheim's personal role during the Second World War. During his presidential election campaign in Austria, for example, the Waldheim camp itself sought to reduce all questions related to his wartime service to that of his personal guilt for war crimes, a charge far easier to parry or "refute" than allegations of postwar dishonesty. At the same time, Waldheim's critics (such as the World Jewish Congress) who were insisting on this latter charge were made to appear as advocates of the former. Such an amalgamation was plausible not only because of the lacunae in reliable information, but also because the debate on Waldheim's past and its significance was more frequently characterized on both sides by Manichaean certainties born of much conviction but substantially less intellectual rigor. A discussion of the broader issues of criminality in Chapter Five can therefore help explain both why public suspicion of Waldheim's criminal behavior could become so quickly established as well as why such suspicion was largely based on mistaken assumptions. It is, however, also intended to show that Waldheim's exoneration from criminal misconduct during the war merely initiates, rather than concludes the debate on the "moral" issues involving Waldheim's postwar dissimulation.

In Chapter Six we examine the role of the World Jewish Congress, using its press releases and the documents appended to them as our principal sources. By reconstructing in detail the WJC's disclosures of documents and the evolution of its views about them, it is possible to indicate the nature and content of the Waldheim camp's misrepresentation of the claims and criticisms—particularly on the issue of criminality—the WJC in fact made. The distorted way in which the activities of the WJC were presented in the Austrian public media also helped reinforce corollary stereotyped images about Jews which, we argue later, completed the antisemitic *Feindbild.*

A similar motive informs the analysis of the *New York Times* in Chapter Seven. It is not merely our task to contrast the *Times's* reporting with the way it was received in certain Austria public media, but also to examine all aspects of the newspaper's coverage of the Waldheim affair for mistaken assumptions or biases which lent themselves most easily to misinterpretation, or, in other words, which most readily appeared to corroborate the *Times's* alleged journalistic malefaction.

The details presented in these chapters suggest that even under the best of circumstances, the barriers to knowledge about Waldheim's past were considerable. The fragility of this knowledge, in turn, favored the adoption in Austria of explanations incorporating a theory of the international Jewish conspiracy whose principal virtue was the dubious one of simplicity. It was all the more favored, as the conceptual framework of the debate had been determined by Waldheim and his supporters, substantially limiting the possibilities for shifting the terms of debate in a way which would call these assumptions into question. Thus in Chapter Eight we examine in detail the mutations in public discourse in Austria during the Waldheim election campaign itself.[3] We show how out of the interplay of accident, guess, prejudice and cold-blooded political calculation, the composite antisemitic explanation of the Waldheim affair emerged; in other words, we examine how the Waldheim phenomenon could make the Waldheim affair possible.

Our remarks in Chapter Nine should be read as an afterword of sorts. In it we attempt to bring the Waldheim controversy a bit up to date, and take up some of the more general issues posed by the Waldheim phenomenon.

This book, which describes what I have termed the Waldheim phenomenon in Austrian politics, is not the story of Waldheim's shifting biography. The debate on Waldheim also offered an important insight into how history is created and revised, and how and why one version of Austria's past conformed to and in important ways confirmed some significant shared assumptions of postwar Austrian political culture. Waldheim's own career before and during the Second World War must be examined alongside the broader questions of duty, collaboration, obedience and resistance under the Nazi dictatorship as well as those features of Austrian political culture, in particular the traditions of antisemitic prejudice, which proved so receptive a breeding ground for the various Nazi messages. Only then can one explain how an official Austrian "history" became the actual Austrian *Lebenslüge.*

It is true that the specific contours of the debate inside Austria have a unique character, as does the past which is at the center of debate (i.e., the Nazi period), but the discussion of the broader issues can also help illuminate processes by which societies cope with the past through the creation of historical myths. Discussions of the war in Austria are frequently described as an *"Aufwühlung,"* a stirring up of the past, an expression which connotes the disinterring of long-decayed bodies, skeletons which are better left buried, or a rousing of the furies, the consequences of which cannot be foreseen and should therefore be avoided, rather than as a *"Bewältigung,"* coming to terms with that past, a word which, despite its difficulties, in this context implies an honest and informed retrospective look at how things happened and why. It is important to see how Austrians have "coped" with their past, but also to offer an idea of how it might have been different. The very vocabulary employed by the hardline Waldheim defenders, however, is not unique, and this suggests that the relationships between power, values, political culture and history, which the Waldheim affair illustrates so graphically, are problems which do and should involve us all. And in these matters, neither facile moral revulsion nor selective historical amnesia has any place.

Notes

1. Friedrich Nietzsche, *Vom Nutzen und Nachteil der Historie für das Leben* (1873) (Basel: Diogenes, 1984), p. 12.

2. I have borrowed the expression *"Feindbild 'Jud'"* from Leopold Spira's book of the same title, *Feindbild 'Jud'* (Vienna: Löcker Verlag, 1981). *Feindbild* is a German word for which there is no real English equivalent. It is the image one has of an enemy, but conveys a certain fixity of the stereotypes which go to make up this picture, and a very strong negative connotation. I have chosen to use the German expression in the text rather than attempt to contrive inadequate English renderings. *'Jud'*, of course, is the pejorative German expression for Jew (*Jude*).

3. The very nature of an investigation such as this necessarily requires one to examine how similar or even identical events or pieces of information were "handled" by various media and politicians in the United States and Austria, making a certain amount of repetition unavoidable. I have attempted to keep this to a bearable minimum, but it could not be dispensed with altogether.

2

Austria Past and Present

At the time it entered the First World War, the Austro-Hungarian empire numbered fifty million inhabitants and comprised parts of present-day Austria, Hungary, Italy, Yugoslavia, Rumania, Poland, and Czechoslovakia. By the time Emperor Karl renounced his claim to govern at the close of the war, ending six hundred years of Hapsburg rule, the state over which he presided could not even exercise authority over all the German-speaking areas of his former realm. Karl departed quickly from the scene, and his family has for the most part followed his lead, though in this they have been assisted by republican Austrian law. The job of sorting out the political heritage he left behind, however, fell to others. The fortunes of the state of Austria in the twentieth century form the backdrop to the political and media events which have come to be known as the Waldheim affair. To those possessing a more comprehensive knowledge of "many times tested Austria," as the national anthem of the Second Republic puts it, neither the direction nor the success of Kurt Waldheim's electoral propaganda should have come as any great surprise. It seems, therefore, advisable to examine the elements in this history, or, more accurately, particular interpretations of these events, which have an immediate relevance for the discussion surrounding Waldheim's past. It is impossible in this short space to give an adequate chronological narrative summary of Austrian history.[1] Our purpose is to provide enough historical reference points to enable readers to understand the allusions which emerged during the Waldheim controversy, as well as to indicate certain aspects of Austria's past which have contributed to what might be called a popular memory about Austrian history, and which, aided by an effective propaganda effort, provided a general framework for categorizing, labelling and explaining the events of 1986.

Representatives of Austrian Liberalism dominated imperial cabinets from 1867 until 1879, when they were isolated by Count Taaffe's conservative coalition known as the "Iron Ring."[2] The immediate result of the routing of the Liberal party was a process of political differentiation within its ranks. In the long term, the collapse of Liberalism was both a measure of its programmatic weaknesses and at the same time served as organizational midwife for the three political currents, or "camps," which defined politics in twentieth-century Hapsburg and later republican Austria.[3] The three most important political tendencies to issue from the Liberals were the Christian Socials, the Social Democrats, and those representing a more explicit pan-German nationalism. All three shared a commitment to German cultural predominance in the empire, but each spoke for and addressed very different audiences.

The Christian Social movement originated as the Christian Social Union, which had formed in 1887 as a coalition of disparate and sometimes conflicting constituent groups (artisans, lower clergy, disaffected Democrats, etc.) and was molded into a potent electoral force by Karl Lueger, mayor of Vienna from 1897 until his death in 1910. Lueger had entered politics as a Liberal nationalist, but soon came to see his future as a more populist pro-(Hapsburg) Austrian anti-Liberal leader. The program of his movement amalgamated several anti-Liberal elements: democracy (for a less restricted, but still not universal, suffrage), social reform, antisemitism, dynastic loyalty, etc. From 1895 until 1919, the Christian Socials dominated Vienna's municipal politics. As a national party, it later incorporated peasants from the provinces and attempted to compete with the Social Democrats for working class support. Once in power, however, whatever radicalism had been promised or feared was quickly forgotten, and, although Lueger carried through an impressive list of municipal achievements, the Christian Socials soon became the conservative Catholic political movement it was to remain until the fall of the First Republic.[4]

The Social Democrats in the empire were led by Viktor Adler, a former radical Liberal and German nationalist, and produced a broad range of talented thinkers and politicians, the two most important of whom for later developments were Otto Bauer and Karl Renner. In addition to representing the economic interests of the working class (with a corresponding Marxist vocabulary), the principal political demand of the Social Democrats was for universal manhood suffrage. After the 1907 elections to the Imperial Parliament (*Reichsrat*), held under the extended franchise, the Social Democrats became the largest party in the *Reichsrat*, but they never held government office under the monarchy. They defended the necessity of the empire's existence, but on economic rather than dynastic grounds. Moreover, although they promoted the idea of autonomy for nations inside the empire, social democratic leaders were never in any doubt about the privileged cultural mission of the Germans. Emblematic was the title of the editorial in the Austrian party paper *Arbeiter-Zeitung* commenting on the approval of war credits in the German Reichstag (passed with the votes of their German sister party the SPD) in August 1914: the paper celebrated "the day of the German nation."[5]

Pan-Germanism was a residual category encompassing a wide variety of specific positions, but in fin-de-siècle Austria came to be broadly identified with the politics, if not the person, of Georg von Schönerer. Schönerer had originally been elected to the *Reichsrat* as a progressive Liberal and was an able defender of the interests of his largely agrarian smallholder constituency, but he soon became a bitter critic of the Liberal establishment. Along with Viktor Adler, Engelbert Pernerstorfer, both later leaders of the Social Democratic movement, and Heinrich Friedjung, a Liberal historian, Schönerer drafted the Linz program, adopted by his "German National Union" in 1882, which called for a closer union with Wilhelmine Germany. From this relatively moderate beginning, Schönerer and his program became increasingly more radical in their pro-German orientation and their hostility to the multi-national Austrian empire. Schönerer and his earlier colleagues also parted ways very soon, for in 1885 he amended the Linz program to exclude Jews. Schönerer's radicalism also extended to his antisemitism, and he articulated and came to be identified with a virulent racial variety. Though Schönerer himself never achieved any real political power in his lifetime, he bequeathed a political legacy not only of racial antisemitism but one which redefined German nationalism in Austria. Its focus shifted away from mere cultural supremacy in the multi-national state and its fortunes became explicitly linked to those of the German empire. With some variations, these three camps remained the principal political currents into the first and even second Austria republics.[6]

The collapse of the Hapsburg empire confronted Austria's new leaders with enormous problems. One of the first acts of the first postwar government was to declare the new polity the "German-Austrian Republic," and to announce its intention to join together with the nearly simultaneously proclaimed German Republic. If the new German-Austrian government had hoped to take advantage of U.S. President Woodrow Wilson's stated commitment to the principle of self-determination, the Entente powers themselves had other ideas, and quickly moved to prevent an *Anschluss.* This first debate over an *Anschluss* between Austria and Germany was motivated by obvious perceived cultural affinities, which had been present in all three camps, but also by some far more mundane questions of survival. On the one hand, as the rump leftover from a collapsed multi-national empire, an Austrian Republic standing alone, cut off from its former sources of raw materials and food and facing the tariff barriers of the Hapsburg successor states, appeared economically unviable. Joined to a greater Germany, on the other hand, Austria's economic prospects seemed, if not exactly rosy, at least tolerable. Then there was the legal question of war guilt: if the new republic was the legitimate successor to the Hapsburg monarchy, it would be expected to shoulder the costs for any reparations payments which its former enemies would surely demand.

The arguments of the Austrian representatives to the negotiations of the Austrian peace treaty of St. Germain, however, carried little weight against Allied interests and French fears of Germany, and the treaty was imposed against the wishes of the entire Austrian delegation. All border changes were, from the Austrian point of view, either negative (German-speaking areas of the former empire [Sudetenland] and parts of Upper and Lower Austria went to Czechoslavakia; the Brenner frontier went to Italy; Maribor areas of South Styria went to Yugoslavia) or uncertain (areas of southern Carinthia were to be decided by a plebiscite). *Anschluss* with Germany was prohibited except with the consent of the League of Nations. Moreover, the Allies included a war guilt clause in the treaty, based on the assumption of the collective responsibility for the war of the German-speaking inhabitants of the former empire. The treaty, which was adopted by the Austrian parliament on 10 September 1919, was viewed and presented by all parties in Austria as a *Diktat* of the victorious powers and in flagrant violation of the principles of self-determination.[7] The *Anschluss* idea, moreover, which had both positive and negative elements in it, was never dismissed by the Austrians in principle, and the attractions of union with an economically viable Germany would not fade as Austria struggled against the privations of the 1920s and 1930s.[8]

Austria as a victim of power politics, unjustly accused of guilt for a war not of its making, is a part of the history of the Austrian Republic which dates from its inception. The belief that Austria was subject to *Diktat* remained a continuous theme throughout the 1920s, as the government was forced to look abroad for credit and to impose the draconian austerity measures demanded by lending conditions, all of which could be fit into this mold.

The unity inside German-Austria against the common foe, the victorious Entente powers, however, quickly broke down. Although the electoral support of the three major groups did not vary significantly prior to 1934, the First Republic witnessed a recomposition of political representation inside both the Christian Social and German nationalist camps, as well as a growing polarization and consolidation of the "bloc" of conservative parties against the Socialists. On the one hand, the Christian Social party in the 1930s came increasingly under pressure from extra-parliamentary groups, such as the Heimwehr,[9] while inside the National camp a widespread radicalization was underway, which ended in the Nazis becoming hegemonic. After 1920, moreover, the Socialists were excluded from power altogether at the national level, although they regularly polled a third of the votes. At the same time, because of the strongly federalist constitution, the Socialists were able to establish a quasi-autonomous power base in the capital Vienna, to the everlasting wrath of the Christian Socials. Politics in the First Republic became increasingly bellicose, and with both major camps able to enlist the support of para-military groups, there was a kind of permanent standoff, which bred and nourished a fundamental political hostility and mistrust. Christian Social politicians from Ignaz Seipel, a priest turned politician, to Engelbert Dollfuss—dubbed "Millimetternich" to correlate his physical with his political stature—openly expressed their contempt for constitutional government, while the Socialists warned of the possible necessity of imposing the dictatorship of the proletariat, should the conservatives attempt to destroy the Republic.[10]

For our purposes it is probably best to view the events of the First Republic as a series of *journées* which led to the destruction of the Austrian Republic and the inauguration of an "Austro-fascist" regime. In July, 1927, a jury acquitted the defendants in a trial in Schattendorf who had been accused of killing peaceful demonstrators. To protest what was seen as class justice, Socialist and Communist workers marched in Vienna. When the police attacked the demonstrators with live ammunition, some set fire to the Palace of Justice. Altogether, about eighty demonstrators were killed, but Seipel, then Chancellor, declared that his opponents could expect "no mercy" from him.

In the late 1920s, several prominent Christian Social politicians were calling openly for authoritarian changes in the Austrian constitution. On the defensive, the

Socialists, represented by Robert Danneberg in the negotiations with then Chancellor Johann Schober, were nonetheless able to prevent some of these more extreme measures from being implemented. The compromise result, known as the "Schober Constitution," was adopted in 1929. It replaced the parliamentary republic which had been established in 1920 with a modified presidential one. With an acquiescent president, which then President Wilhelm Miklas certainly was, the shift of responsibility for appointing governments from parliament to the president facilitated the implementation of measures which were a threat to the constitution itself.

The Socialists refused a final offer from the Christian Socials to join a coalition in 1931, because they felt the price too high. In 1932, Engelbert Dollfuss became chancellor. His enthusiasm for fascist Italy was as unconcealed as his hostility towards the Socialists. Under continuous pressure from Mussolini to implement fascist reforms as the only way to outflank the Nazis on the right, Dollfuss has the distinction of being both the gravedigger of the Republic as well as a personal victim of a Nazi putsch attempt.

In March 1933, Dollfuss took advantage of procedural chaos in parliament to declare that the assembly had "dissolved itself." Further sessions were prevented by force. The stage was thus set for the Austrian civil war. An attempt by the Socialist paramilitary organization, the *Schutzbund,* in Linz to resist a police raid in February, 1934, became the occasion for a massive attack by the Austrian police, army and some Heimwehr troops on an unprepared and poorly coordinated opponent. The Socialists were forced underground, their leaders forced to flee, or were imprisoned or killed. For many Socialists of the First Republic, the civil war was the blackest day of the 1930s, blacker even than the *Anschluss* four years later. After it, an unbridgeable gulf existed between the two major camps in Austrian politics.

Dollfuss followed up this success against the Socialists with the introduction of a corporatist constitution and the founding of the Patriotic Front, which was the Austrian dictator's answer to the Italian fascist party. Moreover, with the Socialists out of the way, Dollfuss could attend to the danger on the right, which, especially after Hitler's accession to power in January 1933, had been gaining support in Austria. On 1 June 1934, all Nazi organizations were outlawed in Austria, but they were able to continue work underground, with operations based in Bavaria. On 25 July, the Austrian Nazis attempted to seize power. The putsch attempt failed, but in the course of it Dollfuss was murdered. The main leaders of the putsch were hanged, and Austria temporarily enjoyed the protection of Mussolini, who had sent troops to the Brenner Pass to prevent the Germans coming to the Austrian Nazis' aid.

Dollfuss's successor as chancellor, Kurt Schuschnigg, continued his predecessor's policies, but came under increasing pressure from Germany as Italy gradually distanced itself. Externally, Schuschnigg continued to rely on Mussolini's support, but failed to appreciate the extent of Mussolini's rapprochement with Hitler, especially after 1937. Internally, Schuschnigg had to steer a course between the illegal Social Democrats and the underground Nazis, while retaining a very narrow base of support himself. As a consequence, he was forced to rely increasingly on the Heimwehr, the army and the police. Although neither Dollfuss nor Schuschnigg had any great sympathy for National Socialism, neither rejected the idea of a greater Germany. Schuschnigg was convinced of the closeness of intellectual and cultural ties linking the entire German community, and hoped to establish an acceptable relationship with Nazi Germany. In pursuit of this objective, he tried to entice "moderate" elements from the nationalist camp into working with him, hoping thereby to outflank the more radical Nazis. Yet these measures only resulted in the further erosion of his domestic base, and increased powerlessness in the face of the pressure from Nazi Germany. No bridges were built to the Socialists, and the Patriotic Front proved a flop. The situation worsened after the Austro-German agreement of July, 1936, even though Germany had explicitly recognized Austrian independence and sovereignty. The Austrian government was isolated both domestically and in the international arena. When the *Anschluss* finally came, in March, 1938, Schuschnigg did not resist: he refused to shed "German" blood.[11]

As anyone watching the archive footage from March, 1938, could see, Hitler was met in Austria with enthusiasm by many, resignation by most others.[12] Schuschnigg's ambivalent attitude towards German nationalism itself suggests that the *Anschluss* idea could in principle be retained by Austrians, even though they may have rejected joining a Germany under the Nazis. Once the *Anschluss* became an accomplished fact, moreover, political opposition to the German regime could give way to support for or acquiescence in the greater national "good."[13] Austrians suddenly became part of a great power, and the preparations for war reduced unemployment signifcantly. More importantly for this study, the anti-Jewish policies of the Nazis were able to count on the zealous support of thousands in Austria. Gerhard Botz has suggested that the policies of "Aryanization" and the imposition of legal disabilities against Jews functioned as a sort of ersatz social policy, and could therefore offer positive material rewards for those assisting in the persecution of the Jews.[14] Throughout every stage of the exclusion of the Jews from "Ostmark" society, moreover, this support did not really subside,[15] and in many cases (such as during *"Reichskristallnacht"*) outrages against Jews were more excessive in Austria than in Germany.[16]

During the Second World War, the state of Austria ceased to exist. Many Austrians, like Waldheim, "did their duty" in the Wehrmacht, the SS and the Gestapo. Duty to the Führer, however, precluded commitment to an independent Austria, for the German imperial idea under Hitler had subsumed former Austria into the empire as the "Ostmark." Others, whose sense of duty made rather different demands on their consciences and who took up active resistance against the Nazi regime, were killed or interned in concentration camps. It is true, of course, that Nazi documents themselves record various degrees of hostility to the Nazis or transgressions against Nazi anti-Jewish policies, and that in the course of the war disillusionment with the Nazi occupation authorities increased. However, although individual acts of opposition to Nazi policies should not be minimized, there seems no reason to suspect that in most cases this was in any essential way more politically inspired than the discontent which would arise from the privation and destruction of war or from traditional Austrian animosity to perceived German arrogance. Official Nazi reports recorded that as late as September, 1944, there was no significant demoralization in the western provinces of the Ostmark. Austrians, however, possessed an idiom (i.e., independence, or at least cultural self-assertion) in which they could express their discontent which gave the expression of it a different dynamic than, say, disaffection in an area like Bavaria.[17] In October, 1943, the foreign ministers of the three Allied powers issued the "Moscow Declaration," which for the Austrian Second Republic has acquired quasi-iconographical significance. In this declaration the Allies officially designated Austria the first victim of Nazi aggression, but at the same time reminded it of its responsibility for having fought the war at the side of Nazi Germany.[18] This latter part of the declaration did present some difficulties for postwar status and identity. Yet in the end, the ambiguities, not to say contradictions, in a declaration which vowed to "liberate" an ally of Nazi Germany, were—by the Western Allies at least—resolved in favor of the "victim" passage, an interpretation shared by the post-Nazi political leadership in Austria. The preferred values of a newly constructed Austrian political culture, not surprisingly, tended to stress differences with Germany, and this consorted well with the desire to take one's distance from the Nazi abomination. As wartime alliance gave way to cold war, the very limited de-Nazification in Austria was quickly and quietly abandoned, with the collusion of the Western powers. All this, and much more, impeded Austrians "coming to terms with the past" (in German *Vergangenheitsbewältigung*) commensurate to that which citizens of the Federal Republic of Germany were forced to endure.[19] The postwar political consensus, however, extended to far more than mere unity against the occupying powers. The *Lagerstrasse,* a reference to the "road" running down the middle of concentration camps for political prisoners under the Nazis, signalled to the interned former arch-enemies in the Socialist and Christian Social parties their common Austrian fate and taught them the virtues of cooperation. This stood the politicians in good stead after the Nazi regime had ended. Yet for many in Austria, it was not clear whether May 1945 represented a liberation or a defeat. Austrians could only with difficulty utilize the vocabulary of "national liberation," but could assert an Austrian distinctiveness which, when reinforced or at least not challenged, would eventually lead to a sort of national consciousness.[20]

The end of the war confronted Austrian political leaders with enormous problems: military occupation by foreign powers, economic recovery, de-Nazification, compensation of those who had been forced to leave, etc. In official mythology the awkward questions from this period have been smothered in more inspirational terms like "reconstruction." The dilemmas were, however, real enough. Over 500,000 former members of Nazi organizations had to be "de-Nazified" and somehow integrated into the political system. Once enfranchised in 1949, the major political parties had to solicit their votes in competition with the Union of Independents (later the Freedom Party of Austria, or FPÖ, which became the former Nazis' principal political home). The vocabulary they employed stressed areas of agreement, not moral censure, and they looked ahead to the future rather than dwelling on the past. It is no accident that the category of "collaboration" has played virtually no role in official postwar Austrian discourse on the Nazi period, although officially Austria was Hitler's first victim.

From 1945 to 1966, all elected Austrian governments were grand coalitions of the Austrian People's Party and the Socialists.[21] Other institutionalizations of cooperation, such as the "social partnership," made parliament more or less superfluous. In 1966, the ÖVP was able to win an absolute majority of votes, and formed the first one-party government since the war. The Klaus government, in which Waldheim served as foreign minister, was in office only four years. In 1970, the Socialists under Bruno Kreisky won a plurality of votes and remained in power as a minority government, inaugurating what is known today as the "Kreisky era." A few months later, the Socialists were able to win an absolute majority, and the Socialists governed alone until 1983, when Kreisky resigned as chancellor and was succeeded by Fred Sinowatz, who formed a coalition with the FPÖ. This government was in office at the time of Waldheim's election in 1986.

Toward a History of Antisemitism in Austria: Hostilities in Search of a Concept

As in the survey of the general historical context of the Waldheim affair, our consideration of the origins and development of antisemitism in Austria cannot be an exhaustive one. However, both the historical vicissitudes of antisemitic prejudice as well as the continuities this prejudice has evinced are relevant to understanding the "Jewish question" in Austria after the end of the Second World War. The development of several antisemitic organizations in nineteenth-century Austria, for example, bears only tangentially on the remarks made here, for we concentrate more on the substance of anti-Jewish hostility which found corresponding political expressions in varying historical contexts than on these political formations themselves. The various motifs of anti-Jewish hostility (religious, economic, cultural, racial) do not appear to have had a sharply delineated causal significance for political practice, which in Austria prior to 1945 ranged from the advocacy of the reimposition of pre-emancipation disabilities on Jews to participation in industrialized mass murder. This is not to argue either that the history of anti-Jewish prejudice is teleological, with the attempted annihilation of the European Jews serving as the ultimate end, or that the Nazi execution of its planned "final solution" did not represent an unprecedented qualitative dimension in the persecution of the Jews. What I would like to suggest here is that even the commission of such barbaric acts against Jews neither required nor presumed a specific antisemitic belief system. Moreover, those who carried out (as opposed to having conceived) such acts would not necessarily have subscribed to a similarly specific antisemitic ideology, though in both cases the range of possibilities for such beliefs was not unlimited. Put another way, not everyone who viewed Jews as a separate race whose presence had deleterious effects on the non-Jewish population would necessarily have endorsed the Jews' physical elimination. Likewise, those who might have advocated severe discriminatory measures against Jews, including their physical exclusion (even if not their extermination) from Europe need not have justified this by reference to a specific racial theory. The register of traditional antisemitic prejudices had always offered sufficient possibilities to justify a wide spectrum of measures undertaken against Jews. A strict separation between racial and other forms of hostility in this sense was less important than the ways in which they commingled with one another and were continually deployed and redeployed in different combinations explicitly to further political ends or merely, in the manner of a *Iudeus ex machina,* to explain otherwise inexplicable social phenomena.

An explanation of the causes of the persistence of antisemitic prejudices in milder or more virulent forms in more recent Austrian history, and more specifically, why so much aggression can still be directed against a specific minority which has nearly disappeared[22] is elusive in any case. However, wherever one traces the origins and causes of antisemitic prejudice, both open and coded expressions of it could be found in the discourse on the Waldheim affair. What we hope to outline below is the historical reservoir of prejudices against Jews upon which "post-Auschwitz" antisemitic beliefs could draw, and indicate some of the reasons why the Waldheim campaign could allude to these sentiments with such powerful effect. A study of the contours of post-Auschwitz political functionalization of antisemitic prejudice, it is argued here, represents an initial and tentative attempt to delimit the linguistic conventions (in Quentin Skinner's sense)[23] proper to one important way of writing and speaking about Jews and things Jewish in post-World War II Austrian political culture.

Hostility Toward Jews Prior to the Emancipation

Components of modern antisemitic prejudice can be traced to antiquity. Although it would be mistaken to speak of a fully elaborated anti-Judaism, the exclusionary language which it inaugurated, having gradually become divorced from its ancient origins, has long served well in the arsenal of prejudiced discourse. Authors as diverse as Plutarch, Seneca and Tacitus criticized Jews, among other things, for being descended from lepers, for hating the gods, for being a people without a god, for refusing to accept the imperial cult (which came to be equated with disrespect towards all things held in esteem), for wasting the seventh day of the week, for revering swine, and for being both a stubborn, seditious and fearless as well as a cowardly and contemptible group, etc.[24] Philo of Alexandria, whose polemical writings defending the Jews is the source of most of our information about anti-Jewish sentiment, recorded an "instinctive" rejection of Jews by non-Jews.[25] Although discriminatory measures against Jews were frequent enough (for example, the edicts which followed the Bar-Kochbar uprising in the year 135 A.D. or the provisions of the *Codex Theodosianus* of 438 A.D.), the Roman Empire in general appears not to have pursued systematic or even consistent anti-Jewish policies despite frequent Jewish uprisings against Roman rule.[26] To these negative attitudes towards Jews which the ancients had bequeathed were added, in the period of early Christianity, specifically Christian prejudices. These attitudes, based on New Testament writings, were in many cases ambivalent: on the one hand, the Jews played a special role in Augustine's accounts of Christian salvation (i.e., that Jews were witness to the truth of Christianity), but they were at the same time accursed and damned. Several Church fathers emphasized the responsibility of the Jews for the murder of God and the "evil character" of Judaism.[27] The basic elements of a Christian anti-Jewish ideology were thus firmly in place.

In the Middle Ages, this ideologically colored tradition of prejudice was expressed both in discriminatory acts against Jews and periodic attacks on Jews. The church councils issued numerous acts to discourage or prevent contacts between Christians and Jews, required Jews to wear a distinguising mark, and imposed restrictions on the exercise of professions, relegating, for example, at least officially, the practice of usury to the Jews.[28] These were, however, frequently coupled with a degree of pragmatic tolerance because of the financial services the Jews could offer to penurious secular princes, and on occasion individual urban notables could even view Jews in thoroughly positive ways.[29] In addition to the legal disabilities Jews suffered, in the wake of the plague or in times of general dearth, charges of poisoning of wells or desecration of the sacraments and ritual murder of Christian children accompanied periodic massacres of the largely helpless Jewish population.[30]

Essential features of prejudice and discrimination more familiar from their expressions in the Third Reich were also firmly anchored in the practices of the Middle Ages. Measures implemented in Spain after the Christian conquest bear nearly prototypical similarity to the Nuremberg laws. In the wake of massacres of Jews in Toledo from 1391, Jews there were faced with the alternatives of forced conversions, exile or death. Later, in order to limit the influence of these "Conversos," Pedro Sarmient, commandant of Alcazar of Toledo, promulgated a statute in 1449 concerning the "purity of the blood." The criteria contained in Sarmiento's regulations, however, recall a modern context: whoever had even one Jewish ancestor within the previous three generations was excluded from public office. In 1492, all Jews were officially expelled from Spain and shortly thereafter from Portugal at Spain's behest. Expulsion of Jews itself merely continued a long-standing medieval tradition, but the extent of the measures (the country was officially free of Jews) established a precedent of another sort in the history of European antisemitism.[31] In the event, the Spanish crown soon rescinded the Toledo statute of *limpieze de sangre,*[32] and the persecution of the "Conversos" was officially justified on character grounds, not those of blood, i.e., that the conversions were not sincere. The option of conversion contradicted the assumptions underlying the Toledo statute in any case. This chapter in the history of the persecution of Jews is relevant above all for illustrating the interchangeablity of a religious and a "proto-racist" (Geiss) justification of discriminatory measures, and the adaptability of various strains of argument used to justify measures against Jews.[33]

Such a cluster of both explicit and more inchoate anti-Jewish prejudices, which included the acceptance of racially conceived notions such as "purity of blood," the contemning by church authorities of genuine Jewish religious practices and customs and the inveighing against invented ones (ritual murder, desecration of the host, etc.), and the ascription of other character traits to Jews *qua* Jews, may be assumed to have formed a sort of antisemitic intellectual heritage, whose principal cultural bearer was European Christianity (in both its Catholic and Protestant forms).[34] Negatively connotated features of Jewish religion or culture could thus come to be described as an "essence" or "national character" of "the Jews" as soon as a language had developed in which such meanings had become, as it were, ideological conventions. "Modern" antisemitism must therefore be integrated into a more broadly conceived intellectual history which explains the emergence and eventual adoption of such concepts as "essence," "nation," "race," etc. For these concepts made (ideologically) possible modern notions of antisemitism and it is in terms of them that antisemitic beliefs found independent justification and legitimation.

The Reformation and the Enlightenment are of interest in this brief discussion of the history of antisemitism principally because it was in the course of these broad intellectual movements that a concept of the "spirit" of Judaism, which was conceived as a national or cultural spirit, or even as a world-historical principal, gradually displaced the hitherto nearly exclusive religious semantics of the terms Jew and Judaism. Distinctions between Israelites, members of a religious community, and Jews, which emphasized the individual's parentage, offered a new justification for an old problem, namely, that in the eyes of their castigators, Jews could not escape merely through baptism the disadvantages to which their heritage had consigned them. Since the eighteenth century, moreover, Jews have been described as a nation with a specific "national character."[35]

"Modern" Antisemitism

The word "antisemitism" itself is a neologism of the nineteenth century, and was a logical extrapolation from the linguistic concepts "Semitic language," "Semites" and even "Semitism," all of which dated from the eighteenth century. The term Semite and its derivatives were soon adopted by ethnologists. Analogous with other peoples, which also possessed their own essence and possessed peculiar characteristics, the "Semitic" spirit and character became an object of scholarly research and publicistic adulteration. Gobineau represented a particularly radical current in this general intellectual development, because he claimed to have grounded the linguistic and ethnologic concepts such as "Semite" naturalistically by means of the concept of "race."[36]

In the course of the nineteenth century, the concepts "Jew" and "Judaism" (*Judentum*) gradually but definitively took on a secular character. From around 1870, the concepts Semite and Jew became quasi-synonymous and largely interchangeable, and became linguistic vessels for transporting the condensed register of negative qualities which the occidental hatred of Jews had accumulated. As a consequence of the ending of legal disabilities against Jews (the "emancipation"), the words became general pejorative connotations for perceived negative features of modern society itself.[37]

The writings of Houston Stewart Chamberlain, Julius Langbehn and Paul de Lagarde, among others, were influential in their respective ways in consolidating the racist content of these concepts. Langbehn's main work *Rembrandt als Erzieher* offered a cultural nationalist or "völkisch" reference point in Germany. His antisemitism was directed principally against assimilated Jews, for they embodied the modern materialistic spirit he deplored. Chamberlain argued that the dominant factor of human development resided in the necessity of preserving the essential character of one's race. The two races which had best succeeded, he believed, were the Teutons (*Germanen*) and the Jews. The struggle between these two races formed an important topos of his book *Die Grundlagen des Neunzehnten Jahrhunderts.* In this work Chamberlain linked a theory of the master race, which had retained its characteristics through natural selection, with the belief that such a master race possessed its own historical mission: the Teutons were the creators of a new culture. "Juda," which itself strove for world domination, contested this mission of the Teutons, in which effort they must be hindered through concrete measures. In 1925, Chamberlain even praised Hitler as one of the only antisemites capable of appropriate action.[38] Cultural critic Paul de Lagarde wrote in a similar vein that the Jews threatened the exclusivity of German domination. He distinguished in his writing between Jews and Semites, but in the final analysis linked notions of people (*Volk*) and nation to a rejection of the Semities based essentially on religious grounds.[39]

The coining of the word "antisemitism" has traditionally been attributed to Wilhelm Marr, although the word itself does not appear in his book *Der Sieg des Judenthums über das Germanenthum.* Its first usage was probably in 1879 in the *Allgemeinen Zeitung des deutschen Judentums.*[40] The term soon assumed conventional status as defining the array of anti-Jewish prejudices of both an old and new kind. For many it was a synonym for a certain strain of criticism of modern liberal capitalist society, a reaction to the "Jewish question" as it had been reformulated by the end of legal disabilities against the Jews. It became representative of all possible forms of behavior or opinion whose common denominator was aversion to, hatred of, or hostility towards Jews and Judaism, whether they stemmed from antiquity, the middle ages or the modern period.[41] The German antisemite Theodor Fritsch, in his *Antisemite's Catechism* published in 1888, illustrated interchangeability of the words Jew and Semite within this discourse: "'Anti' means 'against,' and 'Semitism' refers to the essence of the Semitic race. Thus, antisemitism means combatting Semitism. Since the Semitic race in Europe is represented almost exclusively by the Jews, we understand by the term 'Semites' in a narrower sense the Jews. In this case, antisemite means thus 'opponent of the Jews' or enemy of the Jews."[42] Fritsch, of course, stressed the "racial" elements of antisemitism, but his use of Semite and Jew was not an exclusive property of racist theories, and was found in the Austrian literature as well.

Antisemitism in Austria

Although there were affinities between the antisemitic ideologies in Germany and in German-speaking Austria (especially regarding racist notions), certain features peculiar to Austria's historical development (predominance of the Catholic Church and the nature of Church-State relations, the specificities of the nationalities question in the multi-national empire, migration of Jews from Galicia, Moravia, etc.) gave antisemitism in Austria a distinctive character. Without wishing to minimize the features common to both, we will concentrate on the currents in Austria which rested on a variety of old and new hostilities and which antisemites of various stripes shared.[43]

The development of capitalism in the nineteenth century, the short-lived ascendency and disastrous fall of Liberalism, the conflict of nationalities in the empire, the emancipation of the Jews, the growth of a large and unified Social Democratic movement, and the over-arching emergence of mass political parties, all were decisive in determining the context and to some extent the nature of antisemitism in Austria.[44] The relatively late and uneven industrialization in Austria, together with the ending of Jewish disabilities in 1867, created conditions which promoted the spread of antisemitic resentments. Jews achieved leading (visible) positions in the economy (especially in banking and on the stock exchange), in intellectual and cultural life (especially the press) and in certain professions (doctors and lawyers), and were leaders of the Social Democratic Party. Other Jews were peddlars who were thought to undermine artisans and small shopkeepers. There were Jews who wished to assimilate fully (and, as bearers of German culture, believed themselves to have assimilated), others, the *Ostjuden* from Galicia and elsewhere, stood out as Jews because they wished to retain their traditional customs and dress.[45] This spectrum of Jewish existence and identity offered no antidote to beliefs about a unified "essence" of the Jew; on the contrary, it formed the basis of the protean mixture of religious, economic, cultural and racial hostilities which constituted the specific Austrian variant of antisemitism and merely multiplied the occasions for confirming the heritage of prejudice to explain a myriad of social and cultural problems.

The distinction between the national racial form of antisemitism and the less systematic, pragmatic Christian Social variety, was far less strict than much of the writing on the subject implies. In general it could be said that although certain currents representing the purest form of racial antisemitism (above all Georg Schönerer and his followers) ideologically differentiated their own brand from other less consistent or non-racial opponents within the antisemitic movement, these opponents were far less keen to draw hard and fast ideological lines. Where Christian Social antisemites did distance themselves from Schönerer, it was for political reasons which had little to do with the assumptions underlying the shared beliefs about the Jews.

Indeed, several men who later played leading roles in the Christian Social party had worked politically very closely with Schönerer, and there is no evidence that the origins of the disputes which led to their falling out related to fundamental differences over the nature of antisemitic beliefs themselves (at least on the part of Schönerer's former allies). Moreover, there are numerous examples of individual representatives of "religious" antisemitism, such as the priest Josef Deckert, who constructed an elaborate theological defense of racial antisemitism. Finally, inside the Christian Social party itself, some (even if not all) leading figures defended openly racist views into the First Austrian Republic.

In any event, it is doubtful if all members or supporters of expressly antisemitic parties in Austria concerned themselves with the fine points of antisemitic theory. Any leader or member of political movements who wished to restrict or repeal Jewish emancipation could draw upon more than one of the available interpretive frameworks to justify the prescribed actions against the "Jewish danger." But identical beliefs need not be ascribed to every individual member of such parties, nor did the support of anti-Jewish measures or propaganda necessarily require an explicit ideological justification, though such measures or utterances, if not merely isolated faux pas, would have presumed such a justification. This syncretic antisemitism, as I would like to call it, enabled one (simultaneously, if need be) to loathe Jews, or support laws against them, because they were capitalists or because they were socialists, or because they belonged to a false religion, a foreign nation or a degenerate (and/or powerful and threatening) race. The common denominator was the antipathy towards Jews. The intellectual procedures and social-psychological mechanisms involved in adopting antisemitic beliefs, as well as the relations between such beliefs and discrimination against Jews, lie beyond the scope of this study. Our interest lies rather in reconstructing the range of contemporary possibilities for the construction of a syncretic antisemitic ideology.[46]

Among the members of the *Österreichischer Reformverein,* a forerunner of the Christian Social party founded in 1882, were Schönerer, Karl Lueger, Robert Pattai, later a prominent Christian Social politician, and Ernst Schneider, a representative of Viennese artisans and leader of the *Gesellschaft zum Schutz des Handwerkes.* Initially, Pattai belonged to the Schönerer wing in the union. Known as a national and racial antisemite, Pattai, a lawyer, had defended a number of prominent antisemites such as Franz Holubek, Ernst Rohling, Josef Deckert, and Schönerer, who had been charged with slander of Jews or with anti-Jewish agitation. Pattai's later falling out with Schönerer was over the former's embrace of an Austrian (i.e., pro-Hapsburg) orientation, not differences over antisemitic ideology or anti-Jewish policies. The same held for Schneider, who also continued to espouse racial antisemitism. In general, the principal ideological dividing line between the Schönererist party and the Christian Socials centered on the attitude towards Catholicism and the Hapsburg monarchy.[47]

It is true that Schönerer left the *Verein* because it did not "primarily pursue antisemitism,"[48] but the character of the antisemitism the union represented was at that time apparently not in dispute. Schönerer and his former colleagues from the reform union came together again in 1887 to form the "United Christians," an "electoral coalition of all antisemitic and also those conservative elements who fight against Jewish Liberal candidates."[49] The first official program of the United Christians, published in 1889, in addition to fifteen points favoring artisans and peasants which cropped up regularly in antisemitic organizations, demanded the exclusion of Jews from the civil service, the officer corps of the army, the judiciary; the prohibition of the teaching of non-Jewish children by Jewish teachers, the "de-Jewing" (*Entjudung*) of the retail trade and the professions of lawyer, doctor, pawn broker, as well as the restriction of further Jewish immigration and the reimposition of special legal disabilities for Jews.[50]

The early interconnection between persons representing various currents in the antisemitic movement suggests, as was mentioned earlier, that specific sectarian differences of opinion about the Jews themselves were far less significant than agreement on what political aims the antisemitic agitation should pursue.[51] All currents inside this movement were agreed on the importance of the "necessary" struggle against the alleged Jewish "domination" of modern society. But there was no particular interest in the consistency of one's arguments, nor were those who explicitly renounced racial antisemitism (in its Schönererian form) free from opinions with racist implications.

One example of this was Freiherr Karl Emil von Vogelsang, born in 1918 in Mecklenburg in then East Prussia. Raised a Protestant, in 1850 Vogelsang converted to Roman Catholicism and later settled on an estate near Vienna. From 1875, Vogelsang edited the conservative Catholic paper *Das Vaterland.* Exponent of a defensive "neo-feudalist," corporatist anti-capitalism, Vogelsang became something of an *eminence grise* for several Christian social politicians (Pattai, Prince Alois Liechtenstein, Lueger), and for a few Catholic priests ranging from the mere conservative Prälat Schindler, to the more vigorous Josef Scheicher and Josef Deckert. These and others took part in the regular soirées initiated by Franz Schindler at the Vienna cafe Zur goldenen Ente.[52]

Vogelsang's antisemitism was a constitutive element of his overall social theory, which was directed against atomizing tendencies of modern society. Jews, in this view, were the vanguard of capitalist ideology and practice (a position not far from that defended in 1843 by Marx in "On the Jewish Question"),[53] but as a devout Catholic he rejected racial antisemitism. He, like Lagarde, distinguished between the traditional "Israelite" religion, with which he had no fundamental quarrel, and the "Jewish" spirit, which he considered modern and corruptive. In spite of this, his writings contained recognizable racist elements. Unrestricted freedom to sell one's labor, he wrote, privileged the lower "races" such as the Chinese and "Semites" and excluded Aryans. Elsewhere he wrote that "we are tributary to an inimical race," meaning the Jews.[54] In addition, *Das Vaterland* under Vogelsang's editorship published stories on alleged Jewish practices of ritual murder or on an ostensible secret meeting of Rabbis in Cracow to plan world domination.[55] Vogelsang's antisemitic ecumenism would seem to have been a more lasting bequest to his Christian Social followers than his program as such.[56]

This syncretic antisemitism in Austria in the nineteenth century also owed something to the efforts of the priests Joseph Scheicher and Josef Deckert. Both were actively involved in the clerical paper *Correspondenzblatt für den katholischen Clerus in Österreich,* and were known to and respected by leading personalities of the Christian Social party from around 1890.[57] Deckert in particular was one of the most fanatical antisemites in the Christian Social milieu, but, more importantly for our purposes, his writings exemplify the catholic nature of antisemitic discourse in this period. Not only do Deckert's tracts show that arguments for the exclusion of Jews from society did not necessarily require racial assumptions à la Schönerer, they catalog a personal evolution from one who rejected racial antisemitism to one who advocated it, offering quasi-theological legitimation for the entire package.[58] In the 1890s Deckert wrote a number of articles and pamphlets in which he attempted, partially on the basis of forged evidence, to prove an incident of ritual murder.[59] In 1893 Deckert wrote in *Vaterland* that "my experience has made me into an antisemite, not into a racial antisemite."[60] In later pamphlets, however, Deckert argued for the compatibility of Christian teachings and racial antisemitism. "The Jews," he wrote in 1896, "in spite of their dispersal, constitute a separate race which distinguishes itself from other peoples through specific racial characteristics, [both] good and bad . . . Jew remains Jew, whichever language he may speak. . . ." [61] When Deckert died in 1901, the entire Christian Social prominence, including Lueger, Prince Alois Liechtenstein, and vice-mayor Rudolf Neumayer attended his funeral. In its obituary, the *Deutsches Volksblatt* praised Deckert as one who had had "the courage to defend antisemitism fearlessly and single-mindedly with flaming words at a time when anyone who declared himself an antisemite was exposed to the persecutions of the Jews."[62]

Deckert's personal ideological migration illustrated the shifting and overlapping boundaries between religious and racist currents within the antisemitic movement at the turn of the century in Austria. This same lack of clear differentiation continued into the Austrian First Republic, whatever other political differences might have existed. The manifesto of the Christian Social party, published in 1918, stated: "The corruption and power-mania of Jewish circles, evident in the new state, forces the Christian Social Party to call on the German Austrian people for most severe defensive struggle against the Jewish peril. Recognized as a separate nation, the Jews shall be granted self-determination; they shall never be the masters of the German people."[63]

The Schönererist Pan-German Peoples party, on the other hand, declared itself far more openly racist. "The Party," the program declared, ". . . is in favor of a campaign of enlightenment about the corrupting influence of the Jewish spirit and the racial antisemitism necessitated thereby. It will combat Jewish influence in all areas of public and private life."[64]

Neither the (German) national nor the Christian Social wings, however, held strictly to these ideological differences. The Christian Social politician Richard

Schmitz declared on 27 June 1919 in the Vienna municipal council that his party's antisemitism was directed against the "extraordinarily dangerous and spiritually unjustified phenomenon . . . that the members of another people, even another race, appear as pseudo-Germans . . . [and] create a culture which is not German, but also no longer Jewish."[65]

Similarly, Leopold Kunschak, head of the Christian Social Laborers' association in Linz, demanded a "clear separation between Jews and Germans." Jews should be prevented from "denying their group membership [*Volkszugehörigkeit*] merely by leaving their religious community."[66] Ignaz Seipel, priest and Christian Social prime minister in the 1920s, represented a somewhat more ambiguous position. Early on, Seipel had conceived of the "Jewish question" as a type of class question: Jewry represented a class which encompassed mobile big capital and a "certain type of trading practice [*Händlertum*]."[67] He also referred to the Jews as a nation which should be granted the same rights to autonomy in educational and cultural matters as other nations, should they demand them. If they decided not to establish their own "national" schools, however, the Jews should receive the right to study in public institutions according to quotas which corresponded to their percentage in the population. At the same time, Seipel, in a marginal comment on a draft law concerning "the legal situation of the Jewish nation," conceded Jews the possibility of changing their national affiliation, which implicitly recognized that one could cease to be a Jew, a non-racial assumption.[68]

Emmerich Czermak, Christian Social education minister in several governments of the First Republic, also exemplified this ambiguity. "We Germans," he wrote in 1933, "gladly encounter the Jewish people and its national religion with full respect; we wish to see them protected, but also to protect ourselves . . . . In future [the Jews] will have to leave us to ourselves in our own concerns . . . in our national culture they will not be allowed to have their say except as guests. . . . The religious German must decisively reject baptism as an 'entrance ticket' for the Jews."[69] The antisemitic ideological heritage of the Christian Social movement was neither uniform nor clear-cut. Religious, economic, cultural as well as racial prejudice were all represented inside the party, and could be adduced in various combinations to support propaganda needs or programmatic goals. However, such a diffuse amalgamation was at a disadvantage against the quite explicitly racial "antisemitism of reason" (Hitler). Yet the *stated* objectives of these two (politically) separate strands of antisemitism were at that time not essentially dissimilar. Hitler described these in 1919, for example, as "the systematic legal combatting and eliminating of the privileges of the Jews . . . Its [antisemitism's] final goal, however, must be the removal of the Jews altogether."[70] The Lower Austrian Farmers Union [Bauernbund], for example, an organization affiliated to the Christian Social party, advocated "the exclusion of the too extensive Jewish-capitalist influence in finance and administration," and demanded the "carrying through of antisemitism in all areas."[71] Of course, "removal of the Jews altogether" did not have to signify mass murder, and it is a fact that the sometimes extreme antisemitic propaganda of Christian Social politicians or officials of affiliated organizations was not accompanied by corresponding legal measures against Jews.[72] However, the ambiguous vocabulary of Christian Social antisemitism could have offered enough arguments to justify the systematic exclusion of Jews from Austrian society.

Apart from the Christian Socials and German Nationalists, the third political camp in the German-speaking areas of the Hapsburg monarchy and in the Austrian First Republic was the social democratic movement. Officially against all forms of discrimination, and with several leaders from a Jewish background, the Socialists in fact had an ambivalent attitude towards the antisemitic movement, and sometimes had trouble differentiating itself from antisemitic agitation. Karl Kautsky, heavily involved in the negotiations leading to the unification congress of the Austrian Social Democrats in 1889, wrote to Friedrich Engels, "we are having trouble preventing our people from fraternizing with the antisemites. The antisemites are at present our most dangerous opponents, more dangerous than in Germany, because they appear democratic and oppositional, thus appealing to workers' instincts."[73]

The Social Democrats' application of historical materialism to the problem had convinced them that, ideologically, antisemitism was a phenomenon corresponding to a particular stage of capitalist development (Ferdinand Kronawetter's characterization "the socialism of fools" was quickly taken up by Social Democrats like Engelbert Pernerstorfer). Politically, antisemitism was seen as an instrument for promoting and defending certain privileges of the petty bourgeoisie (*Kleinbürgertum*). According to this logic, it would have been not only reactionary, but also fruitless to attempt to counter the historical processes at work. The same processes—i.e., the further development of capitalist society—which reduced the *Kleinbürger* to proletarian status would also eliminate the historically conditioned Jewish professional profile, thereby removing the objective basis of antisemitic prejudice, and, at the same time, would fully assimilate Jews into secular culture, because it would undermine the basis for Judaism itself. Instead of waging a struggle against Jewish capital, as the antisemites did, the Social Democrats counterposed a proletarian fight against Jewish and non-Jewish capitalism. Tactically, however, one could exploit the confused anti-capitalism of the antisemitic movement.[74] This strategy, however, was fraught with dangers. The leadership of the party, largely of Jewish origin, minimized the significance of antisemitism, so that the party would not be seen to be defending specifically Jewish interests. At the same time, in their attempts to expose the Christian Socials' hypocrisy on the Jewish question, the Social Democrats—even into the First Republic—employed a language which was frequently indistinguishable from that of their antisemitic opponents. The results of this tactical maneuvering, as Robert Wistrich points out, was that "antisemitic stereotypes of radical provenence which equated 'capitalist' and 'Jew' received a new kind of respectability and legitimacy precisely because they were used by those who claimed that they were actually fighting against antisemitism."[75] Thus, although the ideological conventions of orthodox Marxist Social Democratic theory offered a framework to explain the phenomenon of antisemitism, at the same time, precisely because their theoretical vocabulary accepted notions of nation, race, etc.—all important presuppositions for antisemitic ideology—the Social Democrats themselves were not immune from contamination by anti-Jewish stereotypes. More importantly, however, they could offer no consistent ideological or political response to the increasingly virulent antisemitism of the 1930s.

Writers and cultural critics of the period were also part of the linguistic context of the syncretic antisemitism in Austria, especially in Vienna, prior to 1938. The works of Otto Weiniger, which contained passages contemptuous of Jews, or the biting wit of Karl Kraus, who reserved his most derisory concinnity for Jews in leading positions in the Viennese press, are merely the best known examples of a much broader phenomenon. Whatever the origins or immediate causes of this type of writing, which is mentioned here only in passing, there can be no doubt that it provided a legitimacy to the antisemitic prejudices of others.[76]

These diffuse ideological currents all helped create an everyday texture of antisemitic prejudice in Austria whose gamut reached from generalizations about Jews in the professions to allegations of actual ritual murder to calls for the reimposition of legal disabilities against racially-defined Jews. Moreover, antisemitism in Austria retained its syncretic character under the Nazi regime, even though racial elements—Hitler's "antisemitism of reason"—assumed a hitherto unheard-of political prominence. Religious hostilities did not disappear in the press of the more secular Nazis, but were reformulated in racial terms. Martin Luther's writings against Jews received coverage otherwise uncommon for religious figures.[77] Julius Streicher's *Stürmer* devoted regular attention to religious themes, continuing a tradition established during Weimar.[78] The headline in a special issue of *Stürmer* for the Nuremberg Nazi party rally in 1935, for example, records the eclectic nature of anti-Jewish sentiment in Nazi Germany in a paper whose name is synonymous with monstrously crude racial hatred: "Murderers from the Beginning. International Jewish Bolshevism from Moses to the Comintern."[79]

More "scholarly" works published under the Nazis also conflated religious and racial assumptions. Exemplary for this genre was the introduction by Professor Johann von Leer to a book on ritual murder. The book rehearsed familiar "evidence" of such stories, but its introduction illustrated how fluid the boundaries were between prejudices from the most varied sources, as well as how easily religious arguments could be mustered to legitimate racial discrimination. Hitler himself had written that his conduct was "in accordance with the will of the Almighty. In standing against the Jew I am defending the handiwork of the Lord."[80] "Judaism," von Leer wrote, following this lead, "is, biologically, hereditary criminality, religiously, syncretism with a dose of demonism. Whoever fights against Judaism 'does God's work' and fights a holy fight."[81] There is no disputing the diminutive importance which Nazi ideologues (particularly Rosenberg) attached to religious antisemitism.[82] Yet on the whole, the Nazis appear not to have been particularly doctrinaire in practice about their hatred of Jews: there were sufficiently potent justifications from other traditions which could contribute to the intellectual and psychological stigmatization of the Jews preparatory to the political exclusion of the Jews from the Third Reich and their physical elimination from Europe. In Austria this entailed a series of steps in a process, and was not teleological.[83] After the *Anschluss,* Austrian antisemites, however, surprised even their *"Altreich"* co-thinkers with the alacrity and zealous ingenuity with which they pursued anti-Jewish measures not yet undertaken in Germany itself.[84] At no stage, however, and this is the essential point, would the concrete achievement of the Nazis' stated political objectives have required a purely racial justification which could not have been found among the ideological arguments of their Christian opponents.

"Antisemitism" in Austria After the Second World War

After the full horror of the Nazi anti-Jewish policies became known, the "Jewish question" could no longer be seen in the same light as before. The Austrian Second Republic foreswore all political and ideological ties to Nazi Germany and emphatically renounced the anti-Jewish policies associated with it. Indeed, antisemitism was considered officially as a relic of a hated regime, and the juridical independence of Austria, enshrined in the Moscow declaration, brought forth a corresponding explanation of the new Austria's ideological tabula rasa.[85] Leopold Figl, first elected chancellor of the Second Republic, felt it "foolish to deny that Nazi racial propaganda [had] found an echo among some Austrians. However, when they saw the means by which antisemitism was implemented, they were cured. One could safely say that the sympathy with the persecuted Jews eradicated antisemitism in Austria. I don't think this question will ever acquire even the slightest significance."[86]

Antisemitism was no longer considered a legitimate positive self-definition in public discourse in postwar, that is to say, post-Auschwitz Austria, but politicians with an antisemitic past continued to be honored because of their anti-Nazi stance.[87] Figl's statement, however, narrowly and arbitrarily redefined antisemitism as coterminus with racially defined Nazi measures of persecution. This had several important implications. One was the ability to minimize the significance of non-racial anti-Jewish hostilities, which no longer counted as antisemitic. Moreover, by defining the term this way, the Austrian population (with the exception of the few such as Adolf Eichmann, Ernst Kaltenbrunner, Franz Stangl, etc.) could be absolved of any responsibilty for or complicity in lesser forms of discrimination, and this in turn obviated any consideration of the moral burden incurred for having sanctioned or applauded Nazi measures. Finally, the identification of antisemitism with Nazism *tout court* implied that legitimate anti-Nazi credentials, which the founders of the Second Republic undoubtedly possessed, made one into an opponent of antisemitic prejudice. These assumptions, however, are open to some question.

First, it is difficult to ascertain just how deeply ingrained the offically sanctioned *Verdrängung* of the history of antisemitism in Austria after the end of the war had become among the population as a whole. Austria's status as the first victim of Hitler, the distance it took from its former relationship to Nazi Germany, together with the ineffectual de-Nazification, enabled it to skirt any responsibility for the antisemitic atrocities of the Nazi regime (and attendant compensation payments), while, on the other hand, the prejudices against Jews, which had been around for centuries but which had been hammered in day in and day out for the seven years of the Nazi dictatorship in Austria, remained, or at least there is no indication that they did not remain, notwithstanding Figl's assurances to the contrary.

The official negative connotations associated with the term antisemitism, however, did not eliminate the "Jewish question" in Austria after the war. Antisemitic prejudice has remained a permanent feature of Austrian political culture, even if after the Second World War it was no longer a constitutive element. The fact of Auschwitz itself threw up new specific problems which both kept the "Jewish question" alive and altered the conventions by which it was viewed and discussed. Apart from the delicate issue of the active and passive support given by Austrians to the "final solution" and the stages of discrimination leading to it, there were fears relating to claims made for the restoration of "aryanized" Jewish property, from which thousands had materially benefitted, or restitution in general; the return of Jews forced into exile but thereby lucky enough to escape the worst; or the question of Austrian citizenship for those who had become citizens of other countries during their exile between 1938–1945.[88]

The existence and re-emergence of anti-Jewish resentments must be seen in the context of the general problem which goes by the name of *Vergangenheitsbewältigung* and the establishment of a post-Nazi political culture, with the corresponding construction of a new official Austrian identity which in turn required both a genetic history and an explication of its political and cultural values. Approximately 500,000 former Nazis were disenfranchised after the war.[89] By 1949, however, most of these had received the right to vote and were thus integrated into the constitutional Second Republic.[90] Apart from the role of the Allied occupying powers in short-circuiting the de-Nazification process, the grounds for postwar Austrian governments lack of serious attempts at re-education or at combatting antisemitic prejudice were straightforwardly political: once the former Nazis had been reintegrated into the electorate, both major parties (the People's Party and the Socialists) had to vie for their votes in the elections.[91] Measures which openly contested the variegated antisemitic heritage in Austria were never implemented, and even those directed against antisemitism as Figl would have defined it were paltry. The existence of broad anti-Jewish sentiment was officially denied, while the periodic open expressions of such beliefs were ascribed to the tiny radical right. At the same time, the postwar governments privately made every attempt to "drag out as long as possible" the negotiations with Jewish authorities over restitution payments.[92]

Until 1986, expressions of anti-Jewish hostility were not seen to have any direct relation to Austrian political culture, but rather were attributed to political slips, as in the case of the People's Party parliamentary deputy Alois Scheibenreif; to personal psychological instability, in the case of then Chancellor Bruno Kreisky's attacks on Simon Wiesenthal; or, in the case of the antisemitic Professor Taras Borodajkowycz, to isolated exceptional personal remnants of Nazi ideology. All such instances trans-

gressed, at least implicitly, recognized normative expectations of Austrian public discourse, and as such were seen in Austria as largely unrelated to the wider political culture.[93] Sociological studies such as that of Hilde Weiss have attempted to register the persistence of anti-Jewish prejudice in contemporary Austria. Weiss's results suggest that, although only seven percent of the Austrian population had "very strong prejudices" against Jews, eighty-five percent were prejudiced in some way or another towards Jews.[94] Bernd Marin offered a model to explain what he rightly called a "paradoxical" phenomenon. According to Marin, postwar antisemitism is an "antisemitism without Jews": such prejudices persist in the face of a sinking Jewish population in Austria, and are usually more widespread in regions where no Jews live and among people who do not know Jews. In addition, it is an "antisemitism without antisemites" in that it is a mass prejudice without legitimacy, without a public subject, without means of propagating it and without the self-confidence of an ideology. Finally, he claims, there is nonetheless an "antisemitism in politics" without their being a "political antisemitism," by which he means that there is a larger tolerance for political lapses, while antisemitism is appealed to indirectly in Austrian election campaigns.[95] Although pioneering in its own terms, at this level of abstraction Marin's model cannot explain the specific processes involved in the transport and realization of antisemitic prejudice. By viewing antisemitism largely as incidence of remnants of Nazi ideology in contemporary Austrian political culture, moreover, he tends to neglect what I have termed the "syncretic" aspect of antisemitic prejudice.[96] Weiss's results have, however, confirmed that antisemitic prejudice is more helpfully viewed as a range of attitudes, predilections and hostilities rather than as specific antisemitic ideologies.[97]

Apart from the normal bias inherent in such undertakings, all such quantitative studies face the difficulty of ascertaining and measuring (from the instruments available, i.e., questionaires) the precise impact of the official taboo on antisemitic prejudice. Thus, such studies may not reliably show how extensive anti-Jewish opinions in fact are, as much as how well the subjects in the study were aware of the preferred response. The inactivity of successive postwar governments' in combatting the prejudice which had existed uninterrupted for centuries, but which had been particularly virulent during the seven years of the Nazi dictatorship, suggests that these beliefs would have continued to exist as a kind of reservoir of hostility toward Jews up to the present, and, given a favorable constellation of circumstances, such as in 1986, could erupt into the open, extending the limits of tolerance for the kind of remarks that certain previously existing taboos against explicit antisemitic remarks had enjoined. The remainder of this book examines how one such opportunity was utilized to turn such vague and unarticulated prejudices into a composite antisemitic *Feindbild.*

Notes

1. Reliable general introductions in English are Elisabeth Barker, *Austria, 1918–1972* (Coral Gables: University of Miami Press, 1973); Karl R. Stadler, *Austria* (New York: Praeger Pub-

lishers, 1971); and Barbara Jelavich, *Modern Austria. Empire and Republic, 1800–1986* (Cambridge: Cambridge University Press, 1987). In addition to those books listed above, good background works are Charles Gulick, *Austria from Hapsburg to Hitler* 2 Vols. (Berkeley: University of California Press, 1948) and Heinrich Benedikt, ed., *Geschichte der Republik Österreich* (Munich: R. Oldenburg, 1954).

2. See William A. Jenks, *Austria Under the Iron Ring, 1879–1907* (Charlottesville: University Press of Virginia, 1965).

3. See Adam Wandruszka, "Österreichs politische Struktur. Die Entwicklung der Parteien und politischen Bewegungen," in Benedikt, ed., *Geschichte,* pp. 289–485.

4. The best treatment of the origins of the Christian Social party is John Boyer, *Political Radicalism in Late Imperial Vienna* (Chicago: University of Chicago Press, 1981). See also Albert Fuchs, *Geistige Strömungen in Österreich 1867–1918* (Vienna: Löcker Verlag, 1984 [reprint of 1949 edition]), pp. 43–82.

5. *Arbeiter-Zeitung,* 5 August 1914, "Der Tag der deutschen Nation," editorial by editor-in-chief Friedrich Austerlitz. See Peter Kulemann, *Am Beispiel des Austromarxismus. Sozialdemokratische Arbeiterbewegung in Österreich von Hainfeld bis zur Dollfuss-Diktatur* (Hamburg: Junius Verlag, 1979), pp. 120–211; Norbert Lesér, *Zwischen Reformismus und Bolschewismus. Der Austromarxismus als Theorie und Praxis* 2nd edition (Graz and Vienna: Böhlau, 1985), pp. 95–133; Anson Rabinbach, *The Crisis of Austrian Socialism. From Red Vienna to Civil War 1927–1934* (Chicago: University of Chicago Press, 1983), esp. pp. 7–31.

6. On Schönerer see A.G. Whiteside, *The Socialism of Fools: Georg Ritter von Schoenerer and Austrian Pan-Germanism* (Berkeley and Los Angeles: University of California Press, 1975).

7. For the background on these negotiations, see Karl Stadler, *The Birth of the Austrian Republic* (Leyden: A.W. Sijthoff, 1966).

8. This aspect of the political culture of the Austrian First Republic is discussed thoroughly in Alfred D. Low, *The Anschluss Movement 1931–1938 and the Great Powers* (New York: East European Monographs, 1985).

9. The Heimwehr were paramilitary formations which had formed in several border areas at the end of the war initially to protect their local areas, but persisted into the First Republic. Although there were attempts to unify the various formations, the Heimwehr remained largely regional, and some inclined to Italian fascist models, while others were sympathetic to the Nazis. On the Heimwehr, see F.L. Carsten, *Fascist Movements in Austria: From Schönerer to Hitler* (London and Beverly Hills: Sage Publications, 1970); C. Earl Edmondson, *The Heimwehr and Austrian Politics, 1918–1936* (Athens, Ga.: University of Georgia Press, 1978).

10. Gulick, *Hapsburg to Hitler,* provides a survey of the developments in the First Republic summarized in the next several paragraphs. See also Benedikt, ed., *Geschichte,* and Rabinbach, *Crisis.*

11. The events leading to the *Anschluss* are catalogued in Gulick, *Hapsburg to Hitler;* see also Gordon Brook-Shepherd, *Anschluss. The Rape of Austria* (London: Macmillan & Co., 1963); and Erwin A. Schmidl, *März 38. Der deutsche Einmarsch in Österreich* 2nd edition (Vienna: Bundesverlag, 1988).

12. See Norbert Schausberger, *Der Griff nach Österreich: Der Anschluss* (Vienna and Munich: Jugend und Volk, 1978); Gerhard Botz, *Wien vom Anschluss zum Krieg: Nationalsozialistische Machtübernahme und politisch-soziale Umgestaltung am Beispiel der Stadt Wien 1938/39* (Vienna/Munich: Jugend und Volk, 1978).

13. See Lonnie R. Johnson, "Die österreichische Nation, die Moskauer Deklaration und die völkerrechtliche Argumentation. Bemerkungen zur Problematik der Interpretation der NS-Zeit in Österreich," in Siegwald Ganglmair, ed, *Jahrbuch 1988* of the Dokumentationsarchiv des österreichischen Widerstandes (Vienna: Österreichischer Bundesverlag, 1988), pp. 40–51.

14. See Gerhard Botz, *Nationalsozialismus in Wien. Machtübernahme und Herrschaftssicherung 1938/39* 3rd revised edition (Buchloe: Druck und Verlag Obermayer, 1988). For an overall picture of Austria's fate under the German occupation, see Radomír Luza, *Austro-German Relations in the Anschluss Era, 1938–1945* (Princeton: Princeton University Press, 1975).

15. See the essay by Gerhard Botz, "The Jews of Vienna from the *Anschluss* to the Holocaust," in Ivar Oxaal, Michael Pollak and Gerhard Botz, eds., *Jews, Antisemitism and Culture in Vienna* (London and New York: Routledge & Kegan Paul, 1987), pp. 185–204. See also Herbert Rosenkranz, *"Reichskristallnacht." 9 November 1938 in Österreich (Vienna, Frankfurt, Zurich: Europa Verlag, 1968); Hans Safrian and Hans Witek, eds., Und keiner war dabei* (Vienna: Picus Verlag, 1988); Erika Weinzierl, *Zu weinig Gerechte. Österreicher und die Judenverfolgung 1938–1945* (Graz and Vienna: Styria Verlag, 1969).

16. For this aspect see Herbert Rosenkranz, *"Reichskristallnacht." 9 November 1938 in Österreich* (Vienna, Frankfurt and Zurich: Europa Verlag), 1968; Safrian and Witek, *Keiner,* passim.

17. See Weinzierl, *Zu wenig,* pp. 113–128 and passim; see also Karl Stadler, *Österreich 1938–1945 im Spiegel der NS-Akten* (Vienna and Munich: Herold, 1966) and William T. Bluhm, *Building an Austrian Nation: The Political Integration of a Western State* (New Haven: Yale University Press, 1973).

18. See Robert H. Keyserlingk, *Austria in World War II. An Anglo-American Dilemma* (Kingston and Montreal: McGill-Queen's University Press, 1988), pp. 123–155; Fritz Fellner, "Die auenpolitische und völkerrechtliche Situation Österreichs 1938. Die Wiederherstellung Österreichs als Kriegsziele der Alliierten," in Erika Weinzierl and Kurt Skalnik, eds., *Österreich. Die Zweite Republik* (Graz, Vienna and Cologne: Styria Verlag, 1972), pp. 53–90; and Audrey Kurth Cronin, *Great Power Politics and the Struggle over Austria, 1945–1955* (Ithaca and London: Cornell University Press, 1986), pp. 15–42.

19. The success of de-Nazification in Germany, of course, should not be exaggerated. See Lutz Niethammer, *Entnazifizierung in Bayern. Säuberung und Rehabilitierung unter amerikanischer Besatzung* (Frankfurt am Main: S. Fischer Verlag, 1972); and Frank Stern, *Im Anfang war Auschwitz* (Gerlingen: Bleicher Verlag, 1991).

20. See Bluhm, *Building,* pp. 52ff.

21. With one exception: in the first government after the war, elected in November 1945 and approved by the Allied Council in December, the Communist Party, which had won four seats in the National Assembly, held the portfolio for electrification and energy. See Manfried Rauchensteiner, *Die Zwei. Die Grosse Koalition in Österreich 1945–1966* (Vienna: Österreichischer Bundesverlag, 1987), pp. 68–78.

22. Within the borders of present-day Austria there were 194,584 registered members of the Jewish religion in 1910. By 1934, their numbers had dropped to 191,481. According to the Nazi paper *Völkischer Beobachter,* around 100,000 Austrian Jews were able to "emigrate" from Austria between the *Anschluss* (March 1938) and May 1939, around another 10,000 before the outbreak of war. After the war began, the remaining Jews were by and large trapped. Altogether approximately 125,000 Austrian Jews succeeded in escaping from the Third Reich. 65,459 Austrian Jews were killed during the Nazi period. On the basis of census figures, the Jewish population in

Austria was 11,224 (including displaced persons) in 1951, 9,049 in 1961, 8,461 in 1971, and 7,123 in 1981. These figures are taken from Johnny Moser, "Die Katastrophe der Juden in Österreich 1938–1945." *Studia Judaica Austriaca.* Vol. V (1977), pp. 67–133, here pp. 122ff. See also idem, "Österreichs Juden unter der NS-Herrschaft," in Emmerich Talos, Ernst Hanisch and Wolfgang Neugebauer, eds., *NS-Herrschaft in Österreich. 1938–1945* (Vienna: Verlag für Gesellschaftskritik, 1988), 185–198; Herbert Rosenkranz, "The Anschluss and the Tragedy of Austrian Jewry 1938–1945" in Joseph Fraenkel, ed., *The Jews of Austria* (London: Valenine, Mitchell, 1970), pp. 479–545; and idem, *Verfolgung und Selbstbehauptung. Die Juden in Österreich 1938–1945* (Vienna and Munich: Herold, 1978), especially Chapters XIII–XVII, XXIV, XXVI-XXXIII.

23. See Quentin Skinner, "Some Problems in the analysis of political thought and action"; idem, "A reply to my critics"; and James Tully, "The Pen is a mighty sword: Quentin Skinner's analysis of politics," in James Tully, ed., *Meaning and Context. Quentin Skinner and his Critics* (Cambridge: Polity Press, 1988).

24. Jürgen Ebach, "Antisemitismus," in Hubert Cancik, Burkhard Gladigow and Matthias Laubischer, eds., *Handbuch religionswissenschaftlicher Grundbegriffe* Vol. 1. (Stuttgart/Berlin/Cologne/Mainz: W. Kohlhammer, 1988), pp. 495-504; Leon Poliakov, *Geschichte des Antisemitismus* (translation of *Histoire d l'Antisémtisme*), Vol. 1: Von der Antike bis zu den Kreuzzügen (Worms: Georg Heintz, 1979), pp. 1–23.

25. Ebach, "Antisemitismus," p. 499.

26. Poliakov, *Geschichte,* Vol. 1, pp. 8ff.

27. Ebach refers to the writings of, among others, Justin, Tertullian, Hippolytes, Origen, Euseb, Chrysostomus, Isaac of Antioch and Augustine as representatives of this tradition. "Antisemitismus," pp. 500–502.

28. Kurt Schubert, "Die Voraussetzungen. Von der Entstehung des Judentums bis zum Ende des ersten Jahrhunderts n. Chr.," in Anna Drabek, Wolfgang Häusler, Kurt Schubert, Karl Stuhlpfarrer and Nikolaus Vielmetti, *Das österreichische Judentum. Voraussetzungen und Geschichte* (Vienna and Munich: Jugend und Volk, 1974), pp. 16–17. The general view of Jews being the only usurers in Europe of the Middle Ages has been qualified in the recent work by Joseph Schatzmiller, *Shylock Reconsidered: Jews, Moneylending and Medieval Society* (Berkeley: University of California Press, 1990).

29. Anna Drabek, "Judentum und christliche Gesellschaft im hohen und späten Mittelalter," in Drabek, et al., *Das österreichische Judentum. Voraussetzungen und Geschichte,* p. 54, note 2.

30. Ebach, "Antisemitismus," pp. 496-497; Poliakov, *Geschichte,* pp. 36–93. Historian Immanuel Geiss, surveying the entire history of occidental racism, views the various pogroms which the first crusade (in the eleventh century) inaugurated as a decisive legitimating precedent for the Nazi persecution of the Jews. Imanuel Geiss, *Geschichte des Rassismus* (Frankfurt am Main: Suhrkamp, 1988), p. 106.

31. Apart from the expulsion of the Jews from England in 1290. See Drabek, "Judentum und christliche Gesellschaft," p. 56, note 27; Poliakov, *Geschichte,* p. 76.

32. In Portugal, however, it was repealed only in 1773. Geiss, *Geschichte,* p. 120.

33. Geiss, *Geschichte,* pp. 114–121; See also Frantisek Graus, "Judenfeindschaft im Mittelalter," in Herbert A. Strauss and Norbert Kampe, eds, *Antisemitismus. Von der Judenfeindschaft zum Holocaust* (Frankfurt/Main and New York: Campus Verlag, 1985, pp. 29–46; Poliakov, *Geschichte,* Vol 2.

34. See, for example, Ernst Ludwig Ehrlich, "Luther und die Juden," in Strauss and Kampe, eds, *Antisemitismus,* pp. 47–65; Poliakov, *Geschichte,* Vol. 2, pp. 113-148.

35. These developments are described in Reinhard Rürup and Thomas Nipperday, "Antisemitismus: Entstehung, Funktion und Geschichte eines Begriffs," in Reinhard Rürup, *Emanzipation und Antisemitismus. Studien zur "Judenfrage" der bürgerlichen Gesellschaft* (Frankfurt am Main: Fischer, 1987), pp. 120–144 (originally published in 1975). Rürup and Nipperday focus primarily on developments in Germany, but this aspect of their research is relevant to the Austrian case as well.

36. See Geiss, *Geschichte,* pp. 168–169.

37. Nipperday/Rürup, "Antisemitismus," pp. 128–136.

38. See Letter from Chamberlain to Dr. E. Boepple, in January, 1925, cited in Doris Mendlewitsch, *Volk und Heil. Vordenker des Nationalsozialismus im 19. Jahrhundert* (Rheda Wiedenbrück: Daedalus Verlag, 1988), p. 45.

39. Paul de Lagarde, *Schriften für das deutsche Volk,* cited in Mendlewitsch *Volk und Heil,* p. 148. See also Jacob Katz, *Vom Vorurteil bis zur Vernichtung. Der Antisemitismus 1700–1933* (transl. Ulrike Berger) (Munich: C.H. Beck, 1989), pp. 307–330. This is a translation with a new preface of *From Prejudice to Destruction. Antisemitism, 1700–1933* (Cambridge, Massachusetts: Harvard University Press, 1980).

40. See Theodor Fritsch (T. Frey), *Antisemitischer Katechismus* (Leipzig, 1888); Nipperday and Rürup, "Antisemitismus," pp. 128–129; P.J.G. Pulzer, *The Rise of Political Antisemitism in Germany and Austria* (New York/London/Sydney: John Wiley and Sons, 1964, New revised edition 1988), p. 49; Katz, *Vom Vorurteil,* p. 268. The evidence on the source of the word "antisemitism" is given in I.A. Hellwing, *Der konfessionelle Antisemitismus im 19. Jahrhundert in Österreich* (Vienna/Freiburg/Basle: Herder, 1972), pp. 22–25 and Nipperday and Rürup, "Antisemitismus," pp. 128–130.

41. Katz, *Vom Vorurteil,* p. 236; Nipperday and Rürup, "Antisemitismus," pp. 130–141.

42. Thomas Frey [T. Fritsch], *Antisemiten-Katechismus,* p. 5, cited in Hellwing, *Der konfessionelle Antisemitismus,* p. 23 n. 20.

43. The best overall histories of antisemitism in Austria remain Dirk van Arkel's "Antisemitism in Austria." Dissertation, University of Leyden, 1966 and Pulzer's *The Rise of Political Antisemitism.* Also of value are Albert Fuchs, *Geistige Strömungen,* and the collection of essays in Nikolaus Vielmetti, ed, *Das österreichische Judentum. Voraussetzungen und Geschichte* (Vienna and Munich: Jugend und Volk, 1974). A concise account of the origins of Austrian antisemitism is also given in Robert Wistrich, *Socialism and the Jews. The Dilemmas of Assimilation in Germany and Austria-Hungary* (East Brunswick, London and Toronto: Associated University Presses, 1982), pp. 187–203. More recent works dealing with different aspects of the development of the early antisemitic movement or the history of the Austrian or Viennese Jews have filled in several gaps in our knowledge. John Boyer's *Political Radicalism in Late Imperial Vienna. Origins of the Christian Social Movement 1848–1867* (Chicago and London: University of Chicago Press, 1981) is indispensable for understanding the subtleties of antisemitic politics among the various constituents which made up the Christian Social movement. Two other important works are William O. McCagg, *A History of the Hapsburg Jews, 1670–1918* (Bloomington and Indianapolis: Indiana University Press, 1989) and Robert Wistrich, *The Jews of Vienna in the Age of Franz Josef* (Oxford: Oxford University Press, 1989). See also the essays in Oxaal, Pollak and Botz, *Jews.*

44. See Schorske, "Politics in a New Key," pp. 116–180. See also van Arkel, "Antisemitism," pp. 9–14; Pulzer, *Rise of Political Anti-Semitism,* pp. 127–187.

45. See Pulzer, *Rise of Political Anti-Semitism,* pp. 3–73; van Arkel, "Antisemitism," pp. 9–14; Hans Tietze, *Die Juden Wiens* (Vienna: Wiener Journal Zeitschriftenverlag, 1987 [origi-

nally published in 1933]), pp. 181–283; more thoroughly: Marsha Rosenblit, *The Jews of Vienna: Assimilation and Identity, 1967–1914* (Albany, New York: State University of New York Press, 1983); Wistrich, *Jews of Vienna,* pp. 38–61; Steven Bellor, *Vienna and the Jews, 1867–1938. A Cultural History* (Cambridge: Cambridge University Press, 1989), pp. 1–70.

46. See in general on this point, Richard Coudenhove-Kalergi, *Judenhass heute* (Vienna/Zurich, 1930), passim. John Boyer has painstakingly reconstructed the social context (among Viennese artisans) which could and did give rise to explanations of social ills which drew upon antisemitic prejudice or remedies incorporating discriminatory measures against Jews. His analysis is suggestive in several respects, but the problem I wish to address here is a rather different one, and may be formulated thus: If I, as an artisan, can view the Jews as the source of my misery—however I define it—it is principally because they represent (or embody) the things which are the cause of my misery. If an alternative, less personalized structual account is ipso facto excluded—otherwise I would not have singled out the post-emancipation Jews—then, merely by asking the question why, I would be forced to seek the explanation of the Jews' exploitative behavior in the characteristics of the Jews themselves. In this endeavor, I could draw upon a wide variety of suitable and accessible prejudices from several different sources. See Boyer, *Political Radicalism,* pp. 40–121.

47. Van Arkel, "Antisemitismus," pp. 81–193. Boyer is right to consign Schneider to what he describes as a "sub-elite" inside the Christian Social party. This, of course, does not mean either that Schneider's views on Jews were the reason he did not rise higher in the party hierarchy, nor that his views were discordant with others in the central leadership. Pattai's own history suggests that rabid Jew hatred, even of a racial kind, did not endanger one's chances for a career in the party. See Boyer, *Political Radicalism,* p. 72.

48. *Unverfälscht Deutsche Worte,* 15 March 1884, quoted in Pulzer, *Rise of Political Anti-Semitism,* p. 171.

49. Letter from Schönerer to Ernst Vergani, probably March, 1889, cited in Pulzer, *Rise of Political Anti-Semitism,* p. 173. See also van Arkel, "Antisemitism," pp. 81–108, 186–193.

50. Pulzer, *Rise of Political Anti-Semitism,* p. 174. See also van Arkel, "Antisemitism," pp. 186–190; Boyer, *Political Radicalism,* pp. 219–226.

51. Schönerer excepted, of course. For a representation of how these cross-currents look graphically, see the diagram between pp. 80–81 in van Arkel, "Antisemitism."

52. See van Arkel, "Antisemitism," pp. 56–67; Pulzer, *Rise of Political Anti-Semitism,* pp. 132–137, 168-169; and Boyer, *Political Radicalism,* pp. 166–180, which offers the best brief discussion of Vogelsang's social theory. The term "neo-feudalist" is van Arkel's.

53. Van Arkel, "Antisemitism," pp. 58–59. See Karl Marx, "On the Jewish Question," translated by Gregor Benton, in *New Left Review* (Quintin Hoare), ed., *Early Writings* (London: Penguin Books), pp. 211–241.

54. Wiard Klopp, *Die sozialen Lehren des Freiherrn Karl von Vogelsang. . .,* pp. 268, 96, quoted in Van Arkel, "Antisemitism," p. 59.

55. Ibid. See also Pulzer, *Rise of Political Anti-Semitism,* pp. 133–134.

56. Boyer, in *Political Radicalism,* p. 180, writes: "The joining of Catholicism to antisemitism with the mediation of Catholic social theory and lower clerical politics helped to justify the movement in terms other than the impoverished eclecticism of *Kleinbürger* Jew hatred."

57. Ibid. pp. 156–161.

58. On Deckert see Hellwing, *Konfessioneller Antisemitismus,* pp. 185–197; Van Arkel, "Antisemitism," pp. 29–32.

59. Deckert was convicted and fined for his role in disseminating this forgery in 1893. Hellwing, *Konfessionelle Antisemitismus,* pp. 218–220.

60. *Das Vaterland,* Nr. 123. Beiblatt, 5 May 1893, cited in Hellwing, *Konfessionelle Antisemitismus,* p. 205.

61. Josef Deckert, *"Der wahre Israelit" vor den Geschworenen,* cited in ibid., p. 246.

62. *Deutsches Volksblatt,* 23 March 1901, cited in ibid., p. 297.

63. *Reichspost,* 24 December 1918, cited in Pulzer, *Rise of Political Anti-Semitism,* p. 318.

64. Cited in ibid., p. 318.

65. Cited in Anton Staudinger, "Christlich-soziale Judenpolitik in der Gründungsphase der österreichischen Republik," in Karl Stuhlpfarrer, ed., *Jahrbücher für Zeitgeschichte* (1978) (Vienna: Löcker Verlag, 1979), p. 29.

66. Cited in ibid., p. 31. On Kunschak and the antisemitism of the Christian Social labor movement, see Anton Pelinka, *Stand oder Klasse? Die christliche Arbeiterbewegung Österreichs 1933–38* (Vienna: Europaverlag, 1972), pp. 213–233.

67. Ignaz Seipel, *Volkswohl* (1919) Number 2, p. 49ff, cited in Moser, "Die Katastrophe," p. 84.

68. Pelinka, *Stand oder Klasse,* pp. 298–300; Staudinger, "Christlich-soziale Judenpolitik," p. 47, note 114.

69. E. Czermak and O. Karbach, *Ordnung in der Judenfrage* (1933), cited in Pulzer, *Rise of Political Anti-Semitism,* p. 319.

70. Letter from Hitler to A. Gemlich, 16 September 1919, reprinted in Detlev Claussen, ed., *Vom Judenhass zum Antisemitismus* (Darmstadt: Neuwied, 1987), p. 192.

71. *Volkswohl,* (1919), Number 1, p. 43, quoted in Moser, "Die Katastrophe," p. 83.

72. See Staudinger, "Christlich-soziale Judenpolitik," passim; Bruce F. Pauley, "Political Antisemitism in Interwar Vienna," in Oxaal, Pollak and Botz, eds., *Jews,* pp.152–173; Sylvia Maderegger, *Die Juden im österreichischen Ständestaat 1934–1938* (Vienna and Salzburg: Geyer, 1973), pp. 105–128; Cf. Alfred Diamant, *Austrian Catholics and the First Republic* (Princeton: Princeton University Press, 1960).

73. Benedikt Kautsky, ed., *Friedrich Engels Briefwechsel mit Karl Kautsky* (Vienna: Danubia-Verlag, 1954), p. 125.

74. The best account of antisemitism in Austrian Social Democracy prior to 1918 is Robert Wistrich, *Socialism and the Jews,* Part II. A brief statement of Wistrich's argument is to be found in ibid., "Social Democracy, Antisemitism and the Jews of Vienna," in Oxaal, Pollak and Botz, *Jews,* pp. 111–120. See also John Bunzl, "Zur Geschichte des Antisemitismus in Österreich," in John Bunzl and Bernd Marin, *Antisemitismus in Österreich* (Innsbruck: InnVerlag, 1983), pp. 34–38; Leopold Spira, *Feindbild 'Jud'* (Vienna: Löcker Verlag, 1981), 21–101.

75. Wistrich, "Social Democracy," p. 120. See, however, the comments of Sigurd Paul Scheichl, "The Contexts and Nuances of Anti-Jewish Language: Were all the 'Antisemites' Antisemites?" Oxaal, Pollak and Gerhard Botz, *Jews,* pp. 89–110.

76. See Wistrich, *Jews of Vienna,* pp. 497–536; Sander L. Gilman, *Jewish Self-Hatred. Antisemitism and the Hidden Language of the Jews* (Baltimore and London: Johns Hopkins University Press, 1986), pp. 208–308; and Jacques Le Rider, *Der Fall Otto Weiniger. Wurzeln des Antifeminismus und Antisemitismus* (Vienna and Munich: Löcker Verlag, 1985), pp. 189–219. See, however, Allan Janik, "Viennese Culture and the Jewish Self-Hatred Hypothesis: A Critique," in Oxaal, Pollak and Botz, *Jews,* pp. 75–88.

77. See Ehrlich, "Luther," pp. 61–64.

78. See Dennis E. Showalter, *Little Man, What Now? Der Stürmer in the Weimar Republich* (Hamden, Connecticut: 1982), pp. 103–108.

79. *Stürmer*-Sondernummer 3, Oktober 1935. Cited in Kurt Schubert, "Der Weg zur Katastrophe," *Studia Judaica Austriaca* Vol. V. (1977), pp. 31–66, here, p. 58. See also Nira Feldman, "Motive des 'Stürmer.' Anatomie einer Zeitung," Dissertation, University of Vienna, 1966, pp. 32–38.

80. Adolf Hitler, *Mein Kampf,* quoted in Martin Gilbert, *The Holocaust* (New York: Henry Holt and Company), p. 28.

81. Johann von Leers, "Vorwort" to H. Schramm, *Der jüdische Ritualmord. Eine historische Untersuchung* (Berlin, 1942), p. xvii.

82. See particularly, *Der Mythos des Zwanzigsten Jahrhunderts* (Munich: Hoheneichen Verlag, 1930).

83. Botz, "The Jews of Vienna," in Oxaal, et al., *Jews,* pp. 185–204; Rosenkranz, *Verfolgung und Selbstbehauptung.*

84. See Gerhard Botz, *Wohnungspolitik und Judendeportation in Wien 1938 bis 1945: Zur Funktion des Antisemitismus als Ersatz nationalsozialistischer sozialpolitik* (Vienna: Jugend & Volk, 1975); ibid., *Nationalsozialismus in Wien. Machtübernahme und Herrschaftssicherung 1938/39* (Buchloe: DVO, 1988); Rosenkranz, *Verfolgung und Selbstbehauptung;* Hans Witek, "'Arisierungen' in Wien. Aspekte nationalsozialistischer Enteignungspolitik 1938–1940," in Talos, Hanisch and Neugebauer, *NS-Herrschaft in Österreich,* pp. 199–216, and Gerhard Jagschitz, "Von der 'Bewegung' zum Apparat. Zur Phänomenologie der NSDAP 1938 bis 1945," in ibid., pp. 487–516.

85. Discussions of antisemitism after the war have been marred by some terminological confusion. If antisemitism refers to all utterances, political or ideological currents or movements in history which have been hostile to Jews, then it did exist in postwar Austria (even though explicit discrimination was legally forbidden). Indeed, the term does help emphasize the continuity of such beliefs, and any thesis of overall continuity in anti-Jewish prejudice in the postwar period presupposes the existence of anti-Jewish feelings, politics and public discourse in the period beforehand. The above paragraphs have attempted to retrace in outline form the traditions which were probably carried over into the Austrian Second Republic. On the other hand, for reasons outlined above, the use of the term "antisemitism" seems incapable of fully capturing the nuances of public discourse on Jews and things Jewish in a political culture where the open expression of more vulgar anti-Jewish prejudice is conventionally stigmatized. Antisemitism, as a word describing anti-Jewish prejudice, was always a solecistic misnomer, but was a self-description of the antisemites themselves. However, because it applied to a self-conciousnessly and openly hostile attitude towards Jews, it seems inappropriate for the period after World War II. Terms such as anti-Jewish or antisemitic prejudice, however, emphasize the character of the utterance but abstract from the relationship between these beliefs, whatever form they may take, and any explicit intentionality, i.e., whether the existence of prejudice must necessarily imply discriminatory intent. Although I have some objections to its use, I will employ terms such as antisemitism, antisemitic, etc., in the conventional sense cited above. See Nipperday and Rürup, "Antisemitismus," pp. 144, 233, note 122.

86. *Shanghai Echo,* cited in *Der Neue Weg,* Nr. 10, Beginning of June, 1947, p. 11.

87. Leopold Kunschak, for example, was elected President of the National Assembly in December, 1945. It also bears mentioning here that Karl Lueger still has both a square and a section of the Ringstrasse named in his honor, and that the local ÖVP organization in Vienna to this very day refuses to allow "Pfarrer Josef Deckert Platz" to be renamed.

88. See Dietmar Walch, *Die jüdischen Bemühungen um die materiellen Wiedergutmachungen durch die Republik Österreich* (Vienna: Geyer, 1971); Brigitte Galanda, "Die Massnahmen der Republik Österreichs für die Widerstandskämpfer und Opfer des Faschismus–Wiedergutmachung," in Sebastian Meissl, Klaus-Dieter Mulley and Oliver Rathkolb, eds., *Verdrängte Schuld, verfehlte Sühne. Entnazifizierung in Österreich 1945–1955* (Vienna: Verlag for Geschichte und Politik, 1986), pp. 137–201.

89. Dieter Stiefel, *Entnazifizierung in Österreich* (Vienna/Munich/Zurich: Europaverlag), pp. 84–124.

90. Oliver Rathkolb, "NS-Problem und politische Restauration: Vorgeschichte und Etablierung des VdU," in Meiss, Mulley and Rathkolb, *Verdrängte Schuld*, pp. 73–99.

91. Rathkolb, "NS-Problem," pp. 79–88. See also Spira, *Feindbild*, pp. 103–107.

92. See Robert Knight, ed., *"Ich bin dafür, die Sache in die Länge zu ziehen." Die Wortprotokolle der österreichischen Bundesregierung von 1945 bis 1952 über die Entschädigung der Juden* (Frankfurt am Main: Athenäum Verlag, 1988). See also Ruth Beckermann, *Unzugehörig. Österreicher und Juden nach 1945* (Vienna: Löcker Verlag, 1989), pp. 35–47.

93. See Spira, *Feindbild*, pp.107–152; Martin van Amerongen, *Kreisky und seine unbewältigte Gegenwart* (Vienna: Styria, 1983); Robert Wistrich, "The Strange Case of Bruno Kreisky," *Encounter* (May 1979), pp. 78–85.

94. Hilde Weiss, *Antisemitische Vorurteile in Österreich* (Vienna: Braumüller, 1984); Bernd Marin, "Umfragebefunde zum Antisemitismus in Österreich 1946–1982. SWS-Meinungsprofile aus: Journal für Sozialforschung 23. Jg. (1983)," in Bunzl and Marin, *Antisemitismus*, pp. 226 and unpaginated appendix following.

95. Bernd Marin, "Ein historisch neuartiger 'Antisemitismus ohne Antisemiten?'" and "Nachwirkungen des Nazismus. ein Reproduktionsmodel kollektiver Mentalität," in Bunzl and Marin, *Antisemitismus*, pp. 171–224.

96. See Marin's analysis of a series on the history of the Jews in the leading Austrian daily, in which he makes comparisons between *Stürmer* and the idiom employed by Viktor Reimann. Marin, "'Die Juden' in der Kronen-Zeitung. Textanalytisches Fragment zur Mythenproduktion 1974," in Bunzl and Marin, *Antisemitismus*, pp. 89–169. On other weaknesses of Marin's analysis and other quantitative studies of antisemitic prejudice, see Projektteam "Sprache und Vorurteil," "'Wir sind alle unschuldige Täter!'" Studien zum antisemtischen Diskurs im Nachkriegsösterreich." Project Report, Manuscript (Vienna, 1989), pp. 28–38.

97. Weiss, *Vorurteile*, pp. 105–114.

3

From Election Catatonia to the "Waldheim Affair"

In 1985, Kurt Waldheim's candidacy for president of Austria in the election to be held the following year appeared to have been fated. Waldheim himself, however, was never one to leave such things to chance, and in fact preparations for his campaign had been under way for some time. The principal unanswered question was whether he would run as the candidate of the Austrian People's Party (ÖVP) alone, as he had done in his unsuccessful bid in 1971, or as the joint candidate of both major parties. The advantages Waldheim could bring to such a campaign were considerable. His international reputation was undisputed, even if in the eyes of some international figures he was not exactly an object of admiration. The Austrian daily *Kurier,* for example, reported in May 1981 then Israeli defense minister Ezer Weizman's characterization of Waldheim as "one of the most unlikeable people I have ever met—hostile, ice cold and not very intelligent," but the Austrian press tended to overlook Waldheim's unpopularity in places like the United States and to stress his perceived international achievements.[1]

In 1981, Waldheim still had his sights set on a third term as U.N. Secretary General. As he expressed it to the Vienna daily *Die Presse,* he would consider it a "duty and an honor" to assume the responsibility of that office, should it be offered.[2] The Austrian government, led by Bruno Kreisky, also did its best to support Waldheim's candidacy. Then foreign minister Willibald Pahr sent emissaries to New York to run the international election campaign on Waldheim's behalf, while Kreisky himself wrote to numerous heads of state and government recommending Waldheim for the post.[3] The Austrian press reported some opposition to Waldheim's candicacy, principally in the United States, and it was in this connection that the name of U.S. Congressman Stephen Solarz first appeared in the Austrian press: Solarz, it was reported, considered Waldheim incompetent and far too compliant in his dealings with dictators.[4]

All endeavors of the Socialist Kreisky government to keep the conservative Waldheim in New York, and thereby out of Austria, were to no avail: after sixteen ballots without a clear majority, Waldheim withdrew his candidacy. No sooner had Waldheim, described by one Austrian journalist as the "most successful Austrian diplomat since

Metternich," lost his re-election bid at the U.N., than he began making plans for his candidacy for president in his native Austria.[5] The Socialists and the People's Party soon began outbidding each other to lay claim to him. For the People's Party, hopeful that Waldheim's unchallenged prestige would offset its own discouraging domestic political standing, such a move was both logical and imperative. The Socialists (SPÖ), on the other hand, wanted to pre-empt this very danger by posing as Waldheim's principal benefactor. As the party in government, moreover, the Socialists were better placed to reward Waldheim's party political neutrality. Such calculations were scarcely hidden in discussions about Waldheim's post-U.N. role. Alois Mock, then leader of the ÖVP, deflected discussion about a future presidential candidacy for Waldheim, but only because he considered it "impolite" to speak about the current President Rudolf Kirchschläger's successor so early in the latter's second term of office.[6] For his part, Kreisky repeatedly praised Waldheim and remarked, slightly patronizingly, that "a man like Waldheim will have his part to play within the realm of the available possibilities."[7] Among those possibilities floated were that of a special envoy for Kreisky or the head of a commission on East-West relations.[8] The reasons were not hard to guess. As one provincial newspaper reported, "Kreisky . . . wants to do everything to prevent the former ÖVP minister and candidate for president in 1971 from becoming the People's Party's showpiece."[9] After his return to Vienna in March, 1982, Waldheim quickly became a local foreign policy expert who was frequently consulted about world problems.[10] By March 1983, a suitable position had been found: the Austrian government founded and funded the Interaction Council,[11] with Kurt Waldheim as chair.

If the work of the Interaction Council was quickly forgotten (whether it had ever been noticed is a moot question), Waldheim's ambition to become president was not. By December 1983 several Austrian journalists were convinced that Waldheim would run as the candidate of the ÖVP.[12] In the course of the next two years, the People's Party attempted to cement its ties with Waldheim in ways which can only be described as grovelling. Its fraction in parliament, for example, nominated Waldheim for the Nobel Peace Prize, presumably reasoning that Waldheim's role in the Interaction Council would give him the edge over his rivals that his service as U.N. Secretary General had not.[13]

Although the ÖVP's desire to nominate Waldheim as its candidate for president in 1986 was fairly well known, SPÖ leaders were undecided as to whether they would even nominate someone to run against him.[14] The evidence suggests, in fact, that the SPÖ had not finally excluded supporting Waldheim as a joint candidate until his nomination by the People's Party precluded it. In late winter 1984–1985, there had been rumors about an attempt to oust Alois Mock as head and chancellor candidate of the national ÖVP. By nominating him as candidate for president, effectively kicking him upstairs, the way would be open to elect a new party leader, as by tradition Mock would have resigned this post so as to appear less partisan.[15] The plan was to have been carried out at a meeting of the party leadership in March 1985. Before this ÖVP conclave, Fred Sinowatz, chancellor and head of the Socialist Party, told Waldheim that the SPÖ had not yet ruled out supporting Waldheim as a joint candidate. On the morning of 2 March 1985, Waldheim relayed this information to Mock. That very afternoon, Mock moved to endorse Waldheim as the ÖVP candidate for president, apparently without Waldheim's knowledge. Thus a combination of Mock's instinct for political survival and the desire to utilize Waldheim's obvious attractiveness as a candidate, which even the Socialists recognized, to revive the ÖVP's own sagging political fortunes, led to Waldheim becoming the candidate of the ÖVP alone.[16] This was a fateful decision, for it forced the Socialists to put up their own candidate, and made the contest far more partisan than it otherwise would have been. On 16 April 1985, Sinowatz announced that Kurt Steyrer, incumbent Minister of the Environment, would be the candidate of the Socialists.[17]

Waldheim and Steyrer, as well as Otto Scrinzi, former member of parliament of the Freedom Party (Freiheitliche Partei Österreichs [FPÖ]) and in this election the recognized representative, among other things, of Nazi nostalgia, and Freda Meissner-Blau, the Green candidate, all sought the office of president of Austria. Although largely ceremonial in practice, the office of president in Austria does carry potential sources of constitutional authority which, in a situation where the reigning political consensus of the Second Republic broke down, could devolve increased actual powers on the president in relation to the elected National Assembly.

The current Austrian constitution, which defines and limits the powers of the president, is an amended version of the original constitution of the First Republic, written by the legal theorist Hans Kelsen and adopted in 1920. The 1920 constitution vested all essential powers in parliament, and the presidency was little more than a ceremonial post.[18] In 1929, the constitution was substantially amended, replacing what had been an explicit parliamentary system with a limited presidential one. Prior to the 1929 reforms, the result of intense negotiations between the then Christian Social Chancellor Johannes Schober and the representative of the Social Democratic Party, Robert Danneberg,[19] the president had been elected by the Federal Assembly (*Bundesversammlung*), a joint session of the lower and upper houses of the Austrian parliament. The 1929 amendments provided for the popular election of the president and gave the president the powers to dissolve, call and prorogue the national assembly; to issue and govern by means of emergency decree; and to name and dismiss the government, among others. The president also became commander-in-chief of the armed forces.[20] The events of March, 1933, when then Chancellor Dollfuss suppressed parliament, until the *Anschluss,* provide a negative example of the inefficacy of safeguards against subversion of the constitution by the government when the president is not of a mind to exercise the constitutional powers he or she possesses to defend the institutions of the republic. President Miklas, after all, undertook nothing against Dollfuss' disabling and then destruction of the First Republic, although he at any time could have dismissed him and forced new elections. On the contrary, after Dollfuss had prevented parliamentary government by force, Miklas reaffirmed Dollfuss in office and agreed to his plans to rule by emergency decree.

The provisional Austrian government which had been formed before the end of the second World War initially intended to revive the 1920 constitution, and with it the parliamentary republic, in post-Nazi Austria. However, the Federal Assembly eventually adopted a restricted version of the 1929 constitution for the Austrian Second Republic.[21] The actual legal basis of the Austrian constitution, codified in a document dealing with constitutional and legal continuity (*Rechtsüberleitung auf verfassungsrechtlicher Ebene*), revived the constitutional status that existed prior to 4 March 1933, the date of the so-called "self-elimination" of the Austrian parliament, thus including the 1929 constitution and all constitutional laws passed up to March 1933. This date is relevant in another respect, for it explicitly denies constitutional legitimacy to laws passed subsequent to 4 March 1933. The later governments of Engelbert Dollfuss and all governments of Kurt Schuschnigg, i.e., the so-called "Austro-fascist" governments, were, in terms of constitutional continuity, implicitly condemned.[22]

In a European context, the Austrian head of state exercises somewhat greater power than the president of the Federal Republic of Germany, but considerably less than the president of Fifth Republic France. In addition, there are checks on those powers which the president does exercise. Article 67 of the constitution, for example, specifies that all acts undertaken by the president, excepting those minor prerogatives he or she may exercise independently, must be on the recommendation of the government or a minister authorized to make the proposal, and must be countersigned by the chancellor.[23] The president may indeed dissolve the national assembly, but may do so only once for the same reason. Moreover, new elections must be held within a period which enables the newly elected parliament to assemble within one hundred days.[24]

The Austrian president's specific functions in the legislative, executive and judicial branches of the state do not add up to an independent locus of political authority which could effectively act as a counterweight to the government or the courts. Principally a representative figure who in foreign affairs carries out many of the ceremonial tasks historically undertaken by monarchs, the functions of the Austrian president include officially representing the country abroad, the reception and acceptance of credentials of foreign diplomats, the approval of Austrian consular appointees serving abroad, and the signing of treaties. In addition to these "acts of external authority," as the constitution puts it, the president's duties include officially summoning and dissolving the national assembly (this is normally a routine matter, and is done on recommendation of the legislature), signing bills into law (there is no right of veto), appointing and dismissing the government, the naming and approving of certain officials and the bestowing of professional titles (a rather time-consuming job in Austria), and the granting of pardons, amnesties, and remissions of prison sentences. One curious provision of the Austrian constitution is the authority it bestows on the president to confer "legitimacy" on children born to unmarried parents.[25]

The president, on the other hand, does represent an independent pole of legitimacy, since he or she is directly elected, and the powers of office, although not vast, could tip the political balance in a crisis situation. The much-vaunted moral authority of the presidents in the Austrian Second Republic, however, has derived more from the relatively cautious and limited exercise of the constitutional powers at their disposal. As with any constitution which attempts to anticipate possible emergency contingencies, how much actual power the president in Austria could assume depends on the constellation of political forces inside parliament and the modalities of extra-parliamentary power. Austria's postwar social partnership and experience of coalition government gave Austrian presidents little actual room for political initiative, even had they chosen to use their legally given powers to the fullest. With the disappearance of one-party majorities in the National Assembly, and the increase in the number of smaller parties, the hitherto largely formal power of the president to name and dismiss the chancellor could become more significant.[26] This possibility lay behind the Cassandra-like warnings of the SPÖ on the dangers of a President Waldheim who had stated his intention explicitly to use his constitutional powers to the maximum.[27] The Austrian president is certainly not powerless, but parliamentary constraints on the independent exercise of these prerogatives (the ostensible moral authority which the president may employ is another matter, though there is little danger that Waldheim posed much of a threat here) are so extensive that this argument would normally be dismissed as unserious were it not rendered ludicrous by the fact that the feared "strong man" was Kurt Waldheim.

To most observers, the phase of the election campaign before the disclosures about Waldheim's wartime past bordered on the soporific; the weekly magazine *Profil* termed it the "great yawn."[28] However, it was during this period that a distinctive and aggressive idiom first ermerged which would assume a greater significance later in the campaign. In October, 1985, long before anyone had heard of Army Group E in relation to Waldheim, Thomas Chorherr, writing in *Die Presse,* asked rhetorically whether "this presidential campaign will be the most unpleasant yet in the Second Republic?"[29]

Part of the reason, of course, was the high political stakes riding on the result, at least in the eyes of the ÖVP. Their dilemma was how to draw maximum political advantage from Waldheim's candidacy for the party itself, without identifying him so closely with it that it would endanger either Waldheim's election as president or the hoped-for attendant political "turn." This ambiguity was reflected in the inconsistent labels which the People's Party, and in particular its leader Alois Mock, applied to the Waldheim candidacy. Mock initially attempted to portray Waldheim as the "candidate of the ÖVP, whom we consider non-partisan,"[30] but was apparently quickly persuaded to abandon this formulation. Even papers normally sympathetic to the ÖVP had been puzzled by Mock's behavior. "It would truly have been simpler and more honest," wrote a journalist in the *Salzburger Nachrichten,* "to present Waldheim as the candidate of the ÖVP . . . instead of putting on this act."[31]

One early issue in the Austrian presidential election campaign was the strategy developed for Waldheim by Young and Rubicam, the advertising agency whose Vienna office had taken on the Waldheim account.[32] According to a company spokesperson, the agency saw its main task as making "Waldheim into an Austrian again, because he had worked abroad for so long,"[33] though making Waldheim "appear as someone close to the people," observed Hermann Polz of the *Oberösterreichischen Nachrichten* would not be easy, for it would entail making "him appear as something which he cannot be."[34] In September 1985, the Austrian weekly *Profil* published selections of the agency's draft treatment of the Waldheim electoral advertising strategy. The agency sought to utilize Waldheim's obvious high level of recognition by associating him with the U.N., but to give him the additional image of someone with whom the voters could "identify." Waldheim, a man with experience of the world, should make voters feel they are better able "to confront the challenges of the future." Voters should be able to recognize the Austrian in Waldheim and see in him someone who thinks and feels as they do, someone of whom they can be proud. The advertising treatment also suggested that Waldheim's electoral chances improved the less he was identified with the ÖVP. Associating Waldheim with the People's Party would endanger his "good prospects among liberal and floating voters; among Socialists, for whom Dr. Waldheim's convincing qualifications [for office] would neutralize [otherwise] strong party loyalty; among all Austrians who value humanity above partisan advantage."[35]

Waldheim took this advice to heart and began to take his distance from the ÖVP. Declarations of support for Waldheim from various well-known personalities and targeted interest groups, the various private "initiatives," for example, were organized primarily by Waldheim's daughter Christa, who played a role somewhat akin to that of Maureen Reagan in her father's campaign. At the same time, Waldheim himself went on a media offensive, the central point of which was to emphasize his political independence from the People's Party, with which, however, he shared a common *"Weltanschauung."*[36] People's Party politicians did their part as well. At the official launch of Waldheim's candidacy in November 1985, Alois Mock emphasized that his party would "not claim a single vote [for Waldheim] for itself."[37] Confronted with the statement of the ÖVP provincial governor of Salzburg that Waldheim should dismiss the current government if elected president, General Secretary Michael Graff affirmed that "Waldheim is in no way an ÖVP candidate," but is "merely supported" by the party.[38] The SPÖ and newspapers supporting Steyrer's candidacy, on the other hand, drew their own conclusions from the agency strategy paper and attempted to firm up the association of Waldheim with the ÖVP.[39]

Profil's publication of extracts from the Young and Rubicam advertising paper occasioned the first use of the word "defamation" in the campaign. The People's Party's daily *Neues Volksblatt* (*NVB*) reacted swiftly with the banner headline: "Mud-Slinging Campaign Against the Candidate Dr. Kurt Waldheim." This "defamation campaign" was designed to make Waldheim look "ludicrous," in order "to improve the chances of the candidate of the Socialist Party."[40] This public relations mishap was quickly followed by another. Heribert Steinbauer, Waldheim's ÖVP campaign manager, himself had allegedly received a $15,000 commission from Young and Rubicam for landing the Waldheim contract.[41] Although Waldheim was not personally the target of this criticism, the response from ÖVP General Secretary Michael Graff was illustrative of the instantaneous and invariable riposte he would apply to criticisms of Waldheim later in the campaign: "I consider this a disgraceful slander. I am convinced that not one word of the story is true."[42]

The "great yawn" continued unabated until March, 1986. The principal preoccupation of the press lay in exposing embarassments of the three candidates Waldheim, Steyrer and Meissner-Blau (the national press scarcely covered the candidacy of Otto Scrinzi). For example, at a press conference called to introduce leading Austrian personalities who supported Waldheim's candidacy, Katrin Gutensohn, Olympic skier from Austria, offered a novel reason for endorsing the former Secretary General: she had "eaten frankfurters with him from the same plate" and "was astonished by his naturalness."[43] At the same press conference, Georg Karp, reporter for the West German monthly *Stern,* raised the first questions about Waldheim's unknown past. He asked the persons endorsing Waldheim whether they were aware of the title of his doctoral dissertation or that he had been a member of the Nazi Student Union.[44] Karp's questions were duly reported in some newspapers, but more as a curiosity than a serious allegation. Only *Profil* took the trouble to investigate the charges, but concluded that they were groundless.[45]

Waldheim's role as Austrian foreign minister in 1968, at the time of the crushing of the Prague spring, also came under scrutiny during the final months of 1985. The controversy was prompted by SPÖ general secretary Peter Schieder's remark that Waldheim had acted "inhumanely and cowardly."[46] The background to the controversy was this: After the invasion of the Warsaw Pact troops (20–21 August 1968), Rudolf Kirchschläger, then Austrian ambassador to Czechoslovakia, interrupted his vacation and returned to Prague after having met with Waldheim in Vienna. During this meeting, Kirchschläger requested the foreign ministry (i.e., Waldheim) not to send him any official instructions. Despite assurances that this request would be honored, Kirchschläger soon received a directive not to allow anyone seeking asylum into the embassy. He disregarded the order and over the next four days the embassy staff was able to issue around 20,000 entry visas for Czechoslovak citizens. Shortly thereafter, Kirchschläger received another directive instructing the embassy in Prague not to issue any more visas, period. This one bore then Foreign Minister Kurt Waldheim's signature. The source of this story was Kirchschläger himself (who in the meantime had twice been elected president of Austria) or, more precisely, Kirchschläger's biographer Mario Schenz.[47] Waldheim denied the charges vehemently and claimed that he had given Kirchschläger "a free hand in the matter of the issuing of visas for Czechs."[48]

Michael Graff was quick to respond to Schieder's attack, in the same vernacular which was to become the standard fare of the election campaign: the comment was a "defamation" and a "garbage can campaign."[49] Kirchschläger's own elliptical comment on the events: "I thought that this instruction had come from some pedantic undersecretary in the foreign ministry. This turned out to be an error."[50] One month later, the *NVB* published what it called the "clear explanation of the 'inhuman' directive,"[51] but the suspicion remained. Indeed, this might have become an important issue in the otherwise lifeless campaign had not the other "defamation campaign" overtaken it.

The opinion polls prior to March 1986 offered a confusing picture. Most of them were unreliable, principally because the raw data were not normally published. Instead, the figures and interpretations were left to the clients themselves (in this case the parties or campaign committees) to explain. Polls from April 1985 gave Waldheim 48% to Steyrer's 27%.[52] By August of the same year, Steyrer had cut Waldheim's lead somewhat, but was still lagging far behind (46%–34%).[53] The figures from October and November 1985 were hotly disputed: the ÖVP presented the results of a survey of voters made by the Fessl polling organization which showed Waldheim with 49% and Steyrer with 29%.[54] At the same time, Hubertus Czernin wrote in *Profil* that Waldheim was running consistently ten percentage points ahead of Steyrer, without, however, mentioning any polls to support his claim.[55] In November, the SPÖ published the results of a poll they had commissioned from the IFES organization which it claimed gave Waldheim a mere 3 point lead over Steyrer (42% to 39%).[56] According to the Socialists, by December Waldheim and Steyrer were running neck and neck with 35% each and 20% undecided.[57] Gallup's leading electoral analyst Karmasin showed Waldheim ahead of his main rival 42% to 36% at roughly the same time.[58] The SPÖ, on the contrary, even claimed that Steyrer was running ahead of Waldheim,[59] although they modified this later, showing Steyrer and Waldheim even with 36% each.[60]

Though these results were frequently contradictory and their presentation always bewildering, it was possible to discern the following general trends: because of his undoubted renown and prestige as former U.N. Secretary General, Waldheim enjoyed a significant lead over his principal rival Steyrer in voter preference polls, which Steyrer was able partially to recoup. Around January 1986 most newspapers were writing that Freda Meissner Blau's candidacy would force a run-off election.[61] Given the trends, this news would appear to have been good for Steyrer, but bad for Waldheim, who continued to hope for a victory in the first round.

It is important to underline three points about this early phase which have a bearing on the subsequent development of the election campaign. Firstly, the words slander and defamation first made their appearance in this initial, largely uneventful period of the election campaign. Several newspaper commentators also expressed the view that this campaign would involve a lot of mud-slinging. This suggests that the pattern of attributing any criticism of Waldheim's credibility to a slander campaign, which the ÖVP would later exploit to the maximum, fit into a line of argument that was already partly established, but that was in any case familiar.

Secondly, the campaigns of both major candidates included heavy doses of patriotism. Steyrer as well as Waldheim sought to promote a strong sense of national consciousness. However, as soon as the voters perceived that this national self-esteem was being called into question from abroad by means of the attacks on Waldheim, the injured national pride redounded more to Waldheim's favor than to Steyrer's.

Thirdly, Waldheim's ostensible Nazi past was raised in this early phase of the campaign, and by a foreign journalist. The allegations were, in general, not taken seriously by the domestic news media and were quickly forgotten. The one magazine which did investigate them, *Profil,* found nothing untoward about Waldheim's past. The ÖVP, or newspapers who formed a type of *cordon sanitaire* around Waldheim, could then portray later disclosures which were serious and were supported by documentary evidence in a similarly disparaging way. They, and presumably many voters, could assume that there was much ado about insubstantial and unsubstantiated charges.

The "Ides of March": The Campaign Takes a Turn

As was mentioned above, journalists from the weekly *Profil* had followed up on the allegations raised by *Stern* reporter Georg Karp at the October, 1985, press conference, but had found nothing. Since rumors of one sort or another about Waldheim's past had been circulating for years, however, *Profil* decided to investigate further. In fact, three different areas of Waldheim's past had been the subject of speculation or research since 1985: (1) the possible connection between Waldheim and General Pannwitz, or, more precisely, between Waldheim and the SS units under Pannwitz's control. Waldheim had always acknowledged serving on the eastern front in a reconnaissance unit commanded by Pannwitz, but had denied any contact with the *Einsatzkommandos* operating in the same area. Any later relationship between Pannwitz and Waldheim were matters of pure speculation. (2) Waldheim's alleged membership in National Socialist organizations; and (3) Waldheim's service under Alexander Loehr.[62] Hubertus Czernin, the *Profil* reporter assigned to the story, received Waldheim's permission to inspect his wartime records[63] and did so in late February 1986. Czernin's look at Waldheim's file yielded some sensational details from Waldheim's past which had hitherto been unknown to the public: documents, principally Waldheim's *Wehrstammkarte,* or military service card, suggested that the former Secretary General had indeed been a member of the Nazi Student Union (*Nationalsozialistischer Deutscher Studentenbund,* or NSDStB) and that he had also belonged to a horseback riding unit of the *Sturmabteilung,* or SA, while attending the Consular Academy between 1937 and 1939. Despite some "incomplete, imprecise, and sometimes false" claims to the contrary, as Czernin put it, Waldheim had also been declared "fit for duty" after his wounding on the eastern front in 1941, "had been assigned to the Army High Command 12[64] in Salonika by the end of March, 1942, and only received study leave in December of the same year."[65]

Profil's impending publication of the documents had been announced on Sunday, 2 March 1986, in the Austrian daily *Kurier,* a means of indirect advertising common for a magazine owned by the same media conglomerate. On the same day, that is, before the magazine itself had appeared on the newsstands, the Waldheim campaign office issued pre-emptive denials of the points which the *Profil* article was to raise.[66]

Following the customary practice, that issue of *Profil* appeared on the streets on Sunday evening, 2 March, and on the newsstands the following day. The major wave of reactions to *Profil's* disclosures also came on 3 March. Officials of both the ÖVP and the SPÖ had known of research into Waldheim's wartime career for some time.[67] In addition, it is virtually certain that the ÖVP paper *Neues Volksblatt* responded fully aware of the planned revelations in the *New York Times* (*NYT*).[68] How much the editorial staff of the Socialist *Neue AZ/Tagblatt* (*AZ*) knew of the impending publications is still uncertain. In the event, these initial reactions offered insights as to the overall lines of attack and counterattack among Austria's two major political parties.

The headline of the *NVB* on 3 March announced that "Waldheim was never a Member of the SA!" "The presidential election campaign has scarcely entered its hot phase," the article stated, "and the trashcan campaign of lies against the non-party and independent candidate Kurt Waldheim has already begun." The official Waldheim explanation of the disclosures was laid down by Gerold Christian, who had left his job with the *Salzburger Nachrichten* to run Waldheim's press office. Waldheim, he claimed, had "never been a member of the NSDAP or one of its affiliated organizations. This was established even by the Austrian state police in 1945, after Waldheim's entry into [service in] the Foreign Ministry."[69]

Waldheim himself was busy denying not only the allegations actually made, but a few extra as well. According to a report in the *Wiener Zeitung* (*WZ*), Waldheim said that he had "never belonged to either the NSDAP, the SS or the SA," and denied having had any contact with "events in Yugoslavia," though he failed to specify which ones. Waldheim and Alois Mock also introduced an argument with much explanatory power, precisely because it was not likely to be contradicted, namely that Waldheim's past had been thoroughly investigated by the Austrian security police, the KGB and the CIA.[70]

The new disclosures thus fit into a familiar discursive framework, that of a "campaign of mud-slinging and lies," and were related causally to the "defamations" which had been attributed the the SPÖ earlier in the campaign. This, although the research into Waldheim's past had been done independently of the Socialists and by a magazine most Socialist Party members (as well as many journalists on the magazine) would consider positively hostile to the SPÖ. That there could be an independent civic or even journalistic interest in Waldheim's possible membership in two Nazi organizations or in a hidden wartime service was not, at least in these quarters, acknowledged.

The Waldheim camp also vigorously evaded any serious discussion of the allegations against Waldheim: some charges were simply not addressed, others "refuted" or explained away by introducing irrelevant side issues, still others systematically distorted in a way to insure that those raising serious questions could be made to look foolish or even invidious when these inflated (and arguably invented) "defamations" were "disproved." Waldheim spokesman Gerold Christian, for example, was quoted as saying that Waldheim had had "nothing to do with SS units during his entire military service, nor was he involved in activities which would have violated the laws of war or human rights."[71] According to the official ÖVP newspaper *Neues Volksblatt,* Christian's allusion to the SS units was a reply to *Profil's* revelations, which the *NVB* claimed had mentioned Waldheim in connection with SS units "on the eastern front or in Serbia and Croatia or both."[72] The former reference refers to that part of Waldheim's service prior to his leg injury in December 1941 (the only military service, incidently, that Waldheim had publicly acknowledged until March 1986). At that time, Waldheim was serving under Colonel Helmut von Pannwitz, who commanded the reconnaissance unit 45, of which Waldheim was a part. It is well known that there were SS units operating in geographical proximity to Waldheim's unit during the invasion of the Soviet Union, but there has never been any reliable evidence tying Waldheim to these in any way. Indeed, *Profil* journalist Czernin alluded to (and rejected) this charge in reporting, on the basis of information provided by Hans Kwisda, who had served with Waldheim in the reconnaisance unit, that Waldheim had had nothing to do with partisans. The article also mentioned that Pannwitz later became commander of the First Cossack division, which was integrated into the Waffen-SS and was responsible for numerous war crimes in Yugoslavia. However, Czernin explicitly repudiated any association between Waldheim and Pannwitz's activities in the Balkans, writing that "Pannwitz's and Waldheim's paths had parted at Christmas, 1941," i.e., before Waldheim had even set foot in Yugoslavia. Christian's statement in reply to the *Profil* article in fact contains two distinct propositions, both of which address ostensible accusations concerning Waldheim's involvement in war crimes. At the time of the statement (3 March at the latest),[73] however, the only "allegations" about Waldheim in the public domain were those contained in *Profil.* The central theme of Czernin's article was that Waldheim had not always given completely accurate accounts either of the time he was studying in Vienna or of his service in the Wehrmacht. Neither Czernin nor to my knowledge anyone else at that time had publicly charged Waldheim with having been personally involved with SS units, much less that he had committed violations of the "laws of war or human rights." Thus, in light of *Profil's* explicit statements to the contrary, and in the absence of any other such allegations of wrongdoing, Christian's categorical statement that Waldheim had had "nothing to do with SS units during his entire military service, nor was he involved in activities which would have violated the laws of war or human rights," only makes sense as an attempt to refute or at least defuse an allegation that was entirely of his own making. Christian did not address the specific evidence raised in the *Profil* article, while Mock merely reiterated that Waldheim had "clarified everything."[74] The discussion on the Nazi associations Waldheim might have had in 1938, moreover, centered on his membership in the SA and the Nazi Student Union, but not the Nazi party itself, the NSDAP. Christian's emphasizing that Waldheim had "never been a member of the NSDAP or one of its affiliated organizations," thus enabled the Waldheim campaign to discredit an additional charge no one had raised.

Mock, Christian and Waldheim, this time aided by Simon Wiesenthal, also emphasized that the Austrian security police, the KGB and the CIA had all investigated

Waldheim before he became U.N. Secretary General, and had found nothing.[75] "If there had been anything incriminating on Waldheim," Wiesenthal was quoted as saying, "the Soviets would never have allowed Waldheim's election as U.N. Secretary General."[76] Apart from the fact that neither the CIA nor the KGB was likely to confirm or deny the report, this line of argument was convincing only on the assumptions that the KGB, CIA, the Austrian Security Police and Wiesenthal agreed on what constituted incriminating material, and that these secret services had possessed all relevant documents necessary to make such a judgment. In the event, this explanation of sorts, which sounded convincing, found a strong echo both among Waldheim's critics and his supporters. The related question as to whether Waldheim might have been susceptible to blackmail while Secretary General, which was discussed extensively in the United States, also presupposed that these secret services had been fully informed over the details of Waldheim's past, and that they considered this information sufficiently incriminating to be able to coerce favors from Waldheim, both of which would be extraordinarily difficult to prove.[77]

Waldheim and the ÖVP thus presented *Profil's* disclosures as a continuation of the "defamation campaign" against Waldheim by the SPÖ for domestic electoral reasons. They defended Waldheim against them with a strategy whose main components were to deny all allegations initially as untrue, then condemn the motives of the SPÖ. They also drew on selected expert authorities (Wiesenthal) in support of unproven assertions (which were, however, presented as fact) and argued with a syllogistic logic which could not be proved, but could neither be disproved.[78]

The "Defamation Campaign" Gains International Momentum

While *Profil* was looking into Waldheim's past, John Tagliabue of the *New York Times,* among others, was conducting his own investigation. On 4 March 1986, the *Times* published Tagliabue's article under the title, "Files Show Kurt Waldheim Served Under War Criminal." Some of the documents which formed the basis of Tagliabue's article had been given to him by the World Jewish Congress (WJC).[79] The latter's own urgent interest in possible discrepancies in Waldheim's biography apparently dated only from January 1986, when its attention was drawn to an article in *Profil* in which Waldheim had been described as an "assistant adjutant in the general staff of Army Group E, whose commanding officer was Loehr."[80] The "true" story of how, from whom and for what purpose the WJC received certain of the initial documents it passed on to Tagliabue and later published is less important here than the speculation about it which appeared in the Austrian media. What can be established is that *Profil* journalist Czernin had undertaken his own initial research independent of other individuals or organizations.[81] The initial press reactions in Austria to the reports from abroad conformed broadly to the pattern outlined above. The editors at *Die Presse* did note that the *NYT* article emphasized, as its headline stated, Waldheim's "Balkan Deployment during the Second World War," but reported further that "Waldheim Denies All Attacks [and is] Optimistic Despite the Campaign."[82] "I interpret the whole thing as an attempted slander campaign," Waldheim was quoted as saying. He also found it "interesting" that "these things" had come from abroad. Waldheim declared that he had "repeatedly" claimed to have "served as an interpreter during the time in question" (1942–1943) and that all the allegations against him had been refuted "for 40 years." He had, moreover, "known absolutely nothing" about atrocities committed by the troops of Army Group E.[83] The reporter in the *Die Presse* did not question Waldheim about why these gaps had appeared in his public biography, or at least there is no indication of it in the article, even though Waldheim "confirmed" that "he had served in a unit of General Alexander Loehr, who was condemned as a war criminal by Yugoslavia in 1947." Nor was Waldheim confronted with the actual evidence produced by the *NYT* about his political associations. The paper here served merely as a vehicle for Waldheim's own version of the story without the hindrance of critical reporting.

The banner headline in the *Neues Volksblatt,* "Nazi Fairy Tale about Presidential Candidate Dr. Kurt Waldheim," continued the paper's editorial policy of the previous day. The *NYT* and the WJC were mentioned in the article as the source of the scourge. Although the rubric over the unsigned article, "All Statements are Slanders!" represented the line of the Waldheim campaign managers faithfully, it contradicted the content of the article itself, which reported that Waldheim had "confirmed that he belonged to the staff of General Alexander Loehr." This statement was apparently not a slander. The *NVB* summarized the other allegations contained in the *NYT* article, although the version it presented was somewhat misleading. It also explained Waldheim's failure to mention his wartime service after December 1941 in his memoirs. Waldheim's war injury on the eastern front had represented a caesura in his life, since afterwards he "could no longer serve at the front." As his books were memoirs of his service at the United Nations and not autobiographies, Waldheim deemed the details of his Balkan service unworthy of mention.[84]

On the same day, the *Neue Kronen Zeitung* (*NKZ*) dedicated an article and two opinion columns to the "Campaign against Waldheim." In one of these, a column printed under the rubric "What's behind it," Ernst Trost introduced new arguments in Waldheim's defense. An important one was that any criticism of Waldheim's war service was tantamount to criminalizing the mere donning of a Wehrmacht uniform. If Waldheim were to come under fire, Trost maintained, "then every soldier who saw duty in the Balkans would be unfit for public office, for this partisan war was fought with enormous severity on both sides. However, most soldiers were merely small cogs in the gigantic war machine."[85]

The issue of the Balkan war, and more particularly, the role of Austrian soldiers fighting Yugoslav partisans, was one which not only could call on a long tradition of hostility in Austrian political culture towards South Slavs (*"Serbien muss sterbien"* was a well-known slogan in the first World War), but also one which dovetailed with Waldheim's own trivialization of the Nazi atrocities committed by the Wehrmacht in the Balkans. A widely held image of the Balkan theater historically portrayed in post-Second World War Austria effectively equated the violence of the partisans with that of the occupying Germans, and has served to justify the latter as a defense of civilized German values against the barbaric Slavic hordes. The variety of Waldheim's assignments in the Balkan theater placed him geographically near both criminal acts committed against Jews in which the Wehmacht was complicit (predominantly deportations), and equally heinous acts against Yugoslav "bands" and civilians. In Austria, however, these latter were often not viewed or described as atrocities. Although in principle semantically unobjectionable, in this context the amalgamation of the deportation of Jews with reprisal killings against "bands" under the same rubric "atrocities" appears to have increased the reluctance on the part of Waldheim and his supporters to acknowledge the seriousness of the issue of Waldheim's possible knowledge of or involvement in the deportations of Greek Jews. This was especially intractable in view of another myth widely encountered in Austria, namely, that the Wehrmacht played virtually no role in the "final solution." The ambiguities which the conflation of various categories of atrocities generated were used to good effect by Waldheim both to discredit the charges made against him in regard to Jewish deportations, as well as to cast himself as the persecuted victim of those ostensibly indicting an entire generation.[86]

Other papers exhibited more caution towards the Waldheim line. Journalists from *Kurier*, for example, attempted to clarify the allegations by independently investigating the role of the German Wehrmacht in the deportation of Jews from Greece, while the leading columnist on the paper, Hans Rauscher, even raised doubts about Waldheim's credibility. Two other reporters sought witnesses who might have been able to shed light on the matter and landed on Johann Auf, who had served with Waldheim in Arsakli and who ostensibly could establish "what is true and what is false . . . in the attacks."[87] The *Wiener Zeitung* presented a largely accurate summary of the *NYT* report and a representative sample of politicians' responses to it. It also reported on an interview given by Simon Wiesenthal, head of the Jewish Documentation Center in Vienna. Wiesenthal said that he did not believe Waldheim to be "personally guilty of Nazi crimes during the Third Reich" and considered a membership in the Nazi party "improbable." On the other hand, Wiesenthal found it difficult to believe Waldheim's statement that he had not known about the deportations of Jews from Salonika.[88]

Although the reporting of the Austrian papers was not uniform, the above sample is representative of the range it covered. It is possible to identify an emerging consensus about the allegations against Waldheim from the reactions to the first reports of the *NYT* and the revelations of the WJC. Later disclosures relating to Waldheim's past would continue to be interpreted in terms of these assumptions, which bore a strong resemblance to the explanations offered by the Waldheim campaign and overlapped with and extended those which had appeared prior to the "intervention" from "abroad." The principal elements were the idea that the "reproaches" (*Vorwürfe*) of the *NYT* represented a continuation of the slander campaign that the Socialist Party had been waging against Waldheim for some time, and the notion that the Socialists or their accomplices had fed documents to the WJC and the *NYT* in order to damage

Waldheim's international reputation—his main advantage over his principal opponent, Steyrer. The criticism directed against Waldheim was deemed all the less credible because Waldheim's past had not interested anyone for over 40 years. At the time Waldheim entered the diplomatic service, he had been cleared by the Austrian secret service, and during his candidacy for U.N. Secretary General, the CIA, the KGB and the Israelis had investigated him. If there had been anything in the least incriminating against him, it was asked, would they have allowed him to become Secretary General? Waldheim never denied having served in the German army during World War II. He did not mention his tour of duty in the Balkans, the argument went, because he had had such a minor function and also because his injury on the eastern front had been a far more significant event in his life. He had also known nothing of Jewish deportations and had had nothing to do with other atrocities. But if he were to be blamed for such things, then truly every Wehrmacht soldier would also come under suspicion.

These arguments, advanced for the most part by the Waldheim camp, sounded plausible, even though they rested on a number of questionable and unverified assumptions. Here we should recall that the People's Party had already fingered the SPÖ as the instigator of dirty tricks. It would have been suspicious in any case that the appearance of embarassing material on Waldheim in the midst of an election campaign were merely coincidental. The effect of the Waldheim line on voters was not easy to measure, but its impact on the media was extensive. Further new disclosures were interpreted broadly in light of it.

The explanations offered by the Waldheim team seemed all the more believable because important authorities appeared to confirm them. If Simon Wiesenthal, the famous Nazi hunter, were convinced that Waldheim was not a Nazi, and Josef Lovinger, president of the Jewish community in Greece, had never heard Kurt Waldheim's name mentioned in connection with Nazis, would it not then follow that the allegations made against the former Secretary General were "nothing but filthy lies [*erstunken und erlogen*]?"[89] Incumbent President Rudolf Kirchschläger, who possessed undisputed moral authority among Austrians of all political persuasions, also gave implicit support to the Waldheim propaganda line. Three days after the first disclosures by the WJC and the *NYT*, Kirchschläger was quoted as deploring "the political witch hunt about the past [*politische Vergangenheitsjagd*] we are presently witnessing in the presidential election campaign."[90] Kirchschläger's pejorative and yet indulgent expression, which implied that it was reprehensible merely to raise questions about Waldheim, conceded an essential element of the Waldheim position, namely, that the publication of documents alone amounted to a "vilification."

This pattern, ostensibly or actually supported by authorities as diverse and of such unimpeachable credentials as Simon Wiesenthal, Josef Lovinger and Rudolf Kirchschläger, which in its essentials was taken over by most of the papers and in the electronic media in Austria, buttressed Waldheim's own efforts to show that the disclosures were a "planned slander campaign" undertaken for tactical electoral reasons. If one assumed the existence of such a "slander campaign," however, then several things followed. Firstly, the search for its orchestrators began in earnest. This, in turn, tended to affect attitudes towards the allegations themselves. Finding out who was behind the disclosures displaced the investigation into the allegations themselves. Moreover, since some of the original charges (arguably invented by the Waldheim campaign itself) turned out to be groundless, it then became possible to fit further pieces of documentary evidence into the pre-existing mold of an unjustified attempt to defame; consequently, to take them seriously would be beneath one's dignity. Every new document, every new allegation, could be incorporated into this framework, and not without a certain justification. The questions ultimately raised by these assumptions, however, if they were not to collapse, could really only be answered by resorting to the old bogey of an international Jewish conspiracy.

Notes

1. *Kurier,* 3 May 1981.

2. *Die Presse,* 11 September 1981.

3. *Neue Zeit,* 17 September 1981.

4. *Neue AZ/Tagblatt* (*AZ*), 27 June 1981. Solarz is a member of the U.S. House of Representatives from New York City. His correspondence with Waldheim in the 1980s became one of the major pieces of evidence to support the charge that Waldheim had deliberately misrepresented his army career. See *Profil,* 14 March 1988.

5. See *Profil,* 29 September 1981 and 16 September 1985.

6. *Salzburger Nachrichten* (*SN*), 15 December 1981. Kirchschläger was constitutionally prohibited from seeking a third consecutive term as president.

7. *Kurier,* 16 December 1981.

8. *Neue Kronen Zeitung* (*NKZ*), 1 January 1982.

9. *Südost Tagespost,* 1 January 1982.

10. See u.a., *NKZ,* 11 April 1982; *Die Presse,* 23 July 1982, 23 and 30 August 1982, and 29 September 1982; *Kurier,* 8 August 1982 *AZ,* 9 August 1982; and *Kurier,* 18 October 1982.

11. *Wochenpresse,* 19 July 1983. The "Interaction Council" brought together former prominent "statesmen" who met to discuss the problems of the world under Kurt Waldheim's leadership.

12. *Kurier,* 21 December 1983. See also *Die Presse,* 13 August 1983; *NKZ,* 16 January 1984.

13. *Neues Volksblatt* (*NVB*), 11 February 1985.

14. See *Oberösterreichische Nachrichten,* 19 April 1983; *Vorarlberger Nachrichten,* 16 August 1983; *Die Presse,* 17 January 1984; 17 January 1985; *AZ,* 11 February 1985.

15. *NKZ,* 4 March 1985.

16. *Kurier,* 17 January 1986. Hubert Wachter described the events of the weekend of 2–3 March 1985. Compare the version of events by Heinz Fischer, then Socialist Minister of Science and Research, in the *Wiener Zeitung* (*WZ*), 23 March 1986. See also the *Süddeutsche Zeitung,* 3–4 May 1986.

17. *Die Presse,* 17 April 1985.

18. Ludwig K. Adamovich and Bernard-Christian Funk, eds., *Österreichs Verfassungsrecht* 3rd edition (Vienna and New York: Springer-Verlag, 1985), p. 71.

19. On these negotiations see Charles Gulick, *Austria from Habsburg to Hitler* (Berkeley, California: University of California Press, 1948) Vol. 2, pp. 862–74, and Norbert Leser, *Zwischen Reformismus und Bolschewismus* 2nd edition (Vienna: Böhlau, 1985), pp. 287–292.

20. Gulick, *Habsburg to Hitler,* pp. 875–79; Adamovich and Funk, *Verfassungsrecht,* pp. 73–74.

21. On the evolution of the position against the 1920 constitution, see Hella Postranecky-Altmann, "Wie die Verfassung von 1929 wieder kam," *Wiener Tagebuch* Nr. 12 (December 1985), pp. 19–20, which quotes the declaration.

22. Adamovich and Funk, *Verfassungsrecht,* p. 83.

23. Hans R. Klecatsky and Siegbert Morscher, eds., *Bundesverfassungsgesetz mit Nebenverfassungsgesetzen. Stand 15.9.1983* 2nd edition (Vienna, 1983), 64.

24. Klecatsky and Morscher, *Bundesverfassungsgesetz,* p. 40. See also Adamovich and Funk, *Verfassungsrecht,* pp. 261–264, and Manfred Welan, "Das österreichische Staatsoberhaupt," *Österreichisches Jahrbuch für Politik,* Sonderband 2 (Vienna, 1986), p. 76.

25. Welan, "Staatsoberhaupt," pp. 38–39; Klecatsky and Morscher, *Bundesverfassungsgesetz,* pp. 59–65 and passim; Adamovich and Funk, *Verfassungsrecht,* pp. 262–264. The term "legitimacy" does not appear in the Austrian constitution; the quotation marks signify my own displeasure at the lack of a less pejorative equivalent term in English.

26. Welan, "Staatsoberhaupt," p. 75.

27. See *AZ,* 14 March 1986.

28. This was the title of editor P.M. Lingens' commentary in the 13 January 1986 issue.

29. *Die Presse,* 4 October 1985. See also *Kurier,* 16 October 1985, where it was suggested that this election campaign would be "one of the most brutal in a long time."

30. *WZ,* 11 April 1985. See also *Kurier,* 14 July 1985.

31. *SN,* 4 March 1985. The author was referring to the weekend nomination intrigue.

32. *Die Presse,* 29 June 1985.

33. The *Südost Tagespost,* 24 August 1985 and the *Oberösterreichische Nachrichten,* 29 August 1985. See also *AZ,* 5 September 1985.

34. *Oberösterreichische Nachrichten,* 13 July 1985. See also the interview in *Kurier* on 14 July 1985.

35. Quoted in *Profil,* 16 September 1985.

36. *Wiener,* December 1985; see also *Basta,* December 1985 and *Österreichische Monatshefte,* December 1985; *Vorarlberger Nachrichten,* 17 February 1986.

37. *WZ,* 5 November 1985.

38. *Die Presse,* 15 January 1986.

39. The January, 1986, issue of *Welt der Arbeit* for example, carried a headline, "Mock and Graff come with Waldheim."

40. *NVB,* 17 September 1985.

41. *Wochenpresse,* 8 October 1985.

42. *Kurier,* 9 October 1985.

43. *Die Presse,* 4 October 1985; *AZ,* 4 October 1985.

44. *Die Presse,* 4 October 1985.

45. *Profil,* 14 October 1985.

46. *Kurier,* 8 November 1985.

47. For the background to the story see *Profil,* 14 October 1985. See also Mario Schenz, *Bundespräsident Rudolf Kirchschläger* (Vienna: Böhlau Verlag, 1984), pp. 71–77.

48. *Wiener,* December 1985.

49. *NVB,* 21 November 1985. The original "Schmutzkübelkampagne" appears to have been a new coinage for the German language as well. Freda Meissner-Blau employed a similar idiom when asked about her receipt of a disability pension while she was collecting fees as a consultant for the same company, speaking of a "garbage can" as well. *AZ,* 31 January 1986; See also *AZ,* and *NVB,* 1 February 1986.

50. *Profil,* 14 October 1985.

51. *NVB,* 20 and 21 November 1985. The "explanation" offered in fact confirmed Kirchschläger's, not Waldheim's version, but this was omitted from the article.

52. E. Gehmacher, F. Birk, and G. Orgis, "Die Waldheim-Wahl. Eine erste Analyse," *Journal für Sozialforschung* Vol. 26, No. 3 (1986), 319–331.

53. *Kurier,* 23 August 1985.

54. *NVB,* 23 October 1985.

55. *Profil,* 14 October 1985.

56. *Die Presse,* 15 November 1985; *AZ,* 19 November 1985.

57. *AZ,* 18 December 1985.

58. *Die Presse,* 30 January 1986.

59. *AZ,* 27 January 1986.

60. *AZ,* 11 November 1986.

61. According to Austrian laws, to be elected president a candidate must receive at least 50% plus 1 of the valid votes cast. Should no candidate receive the absolute majority, as happened in 1986, a second election is to be held within 6 weeks. What makes the second election in Austria a bit different from a "run-off" in the normal sense is the provision that the party or group which put up a candidate in the first "round" may choose to nominate a different one for the second. Klecatsky and Morscher, *Bundesverfassungsgesetz,* p. 62.

62. See *Profil,* 17 August 1987 and 24 August 1987.

63. Then Chancellor Fred Sinowatz had previously instructed the chief archivist not to allow access to either Waldheim's or Steyrer's personal wartime records without his, and the respective candidate's, explicit permission.

64. The Army High Command 12 (*Armeeoberkommando* 12, or AOK 12) became Army Group E in January 1943. The various command structures of the Wehrmacht in the Balkans between 1941 and 1945 are not directly relevant here. To avoid confusion, in the text I will refer to the headquarters of the general staff in Arsakli, Waldheim's official home base from 1942 until late 1944 (when the location of the general staff moved as the armies retreated), as Army Group E, even when referring to the period prior to January, 1943. Waldheim's temporary assignments will be distinguished where necessary. For more information on Waldheim's postings see Chapter 4 and Kurz, et al., *Bericht.*

65. *Profil,* 3 March 1986.

66. *Kurier,* 2 March 1986; *NKZ,* 2 March 1986.

67. See *Profil,* 24 August 1987.

68. Waldheim's office knew by Sunday, 2 March, at the latest that the *NYT* planned to do a story, since John Tagliabue interviewed Waldheim about the documents on that day. See *NYT,* 4 March 1986.

69. *NVB,* 3 March 1986.

70. *WZ,* 4 March 1986.

71. Ibid.

72. *NVB*, 3 March 1986.

73. *NVB*, 3 March 1986. Christian's statement is rendered in the *NVB* in the subjunctive used for indirect discourse in German, but it is identical to the statement quoted in *WZ*, 4 March 1986.

74. Ibid.

75. *WZ*, 4 March 1986; *NVB*, 3 March 1986.

76. *Die Welt*, 4 March 1986. See also *NKZ*, 24 March 1986, *Neue Zeit*, 26 March 1986, and *Frankfurter Allgemeine Zeitung*, 26 March 1986.

77. See, for example, Rainer Stepan, "Die Vorwürfe, Daten und Fakten—Eine historische Dokumentation," in Andreas Khol, Theodor Faulhaber and Günther Ofner, eds., *Die Kampagne. Kurt Waldheim—Opfer oder Täter? Hintergründe und Szenen eines Falles von Medienjustiz* (Munich: Herbig, 1987), pp. 327–347; Robert Erwin Herzstein, *Waldheim. The Missing Years* (London: Groton, 1988), pp. 213–231; *NYT*, 8 April 1986.

78. For example: All potential Secretaries General of the U.N. are checked for anything incriminating by the CIA, KGB and the Israelis and eliminated if something incriminating is discovered; Kurt Waldheim was Secretary General; therefore, nothing incriminating can exist against Waldheim. Wiesenthal, by the way, had stated his views in a conditional manner, but his plausible speculation became hard fact in the hands of the Waldheim camp's propaganda machinery.

79. *NYT*, 4 March 1986; "News from World Jewish Congress" (News from WJC), 4 March 1986.

80. *Profil*, 27 January 1986. The quotation was from military historian Manfried Rauchensteiner.

81. An examination of the possible role of individual officials of the SPÖ in the leaking of damaging documents is beyond the scope of this book. The best summary of the evidence is published in *Profil*, 17 August 1987 and 24 August 1987. See also *Jüdische Rundschau Maccabi*, 20 March 1986 and Günther Ofner, "Die Role der SPÖ in der 'Waldheim-Kampagne,'" in Khol, Faulhaber and Ofner, eds., *Kampagne*, pp. 121–175.

82. *Die Presse*, 5 March 1986. There are some difficulties in rendering some of the German words and expressions in this context. The normal German word for an electoral campaign is *Wahlkampf*, and the word used to describe something like an advertising or slander campaign is *Kampagne*. The headline here thus appears slightly puzzling. Although somewhat tedious, the way I will deal with this difficulty is to use electoral as the attributive adjective in front of campaign when it is used in that sense, and use quotation marks where possible to distinguish the one campaign from the so-called defamation "campaign." The reference Waldheim is making, which the *Die Presse* headline quotes, is, of course, to the "campaign," not the electoral contest.

83. *Die Presse*, 5 March 1986.

84. *NVB*, 6 March 1986.

85. *NKZ*, 6 March 1986. The difference between news reports and opinion columns in the *NKZ*, however, is more one of layout than of substance.

86. See Rubina Möhring, "Trauma Balkankrieg. Die Rezeption der Jahre 1941–1945 in den österreichischen Printmedien—ein Pressevergleich," in Walter Manoschek, Hans Safrian, Florian Freund, Pertrand Pelz and Rubina Möhring, "Der Balkankrieg im Zweiten Weltkrieg als Teil der österreichischen Zeitgeschichte," Ms. (Vienna, 1989), pp. 285–323.

87. *Kurier*, 6 March 1986.

88. *WZ*, 6 March 1986.

89. Wiesenthal soon became an all-purpose authority, whose judgment was acclaimed by all sides in the dispute. Wiesenthal's initial statement was balanced, and therefore could be inter-

preted as giving comfort to both Waldheim and his critics. On the one hand, from Wiesenthal's statement that he did not believe Waldheim to have been a member of the NSDAP (which, incidently, no one had alleged), several reporters (and the Waldheim camp) inferred that therefore Waldheim had not been a "Nazi." On the other hand, Wiesenthal found it hard to believe Waldheim's claim of ignorance of the deportations of the Salonika Jews, which gave succor to those criticizing Waldheim's credibility. See *WZ,* 6 March 1986; *NVB,* 6 March 1986; *NKZ,* 5 March 1986; *AZ,* 6 March 1986; *NKZ,* 6 March 1986. The most explicit example of how Jewish sources were manipulated in general is shown by the headline and article of 6 March 1986 in the *Oberösterreichische Nachrichten,* a regional paper which normally supports the ÖVP editorially and stood fully behind Waldheim. The headline read, "Jews exonerate Waldheim." "Prominent Jews," the article stated, "who are very knowledgeable about Nazi crimes, exonerated the People's Party candidate for the presidential election, Kurt Waldheim." Josef Lovinger, mentioned prominently in many of these reports, later repudiated his initial reaction after he had been shown the documentary evidence which the WJC had assembled. His later statement, of course, received a very different press in Austria, if it was mentioned at all. See, for example *NYT,* 10 April 1986 and *NKZ,* 10 April 1986.

90. *Die Presse,* 7 March 1986. *NVB,* 8 March 1986.

4

"What Did You Do in the War, Kurt?"

The publication of the results of an investigation by the British Ministry of Defense in October, 1989, was the occasion for much relieved self-congratulation by Kurt Waldheim. This commission, which had investigated Waldheim's possible role in the murder of Allied prisoners of war while serving as a staff officer of Army Group E in Greece in 1944, found no "evidence of any criminal activity on the part of Lieutenant Waldheim."[1] According to Waldheim, the report proved "once again that all the allegations in connection with my wartime service are without foundation. It has confirmed my previous statements."[2]

Exactly which of the dozens of his frequently conflicting statements[3] Waldheim believes the Mininstry of Defense report to have "confirmed" is not clear, but the Vienna daily *Die Presse's* upbeat judgment that the report had "rehabilitated" the Austrian president was a bit premature.[4] The controversy surrounding Kurt Waldheim's hidden past has nonetheless been plagued from the beginning by confusion over the issues involved, in no small part thanks to Waldheim himself. If for Waldheim the only relevant question related to his wartime service was whether he could be held personally responsible for war crimes, for his critics the issues were by no means clear. The displeasure that might have accompanied the discovery of merely embarassing aspects of a hidden past soon gave way to odium and rancor when the nature of that past became known, while the possibilities for inferring something opprobrious about Waldheim's service in the Wehrmacht from his previously concealed Nazi affiliations were legion. The publication of first the U.S. Army's Central Registry of War Criminals and Security Suspects (CROWCASS)[5] and then the Yugoslav war crimes file, on which the CROWCASS list was ultimately based, however, transformed the vague intimations into concrete juridical suspicion. This Yugoslav War Crimes Commission file, known by its Serbo-Croatian name *Odluka,* or "decision," had been compiled by the Yugoslav authorities to incriminate Waldheim in war crimes and was submitted to and accepted after only cursory perusal by the United Nations War Crimes Commission (UNWCC) in 1948, shortly before it concluded its work. The evidence in Waldheim's file is highly suspect, and the Yugoslav's principal target was probably not even Waldheim personally, but his boss in the Austrian Foreign Ministry at the time, Karl Gruber. Since Gruber, as a leader of armed resistance to the Nazis in Tyrol, was himself invulnerable to political extortion, the Yugoslavs apparently hoped to use the material they had assembled against Waldheim to compromise Gruber and thereby to wring concessions from Austria in their dispute over the postwar borders. The background to the compilation of this file and its fate in the changing political alignments of the postwar world, of course, only became known much later.[6] Although public awareness of the unresolved allegations dating from 1948 would have forced Waldheim to confront the issue of criminality independently of her or his critics' intentions, it nonetheless bears repeating that the issue of criminality was first introduced into the debate in 1986 by Waldheim spokesmen before either the World Jewish Congress (WJC) or the *New York Times* made their own findings public on 4 March 1986 (neither accused Waldheim of criminal activity in any case).[7]

Since these early days of the Waldheim affair, a great deal has been clarified, at least for those capable of sustaining the effort. In order to help us find our way through the labyrinth of the sometimes conflicting evidence and even more disparate range of interpretations, as well as comprehend the arguments and references which arose in the course of the election campaign and how they related to the Waldheim camp's systematic distortion of the allegations made against him, it would be wise to summarize what is now known about Waldheim's affiliations and allegiance to the National Socialists and his service in the Wehrmacht. For only in light of such a discussion is it possible clearly to understand the dynamic of the controversy as well as make an informed judgment about Waldheim and his past.

The two principal questions which have arisen in the course of the debate were: was Waldheim a "Nazi" and was he complicit in war crimes? In this chapter we hope to be able to propose an answer to both. What follows makes no claims to being a comprehensive chronological account of Waldheim's career, or even a fully systematic evaluation of the controversial points of evidence. Reliable works of both types exist and their findings need not be repeated here.[8] On the basis of these, however, we will offer a sketch of Waldheim's whereabouts in the Balkans, and suggest some reasons why the discussion of Waldheim's personal criminal complicity was so often confused.

Waldheim's "Nazi" Past

As was mentioned above, before the 3 March 1986 issue of *Profil* had even appeared, Waldheim had denounced its impending disclosures as an "outrage," merely a "calculated device to wreck my electoral chances."[9] What had so upset the presidential candidate was *Profil's* publication of his military service card, according to which Waldheim had been enrolled in both the (Horseback) Riding Unit [*Reiterstandarte*] 5/90 of the SA and Nazi Student Union.[10] On Tuesday, 4 March, the WJC held a press conference in New York, at which it made public other documents revealing the former U.N. Secretary General's "concealed Nazi past," while the *New York Times*

(*NYT*), on the basis of documents it had received from the WJC, ran an article claiming the same.[11]

Waldheim continued to deny categorically ever having been a member of any Nazi organization, but quickly erected a fallback position. As he told *NYT* reporter John Tagliabue, even if he had been a member, it "would still not be a sign of Nazi thinking or that I was a proponent of theirs. You should not exaggerate. The student union was nothing, a totally harmless, fully uninteresting organization, in which most of those went who wanted to be left in peace."[12] Waldheim was right to adopt this strategy, for the evidence relating to the fact of this membership is compelling. The principal documentary source corroborating it is the "Special Commission File 235" (hereafter SK-235),[13] a dossier containing summaries of materials examined by the Austrian authorities in the course of Waldheim's de-Nazification after the war. (The authorities pronounced him free of any incriminating National Socialist associations.) Many of the items referred to in this summary (for example, a hostile statement on Waldheim by the Nazi *Gauleiter* of the Tulln region) have survived; indeed, Waldheim himself provided some of them to journalists after the controversy broke, all, not unexpectedly, exculpatory. There is an exact correspondence between the excerpts contained in SK-235 and the documents from which they were taken—at least for those that have survived and can be independently verified—which increases the likelihood that the remaining excerpts in SK-235 accurately represented those documents that cannot. Two important original pieces of evidence referred to in this file, however, have apparently not survived. One was a form from 24 April 1940, which Waldheim had filled out as part of his application to become a *Gerichtsreferrendar*, a sort of on-the-job judicial trainee, roughly equivalent to a court clerk.[14] This questionnaire contained the following entry, which not only certified Waldheim's membership in the SA, but strongly suggested that he fully intended to join the Nazi party itself: "NSDAP: not yet possible, since doing military duty," and "SA Reitersturm [sic][15] 5/90 18 November 1938." The office to which Waldheim had submitted his application for acceptance into the judiciary recorded information Waldheim had supplied it. The entries from this *"Personalbogen,"* which were also recorded in the SK-235, stated the following: "SA Reiterstandarte 5é!o [sic][16] SA man since 18 November 1938, NS Studentebnund [sic] 1 April 1938."[17]

In January, 1946,[18] Waldheim submitted a signed statement purporting to explain the "political entries" in his personnel file at the Vienna Provincial Supreme Court (*Oberlandesgericht*). This, too, was summarized in SK-235. Although in this statement Waldheim denied that his participation in the activities of the SA riding organization had constituted real membership,[19] the de-Nazification authorities were less concerned with whether Waldheim formally belonged to the SA than with the political significance of his activities. The evaluation in the SK-235 read: "Required to practice law [*Gerichtsdienst*], therefore only as a former Austrian cavalry man participation of a sporting nature in the SA Reiterstandarte from 18 November 1938 until the summer of 1939."

In the 25 January 1946 statement explaining his Nazi connections, Waldheim did not address his alleged membership in the NSDStB directly, although his allusion to it was unmistakable. "Finally," he wrote, "I would like to state that the grant from the Austrian Chamber of Industry and Commerce to attend the Consular Academy, which I had received prior to March 1938, was cancelled as a result of my unwavering pro-Austrian attitude [*stets positiv österreichische Gesinnung*] and the dismissal of my father which had resulted from the National Socialist seizure of power."[20] The entry in the SK-235 which referred to Waldheim's court personnel file (the *Personalbogen*) dated Waldheim's enrollment in the Nazi Student Union as 1 April 1938. The *Anschluss,* it will be recalled, took place on 12 March 1938. If Waldheim, like his father, had suffered as result of an "unwavering pro-Austrian attitude" after the German invasion, as he claimed, it seems highly unlikely that three weeks later he would have joined the Nazi Student Union. This is certainly the impression Waldheim wished to convey. In 1946, he buttressed this version of events with statements from the former mayor of his hometown Tulln and from local officials of the ÖVP and the SPÖ, all attesting to his exemplary anti-Nazi stance,[21] while in 1986 he collected additional affidavits from former fellow students of his at the Consular Academy, among them Lord Weidenfeld, who likewise offered character references.[22] All these taken together, suggested the *Generalanwalt* Karl Marschall, who offered a legal opinion on the matter, "prove the irreproachable conduct of Dr. Waldheim" during this period.[23]

There are, however, some problems with this view. The first is the assumption that one's private opposition to National Socialism would have excluded membership in any Nazi organization. Official connection to some affiliated group was mandatory for some professions, among them the judiciary, during the National Socialist period, but this would not have applied to Waldheim in 1938. At the same time, there seems no obvious reason to infer that Kurt Waldheim would openly oppose the Nazis at the Consular Academy merely because his father, Walter Waldheim, had suffered disabilities under the Nazis for his political beliefs (he lost his position as an inspector of state schools in the Tulln district). Kurt Waldheim, of course, has utilized this presumed family trait to good effect to strengthen his own claims to have suffered discrimination because of his anti-Nazi views, and succeeded in convincing otherwise critical historians and journalists of it. Hanspeter Born, for example, found Waldheim's postwar explanation "credible," while Robert Herzstein repeated as fact Waldheim's claim that his scholarship to the Consular Academy was "cancelled."[24] More recent research,[25] however, has shattered both Waldheim's claim and the assumptions which underly it. At issue here is the grant to attend the Consular Academy to which Waldheim referred in his January 1946 statement. Far from his grant being cancelled because of his "pro-Austrian attitude," as he stated, Waldheim only received the grant after the "National Socialist seizure of power" in Austria. If it can be shown that Waldheim possessed a material motive for joining the Nazi Student Union, the case for his membership on the basis of other documentary sources would be considerably strengthened.

On 3 November 1937, the director of the Consular Academy, Hlavac von Rechtwall, in a letter to the head of the Austrian Chamber of Commerce, reported on the achievements of three students who had received grants from the Chamber for the academic year 1936–1937 and nominated replacement candidates for 1937–1938. One of the three recipients of the earlier grant, Helmut Guttmann, was to have his grant renewed for the coming academic year, while the two free places were to be filled by Hans Schernhorst and Kurt Waldheim. The criteria adduced in support of these two were scholastic achievement, good character and having relatives involved in commerce, in that order.[26] As the Chamber did not respond to his earlier letter and the summer semester was approaching, on 10 February 1938, that is, one month before the *Anschluss,* Hlavac wrote requesting a decision on the scholarship applications. In this letter he referred to an earlier communication dated 7 January 1938, in which he had apparently recommended a fourth person, Hugo Weihs, for a grant.[27]

On 5 May 1938, slightly less than two months after the *Anschluss,* the Chamber of Commerce wrote to the Academy director setting out new criteria for the four scholarship candidates. Guttmann, Schernhorst, Waldheim and Weihs would receive their grant for the summer semester 1938 only if the academy director reported to the Chamber whether the candidates *"are Aryans and also whether there is anything [to be held] against them."* Those not meeting these conditions, the letter continued, were to be replaced by others who did. *"Primary consideration,"* the letter concluded, *"is to be given to students* who were previously excluded from grants because of their own National Socialist convictions or those of their parents."[28] The academy administration replied to the 5 May 1938 letter of the Chamber of Commerce on the eighteenth. Only Hans Schernhorst and Kurt Waldheim remained from the original list of candidates. "They have brought proof of Aryan descent (four Ayran Grandparents) and were described by the [Nazi] student leader at the Consular Academy as completely suitable." "Hans Schernhorst," Hlavac continued, "has been active in illegal [i.e., Nazi] formations both in high school [*Mittelschulstudien*] and as a student at the Consular Academy; Kurt Waldheim, who likewise has been a convinced National Socialist [*gesinnungsgemäß Nationalsozialist*] for years, has not been able to be politically active since 1936, since he was doing military service." In place of Guttmann and Weihs, "who do not, or not entirely, meet the requirements," Hlavac recommended Gustav Rudolf Bock and Wolfgang Janesch. Both, the letter claimed, had been active as illegal Nazis and, like Schernhorst and Waldheim, were in need of the grant.[29] Janesch, incidentally, was the same Nazi student leader at the Consular Academy who had evaluated Waldheim's political suitability.

On 25 May 1938, the Chamber of Commerce wrote confirming that each of the four candidates, including Kurt Waldheim, would receive a scholarship of 130 Reichmarks for the 1937/38 academic year.[30] On 30 June 1938, the Consular Academy administration replied, thanking the Chamber of Commerce for the students' grants and reporting that the grants had been paid out. In this letter Kurt Waldheim was named explicitly as one of the recipients.[31] The beneficiaries of the *gleichgeschaltete* Chamber of Commerce were, then, three illegal Nazis and Kurt Waldheim, who obviously evinced no scruple about allowing the leader of the Nazis at the Academy to pronounce him politically reliable, or the head of the Academy to infer that he had been "a convinced National Socialist for years," despite his ostensible private "unwavering pro-Austrian" views.

The letter of 18 May 1938 did not state why Weihs and Guttmann were excluded, but the two were almost certainly not excluded on racial grounds. A "porter's report," for example, which is undated but is clearly from the academic year 1937–38,[32] listed "Guttmann Helmut" and "Weiß [sic] Hugo" as "röm. kath." (i.e., Roman Catholic). Proof that one was "Aryan," however, depended not upon a certificate of baptism, but on the religious affiliation of one's grandparents, a racial principle not without its contradictions. Thus, even though Guttman and Weihs had been baptized, theoretically they still could have been excluded as "non-Aryans" if they had not been able to produce the proof of "Aryan" ancestry required by the Chamber of Commerce in its 5 May 1938 letter. Remaining ambiguities evaporate if we examine a circular letter of 16 May 1938. On that day the director of the Academy informed the "non-Aryan" students at the Consular Academy that "in order to bring the procedures of the Consular Academy into line with other secondary schools, from now on *only* Aryans will be allowed to attend lectures,"[33] and named the thirteen students thus affected. Neither Guttmann nor Weihs appeared on this list, confirming that both were denied their grants on the basis of the second, political condition, that there was something "against them." It is not clear what political affiliations Guttmann and Weihs had, or the specific grounds on which they were excluded, but it is clear that students certainly could have been excluded for exhibiting an "unwavering pro-Austrian attitude" or something similar.

Apart from casting even more suspicion on the veracity of Waldheim's own account, this evidence also helps explain why Waldheim joined the NSDStB on 1 April 1938, the date given on all the relevant documents, "in order," as he put it in 1946, when describing his "sporadic participation in events called by" the Nazi Student Union, "not to endanger the continuance or completion of [his] studies." What better way to make certain that he was "completely suitable" to the post-*Anschluss* Nazi student leader at the Consular Academy than by joining the *Studentenbund,* perhaps even at Hlavac's suggestion, in April of 1938? Waldheim, of course, denies to this very day having been a member of the NSDStB, and he and his supporters have their own explanation of Waldheim's relationship with the Nazi Student Union.[34] As for the scholarship itself, Waldheim claimed that he was unaware of the correspondence between Hlavac and the Chamber of Commerce; that Hlavac must have known of his anti-Nazi views; and that, when he was composing his 1946 statement, he "was thinking of the second year," because in that year (1938–39) he "received nothing."[35]

The story of Waldheim's quest for financial aid suggests that there is even less reason to doubt Waldheim's membership in the NSDStB, which the international historians commission, without having examined this additional evidence, held to be "undisputed." Does this or his having joined the SA *Reiterstandarte,* however, make Waldheim a "Nazi?" Here we should recall Waldheim's second line of defense when confronted with the evidence of his membership, namely, that such "would still not be a sign of Nazi thinking or that I was a proponent of theirs." For the WJC and most commentators in the United States, the evidence which established Waldheim's membership incontrovertibly "proved" he was a "Nazi." For many in Austria, however, this very evidence tended to "prove" he was not. How is this possible?

Under the Nazis it was frequently necessary to join some official organization in order not to be penalized, or, perhaps less noble, not to hinder the advancement of one's career. As of January, 1940, that is, after Waldheim had graduated, admission to the Consular Academy itself was conditional on membership in the "NSDAP or one of its affiliated organizations."[36] Such measures confronted thousands of people who did not share Nazi convictions with a moral dilemma of some significance. Yet it would be misleading to infer National Socialist ideological conviction simply from one's membership in one of these affiliated organizations such as the NSDStB and the SA *Reiterstandarte.*

After the war, the de-Nazification authorities in Austria drew fine distinctions between different categories of membership in the various Nazi auxiliary organizations.[37] In general, among persons who had had some sort of official affiliation to the Nazis (and were thus required to register this after the war), the dividing line was between those who had belonged to any "illegal" (i.e., prior to the *Anschluss*) Nazi formation, those who had joined an organization after 12 March 1938 which the authorities judged prima facie incriminating (such as the SS) or those who had held a leadership position at any time in the NSDAP or one of its auxiliary organizations, on the one hand, and those who had not, on the other.[38] The reasoning was that the act of joining either any Nazi organization while membership was still illegal or an incriminated Nazi organization even after 1938, or the exercise of leadership functions in even a less incriminated organization, required more political or ideological commitment. In the course of de-Nazification in Austria, the term "Nazi" came to be applied almost exclusively to those who had been registered in the "incriminated" and "less incriminated" categories. Knowledge of these distinctions, pragmatic and somewhat arbitrary, carried over into postwar Austrian political culture, for they had immediate political and possibly economic ramifications for those affected. Outside Austria, and especially in the United States, such differences were scarcely noted or have been disregarded. Neither rank-and-file members of the NSDStB nor those of the SA *Reiterstandarte,* the two organizations Waldheim joined, were deemed "incriminated" according to de-Nazification legislation, provided they had joined after 12 March 1938. Moreover, although technically membership in such organizations should have been registered as such, the lenient attitude towards fellow travellers, coupled with Waldheim's obviously low-profile memberships and the supplementary exculpatory evidence he submitted to the authorities, would most likely have inclined the personnel clerk vetting him in 1946 to believe his retrospective explanation of his conduct in 1938. All these points taken together help explain why Waldheim was cleared without much ado in 1946, even though the de-Nazification authorities seem not to have doubted his membership per se (though it is not certain

how they would have reacted had they known that Waldheim's statement contained false information).

However, it would be equally misleading to think that these two organizations were mere refuges for those seeking a relatively harmless Nazi alibi. The three other students who received scholarships from the Chamber of Commerce—Hans Schernhorst, Gustav Rudolf Bock and Wolfgang Janesch—had all been active (Schernhorst in Munich, the others in Austria) Nazis at the time the party was still illegal in Austria, were notorious for their bravado, and were all members of the NSDStB.[39] Thus, on the basis of his memberships alone, it would be misleading to say simply that Waldheim had been a "Nazi" or that he had not, without clarifying what one means by doing so.

The available documentary evidence offers no conclusive insights into what Waldheim's personal beliefs were by the time he joined the NSDStB. The affidavits and statements from fellow students suggest that, though his convictions were somewhat mutable, depending on his interests and his audience, at least in private he was something less than a true believer. Indeed, there is no reason to take literally Hlavac's statement that Waldheim had held National Socialist beliefs "for years," for that assumes a courage of conviction that Waldheim likely did not exhibit.[40] It does seem advisable to maintain some way of differentiating between ideological Nazis and their fellow travellers, whatever one may think of the latter. Both, however, were indispensable for the maintenance of the National Socialist system of authority. Waldheim's own version of his quiet but noble opposition to the Nazis at the Consular Academy remains unconvincing. What is striking about this episode, on the contrary, is that Waldheim's readiness to accomodate himself to those who could further his own interests was already clearly discernible even at this early age.

Waldheim's Army Career

The merit of the discussion surrounding Waldheim's service in the Balkans lies not only, and, perhaps, not even principally, in the exposure of the hidden and possibly criminal past of a young Wehrmacht lieutenant. It is rather to be found in the recognition of some hard truths about the conduct of war in general and the scale of legitimate slaughter in the Second World War in particular; the victorious Western powers' postwar *Realpolitik* in dealing with the crimes committed during it; and the inappropriateness of such concepts as justice to describe the reckoning with the legacy of that war. Seen in this context, one of the most important conclusions to be drawn from Waldheim's role as a staff officer in the Balkans is just how much murderous force one was (and theoretically still is) allowed in wartime to employ without incurring criminal liability. Contrary to popular belief, the overwhelming bulk of documents showing Waldheim's intimate familiarity with the most brutal acts of some of the Wehrmacht's most ruthless units did not criminally inculpate him, at least according to the practice of the Nuremberg Tribunals. These documents did call forth a justifiable horror at the nature of the war in the Balkans, together with an incredulity (born, as it were, of either ignorance, naïveté or selective moral outrage) that someone like Waldheim could have "gotten away" after the war.[41]

The authority of the International Military Tribunal at Nuremberg, on the other hand, which in the popular imagination tends to symbolize the triumph of justice over barbarism, has remained largely beyond debate.[42] In any event, virtually no one has called the principles and judgments of the Tribunal into question in the discussion over Waldheim. Yet the logic of such revulsion at the "legal" conduct of the war in the Balkan theater would seem to demand it. Unless one reformulates the terms according to which criminal liability was understood and attributed by the judges at Nuremberg, any attempts to lace Waldheim's wartime activities with the suspicion of criminality expose themselves as either historically untenable or morally discrepant. Although in theory the scope for accomplices to criminal acts incurring liability was sufficiently broad to have included anyone who had provided tools or even information, knowing that they would be used in a war crime—or even reckless indifference as to whether they would be so used—in practice these principles were interpreted in a considerably more narrow fashion.[43]

In evaluating Waldheim's personal role, therefore, the only applicable juridical precepts are those which in fact informed the practice of the Nuremberg Tribunal. It is neither accidental that until now no one has constructed a compelling case against Waldheim on these grounds, nor surprising that Waldheim himself has indefatigably endeavored to reduce all questions dealing with his past to this very narrow one. Waldheim is, however, merely a proxy in this connection for much broader questions. For these, namely, what should the laws of war actually look like, and how might they be best upheld or enforced, the principles of Nuremberg offer the weight of historical factuality, but do not necessarily possess any prior claim to juridical certitude. This need not mean that Axis war criminals ought to get off the hook, or that their crimes be rendered harmless. One must merely cast the net far wider, without thereby "relativising" Nazi atrocities. In order to engage these broader questions using Waldheim as an example, however, it is first necessary to survey his whereabouts in the Balkan theater, then examine the charges which have arisen in relation to his wartime service there.

From the spring of 1942, when he returned to active military service after having recovered from an injury to his leg, until the end of the war, Waldheim filled seven different posts in at least ten locations in parts of postwar Yugoslavia, Greece and Albania. He served as a liaison officer of the General Staff of the Wehrmacht Battle Group "Bader" to the Italian "Pusteria" Division, based in Plevlja, Bosnia-Hercegovina; as an assistant adjutant (the second *Ordonnanzoffizier,* or O2) in the quartermaster's department of the Battle Group "West Bosnia," based originally in Banja Luka, then in Kostajnica and finally Novska, in Bosnia-Hercegovina; as an interpreter attached to the Military Intelligence department of the Army High Command of the southeast region,[44] based in Arsakli near Salonika; as an interpreter in another German liaison staff to a different Italian army, the ninth, based in Montenegro and Albania; as the first assistant adjutant (first *Ordonnanzoffizier,* or O1) in the operations department of yet another German liaison staff with the 11th Italian army High Command, based in Athens (this liaison staff became the Army Group South Greece after the Italian capitulation in September, 1943, in which Waldheim performed the same function); and as an assistant adjutant, the third *Ordonnanzoffizier,* or O3 in the military intelligence department of the command headquarters of Army Group E, based initially in Arsakli, but which moved around in the course of the retreat. This latter position is the one Waldheim held until he was finally called back to the front, which, however, he never reached. Merely keeping track of Waldheim's various postings in the Balkans, interspersed as they are with personal, educational and medical leaves, is arduous enough; making the military significance of these various assignments comprehensible to a non-specialist has proved beyond the expository talents of most. Without making any claims to completeness, we will attempt to provide a few helpful points of reference in understanding why the discussion over Waldheim's possible criminal responsibility was in many instances confusing, even if impassioned.[45]

The Battle Group "Bader"

From April 1942 until it was dissolved in late May of the same year, Waldheim was attached to the Battle Group "Bader" (named after the German commander Paul Bader). He was assigned as interpreter and head of liaison staff number 5 with the Italian Army Pusteria division. Battle Group Bader had been set up to lead a tripartite (German, Italian, and Croation) offensive against partisans in areas of eastern Bosnia. Waldheim's duties were to transmit orders, situation reports, etc., from the German command of the battle group to the Italian generals, thereby facilitating the coordination of the attack, as well as to inform the German commanders of his own impressions and observations.

In the course of the brutal and frequently criminal campaign undertaken by the battle group against suspected partisans and their civilian supporters, a great many prisoners were taken. The commanding general of the Wehrmacht southeast region agreed to Bader's recommendation to gather the prisoners in concentration camps in preparation for their shipment to Norway to be used for slave labor, which the International Military Tribunal at Nuremberg defined as a war crime, and was clearly in contravention of the Geneva convention of 1929.[46] According to German Army documents, the Italian Pusteria division provided 488 prisoners who were eventually sent to Norway.

By virtue of his duties as a liaison officer, there is little doubt that Waldheim would have been informed of the fact that the Pusteria division had taken prisoners, including civilians, though it cannot be proved that he was aware of their ultimate fate. This was sufficient for the OSI to judge Waldheim guilty of complicity in the transfer of civilian prisoners to the SS for exploitation as slave laborers.[47] The precedents of the Nuremberg trials suggest, to the contrary, that Waldheim would not have been criminally liable in these deportations, even had the Pusteria division been following a direct order from the commanders of Battle Group Bader, and even if Waldheim had personally transmitted it. The reasoning being that, however gruesome or criminal the order given, someone who merely passes it on along the chain of command does not act unlawfully by doing so.[48]

The Battle Group "West Bosnia"

The Battle Group "West Bosnia," established by an order of 20 May 1942 under the command of Major General Friedrich Stahl, was to continue the fight against partisans and was scheduled to be ready for action by the middle of June. Waldheim, along with several others, was transferred directly from Battle Group Bader to Battle Group West Bosnia. Unlike the previous campaign, however, the orders for the Battle Group West Bosnia specified that the Germans were to undertake the "cleansing" and "pacification" of the area around the Kozara mountains without Italian, but with some Croation assistance. Thus came Kurt Waldheim to his new assignment as deputy assistant adjutant (O2) to the head ([Roman numeral] Ib) of the quartermaster's department of Battle Group West Bosnia.

The campaign of the Battle Group West Bosnia against those who lived or had taken refuge in the Kosara mountains quickly took on the characteristics of a massacre. After the Kozara mountain area had been "cleansed," there were additional "mopping-up" operations [*Nachsäuberungen*] around the area where the Una River joins the Sana, in Samarica and in the Psunj mountains, which lie northwest of the Kozara range across the Sana River. The official divisional history of the 714th Infantry Division, commanded by Stahl and principally responsible for the carnage in western Bosnia, itself described the Kozara action as "a battle without mercy, without pity."[49] In the final report on the successes of the Battle Group West Bosnia's eight weeks' fighting, the German losses were put at 71, against 4,735 Yugoslavs killed and 12,207 captured, and even these figures are drastically understated.[50] Here as well, civilians were deported to concentration camps or prisons in Prijedor, Gradiska, Banja Luka and Semlin. The German army was assisted in the treatment of the prisoners by the Croation Ustasha, whose brutality was extreme even by prevailing German standards.[51]

Waldheim's service in western Bosnia has been the subject of much speculation and even the occasion for a forgery.[52] One reason for the uncertainty regarding Waldheim's activities is the absence of virtually all important documents relating to the Ib department of this battle group.[53] Though interpretations vary, the more or less sufficient available documentary evidence relating to Waldheim's activities between 1942 and 1945 has enabled historians, journalists or jurists to offer relatively authoritative judgments on possible criminal activity in most areas where Waldheim saw duty in the Balkans. With Battle Group West Bosnia, on the contrary, the lack of evidence prevents a number of detailed questions from being answered with certainty, allowing no other conclusion than that possible allegations remain not proven. Still, the charges are grave enough, and the historians commission and the work of others[54] have at least suggested grounds for suspicion. There are two general areas of responsibility where the quartermaster's department of Battle Group West Bosnia might have incurred criminal liability: (1) in the illegal deportation of civilian prisoners, and (2) in the illegal shooting of suspected partisans.

Though Waldheim first admitted, then retracted, then grudgingly conceded the possibility that he had been the 02 in the Ib department of the Battle Group West Bosnia, led by a captain Plume, the documentary record has established this beyond any doubt.[55] However, none of the surviving documents specify the precise details of Waldheim's duties as 02. As a consequence, the duty roster of the previous quartermaster's department of Battle Group Bader, in which then first lieutenant Plume had served as 02 himself, takes on added significance, for it can be used by analogy to reconstruct the duties which Waldheim had as 02 in the Battle Group West Bosnia. According to this duty roster, one of the responsibilities of the Ib department was "removal of prisoners."[56] Other documents from Battle Group West Bosnia itself confirm this conclusively, among them the "Guidelines for the Operations in West Bosnia," which define one of the "supply" tasks of the troops to be assistance in the removal of prisoners.[57] Indeed, there is evidence to suggest that the rugged terrain of the battle zone, which required that the troops carry their own provisions with them in the field, heightened the possibility that the Ib department would have devoted more time to the transport of prisoners.[58] An additional point of significance is that a 21-man-strong group of the military police (*Feldgendarmerie*) was seconded to the Ib section. The *Feldgendarmerie's* principal assignment was to "maintain military order" as well as general public order in the area in the rear. According to the orders from the Army High Command (AOK 12), such police forces were also responsible for "combatting rebels in the rear,"[59] and, according to other documents, for "cleansing" operations under the aegis of Battle Groups Bader[60] and West Bosnia.[61]

It is, of course, normal that an army should make arrangments to intern, feed and transport captured prisoners, and the quartermaster's department would be the logical one to perform this function. Yet these were not normal battles, and the prisoners were largely civilians. According to international law expert Christopher Greenwood's interpretation of the Nuremberg judgments, even the evacuation of civilians to other areas of the occupied territory was not illegal, provided they were not maltreated and the move was necessary to protect the security of the occupying powers. At the same time, the deportation of civilians who were not partisans or suspected partisans outside the territory clearly was illegal.[62] Though such criteria seem very generous towards the occupying powers, the Wehrmacht did not even meet these standards. The mass deportations of civilians were thus criminal according to the principles laid down at Nuremberg,[63] and were judged to be so by the court in the "Hostages Case" (Case 7) against the commanding officers of the southeast European theater.[64]

There is no clear answer as to the possible criminal complicity of the Ib department in illegal deportations of civilians. In general, the Nuremberg courts held that those who had organized the supply and organization of such transports would not be held criminally liable if they had not in fact ordered them.[65] If so, then the judgment of the international historians' commission that investigated Waldheim's past, that "participation in a crime would be assumed if one acted, knowing that 'forced labor' meant working the prisoners to death [*Vernichtung durch Arbeit*],"[66] is open to some doubt. There is even some reason to believe that the officer involved would not have incurred any criminal liability, even if he had been aware of the ultimate destination of these prisoners, unless it were shown that he had personally ordered the deportation, selected prisoners to be used for forced labor, or incited or permitted ill-treatment of the prisoners being transported.[67]

As for the "cleansing" operations of the *Feldgendarmerie*, or, for that matter, the Croation police, the issues are even less clear, because it cannot be established on whose orders they acted. On the assumption that the shootings were themselves illegal,[68] the Ib or someone acting in his stead could have been held criminally liable if there were evidence that such orders had been given by the Ib himself, that the Ib had been personally involved, or if he could have been in a position of command authority to have prevented the commission of acts he knew were taking place and knew to be criminal, and had not done so.[69]

Thus, the scope for criminal activities on the part of the Ib is somewhat circumscribed, though room for dispute remains, and essential evidence is missing. Waldheim's criminal responsibility in this case would, however, still be theoretically one step removed. However, it is legitimate to infer from the duty roster of Battle Group Bader, which listed the O2 as the quartermaster's deputy (*Vertreter*), that Waldheim as O2 would have taken over for Plume in the latter's absence, making Waldheim potentially liable for his actions as the "acting" Ib. Most, in fact, have assumed that Plume remained as Ib until the battle group was dissolved in August 1942. It followed that as long as he remained Plume's subordinate and his responsibilities involved the transmission of orders and the arrangement of transport of these prisoners on Plume's instructions, Waldheim could probably not be held criminally liable according to the courts in Nuremberg, even though the deportation of civilians to forced labor was itself considered criminal.

However, in an interview with a researcher for the Thames Television–Home Box Office program *Waldheim: A Commission of Inquiry*, Waldheim's former superior, Plume, claimed that he had left his post as Ib with the Battle Group West Bosnia on 18 July 1942.[70] If Plume's statement could be verified, and if it could be shown either that Waldheim was appointed Ib after this date, or that he was, as Plume's deputy, left in de facto charge of the Ib department after Plume had left—the period of "mopping up" operations conducted after the troops had been transferred to Kostajnica at the end of July—then Waldheim would have to answer for those acts that had been thought to fall under the responsibility of Plume during this period.

This lead might yield some new evidence as to Waldheim's proximity to atrocities, especially since during the specified period the *Feldgendarmerie* would theoretically have been under his command. It might also throw additional light on Waldheim's personal involvement in the transports of civilian prisoners. However, it is scarcely likely that this would have any substantial bearing on the legal questions involved, in other than a purely academic sense. The practices followed by the judges in the Nuremberg trials suggest that, even if the personal involvement of Waldheim during his duties as the O2 could be established, and be shown to have violated the principles the tribunal had laid down, he would never have been brought to trial, much less convicted. For it cannot but be sobering to recall that the commanding officer of the Battle Group West Bosnia, Friedrich Stahl, the author of the very orders that Waldheim would have been carrying out, who admitted under oath that "it was clear to all of us that such orders [he is speaking here of the orders requiring a fixed number of reprisal killings and the burning down of neighboring villages in retaliation for the death or injury of a German soldier] also violated the Hague Laws on land warfare,"[71] himself was not indicted at Nuremberg.

Waldheim in Athens

After the Battle Group West Bosnia was dissolved, Waldheim returned to Arsakli to resume his duties as interpreter in the military intelligence section ([Roman numeral] Ic/AO) of Army Group E. He did not remain long. On 13 November 1942, Waldheim was granted a four-month study leave, which he began on the 19th. In April 1943 he returned to Belgrade, whence he was immediately assigned as an interpreter on the German liaison staff to the 9th Italian Army, based in Albania. This assignment became famous above all because of a photograph of Waldheim standing between the Waffen-SS General Artur Phleps and the Italian General Roncaglia on the airfield in Podgorica, which the *New York Times* published with its first article on Waldheim's past on 4 March 1986.[72] The meeting had been called to iron out differences between the Germans and the Italians over diverging tactics for combatting the partisans, and to discuss the upcoming campaign "Operation Black." Although it has been suggested that Waldheim might have been involved in the planning of this operation, the evidence does not support it.[73]

Waldheim returned to Arsakli from Tirana at the beginning of July, 1943, and remained there for three weeks. On 19 July, the commanding general of Army Group E, Alexander Loehr, ordered the formation of a new German liaison staff with the 11th Italian Army, based in Athens. General Gyldenfeldt was to head it, and was seconded by, among others, Colonel Bruno Willers, the head of the operations department ([Roman numeral] Ia). First Lieutenant Waldheim was assigned to Willers as the first assistant adjutant (*Ordonnanzoffizier*, or O1) in the operations department. The staff flew to Athens on 26 July, the day after Mussolini had been arrested. Wehrmacht commanders had been suspicious of the Italians for some time. The Army High Command in Berlin wasted no time. The day after the fall of Mussolini, on 26 July 1943, it issued orders placing the 11th Italian Army under the overall control of Army Group E, although the liaison staff in Athens, in which Waldheim served, remained subordinate to the 11th Army command.[74] In addition, the Wehrmacht made preparations for the anticipated Italian capitulation by drawing up plans for an operation with the code name "Axis." During the period between Mussolini's arrest (25 July) and the day the news of the capitulation reached the Germans, on 8 September,[75] the liaison staff played an especially important role in keeping the Army Group E fully informed about their Italian allies. At the same time, the principal military activity of the staff was to coordinate the fight against Greek partisans in the area around Athens. Waldheim has been criticized in connection with criminal acts related to the duplicitous shipment of Italian prisoners to forced labor, and for possible complicity in a massacre in the Greek village of Komeno,[76] but, as in other areas as well, on closer inspection the charge of criminal conduct has not held.

His position as *Ordonnanzoffizier* in the operations department of the liaison staff brought Waldheim very near to those responsible for issuing orders to combat troops, and kept him thoroughly informed as to the nature of the fighting against the Greek "bands," as they were called. Among Waldheim's initial duties, which he began while the staff was still in Arsakli, was to keep the war diary, a task he carried out from 19 July to 21 August 1943. If Waldheim's intimate knowledge of criminal acts cannot be doubted, his personal criminal involvement in them is nearly as improbable. Waldheim was always one step removed from any real authority, and this would have insulated him against liability.

The exact status of the Italian army after Italy's capitulation, but before it declared war on Germany on 13 October 1943, was unclear. It cannot be said with certainty under what category the soldiers of the 11th Army fell. Still, the policies the Germans followed, in particular their shipment of the disarmed Italian soldiers to forced labor in Germany or in Eastern Europe, would have violated the relevant conventions whether the Italians had been considered combatants or civilians under an army of occupation.[77] Although the Italians had surrendered under the assumption that they would be sent home, the High Command of Army Group E never intended them to be returned. Hubert Lanz, the acting commanding officer of the Army Group South Greece, which is what the liaison staff became after the Italian capitulation, negotiated with the Italian General Vecchiarelli with a *ruse de guerre,* of which Waldheim was probably aware. Waldheim, however, would not have been criminally complicit in the decisions made, whether willfully to deceive the Italians, to transport them to forced labor, or to shoot those resisting disarmament. It is not even certain to what extent Willers, the Ia and Waldheim's superior, himself would have incurred liability under the principles laid down at Nuremberg. Waldheim was, legally, yet again a safe distance away.

In Arsakli: The Deportation of Jews

Of all the areas of Waldheim's wartime service that have come under scrutiny, perhaps the most fateful is the suspicion of his involvement in the deportation of Jews from Greece. During the time that Waldheim was attached to the staff of Army Group E, Jews were shipped to concentration camps from Salonika, Athens, Rhodes, Corfu and Ioannina, as well as from smaller Greek islands in the Peloponnese. One of the more severe poundings that Waldheim's credibility has taken in the whole affair has been his consistent denial of any knowledge of the forcible removal of a single Jew from Greece, including the islands. The evidence that exists suggests no grounds for assuming Waldheim to be personally, criminally complicit in the deportations, although "involvement" of a more general kind, by virtue of his job as O3 in the military intelligence (Ic) section of Army Group E, cannot be excluded, depending on how broadly one defines the term. Considering the nature of his job it is virtually certain that he would have been exposed to information detailing at least one deportation of Jews. Whether that means that he did not "know" of the deportations may be debated, but only on the most tenuous of epistemological grounds.

For a time, the controversy over Waldheim's relation to the deportations centered on those from Salonika. Over 46,000 Jews, one-fifth of the city's population, were deported to Auschwitz between March and August 1943. Prior to that, in February 1943, the Jews had been ordered to wear a yellow star and were shortly thereafter herded into ghettos, in preparation for the impending deportations.[78] Among the documents first published on Waldheim's past were records showing Waldheim's assignment to the Army Group E during the very months of 1943 that the transports carrying Salonika's Jews were leaving the train station. At that time, no further details were known about Waldheim's various postings in the Balkans and there was little public knowledge about the Army Group E itself. Moreover, Waldheim offered nothing to help clarify matters. Consequently, all (including Waldheim) assumed Waldheim to have been serving in Salonika during the deportations, and most found his adamantine denials of any knowledge of these events incredible.

The assumption that Waldheim had been serving in Salonika at that time, however, turned out to have been mistaken. Although most of the staff and troops of Army Group E (and its predecessor AOK 12) were stationed in Salonika, the general staff, to which Waldheim was attached, resided in a small village, Arsakli, three miles away. Moreover, with the exception of three weeks in July, Waldheim was absent from the Salonika area during the deportations, either on study leave in Vienna, or on military assignment in Albania or Athens. None of this, of course, necessarily bears out Waldheim's claim to ignorance of the Salonika deportations, and informed opinions on the probability of his knowledge vary.[79] But there can be no question of direct involvement of any kind.

After the capitulation of Italy, the Wehrmacht occupied the former Italian territory in Greece. This brought the remaining Jewish population under its control: around 8,000 in Athens, 1,700 on the island of Rhodes, in Ioannina 1,950, on Corfu 2,000, as well as smaller groups on the Peloponnese.[80] The involvement of the Wehrmacht in the deportations of these Jews, which took place between March and August 1944, either through the organization of transport or the rounding up and removal of the Jews themselves, cannot be disputed. Waldheim's claim not to have known about these deportations is thus especially unconvincing in these cases. Even though he could conceivably utilize the fact of his absence from Arsakli during the deportations from Ioannina to buttress his claim of ignorance, the nature of his duties in the military intelligence section (especially that of a clearing house for incoming information from troops in the field) effectively vitiates his denial of knowledge concerning the transport of Jews from Corfu and Rhodes, when he was present in Arsakli.

Take for example what happened on Corfu.[81] In March 1944, Waldheim's immediate superior, military intelligence officer ([Roman numeral] Ic) Lieutenant Colonel Herbert Warnstorff, reported to Army Group F, based in Belgrade—and to which Army Group E was subordinate—on the "ethnic breakdown" (*völkische Aufgliederung*) of Greece. In this report he identified 22,770 Greek Jews according to the 1940 census, a figure which he considered an underestimation. At the time of this report, Waldheim was on sick leave, dividing his time between the military hospital in Semmering (where he was recovering from a thyroid complaint) and Vienna (where he was finishing work on his law degree, which he completed in April, 1944). He returned to the staff of Army Group E on 16 April. Warnstorff's report is significant because it suggests that the military intelligence section (Ic/AO) to which Waldheim was attached had been intimately involved in identifying the Jewish population on the Greek islands. Five days after Waldheim had returned to Arsakli from Vienna, Major Wilhelm Hammer, the counter-intelligence officer (Abwehroffizier, or AO) in the Ic/AO department of Army Group E, informed the Corps Group Ioannina that "according to reports at hand there are 1,600 Jews, many English, 562 Anglo-Maltese and 17 French" on Corfu. Hammer sent this information on behalf of the Army Group E Chief of Staff, Schmidt-Richberg, which suggests that the general staff continued to be involved in gathering the information necessary to organize sufficient transport for the deportations of the Jews from the Greek islands. It is highly probable that the "reports at hand" to which Hammer referred had crossed Waldheim's desk, since the Ic/AO section was as a matter of course concerned with such information and Waldheim, who served as O3, would have seen every incoming report of any consequence.[82] Most compelling of all is a report from 28 April 1944, sent by the Ic of the Corps Group Ioannina, first lieutenant Ziegler, to the Ic/AO department of Army Group E. Ziegler reported that the deportation of the 2,000 Jews on Corfu "would also represent a not inconsiderable alleviation of the food situation. SD [*Sicherheitsdienst*] and GFP [*Geheimfeldpolizei*] are in the process of making preparations for a deportation of the Jews. . . . With the aim of regulation of the Jewish question, the Corps Group requests that the SD procure the appropriate measures for execution [*Zwecks Regelung der Judenfrage bittet Korpsgruppe Durchführungsmaßnahmen beim SD erwirken zu wollen*]." It was Waldheim's duty to sort through exactly such reports as they came in from the field and to synthesize the important points for his superior. It is therefore virtually certain that Waldheim would have seen a report addressed to the Ic/AO of Army Group E.

An 11 August 1944 report by the Ic of the Storm Division Rhodes, which stated that "the deportation of the Jews from Rhodes and Coo [i.e., Kos] was accepted [i.e., by the local population] with mixed feelings," was also addressed to Waldheim's department in Arsakli. Although Waldheim's name appears nowhere on these documents, he would have to have been aware of such reports merely to have done the job he by all accounts performed exceptionally well. There can be little doubt, then, that Waldheim must have known of the deportations of Jews from at least Corfu, Rhodes and Kos.[83]

The documents relating to the deportation from Rhodes, moreover, have raised questions beyond Waldheim's mere knowledge of these events. The contribution of the Ic of the Wehrmacht command of the East Aegean region to the "counter-intelligence" section of a 22 September 1944, report stated: "End of July, 1944, deportation [*Abschub*] of Jews not holding Turkish citizenship out of the entire area of command on the orders [*auf Weisung*] of the Army Group High Command [section] Ic/AO. Execution in the hands of the SD-Greece, which set up a special unit [*Sonderkommando*] for this purpose in the area of command. Documents retained, because still required." This document appears to show that Waldheim's unit, the Ic/AO, had ordered the deportation of Jews from Rhodes. Waldheim himself has not disputed the accuracy of this report, arguing merely that it would have been the function of the counter-intelligence officer (AO), not the military intellegence officer (Ic), to have issued such orders.[84] Born, on the other hand, argued that Waldheim's department was "directly involved in the deportations."[85] Czernin, on the strength of a statement of Karl-August Müller Mangeot, who served in the Storm Division Rhodes, where this report originated, suggested that the reference to the Ic/AO was an error.[86]

The background to this document, according to Müller-Mangeot, was this: two high-ranking SS officials concerned with Jewish deportations, Dieter Wisliceny and Anton Burger, had travelled together[87] to Rhodes and attempted to organize these deportations without first having contacted the commanding officer of the Storm Division Rhodes, General Ulrich Kleemann. Angered at what he saw as an SS attempt to usurp his authority, Kleemann initially opposed the deportations of Jews. Kleemann phoned the general staff of Army Group E, and was informed that he should not oppose the deportations. Kleemann then told the SS men, "I cannot stop you." According to the 22 September 1944 report quoted above, the directive for the deportations came from the Ic/AO department. Müller-Mangeot, who claims knowledge of this report itself, suggested on the contrary that Kleemann probably spoke with Schmidt-Richberg, the chief of staff, on this occasion, not with someone from the Ic/AO department. He explained the entry in the report as carelessness on the part of whoever wrote it. On that day, 22 September, Kleemann and his staff were relieved by a new commander and his staff, and this document was one of many hastily prepared to brief new staff officers.[88]

Müller-Mangeot's explanation does clear up some gaps in the previous versions, but a necessary assumption would appear to be that Kleemann would only have turned to someone of Schmidt-Richberg's rank and position in order to settle a conflict with the SS. This, however, is by no means certain. The research of Hans Safrian on the involvement of the Wehrmacht in the Jewish deportations from the Balkans suggests that by the summer of 1944, the deportations of Jews had become such a routine matter for the Wehrmacht that the Ic would have been the post to which one normally turned for such information or directives.[89] Even if Safrian's general point is correct, however, it would not necessarily invalidate Müller-Mangeot's explanation of Kleemann's reaction in this particular case. The surviving documentary evidence is insufficient to prove precisely who communicated with whom in July, 1944, and thus the exact nature of the Ic/AO's involvement in these deportations remains legally equivocal. Yet however inconclusive the evidence against Waldheim's superior in the Ic/AO department, it is all but excluded that Waldheim himself would have incurred any criminal liability in the deportations of Jews from Rhodes or anywhere else in Greece. Throughout this period Waldheim served as the third assistant adjutant (O3) to the military intelligence officer (Ic), Warnstorff. Waldheim's personal complicity would depend in the first instance on the extent and nature of involvement the Ic/AO department, and in the second on Waldheim's specific activities. Waldheim's status as an *Ordonnanzoffizier,* without authority to issue directives of any kind to troops in the field, or of shaping the decisions regarding the deportations themselves, rather than merely scrutinizing orders as to their accuracy or communicating them to such troops or both, would have effectively insulated him from incrimination according to the Nuremberg principles.[90] Whether Waldheim's certain contemporaneous knowledge of the deportations from the Greek mainland and islands would imply a more broadly defined moral responsibility for these events, however, is a different matter altogether.

In Arsakli: Military Intelligence for Reprisal Killings

Another suggestion of Waldheim's possible criminal involvement in the Balkans relates specifically to his duties in the intelligence-gathering process. The *Odluka* was the first to raise this possibility, and Eli Rosenbaum of the WJC attempted to corroborate it.[91] Although both the Yugoslav War Crimes Commission and Rosenbaum only applied their investigations to the case of a massacre in October, 1944, along the road between Stip and Kocane in Macedonia, the basic parameters of the argument have wider application. According to the reasoning contained in the *Odluka,* because Waldheim's intelligence reports on the activities of the partisans formed the basis for the operational orders of the Wehrmacht command, and because he must have been aware of the standing policy of the Army Group E, which included reprisal killings and destruction of villages, Waldheim could not but have known that reports he authored identifying pockets of partisan activity would result in reprisal killings that at least in some cases were criminal. Consequently, according to this view, Waldheim could be held complicit in any criminal murders which ensued. Waldheim's duties as a military intelligence officer undoubtedly led to such reprisal killings, and it is inconceivable that he was unaware of the Wehrmacht "punishment" (*Sühnemassnahmen*) of suspected partisans and their supporters. It is, however, equally clear that the preparation of military intelligence reports, even if their likely result was known, was not held to be criminal by the courts at Nuremberg. Waldheim's position as subaltern in the military intelligence section of the general staff of Army Group E would have shielded him even further. The report of the international historians' commission recognized this legal ambiguity, and characterized such activity, as "consultative support of repressive measures."[92] Commission member Manfred Messerschmidt referred to it elsewhere as "moral complicity."[93] All this conceptual opacity, however, merely underlines the difficulty of reconciling the juridical legacy of Nuremberg with instinctive moral revulsion at the nature of the war in the Balkans, but in this case, as in all the others, Waldheim's complicity was not of a criminal kind. Waldheim has become a convenient symbolic target for those who sense the moral equivocation of the Nuremberg judgments, but cannot or dare not question them, for fear of relativizing or "historicizing" Nazi atrocities. It has, in fact, become Waldheim's personal fate to stand as the symbol of a postwar unwillingness or inability to adequately come to terms with the implications of the National Socialist abomination. Coming to terms with this past, however, must comprise not only legal, but also political, ideological, psychological, and moral moments as well. The attention devoted to Waldheim's possible criminality as an officer in the Wehrmacht, while it has brought some ancillary intellectual benefits, tends to divert our attention away from this broader task. This is not accidental, for the hard questions about the postwar political "settlement" all too frequently expose the fragility of putative moral considerations when confronted by questions of power and interest.

Our purpose here has been to redirect our thinking away from the attempt to find a "smoking gun" and towards this more comprehensive appreciation of Waldheim's previously hidden past. Though he was arguably not a "Nazi" in the ideological sense, nor someone the Nuremberg Tribunal would have convicted of war crimes, Waldheim does not escape censure. He was not merely duplicitous for forty years. Perhaps far more important was his unwillingness to use his considerable international profile to address even his own minor part in the Nazi horror, much less provide insights into the broader issues his personal past would imply for a new generation without personal experience of the Second World War. Waldheim appears to have forfeited whatever opportunity he might once have possessed to contribute something positive to a heightened political or moral awareness of the Nazi legacy, or to a rethinking of the ways in which we debate it. But for having helped, willy-nilly, revive the questions we have discussed here, we should at least thank him. There is little danger that Waldheim will not remain "in the dock." But he will not be alone.

Notes

1. Ministry of Defence, United Kingdom [MOD], "Review of the results of investigations carried out by the Ministry of Defence in 1986 into the fate of British servicemen captured in Greece and the Greek Islands between October 1943 and the involvement, of any, of the then Lieutenant Waldheim" (London: Her Majesty's Stationery Office, 1989), p. 9.

2. Cited in *Neue Kronen Zeitung,* 18 October 1989.

3. For a useful catalogue of these see Bernhard Heindl, "Leutnant, Lügner, Präsident," *Forum,* Year XXXVI, Numbers 436/427 (June/July 1989), pp. 44–55; idem, *"Wir Österreicher sind ein anst'auandiges Volk"* (Vienna: Edition Sandkorn, 1991).

4. *Die Presse,* 18 October 1989.

5. Technically merely making public the contents of a list which had been accessible to the public for years. See "News from World Jewish Congress" (News from WJC), press release, 22 March 1986.

6. This background is carefully reconstructed in Robert E. Herzstein, *Waldheim. The Missing Years* (London: Grafton Books, 1988), pp. 193–211.

7. *Wiener Zeitung,* 4 March 1986; News from WJC, 4 March 1986; *New York Times,* 4 March 1986. See also Heindl, "Leutnant, Lügner, Präsident," pp. 46–47, who, however, mistakenly dates Waldheim's introduction of the "war criminal" issue a day later.

8. The literature on Waldheim's wartime career is of uneven quality. In addition to my own research I have relied most heavily on the following for the chapter here: Walter Manoschek [Neues Österreich], ed., *Pflichterfüllung. Ein Bericht über Kurt Waldheim* (Vienna: Löcker Verlag, 1986); Hanspeter Born, *Für die Richtigkeit. Kurt Waldheim* (Munich: Schneekluth, 1987); Hubertus Czernin, "Waldheims Balkanjahre," *Profil,* Nos. 49–52, 1987, and 1–4, 1988; Hans Kurz, James Collins, Jean Vanwelkenheuzen, Gerald Fleming, Hagen Fleischer, Jehuda Wallach and Manfred Messerschmidt, *Der Bericht der internationalen Historikerkommission,* Manuscript, 202 pp. plus addenda, Vienna, 1988. The report was printed as a supplement to *Profil,* 15 February 1988. All references to the report will be to this version, which was published without the documentary addenda; MOD, "Review"; and Herzstein, *Missing.* Some documents of interest are reproduced in the Waldheim apologia compiled by Karl Gruber, Ralph Scheide and Ferdinand Trautmannsdorff, *Waldheim's Wartime Years. A Documentation* (Vienna: Carl Gerold's Sohn, 1987). For a general evaluation of the Waldheim literature see Richard Mitten, "L'affaire Waldheim," *Times Literary Supplement,* 7–13 October 1988, pp. 1119–1120.

9. *Neue Kronen Zeitung,* 2 March 1986.

10. *Profil,* 3 March 1986.

11. News from WJC, 4 March 1986. *NYT,* 4 March 1986. *Profil,* the WJC and the *NYT* all published additional material relating to Waldheim's military service, but this is not relevant to the present discussion.

12. *NYT,* 4 March 1986.

13. *Sonderkommissionsakt* 235, reproduced in *Profil,* 10 March 1986, but not in Gruber, et al., *Wartime Years.*

14. Technically, a *Gerichtsreferendar* is someone in training to be a professional judge who has passed her or his first state qualifying exams, but who, after completing this training, must take a second exam.

15. This entry should, of course, read SA "Reiterstandarte." The dates in these documents were all written in the style common in Austria (18.11.38), but I have written the name of the month and the full designation of the year.

16. This should read 5/90.

17. Generalanwalt Dr. Marschall, who wrote an expert opinion for Waldheim "concerning the non-existence of alleged membership of Dr. Waldheim in NS organizations," does take note of the entries in the SK-235, but argued that the positive result of Waldheim's de-Nazification procedure effectively obviates serious consideration of them as evidence. However, he himself cannot explain how these very precise entries appeared in Waldheim's special commission file. Though the evidence concerning Waldheim's Nazi affiliations is not without its puzzling aspects (e.g., that the Gauleiter of Tulln did not mention them in his letter), Marschall's conclusion rests on the assumption, which is by no means self-evident, that such memberships would have precluded a favorable ruling by the de-Nazification commission. On the extremely indulgent atti-

tude of postwar Austrian authorities towards fellow travellers, see Dieter Stiefel, *Entnazifierung in Österreich* (Vienna/Munich/Zurich: Europaverlag, 1981), pp. 57–75. Marschall's expert opinion is printed in Gruber, et al., *Wartime Years,* pp. 84–98.

18. The date of this explanation was mistakenly recorded in SK-235 as 23 January, although it was actually 25 January. There is, however, no doubt that this is the document referred to in the Special Commission's file. See *Profil,* 24 March 1986.

19. A transcript of this document, which Waldheim allowed selected Austrian journalists to inspect but not photocopy, was printed in *Profil,* 24 March 1986. The relevant passage reads: "This riding duty [*Reiterdienst*] had an exclusively sporting character. My participation was also very short-lived, as I was inducted into the military in the summer of 1939 and served in the field until the end of the war. Therefore, it cannot be a question of membership in this formation, since a certain amount of participation and/or a period of time for candidacy membership were required, which, because of the brevity of my participation in riding exercises, I would not have been able to demonstrate."

20. *Profil,* 24 March 1986.

21. These are reproduced in Karl Gruber, et al., *Wartime Years,* pp. 111–114.

22. Ibid., pp. 101–109.

23. Ibid., p. 91.

24. Born, *Richtigkeit,* p. 23; Herzstein, *Missing,* p. 55.

25. Richard Mitten and Hans Schafranek, "Waldheim ist doch ein Lügner," *Die Weltwoche,* 10 November 1988.

26. Memo, "Direktion der Konsularakademie" to "das verehrliche Präsidium der Kammer für Handel, Gewerbe and Industrie, Wien," and Helmut Guttmann, Kurt Waldheim and Hans Schernhorst, 3 November 1937. File "Konsularakademie" in the Haus-, Hof- und Staatsarchiv, Vienna, (hereafter "Konsularakademie") Box 64.

27. Letter from Hlavac von Rechtwall to the "Kammer für Industrie, Gewerbe, Handel, Verkehr und Finanz, Wien," 10 February 1938. "Konsularakademie," Vienna, Box 64.

28. Letter from the "Handelskammer für Wien (Kammer für Industrie, Gewerbe, Handel, Verkehr und Finanzen)" to the "Konsolarakademie, zuhanden des Herrn kommissarischen Leiters" (i.e., Hlavac), 5 May 1938. "Konsularakademie," Box 64, emphasis in original.

29. Letter from Hlavac von Rechtwall to the "Präsidium der Handelskammer," Vienna, 18 May 1938. "Konsularakademie," Box 64.

30. Letter from the "Handelskammer für Wien" to the "Direktion der Konsularakademie, zuhanden des kommissarischen Leiters," 25 May 1938. "Konsularakademie," Box 64.

31. Letter from Hlavac von Rechtwall to the "Handelskammer, Wien," 30 June 1938. "Konsularakademie," Box 64.

32. Kurt Waldheim is listed as a first-year student and his age as of 31 December 1937 is given as "19." Konsularakademie "Portier-Rapport," "Konsularakademie," Box 64.

33. "Rundschreiben" from the "Direktion der Konsularakademie," 16 May 1938. "Konsularakademie," Box 64, emphasis in original.

34. For Waldheim's version, see Gruber, et al., *Wartime Years,* pp. 12, 25–29, and the relevant Annexes, pp. 84–115.

35. *Profil,* 14 November 1988. For a rejoinder to Waldheim's explanation, in which he alleges that the authors of the original article are part of the "defamation campaign" against him, see Richard Mitten and Hans Schafranek, "Wer sind die Verleumder?" *Falter* (Vienna) 23 November 1988.

36. Only as of 10 January 1940, long after Waldheim had graduated from the Academy, did it become mandatory for students at the Consular Academy to join a Nazi organization. The immediate occasion for Waldheim's joining the NSDStB appears, then, to have been a perceived, rather real, case of necessity, and it is doubtless true that his membership had a favorable effect on his application for a student grant. See "Konsularakademie," Box 49.

37. See in general Dieter Stiefel, *Entnazifierung,* and the collection of essays in Sebastian Meissl, Klaus-Dieter Mulley and Oliver Rathkolb eds., *Verdrängte Schuld, verfehlte Sühne. Entnazifierung in Österreich 1945–1955* (Vienna: Verlag für Geschichte und Politik, 1986).

38. In the first de-Nazification law, adopted in 1945, the principal dividing line was between those who had been active as "illegal" Nazis, and those who had not. In the law adopted in February 1947, however, this distinction had given way to that between the "incriminated" [*Belastete*] and "less incriminated" [*Minderbelastete*]. The 1947 law thus emphasized one's actual function and role in the Nazi hierarchy rather than merely the length of one's membership in the NSDAP, etc. See Stiefel, *Entnazifierung,* pp. 79–124.

39. See Born, *Richtigkeit,* pp. 20–24.

40. Neal Sher, of the Office of Special Investigation in the U.S. Department of Justice, is quoted in the 29 April 1990 *New York Times* International as saying that Hlavac's letter "shows the big lie as to Waldheim's claim that he was not a Nazi supporter" while at the Consular Academy. Though I was cited by Sher as the source of this document, his interpretation of it, as the present discussion shows, is significantly at odds with my own. To set the record straight, it was in fact my colleague Hans Schafranek who discovered this document in the Vienna archives, though it was I who made a copy of it available to the World Jewish Congress.

41. This, at least, seems to underlie the attempts, most recently by Robert Herzstein and Michael Palumbo, to show that Waldheim was an intelligence source for several powers after the war. The circumstances surrounding the compiling and delivery of the *Odluka,* however, suggest (1) that Waldheim's actual position and responsibilities themselves were not sufficient to warrant criminal proceedings (otherwise why employ tainted evidence?), and (2) that evidence of activity which might have been judged criminal at Nuremberg was in any case largely irrelevant to an attempted extortion of Waldheim, had any power actually wished to do so. Cf. Mitten, "L'affaire Waldheim," p. 1119.

42. See, however, Bradley F. Smith's *Reaching Judgment at Nuremberg* (New York: Basic Books, 1977), esp. pp. 302ff; and *The Road to Nuremberg* (New York: Basic Books, 1981), pp. 247ff.

43. Christopher Greenwood, "In the Matter of Kurt Waldheim. Report Regarding the Practice of the Tribunals Established for the Trial of War Crimes Following World War Two," Ms., Cambridge, 1988, pp. 2–4.

44. This was then known as Army High Command 12, but was renamed Army Group E in January, 1943. Kurz, et al., *Bericht,* pp. 5–7.

45. Archival references to individual documents will not be given, unless they are not noted in either Kurz, et al., *Bericht,* MOD, "Review," or the Thames Television Document Collection (hereafter TTDC), or there is a compelling reason to do so.

46. Part II, Article VI(c) of the Charter of the stated that war crimes included the "deportation to slave labor or for any other purpose of civilian population of or in occupied territory." "Charter of the International Military Tribunal," in Leon Friedman, ed., *The Laws of War. A Documentary History* 2 Vols. (New York: Random House, 1972), Vol. I, p. 887; "Convention on Treatment of Prisoners of War," Geneva, 27 July 1929, in ibid., p. 493.

47. See *Profil,* 18 May 1987; *NYT,* 28 April 1987.

48. See "Opinion and Judgement of United States Military Tribunal at Nuremberg in United States vs. Wilhelm von Leeb u.a." [U.S. vs. von Leeb], in Friedman, *Laws,* Vol. II, pp. 1421–1470; Greenwood, "Matter," p. 17.

49. Cited in Herzstein, *Missing,* p. 75.

50. Yugoslav sources put the number of persons interned in concentration camps at over 68,000, and these were predominantly women and children, many of whom did not survive the long marches to the camps. See Manoschek, *Pflichterfüllung,* pp. 17 and 34, n. 12 and 13. Yugoslav historian Vladimir Dedijer's estimate is over 90,000. Herzstein, *Missing,* p. 75. For a description of these and other atrocities committed by Wehrmacht units in Yugoslavia see Yugoslav War Crimes Commission, ed., *Report on the Crimes of Austria and the Austrians against Yugoslavia and her Peoples* (Belgrad: Yugoslav War Crimes Commission, 1947). Cf. Walter Manoschek, Hans Safrian, Florian Freund, Pertrand Pelz and Rubina Möhring, "Der Balkankrieg im Zweiten Weltkrieg als Teil der österreichischen Zeitgeschichte," Ms. (Vienna, 1989), esp. pp. 19–32 and 109–139.

51. See Born, *Richtigkeit,* pp. 50–69. Cf. Edmond Paris, *Genocide in Satellite Croatia, 1941–1945* (Chicago: American Institute for Balkan Affairs, 1961).

52. The by now (in)famous "Plenca telegramm," "discovered" by the Yugoslav historian Dusan Plenca, duly published by the West German weekly *Der Spiegel* and soon afterwards exposed as a forgery. See *Der Spiegel* No. 5, 1 February 1988; *Profil,* 8 February 1988; Cf. Kurz, et al., *Bericht,* pp. 35–36.

53. Other departments, such as the military intelligence section, are thoroughly documented. Kurz, et al., *Bericht,* p. 45.

54. Two Austrian historians, Walter Manoschek and Hans Schafranek, have made careful and painstaking studies of various aspects of Waldheim's service with the Battle Group West Bosnia. In some cases their research is based upon documents which the historians' commission did not see, and in others on different hypotheses as to what the available evidence might suggest. I am grateful to both for having shared their evidence and views with me. The discussion in this section is heavily indebted to the research of both.

55. The brief filed by Waldheim's lawyers "In the Matter of Kurt Waldheim," dated 1 August 1986, stated that Waldheim had served as 02 in the Ib (Quartermaster's) department with the Battle Group "West Bosnia." Later, ostensibly on the strength of an affidavit of Ernst Wiesinger, a former clerk in the same department, Waldheim revised this earlier statement and claimed that he had not been the assistant to the Ib, but rather to the IVa, involved only with supply questions. In Gruber, et al., *Wartime Years,* the distinction between the Ib and IVa is misleadingly labelled a "detail of nomenclature," although it does not deny categorically that Waldheim served as the assistant to the Ib. The difference is extremely significant: the IVa section, which was staffed by army administrative personnel, not serving officers, was concerned with such matters as clothing and supply requisition. The Ib, on the other hand, in addition to overseeing the work of the IVa, which was subordinate to it, also dealt with other items listed in orders organizing the battle group under the rubric of "supply" (*Versorgung*), among them transfer of prisoners. See "In the Matter of Kurt Waldheim," Ms., Washington, D.C., 1 August 1986, pp. 36ff; Gruber, et al., *Wartime Years,* pp. 38–39; Born, *Richtigkeit,* pp. 57–60; *Profil,* 18 May 1987; Kurz, et al., *Bericht,* p. 30; Manoschek, "Zeitgeschichtliches Gutachten zum Verfahren Kurt Waldheim gegen Walter Oswalt" Ms. (Vienna, 1989), pp. 1–3.

56. See Kurz, et al., *Bericht,* p. 32 and Manoschek, *Pflichterfüllung,* pp. 11–18.

57. Manoschek, "Gutachten," p. 3. Cf. Born, *Richtigkeit,* p. 59; Kurz, et al., *Bericht,* p. 30.

58. See Hans Schafranek, untitled Ms., Vienna, 1988, 2, citing the "Operationsplan für die Vernichtung der Partisanen in der Kozara," from 28 June 1942.

59. Manoschek, "Gutachten," p. 7.

60. Kurz, et al., *Bericht*, p. 33.

61. Manoschek, "Gutachten," pp. 7–8, citing a Croatian document which the historians' commission had not seen.

62. Greenwood, "Matter," p. 16.

63. It apparently made no difference legally that some prisoners were sent to slave labor in Norway. This made the matter worse, but merely the removal itself under inhumane conditions or of civilians outside the occupied territory even under humane conditions violated recognized conventions on the treatment of civilian population. Greenwood, "Matter," p. 16.

64. "Opinion and Judgement of United States Military Tribunal at Nuremberg in United States vs. Wilhelm List et al." [U.S. vs List, et al.], in Friedman, *Laws,* Vol. II, pp. 1303–1343.

65. Greenwood, "Matter," pp. 18–21.

66. The Austrian government established and funded a commission of historians to investigate Kurt Waldheim's wartime service. The commission originally comprised six members, and was later expanded to seven. The commission completed its work and submitted its report on 8 February 1988. The term "forced labor" in the passage cited is quoted from an undated document which appears to be a Croation translation of a message from the Ic (military intelligence) department (signed by a Captain Konopatzki) to the Ib (Waldheim's department) of Battle Group West Bosnia. According to this document, eight persons taken prisoner in the course of the Kozara campaign were to be sent to carry out forced labor in Germany "at their own request." Kurz, et al., *Bericht*, pp. 1–2, 34–35.

67. Greenwood, "Matter," pp. 20–21, citing the "High Command" case.

68. Which would probably not have been the case had those being shot actually been partisans. See "U.S. vs. List, et al.," Friedman, *Laws,* Vol. II, p. 1311. In this connection see Zentrale Stelle der Landesjustizverwaltungen in Ludwigsburg, "Geisel- und Partisanentötungen im zweiten Weltkrieg. Hinweise zur rechtlichen Beurteilung." Bound Ms. (Ludwigsburg, 1968), esp. pp. 81–82.

69. Greenwood, "Matter," pp. 19–20.

70. Interview, N. Goodrick-Clarke with Plume, 23 March 1988. TTDC, File 11. There is no documentary corroboration of Plume's statement. Consequently, there can be no talk here of any definitive "proof," merely questions which to my knowledge have never been addressed publicly by those who have examined Waldheim's past.

71. Document NOKW 1714, Statement of Friedrich Stahl, 12 June 1947. Stahl's own testimony at the trial of the Southeast Generals suggested his personal involvement in the events he described. Nonetheless, Stahl did not stand trial for any actions he had taken as commander of the Battle Group West Bosnia.

72. Also present at the meeting were Waldheim's chief in the liaison staff, Colonel Macholz, who was pictured in the photograph, and the German General Lüters, who was not.

73. Kurz, et al., *Bericht*, p. 37.

74. See ibid., p. 23.

75. In fact, the Italians had officially capitulated some days earlier, but General Badoglio announced it at 7:45 p.m. on 8 September 1943.

76. Historian Mark Mazower has attempted to establish the de facto role of the Ia (and, thereby, the Ia's 01, i.e., Waldheim) in the formulation of orders which, Mazower claimed, pre-

scribed guidelines for reprisal measures for units merely technically subordinate to the 11th Italian Army Command before Italy's capitulation. These guidelines, he argued further, authorized criminal actions such as that committed by a military detachment (Gruppe Salminger) at the village of Komeno in August, 1943. Mazower's argument depends on three crucial assumptions: (1) that the real command structure between the Italian 11th Army and the German troops fighting with them operated contrary to the formal one contained in the relevant orders, according to which these German forces were subordinate to the Italian 11th Army; (2) that the Ia Department of the German-Italian Liaison Staff was the source of an order authorizing criminal acts; and (3) that this order could be causally connected to a massacre carried out by a detachment of a regiment of a division in Komeno. In my view, the principal difficulty with Mazower's interpretation derives from the inability to demonstrate the functioning of this informal chain of command which bypassed the Italian commanders of the 11th Army. Moreover, Mazower could have implicated Waldheim in criminal activity only by demonstrating either that Waldheim had played a substantial part in constructing the order itself (which would be giving effect to an essentially criminal idea), or that he had been in a position significantly to influence policy, neither of which would have applied to O1 Waldheim. See Thames transcript, 16 April 1988, TTDC, File 11. See also Mark Mazower, "Waldheim goes to war," *London Review of Books,* 23 June 1988, p. 8; Greenwood, "Matter," p. 6.

77. The picture becomes a bit more complicated with the soldiers who refused to hand over their arms or resisted disarmament. The conclusion of the historians' commission that they were legally entitled not to hand over their arms when ordered to do so by the Germans, appears to me open to question, so long as the status of the Italian government itself remains unclear. Greenwood has even suggested that an order to have treated these Italians as mutineers "would not have been manifestly unlawful." The legal position of those soldiers who took up arms against the Germans without a formal declaration of war, however, would seem even more precarious. In any event, German orders to shoot prisoners who had fought properly, obeying the orders of their government, were illegal by any standard. See Kurz, et al., *Bericht,* pp. 25–26; Greenwood, "Matter," p. 21.

78. On these deportations see Gerald Reitlinger, *The Final Solution: The Attempt to Exterminate the Jews of Europe 1939–1945* (New York: A.S. Barnes, 1961), pp. 370–378; Raul Hilberg, *The Destruction of the European Jews,* revised and definitive edition (New York and London: Holmes and Meier, 1985), Vol. 2, pp. 692–718; Michael Molho, ed., *In Memoriam,* German translation by Peter Katzung of the 2nd edition (revised by Joseph Nehama) of the Greek translation of 1976 (by Georgios K. Zographiakis), Bound Ms. (Essen, 1981), pp. 158–192, 252–373. See also Hans Safrian, "Wiener Täter, Wiener Methode: Die Deportationen der Juden aus Saloniki," in Manoschek, et al., "Der Balkan," pp. 140–195; idem, *Die Eichmann-Männer* (Vienna: Europaverlag, 1992, forthcoming).

79. Simon Wiesenthal has doubted Waldheim's claim from the very beginning. Both Born and Czernin tend to accept that Waldheim might not have known of the deportations in 1943, while Yehuda Wallach of the historians' commission is convinced that Waldheim must have known about them, even though he was not physically present in Arsakli. See Simon Wiesenthal, *Recht, nicht Rache Erinnerungen* (Frandfurt am Main/Berlin: Ullstein, 1988), pp. 390–392; Born, *Richtigkeit,* p. 121; Czernin, "Balkanjahre," *Profil* 4 January 1988; Kurz, et al., *Bericht,* pp. 19–22, 47.

80. See in general Hilberg, *Destruction,* pp. 702ff.

81. The documents cited in the following two paragraphs may be found in TTDC, Files 4 and 5.

82. For a more detailed analysis of Waldheim's role in the Ic/AO and the intelligence-gathering process in general in this department, see Czernin, "Balkanjahre," *Profil,* 21 December 1987; and Kurz, et al., *Bericht,* pp. 8–13.

83. The most convincing detailed examinations of the documents relating to these deportations are in Born, *Richtigkeit,* pp. 119–136, and Czernin, "Balkanjahre," *Profil,* 4 January 1988, but see Kurz, et al., *Bericht,* pp. 20–22. Waldheim's explanation is given in Gruber, et al., *Wartime Years,* pp. 47–50.

84. Gruber, et al., *Wartime Years,* pp. 49–50.

85. Born, *Richtigkeit,* p. 135.

86. Czernin, "Balkanjahre," *Profil,* 4 January 1988.

87. Müller-Mongeot's recollection on this point appears to be mistaken. Burger was Wisliceny's replacement at the SS and the latter had not been in Greece for some time prior to the meeting with Kleemann. It is therefore virtually impossible that they travelled together to Rhodes. I am grateful to Hans Safrian for clarifying this point for me.

88. Draft Statement, Karl-August Müller-Mangeot, 4 April 1988, TTDC, File 11. Kleemann's resistance to the SS man was confirmed by both Kleemann and Linnemann in statements given during the preliminary investigations of Nazi crimes in Greece undertaken by the German authorities. See Zentrale Stelle der Landesjustizverwaltung Ludwigsburg, File No. 508 AR-Z 26/1963.

89. See Hans Safrian, "Die Rolle von Wehrmacht und SS bei der Deportation griechischer Juden 1943-1944," Ms. (Vienna, 1989); idem, *Die Eichmann-Männer.*

90. Greenwood, "Matter," pp. 22–23.

91. An English translation of the relevant section of the *Odluka* is in Gruber, et al. *Wartime Years,* pp. 223–236; Rosenbaum developed his argument in a report he submitted to Edgar Bronfman, "Newly-discovered Documents Linking Kurt Waldheim to October 1944 Massacres in Macedonia," May 13, 1986. See also *Profil,* 20 May 1986.

92. Kurz, et al., *Bericht,* p. 42.

93. *Der Spiegel,* Nr. 9, 29 February 1988.

5

Dis"kurt"esies: Waldheim and the Language of Guilt

The issue of Waldheim's possible involvement in criminal activity was first introduced preemptively by the Waldheim camp itself. In the hands of his supporters, questions reasonable people might have been inclined to raise in view of the scanty information then available about Waldheim's wartime career were inflated beyond recognition into extravagent concrete charges which were then peremptorily dismissed. The categorical terms in which these initial questions were framed, however, made a serious discussion of specific suspicions of criminal liability, when they inevitably arose, increasingly difficult. As long as the issue refused to go away, it was to Waldheim's advantage politically to ensure that the debate in Austria proceeded on his terms. By conflating the issues of his individual criminal liability for war crimes with a more broadly conceived moral or political responsibility related primarily to his postwar career, Waldheim succeeded in reducing all possible criticisms to one narrowly conceived question, namely, had anyone been able to prove Waldheim's personal involvement in war crimes? Thus the continued focus on criminality could not but assist Waldheim and his supporters in derailing or clouding these broader issues of moral responsibility. Waldheim's overall ability to determine the terms of the debate, coupled with the general imprecision on the part of his critics as to what issues beyond his mere untruthfulness were actually at stake, meant in addition that those (like the WJC) who raised the subjects of Waldheim's postwar dissemblance and perceived moral failings could be and were successfully portrayed by the Waldheim camp as having alleged his personal guilt for war crimes. As we will see in Chapter Six, the WJC never accused Waldheim of such personal involvement. Others, for example the historian C.M. Woodhouse, did accuse Waldheim of criminal behavior—in this case complicity in the murder of an Allied commando—though he did not raise the charge during the election campaign itself.

It would repay examining Woodhouse's allegations in some detail, but not simply to show that Waldheim did not incur criminal liability for the deaths of any of the Allied commandos which have been examined to date. An analysis of Woodhouse's allegations may also help explain not only why popular suspicion about Waldheim's criminality could have become so quickly established in a situation where reliable information was either absent or incomplete and one side in the dispute was mounting a determined effort to narrow the range of relevant issues, but also why the assumptions underlying this suspicion were mostly mistaken. It allows us further to demonstrate in detail the range of behavior which exists this side of proven criminal complicity. We will then be better placed to evaluate Waldheim's suggestion that his innocence of war crimes necessarily implied that his conduct—either during or after the war—was irreproachable. It will finally enable us to comprehend the extent of the Waldheim camp's distortion of the arguments and motives of the World Jewish Congress during the election campaign, which in turn became a central premise upon which Waldheim's electoral propaganda was able to build the image of an international Jewish conspiracy against him. First, however, to the issue of war crimes in general and Woodhouse's argument in particular.

When the WJC published a copy of the U.S. Army's Central Registry of War Criminals and Security Suspects (CROWCASS), which listed Kurt Waldheim as being sought by Yugoslavia for "murder," the previous ill-defined suspicions of misdeeds suddenly became disturbingly specific. For a time the debate in the media focussed on the allegations against Waldheim contained in the Yugoslav *Odluka,* whose findings had formed the evidentiary basis of both the United Nations War Crimes Commission file and the CROWCASS. The largely uncritical attention given to this file, which military historian Manfred Messerschmidt has rightly described as proving "virtually nothing,"[1] helped fuel the popular perception that Waldheim's wartime service was associated with criminal activity of some kind. The report of the international historians' commission, on which Messerschmidt served, as well as some more recent well-researched accounts of Waldheim's military service, especially that of Robert Herzstein, have collectively delivered this assumption, insofar as it is based on the *Odluka,* a blow from which it ought never to recover.[2]

The discrediting of the Yugoslav file, however, need not have put an end to the discussion on Waldheim's wartime service. In their report, the historians' commission labored valiantly to find a vocabulary which would do justice to both the scholarly and the political aspects of their investigation into Waldheim's past. Although their brief from the Austrian government was broadly formulated, there seems little doubt that the commission had been expected to pronounce Waldheim guilty or innocent of war crimes. The intellectual scope for rendering such interpretative conclusions was, however, limited. It is one thing, for example, to reconstruct the cable traffic relating to imprisoned Allied commandos, and even argue that Waldheim's actions might have hastened the commandos' execution at the hands of the *Sicherheitsdienst* (SD). One could further demonstrate that the Nuremberg Tribunal found particular acts of certain individual officers criminal according to the principles and practice it established, and argue analogously that Waldheim performed tasks of an essentially similar nature. It is, however, something else again to contend that Waldheim's actions constituted criminal activity.

The members of the commission seem to have recognized their predicament and settled upon categories which were at once sweeping and somewhat arcane. They wrote, for example, "in general, a certain [amount of] guilt can ensue simply by virtue of one's knowledge of violations of human rights in the area in which one served, if the person involved, lacking the requisite strength or courage, fails to observe his human responsibility to intervene against injustice."[3] They spoke later of the "active assistance [*Mitwirkung*] in those cases in which various degrees of participation [*Mitbeteiligung*] could be established. One such was, for example, in the consultative support given to measures related to 'cleansing operations.'"[4] By virtue of his duties, Waldheim possessed a comprehensive overview of military operations, which "in some cases included acts and measures which contravened the laws of war and the basic principles of humanity [*Grundsätzen der Menschlichkeit*]."[5] Waldheim never objected to such measures. "On the contrary," the report stated, "he repeatedly rendered assistance [*mitwirken*] to illegal activities and thereby facilitated their execution."[6] The commission also had pertinent things to say about the principles in light of which Waldheim's activities ought to be interpreted. Such codifications of rules of warfare were incomplete, the historians wrote, and "wherever a concrete guideline could not be inferred from the [Hague] Convention" of 1907 itself, it was necessary, as the Convention itself stated, "to act in accordance with the usages established among civilized peoples, the laws of humanity and the dictates of public conscience."[7]

The Commission's balanced consideration of this problem commands respect, but the moral and quasi-juridical neologisms it offered were no less obscure merely because they were consonant with a widely recognized antecedent scholarly tradition which is itself ambiguous. The determination of what constitutes "a certain amount of guilt," "active participation," "consultative support," etc., is not, nor could it be, uniform or immutable, and it is no great achievement to underline the imprecision of such terms as "usages established among civilized peoples," "laws of humanity," and the "dictates of public conscience." Commission member Manfred Messerschmidt, who as an historian and jurist is in a rare privileged position to comment, seemed at least implicitly to acknowledge the ambiguity of such terms. In an article he wrote for *Der Spiegel* shortly after the Commission's report had been delivered, Messerschmidt suggested: "If the Commission [itself] did not assume any criminally relevant guilt [*strafrechtlich zurechenbare Schuld*], there is still room to debate whether criminal experts might be able to discuss a form of aiding and abetting."[8]

The desire to contribute some of the juridical clarity which was felt to have been missing from previous efforts to illuminate Waldheim's wartime career appears to have provided the elevated justification for the Thames Television–Home Box Office (HBO) coproduction *Waldheim: A Commission of Inquiry,* though like most other commercial television ventures, the principal objective presumably was to make money.[9] Advised officially by, among others, Telford Taylor, former U.S. prosecutor at Nuremberg, assisted by a team of experienced researchers, and armed with a research budget the size of which the historians' commission or, for that matter, the Office of Special Investigation (OSI) of the U.S. Department of Justice could scarcely imagine, Thames TV in London produced a four-hour version of a nine-day commission of inquiry, which was aired on 5 June 1988. Hundreds of documents were submitted as evidence to the panel of five judges by "presenting counsel" Alan Ryan (who "presented" the case against Waldheim) and "challenging counsel" Lord Rawlinson (who "challenged" the case developed by Ryan).[10] The judges also heard testimony from eyewitnesses to atrocities, from veterans who had served with Waldheim or had something material to add, and from legal and historical experts.[11]

Most of the criticism directed against the Thames-HBO production centered on the legitimacy of subjecting a living public figure to a "trial by television." Reactions ranged from opinions in Austria that such an undertaking amounted to a sort of lèse majesté[12] to OSI-head Neal Sher's charge that the whole idea was "preposterous and dangerous."[13] Similar charges were made against the program by C. M. Woodhouse, who judged it a "most lamentable failure."[14] There are, of course, several points on which to take issue with the production, most of which could be summarized under the rubric of presenting counsel Alan Ryan's overconfidence and underpreparedness, and the results of the program were uneven. Those making the *Commission of Inquiry* seem to have wished to offer a televised means of clarifying a widespread popular uncertainty over whether or not Waldheim had committed war crimes.[15] It is possible to dispute whether this concern justified the making of such a program, and whether television is an appropriate medium for such an inquiry, but it can hardly be denied that this popular suspicion did exist, or that the program did clarify some, even though not all, issues relevant to the possible criminality of acts Waldheim committed in the Balkan theater. Since this program was broadcast, the British Ministry of Defense (MOD) has published its long report on Waldheim's activities in Greece in 1944 relating to the deaths of Allied prisoners of war. Although it is unlikely that the conclusions of the historians' commission's and MOD's reports will ever be open to challenge in any serious way, a few questions do remain open about Waldheim's activities from 1942–1945, and opinions differ as to the legal implications these might have.

If, however, Waldheim were eventually to be called upon to answer such charges, it would probably be less because of this activity itself than because of his later international prominence. This need not in the least affect the moral judgment about his wartime activity or his postwar attitude towards it. More importantly, saying this would not imply that the duties Waldheim performed could not be regarded as criminal according to some of the principles which guided the judges at Nuremberg. It merely suggests that the war crimes tribunal most likely would not have done so. The interest of the prosecutors in so-called *Schreibtischtäter*, bureaucratic culprits, of Waldheim's rank was slight: where staff officers were brought to trial, they were usually of a much higher rank, with more substantial responsibilities. This was less a matter of justice than one of expedience.[16]

Waldheim's possible role in the disappearance and death of Allied commandos was always one of the most potentially damaging for him. Not only was his role as superintending officer in the sub-department responsible for prisoner interrogations established beyond any doubt,[17] but those murdered were not anonymous Greek or Yugoslav peasants of dubious political conviction, but quasi-mythical heroes of the Allies. By connecting Waldheim to the deaths of "our boys," one could, at least in Britain, validate one's own patriotic credentials. The cases of Allied commandos actually or reputedly killed by units under the control of Army Group E have been investigated by several scholars, including those on the historians' commission and the British Ministry of Defense, none of whom found any evidence of Waldheim's criminal involvement in the cases they examined. Among those making the strongest contrary charges against Waldheim on this score is C.M. Woodhouse, historian of modern Greece and the wartime commander of the Allied Military Mission to the Greek Resistance. Woodhouse has accused Waldheim of being an "accessory to [the] murder" of Captain D. A. LaTouche Warren in the spring of 1944.[18]

The broad outlines of Woodhouse's case against Waldheim may be briefly summarized. Captain "Bunny" Warren was an Australian-born commando serving with forces of the Special Operations Executive (SOE) under Woodhouse's command operating in Greece. In early 1944, Warren was entrusted with a mission to evacuate a group of escaped prisoners of war from Greece to Italy. Warren's group, however, was captured and sent to Patras. The troops in Patras were under the command of the German XXII Mountain Corps. The report from the Corps military intelligence ([Roman numeral] Ic) department announcing these prisoners' capture referred to them as a *Sabatogetrupp*. The prisoners were eventually sent to Salonika, where they entered Waldheim's area of responsibility. After they had been interrogated by members of the Ic department of Army Group E, a report evaluating these interrogations was drafted, which bears the initial of Waldheim and the signature of Major Hammer, the Ic's official deputy. According to Woodhouse, this report drew conclusions which were not only spurious and "nonsensical," given the nature of the operation, but which were, for the prisoners, fatally tendentious. Warren's murder is not documented, but Woodhouse has received oral confirmation of it from one of Warren's former fellow prisoners, and believes he knows the name of the *Sicherheitsdienst* (SD) officer who killed him.[19]

Any "competent intelligence officer," Woodhouse argued, would have instantly spotted the discrepancies between the facts of the commando's actual mission and their description as a *Sabatogetrupp* in the report from Ioannina. The "mendacious report," which carries Waldheim's initial, was thus "pure fantasy." It not only repeated the ominous terminology of the initial dispatch, but fabricated an elaborate network of spies, which would only have increased the chances that the prisoners would be treated according to the commando order, i.e., handed over to the SD to be shot. Hence, Waldheim was an "accessory" to Warren's murder. As for Waldheim's motives, Woodhouse suggests that "it was simply to ensure that the inevitable execution—that is to say, murder—was legally watertight under Nazi 'law.'"[20]

The "Commando Order"

As Woodhouse asserts, following the judgement at Nuremberg, the so-called "Commando Order" (*Kommando-Befehl*) of 18 October 1942, according to the provisions of which Warren and others were killed, was "incontrovertibly criminal."[21] It specified that all captured Allied commandos be handed over unconditionally to the SD to be killed. The general line of Woodhouse's argument here is unassailable, but warrants a more detailed examination of the implications which such an order might have had on the actions of a staff officer. Until now this aspect has been insufficiently emphasized and Woodhouse himself makes some questionable assumptions about the nature of the commando order itself, the possibilities for circumventing it, and the practices of the general staff of Army Group E, all of which influenced his reading of the evidence in the Warren case.

The *Geheime Kommandosache* issued by Hitler on 18 October 1942, which has become known as the "commando order," opened with a significant passage:

> 1. For some time our enemies have been using in their warfare methods which are outside the international Geneva Conventions. Especially brutal and treacherous is the behavior of the so-called commandos, who, as is established, are partially recruited even from freed criminals in enemy countries. From captured orders it is divulged that they are directed not only to shackle prisoners, but also to kill defenseless prisoners on the spot at the moment in which they believe that the latter as prisoners represent a burden in the further pursuit of their purposes or could otherwise be a hindrance. Finally, orders have been found in which the killing of prisoners has been demanded in principle.[22]

Hitler issued an addendum on the same day, "to make known the reasons for the order."[23] The structure of Hitler's argument as well as the vocabulary he employed are telling. The addendum first recalls the nature of the "partisan war" against which measures had already been undertaken. Expressions such as "a method of destruction of communications behind enemy lines," "this type of combat," and "this equally vile and insidious sabotage work" clearly established Hitler's emphasis on the manner of combat of these "enemy sabotage parties."

"Even when designated differently," Hitler then argued, amalgamating these partisan methods with those of the Allied commandos, "England and America have opted for an identical method of waging war." Though they may employ different means of infiltrating enemy lines, "this method does not differ in essentials from the Russian partisan activities." In the justification Hitler gave for this statement, however, it was the objectives rather than the fighting methods themselves which incriminated the commandos. Yet of those objectives listed (general espionage, setting up and arming of "terrorist groups," sabotage of communication lines, etc.), only the establishment of a "spy network" would appear even suspicious in terms of a "legality" based on internationally recognized laws of war. Thus, even though the carrying out of otherwise legitimate military objectives (say, the destruction of industrial production centers or the disruption of communication lines) utilizing methods which violated the laws of war could conceivably have made the actions themselves illicit, and thereby in fact have deprived those responsible of the protection of the Geneva Conventions, Hitler's amalgamation of the tasks and methods of commandos here merely obscured the line dividing the "legal" from the "illegal" waging of war, and was certainly not accidental.[24]

In the most significant passage for our argument, Hitler not only provided examples of the allegedly abhorrent fighting practices of the commandos, but he stated explicitly that those who employed them placed themselves outside the protection of the Geneva Accords:

> For all that, this type of war is entirely without danger for the enemy. For by on the one hand deploying its sabotage parties in uniform but on the other hand providing them with civilian clothing, [the members of the enemy party] can appear either as soldiers or as civilians as required. While they themselves are under orders ruthlessly to eliminate German soldiers or even local residents who should hinder them, they are in no danger of sustaining serious losses in their work, since the worst that can happen is that, if they are caught, they can surrender and thereby believe that they theoretically fall under the conditions of the Geneva Convention. There is no doubt, however, that this is an abuse of the Geneva Accords of the worst sort. All the more, as we are dealing partly with criminal elements who were released so that they could earn their rehabilitation by carrying out such activities.

The nonsequitur about the recruitment of former criminals, although clearly intended to buttress Hitler's charge that commandos' methods of combat were illegal, was nonetheless plainly irrelevant to the Geneva Convention and to the protection of prisoners of war.

The objective of this order seemed designed to deter prospective volunteers for such operations. Germany's enemies should know, the addendum continued, *"that every sabotage party is without exception to be liquidated to the last man."* A commando could not "simply surrender and be treated according to the rules of the Geneva Convention. Rather, *he is under all circumstances to be exterminated completely."* (emphasis in original) Perhaps sensing that his arguments alone would not convince, Hitler added a passage prescribing severe penalties for those failing to carry out the order with sufficent "energy": "Officers and non-commissioned officers who fail out of weakness of some kind are to be severely reprimanded or, under some circumstances—if there is imminent danger—to be called immediately to the most severe account."[25]

Ten days later, Alexander Loehr, commanding general of the AOK 12 (Army Group E's predecessor), in which Waldheim served, issued his own addendum to the order: "This [form of] combat is in clear contravention of the international Geneva Convention. Accordingly, those who fight by these methods—wherever they come from—are not to be considered members of an armed power." Loehr also promised to visit severe punishment on those showing insufficient resolve. The context of this passage suggests that Loehr was concerned predominantly with the fight against the partisans. Consequently, the unconditional punishment reserved for waverers in this fight, in which "valuable German blood" was at stake, might not have applied with equal force to those hesitating to follow the order's provisions with regard to captured Allied commandos, though this is not certain.[26]

The Nuremberg Tribunal judged the commando order to be "criminal on its face." It simply "directed the slaughter of these 'sabotage' troops."[27] It is undoubtedly true that the order was criminal, but for a low-ranking officer, even one who had studied law, it may have been less clear than it seems in hindsight that it was criminal "on its face."

Article I of the Annex to the "Convention Respecting the Laws and Customs of War on Land," adopted in the Hague in 1907, specified four conditions which armies, militia and volunteer corps had to meet in order to be recognized as legitimate belligerents. These were "(1) to be commanded by a person responsible for his subordinates; (2) to have a fixed distinctive emblem recognizable at a distance; (3) to carry arms openly; and (4) to conduct their operations in accordance with the laws and customs of war."[28] The Hague Convention is usually cited with respect to partisans, and the discussion normally concerns whether the insignia they wore (a red star) was visible at a sufficient distance to entitle them to status as prisoners of war upon capture. In fact, the Nuremberg courts took a rather dim view of partisan warfare as such. In Case 7, for example, the court judged that not only was the red star not "such that it could be seen at a distance," but the partisans did not "carry their arms openly except when it was to their advantage to do so." Although "a few partisan bands met the requirements of lawful belligerency," they continued, the "bands" under consideration in Case 7 "were not shown by satisfactory evidence to have met the requirements. This means, of course, that captured members of these unlawful groups were not entitled to be treated as prisoners of war. No crime can be properly charged against the defendents for the killing of such captured members of the resistance forces, they being *francs-tireurs.*"[29]

With the commandos, notwithstanding Hitler's and Loehr's remarks to the contrary, there is little doubt that they wore recognizable insignia, carried their arms openly, and had a functioning command structure. The issue turns on the interpretation of the fourth condition, that they "conduct their operations in accordance with the laws and customs of war." Thus, though the commando order itself may have been criminal, it does not automatically follow that the execution of persons "in accordance with the Führer order" would be *ipso facto* criminal. It is not inconceivable that an action by an Allied commando would not have fulfilled this fourth criterion, thereby placing him outside the protection of the Geneva Convention. Indeed, in the addendum Hitler himself refers to (probably apochryphal) orders commanding such behavior. In such a case, and only in that case, the Nuremberg Tribunal would have been hard pressed not to have judged the commandos, as it had judged the partisans, as not "entitled to be treated as prisoners of war," and a commando's execution would not necessarily, at least in theory, have been a crime.

There is little reliable evidence to suggest that the actions of any of the commandos in the cases under review failed to meet the Geneva Convention's conditions (although I consider it counter-intuitive to think that all conceivable laws of war were observed completely by all commandos under all circumstances in the Balkan theater). Thus, contributing to the killing of commandos by following the procedures outlined in the order could have been judged criminal by the Tribunal, though no one in Case 7 was actually convicted on this charge.[30] The issue here is, however, what a low-ranking officer in the general staff of Army Group E would have known about the commando order, and how he could have known that it was criminal "on its face." Although Waldheim's knowledge of the essential provisions of the order may be accepted as given, as several documents which bear his signature assume such knowledge, certainty as to the order's criminality would not have been self-evident. To have been able to conclude this he would have been required, at the very least, to reject the assertions Hitler and Loehr had made about the methods employed by Allied commandos, to question their amalgamation of these practices with those of the partisans, and to dissent from their conclusion that the methods and objectives of the commandos deprived them of the protection as prisoners of war under the Geneva Convention.

It is also not entirely clear on what basis such an officer could have disputed such an order. The relevant prewar conventions and postwar judgements themselves offered no uniform principles, and possessed not a few ambiguous formulations. Hence, one could have contested Hitler's and Loehr's orders only by citing the four conditions of the Hague convention and appealing either to a higher logical sophistication than either possessed, or by claiming (by means of an apodictic judgement) that the order "violates international law and outrages fundamental concepts of justice,"[31] the general formulation offered by the judges in Case 7 at Nuremberg. Such arguments, moreover, would provide the only grounds for rejecting the order as criminal under conditions of unimpeded intellectual debate. Even under such circumstances, not everyone would have the knowledge or intellectual confidence to mount such a challenge. Such inhibitions would hold *a fortiori* in a military hierarchy, where these conditions normally do not obtain.

This is an essential point. The judges in Case 7 argued, for instance, that "an officer is duty bound to carry out only the lawful orders that he received. One who distributes, issues, or carries out a criminal order becomes a criminal if he knew or should have known of its criminal character."[32] The officer in question here was List. "Certainly," the court remarked, "a field marshal of the German Army with more than 40 years of experience as a professional soldier knew or ought to have known of its criminal nature."[33] If that was the general criterion, what would have been the minimum level of experience required of a reserve officer to ensure that he "knew or ought to have known" of an order's criminal nature? Quite apart from any intellectual doubts a staff officer might have been able to develop about the commando order, the inculcation of instinctive obedience to one's superiors would probably have disinclined him to think through the ultimate implications of carrying out an order, even a criminal one, if it had been given by his superior. This argument, of course, bears some similarity to the "superior orders" defence frequently offered by defendants at Nuremberg, but is introduced here merely to suggest possible barriers to the moral awareness of junior officers.

The International Military Tribunal, as is well known, in general rejected the defense of superior orders. "The fact that the Defendant acted pursuant to the order of his Government or of a superior," Article VIII of the Tribunal's charter stated, "shall not free him from responsibility, but may be considered in mitigation of punishment if the Tribunal determines that justice so requires."[34] Even where superior orders were considered in principle as a defense, moreover, it was rejected for orders which were manifestly unlawful or if the accused knew them to have been unlawful,[35] though no generally applicable criteria were advanced for determining this. In the High Command case, the court discussed this issue as it related to chiefs of staff. Although it determined that "in the absence of participation in criminal orders or their execution within a command, a chief of staff does not become criminally responsible for criminal acts occurring therein,"[36] the court also argued that "staff officers were indispensable to that end [i.e., "evil and inhumane acts of the last war"] and cannot escape criminal responsibility for their essential contribution to the final execution of such orders on the plea that they were complying with the orders of a superior who was more criminal."[37]

The court in Case 7, which took up the question in more general terms, found that

> Implicit obedience to orders of superior officers is almost indispensable to every military system. But this implies obedience to lawful orders only. If the act done pursuant to a superior's orders be murder, the production of the order will not make it any less so. It may mitigate but it cannot justify the crime. We are of the view, however, that if the illegality of the order was not known to the inferior, no wrongful intent necessary to the commission of a crime exists and the interior [sic, i.e., inferior] will be protected. But the general rule is that members of the armed forces are bound to obey only the lawful orders of their commanding officers and cannot escape criminal liability by obeying a command which violates international law and outrages fundamental concepts of justice.[38]

These judgements not only seem to lack internal consistency, they also beg the question how an inferior staff officer would acquire certain knowledge of an order's criminality.

The practice of the Allied powers themselves was also not such as to encourage critical thought among its soldiers about the criminality of their orders. Until 1944, for example, both the *British Manual of Military Law* and the U.S. *Army Field Manual* listed superior orders as a defense against criminal liability. The British manual stated that "members of the armed forces who commit such violations of the recognized rules of warfare as are ordered by the Government or their commander are not war criminals and cannot therefore be punished by the enemy."[39] In Case 7, the court rejected the view that this provision in military manuals would necessarily be binding on their deliberations, but the unsettling fact that both the U.S. and British armies seem to have considered superior orders a categorical defense against war crimes well into World War II suggests that it would be anachronistic to expect Wehrmacht officers—who arguably would have suffered under an even more onerous pressure to obey blindly than their British or U.S. counterparts[40]—to have shown the predilection for insubordination unwelcome among Allied soldiers. Seen from this perspective, in wartime situations and in cases where the act involved the forwarding of information, the consciousness of an order's criminality (as opposed to revulsion at its provisions) would not be axiomatic. It is true that the German Military Penal Code, which had been adopted in 1872, prescribed obedience to lawful and not criminal orders. The 1940 edition stated that "if through the execution of an order pertaining to the service [*Dienstsachen*], a penal law is violated, then the superior giving the order is alone responsible. However, the obeying subordinate shall be punished as accomplice [*Teilnehmer*]: (1) if he went beyond the order given to him, or (2) if he knew that the order of the superior concerned an act which aimed at a general or military crime or offense."[41] Again, in the present context the key phrase is whether a soldier knew that the act "aimed at a general or military crime or offense." Beyond this difficulty, the penal code made no provisions to protect someone who refused to carry out an order which he held to be criminal, but which his commander did not.

The Nuremberg Tribunal in the High Command Case appears to have recognized this dilemma, and judged that someone called upon to implement an order which he knew to be criminal had the following choices: to issue a countermanding order; to resign; to sabotage the enforcement of the order within a somewhat limited sphere; or to do nothing. The first could not have applied to someone in Waldheim's position. The court acknowledged that "resignation in wartime is not a privilege generally accorded to officers in an army. . . . In Germany, under Hitler, to assert such a ground for resignation probably would have entailed the most serious consequences for an officer," though they were writing about officers of the military High Command, not about lower-ranking staff officers. Sabotage of a criminal order by a staff officer, the court reasoned, would also have been ineffectual. He could have done it "only verbally by personal contacts" and "such verbal repudiation could never be of sufficient scope to annul its enforcement."[42] The fourth choice, to do nothing, seems to have been the one for which Waldheim opted. Theoretically, Waldheim could have made himself liable as an accomplice to war crimes, if his degree of participation in and knowledge of the criminality of a given act were sufficiently well established. In evaluating the evidence, however, we should once again recall the points we have addressed in this section.

The commando order was judged criminal "on its face," because it did not distinguish between those who qualified as combatants and those who did not. Still, the order itself and the various addenda which came from Hitler or Loehr argued in such a way that the criminality of the order was far from self-evident. Moreover, the possibility of challenging the legality of such an order was restricted not only by limited knowledge in face of the order's "logic" and "evidence." The inclination to contest an order's legality would have flown in the face of the instinctive obedience expected in the Wehrmacht. The judgments at Nuremberg provided no insights into how a junior staff officer might have surmised the criminality of an order, and successfully refused its execution. It would, I would argue, under these circumstances, have required a rare intellectual self-confidence for such an officer to have presumed a level of understanding superior to that of the highest authorities in the Wehrmacht as well as Loehr, whose intelligence and knowledge apparently commanded the respect of all those who knew him. To have openly challenged such an order, whose criminality could not have been certain, in a situation where the belief in the defense of superior orders must have been generally shared (despite paragraph 47, quoted above),[43] would have required a courage of conviction which borders on the suicidal.

The crimes of the Wehrmacht in the Balkans were manifold and extreme. Most of these were visible and clear-cut violations of international law and military norms, though the Second World War reached new lows of military norms. The judgment of the court at Nuremberg, which all but legitimated the wholesale slaughter of captured partisans and their civilian accomplices,[44] indicated the gap between the laws of war and standards of conduct which ordinarily count as recognizably moral. The kinds of combat these laws allowed, however, ought to come as no surprise, yet many of the arguments about Waldheim's specific military past have frequently suffered under illusions as to what was clearly criminal in military conduct and the conditions under which officers called upon in borderline cases to execute criminal orders could have known of an order's criminality and been in a position to have dissented.[45] Conflicts between the requirements of military discipline and the demands on conscience are ordinarily settled in favor of obedience. The very fact that the German Military Penal Code directed a soldier not to obey criminal orders but offered no real protection against the consequences should he be wrong, expressed the contradiction most clearly. I have advanced the view that the principles of Nuremberg imply neither an entirely consistent nor comprehensive framework for determining and upholding the laws of war. Wehrmacht military policies in the Balkans, moreover, all but defy such a rubric. It is, however, necessary to ask under what circumstances a subaltern staff officer might have been expected to recognize an order's criminality and might have successfully evaded or even disobeyed it. Then it might be possible to establish ways in which not only the legality of various kinds of warfare could be comprehended clearly by all those called upon to fight, but also adopt measures which protect, even if they do not encourage, the critical thought and action necessary to put into practice the moral imperative which the judgements at Nuremberg enjoin. This, however, demands some hard rethinking about our hierarchy of virtues. When we search for culprits for crimes of war and crimes against humanity, we should not overlook those who strive to instill unquestioning obedience as the highest military "duty."

The Case of Captain Warren

The obstacles which might have lain in the way of someone in Waldheim's position recognizing the criminality of the commando order, as opposed to possessing detailed knowledge of the order's provisions, does not necessarily imply that Waldheim personally did not understand this. The historians' commission, for example, assumed Waldheim's awareness of the order's criminality (which would be difficult to prove in any case), without, however, having engaged the points we have discussed above.[46] Here it is necessary merely to recall that there is some room for dispute as to the certainty of this assumption, which Woodhouse as well as the historians' commission have made. However, nothing in my criticism of Woodhouse's argument about Waldheim's role in the Warren case requires that this assumption be challenged. Even with the aid of it, Woodhouse cannot, in my opinion, sustain his argument on the available evidence.

Woodhouse cites the two most important documents which have survived relating to the case of Captain Warren.[47] The first is the report from 27 March 1944 sent by the Ic department of the Corps Group Ioannina to the High Command of Army Group E. This radio message contained the following entry: "Sabotage party captured 25 March (daily report Ia from 26 March) consists of English, Americans, Russians and Poles. Weapons: 2 machine guns, various sub-machine guns and pistols. Brief interrogation planned for 27 March in Patras. Transfer with captured documents to the Army Group expected 27 March." The second is a report from 8 May 1944 from the Ic/AO department of Army Group E to the High Command of Army Group F. This report, initialed by Waldheim and signed by Major Hammer, summarized the information which the Ic/AO department of Army Group E had gleaned from the interrogation of the prisoners and offered a wide-ranging interpretation of this information as it affected commando activity. On the basis of these two documents, Woodhouse has inferred both Waldheim's criminal negligence as a "competent intelligence officer" and the reprehensible motives which explained his behavior. This, however, is the principal source of Woodhouse's errors. Though it is not clear on what basis he construed his notion of Waldheim's duties as the third *Ordonnanzoffizier* (O3), the syllogistic precision of Woodhouse's reasoning in this case betrays asumptions which presumably derive from unfamiliarity with the details of the operations of the Ic/AO, but are unwarranted in any case. Neither the transcripts of the preliminary interrogations which were carried out in Ioannina nor those of the interrogations conducted in Saloniki have survived (at least they are unknown to me), leaving a large gap in the evidence. Too large, I would argue, to justify Woodhouse's conclusions. In other cases, however, the evidence is more complete and allows us to test some of Woodhouse's assumptions in the Warren case.

Let us examine first of all the contention that the key to Warren's eventual execution lay in the "fatal word" *Sabotagetrupp.* "The word sabotage," Woodhouse writes, "was an instant reminder of the 'commando order.'" Moreover, "the words attributed to Warren implied that he himself took part in 'sabotage' operations."[48] Of the summary of the interrogation of another prisoner, an American civilian, in the report from 8 May 1944, Woodhouse writes, "The only certain conclusion that could be drawn . . . was that he could not possibly have been a member of a *Sabotagetrupp.* But Waldheim did not trouble to make that point (unless, improbably, it was deleted)."[49] The assumption here is that employing the terminology of the commando order meant that the fate of those captured was all but decided, barring some furtive courageous act which contravened the standing policy. This assumption, however, is open to some question.

This can best be shown by examining a few of the documents dealing with an operation by the Special Boat Squadron [SBS] on the island of Calino. The first is the "Ic Contribution to Ia Situation Report" of the "East Aegean Command, Department Ic," from 5 July 1944. In section II of this report, mention was made of an "Assault [*Ueberfall*] by an enemy commando party (3 men) on 3 German soldiers on the road Calino-Vati" on 8 June 1944, as well as a "Commando Raid [*Unternehmen*] of an enemy destruction party [*Stoertrupps*] on Calino: "In the night of 1–2 July unsuccessful raid of a destruction party on a resistance redoubt [*Widerstandsnest*] near Vati."[50] The "Evening report High Command Army Group E" from 2 July 1944 mentioned the assault, and described it as having been carried out "ostensibly by enemy commando party."[51] Details of this "English commando raid on the island of Calino" were contained in a report of the Ic/AO department of Army Group E from 18 July 1944.[52] The "Activity Report for July, 1944" likewise referred to the "registration of the allied commando operations [*Unternehmungen*] in the Aegean," as well as the "interrogation of the captured members of the Anglo-American Military Mission in Greece."[53] Both these latter reports were initialled by Waldheim, the latter was signed by Hammer.

Few designations would appear to be more incriminating under the terms of the commando order than that of "commando party." One of those captured on Calino, Sergeant John Dryden, was indeed to have been, as the 18 July 1944 report stated, "turned over to the SD in accordance with the Führer order,"[54] though he appears to have survived the war in spite of this.[55] The identical "fatal" terminology appeared in the report of the original unit which captured the prisoners as well as the Ic/AO department of Army Group E, also as in the Warren case. Unlike the Warren case, however, copies of the original interrogation reports themselves have also survived. These suggest that the reports which were eventually made corresponded rather closely to the information gathered in the interrogations themselves. In addition, both those filing the interrogation reports as well as Waldheim, insofar as he was responsible for composing the report based upon them, seem to have distinguished between those whom they might have considered commandos in a narrower sense, and those who were not. Nevertheless, the language they used to describe the two was virtually identical.

The interrogation report on Dryden related that he had "volunteered for the Raiding Force (a type of commando party)."[56] The record of the interrogation continued with a description of the Raiding Forces and paid particular attention to the structure of the "Patrols" and the arms and equipment they usually carried. It continued: "The objective of the raids is to take out prisoners [*Gefangene einzubringen*]. Destruction of important military installations is only undertaken when the opportunity presents itself. It is known that these raids are suicide missions, i.e., that there is little chance that one will be taken prisoner if encountered. During the raid all identifying markings are removed with the exception of rank insignias."[57] This passage would appear to contain all information necessary to have ensured Dryden's demise under the terms of the commando order.

James Doughty was interrogated twice before he reached Salonika,[58] and twice by members of the Ic/AO department of Army Group E. The first in Salonika was conducted on 14 July 1944, probably by Hans Wollschläger, who wrote up the notes of it. The report recorded that Doughty had been "captured on the night of 1–2 July 1944 in the course of the English commando raid and was transferred to Army Group E from the commandant of the Eastern Aegean." After noting that Doughty had said nothing which contradicted his earlier interrogations, Wollschläger wrote, "It appears credible that Doughty did not take part in the commando raid as a combatant." Details about Doughty's past service and a description of the American Field Service followed, as well as clear indications that he was not trained in the use of arms. From Doughty, Wollschläger learned that the "leader of the commandos" was a Captain Bethgray, not, as Dryden had told his interrogators in Athens, 1st Lieutenant Smith. Then:

> The description given by the prisoner established that the assault [*Ueberfall*] on the German stronghold was thwarted by the alertness of the German sentry. Doughty declared emphatically that the commando party had no mortars. During the attack he remained behind his comrades, as these had to beat a hasty retreat. He was ordered to remain behind with Sergeant Drydan [sic] who was badly wounded. He spent one night with him in a nearby hut and in the morning told the local residents to inform the Germans of his whereabouts.[59]

The second interrogation took place on 18 July 1944, the day the report was written. Doughty was apparently very reserved and limited his responses to the information he had provided earlier. First Lieutenant Lochner, who wrote up the interrogation report, concluded that Doughty probably knew more details about the operations than he revealed, but added that, "if he carried out his duties as a medic, [he would have been] presumably largely uninformed of the tactical details of the planned raid."[60]

The report of 18 July 1944, which discussed the "English commando raid" on Calino, incorporated the information gleaned from the various interrogations. It contained biographical information on both Dryden and Doughty and registered Dryden's injury and his transfer to Athens. Doughty, the report stated, was a medic who had been "sent to the transit camp in Salonika for further transfer to Germany [for internment] in a German prisoner of war camp, since [he was] unarmed and not involved in the battle." The weapons captured from the commando party were also described, but Doughty's denial that the commandos had used a mortar was also specifically noted. Finally, the report provided sometimes speculative details about the organizational structure of the commandos themselves: "The commando party probably is attached to the 'M' detachment of the Special Boat Squadron (SBS) based in a camp in the immediate vicinity of Alexandria, which comprises 22 English and the American Doughty. The latter belongs to the Royal Medical Corps (English party)."[61]

What can be derived from all this, apart from the casual way prisoners were handed over to the SD? First of all, the initial evaluation of the information given by the prisoners seems to have been done by those in the Ic/AO department who carried out the interrogations. They would have been, after all, in a position to pick out discrepancies more easily.[62] Secondly, in the preparation of reports themselves, Waldheim appears not to have invented things for which there was not at least some evidence in the interrogation or field reports themselves.[63] In this instance, he even repeated Dryden's denial of what might have been an important material fact.[64] Thirdly, in both the interrogation reports and in the final report, exculpatory evidence was cited. Finally, it is clear that the mere mention of one's capture with, or membership in, a "*Commando-Trupp*" was not, at least in this case, sufficient to ensure one's being handed over to the SD. There was no doubt as to Doughty's service with the SBS, as it was mentioned in every interrogation report as well as the final report from 18 July 1944. Yet equally clear is the fact that some distinction was made between those who could be considered commandos in a narrower sense and those who performed other duties but were part of the commando troops. It does not appear as though participation in the raid itself could have been the deciding factor, because, according to an interrogation report, it is unclear whether either Dryden or Doughty had actually taken part in the operation.[65] However, exculpatory evidence, even when provided from the Ic/AO section itself, would not necessarily have saved a prisoner from death under the terms of the commando order, as the Alimnia case shows.[66]

It is not certain which factors motivated Army Group E to condemn Dryden "in accordance to the Führer order," doubtless a crime, while allowing Doughty to be listed as a prisoner of war. Doughty had been referred to as a "medic" in the various reports, but there is no reason to assume that this should have shielded him from the provisions of the commando order.[67] There is even some evidence to suggest that those in Army Group E decided to suppress potentially damaging information which Doughty had given in his second interview in Leros.[68] It is, however, all but excluded that the factor which decided the issue was the mere appearance of a "fatal word" like *Commando-Trupp* in the reports. Waldheim was also in a role to act as a "competent intelligence officer" with the Calino prisoners, just as he had done in the Warren case. The available evidence shows, however, that his personal intervention in preparing the final report on the Calino prisoners was negligible. All the materials at his disposal, of course, would have gone to the chief of staff, Schmidt-Richberg, and almost certainly would have come to Loehr's attention. It seems inconceivable that the decisions announced by Waldheim in the 18 July 1944 report would have been taken in defiance of Loehr's presumed wishes.

The Calino case, therefore, offers some grounds for skepticism as to Woodhouse's assumption that the formulation *Sabotagetrupp* was employed because "the word 'sabotage' was an instant reminder of the 'commando order', and because the words attributed to Warren implied that he himself took part in 'sabotage' operations." Evidence from another case, although spotty, also undermines Woodhouse's insistence on the wording. The telex from the Command of the 22nd Mountain Army corps to the Ia and Ic departments of Army Group E relating to the capture of the commandos Hamilton, Bluett, Davies and Bennett near Asproangeli in May 1944, contained what could easily have been construed as evidence that those captured had been part of a *Sabotagetrupp,* namely, the possession of "2 boxes [of] inflammable material" [*Zundmittel*]. Despite this, the report referred to the four as "captured English."[69] In the Warren case, the evidence is too meager to justify this assumption on Woodhouse's part, while the documents from other cases severely undermine it.

Woodhouse's suggestion that Waldheim willfully refused to amend the usage in compiling his report in order to ensure Warren's death is also questionable in light of the Calino case. What, for example, would explain the discrepancy in the procedure Waldheim followed in the two cases in the writing of the reports? Is it credible that in May, 1944, Waldheim was so determined to send Warren to his death that he was willing to distort findings of interrogations, while two months later he had lost this inclination? The decisions to have Warren killed, and to abandon Dryden to his fate at the hands of the SD, neither of which could have been taken by Waldheim, were both loathsome and in all likelihood criminal acts. It is, however, unproven either that Waldheim would have substantially altered the content of the reports and interrogation records or, if he had, that this would have had any significant bearing on the outcome.

The improbability of Woodhouse's assumption becomes even more evident if we examine the way in which information was handled inside the 03 section of the Ic/AO department. In the preceding discussion, it was necessary to assume that it lay within Waldheim's authority to alter the intelligence reports which he received more or less at will. Without this assumption, Woodhouse's criticisms that Waldheim neglected his duties as intelligence officer, and that he fabricated "a mendacious report" seem difficult to comprehend. Woodhouse's view reflects the widespread conception of Waldheim's role inside the Ic/AO. This view, however, is misleading.

From the beginning of the controversy surrounding Kurt Waldheim's wartime service, the precise nature of his role as 03 in Army Group E has been the subject of much dispute. Waldheim's initial claim that he was just a "little lieutenant" in the organization, who knew virtually nothing, was quickly discredited by the publication of several documents bearing his signature, and has been laid to rest forever by the report of the historians' commission.[70] Confusion over the the meaning of such German expressions as *für die Richtigkeit*, roughly, vouching for the accuracy of the information contained in a document, as well as lacunae in the testimony of those who had worked with Waldheim in the Ic/AO department, tended to bias the assessment of Waldheim's role in the General Staff in favor of the available documentary evidence.

The inference usually drawn was that Waldheim was either a virtually indispensable, or at the very least a highly valued member of the Ic/AO department. Among the many documentary sources contributing to this view of Waldheim, one of the most compelling was the series of Intelligence Bulletins [*Feind-Nachrichtenblätter*] on the partisan enemy which began appearing in Arsakli in November 1943. Hanspeter Born, for example, makes much of these reports, which he rightly sees as exhibiting "a very detailed and surprisingly acute representation of the military and political situation in Greece."[71] Since Waldheim had returned to the general staff in October 1943 from his assignment in Athens, one month before the first edition appeared, Born attributed to Waldheim both the initiation and preparation of this bulletin.[72] Another possible reason for the persistence of this claim is that none of the witnesses who had provided the information to journalists and historians had actually worked directly with Waldheim in his specific area of responsibility. Helmut Poliza, for instance, one of those most frequently interviewed, worked more or less autonomously inside the O3 section, on Allied troop movements. Although nominally subordinate to Waldheim, Poliza actually was responsible to Warnstorff, not Waldheim. In relation to Poliza, Waldheim functioned more as a first among equals.

One of the major investigative achievements of the Thames-HBO *Commission of Inquiry* was the location of Hans Wende, who had been the direct assistant to the O3 in the military intelligence department of AOK 12/Army Group E from the summer of 1942 until the surrender in 1945. He had therefore served not only with Waldheim, but with the latter's predecessors (Merrem, Schollen) and successor (Ziegler). As such, Wende was in a unique position to comment on Waldheim's specific role in the intelligence-gathering process inside the O3 section and thus fill out the documentary record, which has been otherwise so painstakingly reconstructed by the historians' commission. Wende's evidence suggests that the received view of Waldheim's role needs amending. This is a point of some consequence, for while the documentary evidence relating to Warren is too deficient either to prove or to disprove Woodhouse's interpretation, a detailed knowledge of how essentially similar matters were handled inside the Ic/AO department might be able to indicate its probability.

When Wende came to the staff of Army Group E in July 1942, he was 37 years old.[73] From 1934–1938 Wende, a qualified *Gymnasium* instructor, taught in the German school in Athens, during which time he made numerous contacts and acquired a proficiency in modern Greek. Wende was thus more intellectually equipped to provide the expertise on Greece than Waldheim. The intelligence bulletins mentioned above were not the first attempt by the general staff systematically to analyze the Greek partisans. On 9 April 1943, i.e., at which time Waldheim was serving in the German liaison staff with the 11th Italian Army in Albania and Montenegro, the Ic/AO department produced a six-page report which analyzed, as the title indicates, the "Band Situation in Greece."[74] Thus, both the intention and the capacity of the military intelligence department to evaluate Greek partisans in detail predate Waldheim's return to the staff in October 1943. In April, 1944, Wende was sent to Athens to assess public attitudes towards the Germans, and gather what intelligence he could about the various resistance organizations. The report he submitted at the end of this trip presenting his findings, which does indeed show a subtle mind at work, should evaporate any lingering doubts as to his, as opposed to Waldheim's, relative significance as an expert on Greece and the Greek partisans.[75] The intelligence bulletins dealing with the Greek partisans, then, were drafted by Wende, not Waldheim.[76] Insofar as the general staff of Army Group E was concerned with the situation in Greece (which it was until late 1944), the evidence suggests that Waldheim's role in the intelligence-gathering process was primarily that of a conduit of information which Wende provided him.

Wende seems to have played the same role in preparing the essential constituents of what were to become the morning and evening reports. Several passages in a long interview which allude to the intelligence-gathering process support this conclusion.[77] Wende's description in these passages is reinforced by information provided by Hans Wollschläger, who worked with Poliza in his area of competence.[78] The picture which emerged from these interviews with Wende and Wollschläger was that those who were the best informed, specialists like Wende, tended to gather intelligence and make initial evaluations of its significance. Waldheim then sorted the material for Greece again, though frequently enough Warnstorff was in contact with the specialists themselves. Rigid command structures per se appear not to have existed in the exchange of information, for both Wende and Wollschläger painted a picture of relatively autonomous subgroups inside the Ic. Wollschläger also emphasized the central role of Warnstorff as clearinghouse, and Wende's recognized expertise on Greece would seem to have mitigated against an exaggerated superintending role for Waldheim. It is therefore extremely doubtful that there would have been great discrepancies between the information the various specialists provided and that which Waldheim would have passed on to Warnstorff, even had he been in a position to supress information. Likewise, that any such selection on Waldheim's part would have escaped the attention of his superior.

The evidence provided by Wende and Wollschläger on the channels of information inside in the Ic/AO section may assist us, by way of analogy, in trying to reconstruct important details on the Warren case for which there is no direct documentary evidence. The procedures both described suggested at best a narrowly circumscribed freedom for "speculation" on Waldheim's part. Moreover, it is not even certain that Waldheim personally would have drafted the reports based on the interrogation records. One of Woodhouse's central assumptions, namely, that the correspondence between the content of incoming intelligence reports and the summaries prepared for the higher echelons of the General Staff of Army Group E could be, as it were, arbitrary, thus appears thoroughly insecure.

Let us turn finally to Woodhouse's consideration of Waldheim's "speculation." The "only material point extracted by Waldheim from Warren's interrogation report," Woodhouse states, was, as the report itself indicated, that "Warren did not consider it practical to entrust the execution of sabotage operations to the Greeks on their own because of their limited reliability. He would not give an account of his own activity, although the interrogator gave an undertaking that he need not reveal anything about his comrades." Warren, Woodhouse writes, "would certainly not have introduced the word 'sabotage' of his own accord, because they were not so regarded by members of the SOE. They were military operations, carried out by organized units, however, small, and always in recognisable uniform." Whatever the source of the word "sabotage," it was "alone singled out" in the report, "because the word 'sabotage' was an instant reminder of the 'commando order,' and because the words attributed to Warren implied that he himself took part in 'sabotage' operations."

As a consequence of his assumptions that the mere presence of "sabotage" in the final report would necessarily have determined whether Warren lived or died, and that "the only certain conclusion which could be drawn from his [an American captured with Warren] interrogation was that he could not possibly have been a member of a *Sabotagetrupp,*" Woodhouse must seek a motive as to why Waldheim nonetheless would have singled out and ostensibly emphasized this point in his report. As we saw earlier, it is by no means proven that the wording of a report would have had a significant bearing on a prisoner's fate. These justifiable doubts aside, Woodhouse's assumptions also depend on an unnecessarily rigid definition of sabotage, and, perhaps, a belief in the omniscience of Wehrmacht intelligence officers. If, for example, a commando had been sent in to blow up a bridge, destroy communication lines, etc., what may be conceived as military sabotage, completed the mission (and hence had neither explosives nor other such "incriminating" material with him), and was then on the loose for several months before being captured, then to say he is not part of a *Sabotagetrupp* may be true, considered chronologically. It would not, however, be the only possible conclusion, especially if the intelligence officer who captured or interrogated him assumed the presence and operation of groups of soldiers carrying out sabotage. If Waldheim, or other experts working in the Ic/AO department, did operate under such assumptions, it would not have been "pure fantasy," though it may not have been true in Warren's case. One need not ascribe either demonic or criminal motives to explain how someone might have interpreted the mere capture of such troops in light of such an assumption. Rather, it merely requires us to recognize the inevitable gaps in military intelligence, and acknowledge the particular biases which these may have introduced into an otherwise unjaundiced attempt to deduce militarily operative conclusions from spotty and not completely reliable information. It also seems fair to assume that the Ic department of Army Group E was aware that not everything a prisoner said could be taken at face value.

Woodhouse's argument, of course, excludes this possibility. "Waldheim's interpretation" of the information contained in the report, he maintains, is incompatible with remaining "factual details." The passage he quotes from the 8 May 1944 report reads as follows:[79]

> To summarise, it is established that there must exist in Athens and its environs a thoroughly well organized network of secret agents *(Agentennetz)* supported by the English,[80] which influences the Russian and Polish volunteer workers employed by German units, and by means of pressure or promises puts them in touch with the English Military Mission indirectly through the bands.
>
> The treatment of the Russians by the British Military Mission points to the conclusion that the British have a special interest in the Russian volunteer workers located in the Greek region. There is therefore the probability [2 words deleted] the attempt was made on higher orders to convey the Russian prisoners of war back to the Soviet Army. The impression was given that the [deleted] take a wait-and-see attitude towards the relation of the [deletion] to the ELAS bands on the one hand, and the EDES bands on the other. It was repeatedly stated by the captured Russians that the English Military Mission has adopted a very reserved attitude towards both the Communist and the Nationalist groups of bands and is apparently not pursuing a clear objective.
>
> It can reasonably be supposed that the Russians who were on their way back to Cairo from Greece would have been re-infiltrated into Greece later with special instructions depending on the assessment of conditions in the Greek region.

"All this," argues Woodhouse, "was pure fantasy." He continues:

> We had no such *Agentennetz.* For all we knew, the prisoners had all escaped entirely on their own initiative. Not only did we not prompt their escape: their presence in the mountains was in fact a severe embarrassment to us, because the Communist leadership of the "National Liberation Front" (EAM) wanted to enroll them in its "National Popular Liberation Army" (ELAS), and there was nothing that these Russians and Poles wanted less. To avoid friction, our only course was to evacuate them from Greece, and we certainly never wanted to see them back again.

For Woodhouse, this is incontrovertible. Waldheim "could not possibly have derived such nonsensical conclusions, in good faith, from properly and honestly conducted interrogations."

Waldheim may perhaps be forgiven that the above passage did not find its way into his final report. Fortunately for Woodhouse and his comrades, the Ic/AO did not have access to the kind of information Woodhouse possessed about the nature of commando operations. Moreover, had Warren given the above account in a "properly and honestly conducted" interrogation, why should the officers necessarily have believed it? We should examine this document more carefully, without assuming *a priori* that the entire procedure of preparing the report was a charade, and ask how the situation might have looked to an intelligence officer. One should, at least counterfactually, concede the possibility that Army Group E and its military intelligence department could have valued the information such prisoners provided for its usefulness in achieving military objectives, and if we posit such an officer's moral indifference to the fate of the captured commandos, it might be possible to evaluate the reports as military intelligence. We are, of course, hampered in our endeavor, because we do not know what had been said and reported in the interrogation transcripts, nor can we be certain under what assumptions a less recidivist intelligence officer might have been operating. Still, we can examine whether the interpretation was wholly inconsistent with the factual information mentioned in the report.

The first paragraphs described the circumstances of the prisoners' capture and summarized the personal biographies and military service histories of Warren and a member of the U.S. forces, "M." The section on M's activities was precise and very detailed, and suggests that he enjoyed a high degree of mobility. The next passage dealt with the "Russian and/or [deleted] auxiliaries [*Hiwis*]." This section also contains massive deletions, and the remaining passages are extremely difficult to decipher. It states, in part:

> the prisoners unanimously report that they had been taken out of the [illegible] camps and brought to [illegible] by members of the English Military Mission. . . . Russian prisoners were gathered in Viviani. Their [illegible] is to maintain the ground fire at [illegible]. . . . There is a transmitter there. In September and October of last year 2 to 3 times per week, in the last few months every 10 to 12 days. Food and clothing drops are only a [illegible and then deleted] forbid them to establish contacts with or talk to Greek civilians or bandits. . . .
>
> In January of this year the personal details on the Russians were taken down by the interpreter of the English Military Mission, who is fluent in English, Russian and Greek, to be reported to the Soviet Consular Office in Cairo. A short time later these were provided to the Russians by Colonel [deleted]. [Deleted] the Soviet Russian Consul in Cairo [reference unclear] has to bring them to Cairo via Italy.
>
> At the beginning of February, 1944, they set out for Karpenesion, where the English officer hired a Greek truck for 5 gold pounds, with which they drove to Galaxidion.
>
> The entire group remained over a month in Galaxidion waiting for an acceptable boat. The English officer secured uniforms and supplies there.

Then began the passage, quoted above, from the 8 May 1944 report.

Since we do not have the interrogation reports themselves, we cannot check for the correspondence of the "factual details" in the final report with the statements taken by the interrogators, but Woodhouse has confirmed that they were "reasonably near the mark." What does this report show? Apart from perhaps the title (though so much has been deleted that this is uncertain), the word *Sabotagetrupp* did not appear in the report. The one mention of the word "sabotage," when summarizing the information from Warren's interrogation, suggests that it did not have the significance Woodhouse attributed to it. Why, for example, was M's opinion on the reliability of the Greeks in sabotage operations not recorded? Why, indeed, was there no hint of sabotage operations in the very detailed summary of M's movements? From the context, the statement attributed to Warren seems to have been an assessment of the general attitude of the Military Mission towards the "bands," rather than a concerted attempt to contrive a case that the troops had been engaged in sabotage. It did not appear in the final summary, where one would have expected it to, had this been the overriding aim. There is no compelling reason to reject our earlier suggestion that the usage first coined for the captured prisoners in Ioannina had probably been taken over and repeated along the various channels of information inside Army Group E, but room for dispute remains.

Woodhouse's conjecture about Waldheim's "interpretation" is also less clear-cut than he imagines. In order to examine this in light of the report's "findings," however, we must do without the hindrance (or benefit, according to taste) of Woodhouse's premise about Waldheim's intentions. We must, in other words, try to imagine ourselves as such an intelligence officer, whose job it is to do his best to provide useful military information on the basis of intelligence from heterogeneous sources, sporadically received, and of very uneven quality.

The body of the report, as we saw earlier, contained references to extensive travel, provisioning and quartering of both members of the Military Mission and the Russian prisoners, of messengers inside Greece, of radio transmissions and of contacts with the Soviet consulate in Cairo. While the commandos had apparently been able to undertake such activities without an elaborate underground infrastructure, or at least I have inferred as much from Woodhouse's article, might it not have appeared otherwise to an intelligence officer possessed of too little hard information but, for instance, still worried about preparations for a possible Allied landing in Greece? In an interview C.W.R. Bluett, another commando captured in Greece, stated that the members of his party had been instructed to wear the badges of their various local regiments, in order "supposedly to create some sort of strange impression that we were from lots of units, one here, one there."[81] The question, then, could have been: what sort of infrastructure would need to exist in order for this group to have accomplished the tasks which had been detailed in the report? The conclusion of the report initialed by Waldheim, quoted above, seems to have been an answer to precisely such a question. As for the passage's semantic features: the expression, "it is established," is in this context nothing more than a militarily inflected *Amtsdeutsch* (bureaucratic German) and is surely a routine formulation without extravagant epistemological pretentions. Moreover, to argue "that there must exist [*muss bestehen*] in Athens and its environs a thoroughly well organized network of secret agents supported by the British" implies a conditionality not easily captured by rendering the German *muss* as "must." It is certainly plausible that the author had inferred from information in the interrogation reports that such an network would need to exist, and not merely fabricated it to provide a criminal murder with some legalistic window dressing.

Caution is also called for in drawing too strong inferences from *Agentennetz*, which need not stand in any causal relationship to *Sabotagetrupp*. Though it can and often does evoke sinister images of espionage, must it do so ineluctably? More precisely, must it have done so in this instance? If Waldheim had wished to implicate Warren and his comrades in *Spionage,* why should he have chosen a term which is merely redolent of espionage, rather than simply writing *Spionagenetz,* or something similar, a word which would have been far more "legally watertight," and this not only "under Nazi 'law?'" Even conceding the essential affinity of the concepts *Spionage* and *Agentennetz,* Woodhouse would still be unable to demonstrate that the choice of word had, or even would have had, the result for Warren which he claims.

It is also misleading to refer to the conclusions in the 8 May 1944 report as "pure fantasy." Recalling the report's discussion of the communications with the Soviet consulate in Cairo, etc., it is unclear just what is so capriciously inventive about suggesting the probability "that the attempt was made on higher orders to convey the Russian prisoners of war back to the Soviet Army?" On the other hand, there is no obvious visible evidence in the report for the conclusion, contained in the final paragraph, that the Russians were to be shipped back to Greece. The report did apparently mention some tasks which the *"Hiwis"* had performed while in Greece, and Woodhouse himself suggested that the Greek partisans "wanted to enroll" the Russians and Poles in its army. If one assumed the Allies to be preparing for a landing in Greece, such an inference about the reinfiltration of the Russians would not seem unthinkable. At the same time, this part of the report has suffered extensive deletions, and much which remains is illegible, making any judgement a qualified one.

The interpretations themselves thus appear less wildly imaginative than Woodhouse has suggested. He personally, of course, knew and knows how little the conclusions corresponded to the actual situation of the commandos in Greece. Can we, however, assume the same of an enemy intelligence officer? If he did not possess the ulterior motive of legitimating murder, an intelligence officer would have written the report equipped with what information he had elicited from the prisoners and troops in the field, presumably aided by his assistants with more detailed knowledge of partisan movements, and yet intellectually blinkered by the prejudices, beliefs, convictions and fears which informed his analysis. And, it must be emphasized, under the supervision of his superior officer. Woodhouse seemed to assume that Waldheim enjoyed so much authority and autonomy that his superiors would not have noticed grave discrepancies between the information he received and the conclusions offered in his report. Yet why should Warnstorff have been indifferent to what Waldheim had written? After all, such reports went out over Warnstorff's (or, in this case, Hammer's) signature and he, not Waldheim, bore the ultimate responsibility for their contents. Moreover, if the testimony of Wende, Wollschläger, Poliza, Schollen, etc. is to be believed, then what appeared as summaries of reports would have been the result of discussions between various members of the O3, including but not restricted to Waldheim and Warnstorff (and/or Hammer). It follows that the content of such documents would have been the subject of debate, but the general tone of the final version would have reflected the lines approved by the Ic or someone acting in his stead. In any case, the written record would not contain possibly significant pieces of evidence to determine Waldheim's precise contribution to any "interpretation" or "fantasy," making his criminal liability even more difficult to demonstrate.

Let us here briefly recapitulate the main points of our criticism. On the basis of his examination of two surviving documents relating to the Warren case, Woodhouse concluded that Waldheim "was no more than an accessory in the murder of [his] friend." The very paucity of the documentation, however, required Woodhouse to improvise a number of assumptions about intelligence procedures inside the Ic/AO department of Army Group E, about the instrumentality of specific words in reports, and about Waldheim's character, without which his argument would have collapsed. No one should begrudge him this, nor even the speculation in which he himself indulged. One is not, however, bound to accept his conclusions on faith alone, nor to share his confidence in their validity. We have scrutinized these assumptions in detail, referring both to documentary sources and recollections of key witnesses. What is the balance?

We have suggested that factors other than the mere wording of specific reports, and quite possibly external to the intelligence-gathering process as a whole, determined the fates of soldiers captured under rubric of *Commandounternehmen.* The evidence in the Calino, Alimnia and Asproangeli cases seemed to paint, as it were, a consistent picture of inconsistency. There are too many troubling incongruities to accept that the words *Sabotagetrupp* and *Agentennetz* in this report were sufficient to ensure Warren's death. The terminology in the various links along the chain of the intelligence-gathering command, moreover, tended not to vary, putting into some doubt Woodhouse's belief that the O3 could or would have exercised substantial autonomy in drafting reports. The preparation of reports inside the Ic department involved consultation between the officers at every level and the non-commissioned experts with greater mastery of the material. These very procedures would have restricted the possibilities open to anyone's inordinate "speculation." In other cases, moreover, the content of the final reports accorded very precisely with the interrogation reports on which they were based. Woodhouse's confirmation of the factual details in the Warren case would suggest that this policy was also followed here, at least to a degree.

We then asked, free from Woodhouse's determining assumptions about Waldheim's motives, whether the evidence he cited warranted the conclusions he drew. The final report of 8 May 1944, we suggested, did not differ noticeably in structure and in the kinds of information it contained from similar documents in other cases. In the context of the report as a whole, furthermore, the reference to "sabotage" appeared in a less heinous light. There was no attempt to connect *Agentennetz* with *Sabotagetrupp,* as might have been expected under Woodhouse's assumptions, and arguably more incriminating words like *Spionage* had not been employed. Certainly, if one presumes a criminal intent in the preparation of the report, then the words *Sabotage* and *Agentennetz* can indeed appear as sinister semantic deceit. Without this assumption, however, the picture is by no means clear.

Finally, we took up Woodhouse's contention that the conclusions of the report bore no relation to the details from the paragraphs which preceded them. In the end,

Woodhouse could offer no evidence other than his personal knowledge that the contentions were untrue. Still, though one may quarrel over the extent of the imaginative effort involved, we were able to suggest at least two concrete points of reference in the body of the report for the conclusions at the end. We argued that it was not necessary to impute murderous intent to explain such speculation: it is possible that the conjectures contained in the report were the result of enterprising but biased minds under the influence of deficient and unsystematic information.

It is fair to ask whether we, having undermined the probability of the various components of Woodhouse's argument, are in a position ourselves to offer an account with greater explanatory power? The answer is no, but with a clear conscience. Woodhouse set the terms for the debate by ascribing to Waldheim an almost credally rational singleness of purpose. We do not claim to have proved that Waldheim did not act as Woodhouse charges, nor even that the events could not have been as he described. He should be aware, however, of just how shaky the foundations are on which he bases his allegation that Waldheim was an accessory to murder. His ire at the killing of his friend Warren is both understandable and wholly justified. Yet he has not been able to show that it can be pinned on Waldheim. Nonetheless, at every step, we stumbled upon Woodhouse's basic premise, that the only explanation which could reconcile the documentary evidence with the death of Warren was Waldheim's criminal motive. Without it, his case self-destructs. Yet if Woodhouse's subordinate assumptions remain unproven, and in some cases mistaken or at least misleading, and he can offer no compelling proof for his principal one, is there still "a case to answer?" Yes, but it is not that of Waldheim's criminal complicity in war crimes. It is, rather, a case of historical responsibility, and this case is not merely for Waldheim to answer.

Notes

1. *Der Spiegel,* No. 9, 29 February 1988.

2. See Hans Kurz, James Collins, Jean Vanwelkenheuzen, Gerald Fleming, Hagen Fleischer, Jehuda Wallach and Manfred Messerschmidt, *Der Bericht der internationalen Historikerkommission,* supplement to *Profil,* 15 February 1988; Hanspeter Born, *Für die Richtigkeit. Kurt Waldheim* (Munich: Schneekluth, 1987); Hubertus Czernin, "Waldheims Balkanjahre," *Profil,* Nos. 49–52, 1987, and 1–4, 1988; Robert E. Herzstein, *Waldheim. The Missing Years* (London: Grafton Books, 1988); and Michael Palumbo, *The Waldheim Files* (London: Faber, 1988).

3. Kurz, et al., *Bericht,* p. 42.

4. Ibid.

5. Ibid., p. 43.

6. Ibid.

7. Ibid.; see also "Laws and Customs of War on Land," (Hague, IV), in Leon Friedman, ed., *The Law of War. A Documentary History* 2 Vols. (New York: Random House, 1972), Vol. I, p. 309; and Josef Markus, "Die Strafverfolgung von nationalsozialistischen Gewaltverbrechen und die völkerrechtliche Verantwortung Österreichs," in Meissl, et al., *Verdrängte Schuld,* pp. 150–170.

8. *Der Spiegel,* Nr. 9, 29 February 1988. Messerschmidt used a similar formulation in an interview he gave to the *Süddeutsche Zeitung* on 25 February 1988.

9. See Jack Saltman, *Waldheim: A Case To Answer?* (London: Robson, 1988).

10. There was no contact between the challenging counsel, Lord Rawlinson, or his assistant, Tim House, and Waldheim or any of his representatives. Thus, Rawlinson did not "represent" Waldheim, he merely "challenged" the allegations and evidence adduced by the "presenting counsel," Ryan.

11. See *Profil,* 29 May 1988, and Saltman, *A Case.*

12. See Richard Nimmerrichter ("Staberl"), in *Neue Kronen Zeitung* (*NKZ*), 5 June 1988.

13. *New York Times* (*NYT*), 4 June 1988. For a representative sample, see: *Weekend Daily Telegraph,* 4 June 1988, *NYT,* 7 June 1988, *The Kansas City Star,* 5 June 1988. Cf. *Profil,* Nr. 22, 30 May 1988. Jack Saltman, the Tribunal's producer, wrote an account of the making of the programme where he rebutted these criticisms. See Saltman, *A Case.*

14. "The Case of Captain Warren. Waldheim, TV & a Case to Answer," *Encounter* Vol. LXXI, No. 3 (September-October 1988), pp. 27–31.

15. This much, at least, may be inferred from the HBO publicity material, which explicitly posed the question, "Is Kurt Waldheim a War Criminal?"

16. Christopher Greenwood, international law expert from Cambridge University, has stated that he is unaware of a single staff officer of Waldheim's rank having been tried for war crimes committed during the Second World War. See "In the Matter of Kurt Waldheim. Report Regarding the Practice of the Tribunals Established for the Trial of War Crimes Following World War Two," Ms., Cambridge, 1988, p. 7. See also Zentrale Stelle der Landesjustizverwaltungen in Ludwigsburg, "Geisel- und Partisanentötungen im zweiten Weltkrieg. Hinweise zur rechtlichen Beurteilung." Bound Ms., Ludwigsburg, 1968, pp. 47–72. Cf. Alan Ryan's cross-examination of Greenwood, Transcript of *Waldheim: A Commission of Inquiry,* 19 April, 1988. Thames Television Document Collection (TTDC), Wiener Library, London, File 11.

17. See the duty roster (*Führungsabteilungsliste*) of the Ic department of Army Group E. Reproduced in Karl Gruber, Ralph Scheide and Ferdinand Trautmannsdorff, *Waldheim's Wartime Years. A Documentation* (Vienna: Carl Gerold's Sohn, 1987), pp. 206–207.

18. C. M. Woodhouse, "Captain Warren," pp. 27–31.

19. Ibid., pp. 27–28. See MOD, "Report," pp. 39–44.

20. Ibid., p. 31.

21. Ibid., p. 28.

22. Geheime Kommandosache, Der Führer, F.H.Qu., den 18.12.1942, NOKW 498-PS, Prosecution exhibit 124, quoted in Friedman, *Laws,* Vol. II, pp. 1444–1445.

23. This addendum [*Zusatz*] is printed in its entirety in Kurz, et al., *Bericht,* pp. 13–14. All quotations in this and the next paragraphs are taken from this version.

24. See, for example, the discussion in "U.S. vs von Leeb, et al.," Friedman, *Laws,* Vol. II, p. 1467.

25. Kurz, et al., *Bericht,* p. 14.

26. NOKW 2009, Wbfh SO, 28.10.42, "Zusätze Wbfh Südost." Quoted in Born, *Richtigkeit,* pp. 97–98.

27. "U.S. vs. von Leeb, et al.," Friedman, *Laws,* Vol. II, p. 1445.

28. "Laws and Customs of War on Land," (Hague, IV), The Hague, October 18, 1907, in Friedman, *Laws,* Vol. I, pp. 313–314.

29. "U.S. vs. List, et al.," Friedman, *Laws,* Vol. II, p. 1311. See also Zentrale Stelle der Landesjustizverwaltungen in Ludwigsburg, *Geisel- und Partisanentötungen,* esp. 81–82; Martin Zöller, "Introduction," to Martin Zöller and Kazimierz Leszczynski, eds., *Fall 7. Das Urteil im Geiselmordprozeß* (East Berlin: Deutscher Verlag der Wissenschaft, 1965), pp. 50–54.

30. General Hermann Foertsch, chief of staff of Army Group F, to which Army Group E was subordinate, during this period, was explicitly cleared of all criminal liability with regard to the commando order, even though he admitted that he considered the order to be criminal. On the other hand, the reasoning of the judges in the case of Walter Kunze strongly suggests that Loehr would have been convicted, had he been among the indicted. See "U.S. vs. List, et al.," in Zöller and Leszczynski, *Fall 7,* pp. 138, 139 and 127. These passages were not included in the Friedman version.

31. "U.S. vs. List, et al.," Friedman, *Laws,* Vol. II, p. 1307.

32. "U.S. vs. List, et al.," Friedman, *Laws,* Vol II, p. 1323. See also the discussion in Greenwood, "Matter," pp. 8–9, which cites the Peleus and High Command cases to this effect.

33. Ibid. The order in question was one relating to reprisals, but this detail does not bear on the point here.

34. "Prosecution and Punishment of Major War Criminal of European Axis," August 8, 1945. Friedman, *Laws,* Vol. II. p. 887.

35. Greenwood, "Matter," p. 9.

36. "U.S. vs. Von Leeb, et al.," Friedman, *Laws,* Vol. II, p. 1435.

37. Ibid., p. 1437.

38. "U.S. vs. List, et al.," Friedman, *Laws,* Vol. II, p. 1307. The same principle, that an order must have been known to be criminal in order to incur liability, was also held in the 1922 Llandovery Castle case, which the Tribunal in Case 7 cited.

39. *British Manual of Military Law,* 1936 Edition, Paragraph 443, cited in Greenwood, "Matter," p. 8.

40. See, for example, the discussion of military necessity by the judges in Case 7. Zöller and Leszczynski *Fall 7,* p. 104. See also M. Messerschmidt, "Völkerrecht und 'Kriegsnotwendigkeit' in der deutschen militärischen Tradition seit den Einigungskriegen," *Revue de droit pénal militaire et de droit de la guerre,* Vol. XXII, 3–4 (1983), pp. 221–241.

41. Quoted in "U.S. vs. Von Leeb, et al.," Friedman, *Laws,* Vol. II, p. 1431.

42. Ibid., p. 1433.

43. See Zöller and Leszczynski, *Fall 7,* pp. 102–107.

44. See especially "U.S. vs. List, et al.," in Friedman, *Laws,* pp. 90–95; Zentrale Stelle der Landesjustizverwaltungen in Ludwigsburg, *Geisel- und Partisanentötungen,* pp. 47–72.

45. It is important to emphasize that we are dealing here with what I have termed borderline cases, not with criminal activities in general. Though I think it legitimate, *mutatis mutandis,* to debate the issue with regard to events such as reprisal killings, it is not part of my argument that the caveats I advance about the commando order for specific officers in specific positions necessarily have any general application.

46. Kurz, et al., *Bericht,* pp. 13–19.

47. One which Woodhouse did not quote was the Daily Report of Army Group F to the Wehrmacht Military High Command (OKW) on 27 March 1944, which is cited in MOD, "Review," p. 41. This report, however, has no direct bearing on the case presented here, though it might be said to support the claim that there was some direct causal relation between the knowledge of a commando's capture by the OKW and his ultimate murder.

48. Woodhouse, "Captain Warren," p. 30.

49. Ibid. Portions of this report were inexplicably blacked out. Woodhouse sees no consistent pattern in them, and doubts that a particular qualification of the nature of the operation would have been deleted. I see no reason to disagree.

50. TTDC, File 5.

51. Abendmeldung Okdo. H.Gr.E vom 2.7.44. BA/MA, RH24–22/22. This report went to the "OB/Chef," as well as, among others, the Ia/O1, Ic and AO, TTDC, File 5.

52. TTDC, File 5.

53. Gruppe Ic/AO. Nr. 15278/44 g., 1.8.44, Tätigkeitsbericht för Monat Juli 1944. TTDC, File 5.

54. TTDC, File 5.

55. Kurz, et al., *Bericht*, p. 18; MOD, "Review," pp. 74–77.

56. The fact that Dryden had been transferred directly to Athens may provide a clue as to why Army Group E essentially washed its hands of the affair. The report of 18 July 1944 mentions that he was "wounded, flown to Athens on 5 July. To be handed over to the SD in accordance with the Führer order."

57. "Abschrift. Niederschrift über die Vernehmung des engl. Gefangenen Feldw. John Dryden am 11. Juni 1944," TTDC, File 5. There is no way to be certain what is meant by the expression "Gefangene einzubringen." Literally, it would mean to bring in prisoners, although normal German usage would prescribe an additional "hin" or "her" at the beginning. It is possible that infiltrate could be meant, but from the context, it appears that the emphasis was on the taking out of prisoners.

58. Aufstellung über die Aussagen des James Doughty (gefangen beim Kdo.-Unternehmen auf Calino am 1./2.7.44), TTDC, File 5.

59. Vernehmung des Sanitäters (Private) James Doughty, geb. 26.3.18, ledig, amerik. Staatsangehöriger, Volksschullehrer, wohnh. in Ipswich, Mass., signed F.d.R. Wollschläger, Sdf. "G," dated 17.7.44. TTDC, File 5.

60. Vernehmung des amerikanischen Sanitätssoldaten James Doughty. Anlage 4 zu O.B. Südost/Ic Nr. 5557/44g, TTDC, File 5.

61. TTDC, File 5.

62. See in this connection Oberkommando der Heeresgruppe E, Abt. Ic/AO Nr. 7944/43 geh., Guidelines for the Questioning of English and American POWS, 20.7.1943, TTDC, File 4.

63. This correspondence between the interrogation records and final reports is also confirmed by the documentation available from the Alimnia prisoners. See Kurz, et al., *Bericht*, pp. 13–19; MOD, "Review," pp. 45–65.

64. That is, material from the standpoint of military intelligence, not because it would necessarily have had a bearing on Dryden's fate.

65. The German in the document itself is ambiguous and it is not clear whether Dryden had received his injury prior to or during the raid.

66. See the telex "An OB Suedost ("Okdo H.Gr.F Roem 1c/AO" from "Okdo. H.Gr.E Roem 1c/AO Nr. 1053 GKdos, V. 26.4.44," which, among other things, reports, "recommend exempting Greek sailors, because forced to take part." Kurz, et al., *Bericht*, pp. 18–19.

67. It was apparently of no consequence for the Greek sailors in the Alimnia operation that they were referred to as *"Matrosen."* They were murdered anyway. Kurz, et al., *Bericht*, pp. 18–19.

68. For example, Doughty had been captured without a visible insignia as a medical officer, and had been wearing camouflage during the operation itself. This could have even provided just the "legally watertight" justification for him to have been handed over to the SD. Wollschläger, Lochner and Waldheim all seem to have given Doughty the benefit of the doubt and emphasized the credibility of Doughty's statement that he had not taken part in the fighting. "Aufstellung über die Aussagen des James Doughty . . ., Anlage 3 zu O.B. Südost/Ic Nr. 5557/44g; Vernehmung des Sanitäters (Private) James Doughty . . ., Anlage 5 zu O.B. Südost/Ic Nr. 5557/44g. TTDC, File 5.

69. See "Fernschreiben, An Obkdo. Heeresgruppe E Ia gltd. Ic, Saloniki, von Gen. Kdo. XXII. (Geb.) A.K. Ia, 6.5.44," TTDC, File 4.

70. Kurz, et al., *Bericht*, particularly pp. 8–13.

71. Born, *Richtigkeit*, p. 110.

72. Ibid., p. 111.

73. The biographical details come from an interview of Hans Wende with Richard Mitten and Felix Moreau, conducted on 22 March 1988. TTDC, File 11.

74. Hans Wende, "Die griechische Widerstandsbewegung im Urteil der deutschen Heeresführung," Ms. (Bad Wildungen, n.d.), lists the reports which Wende had written while serving on the staff of Army Group E.

75. "Bericht über meinen Aufenthalt in Athen vom 2.4 bis 6.4.44." Feindnachrichtenblatt H.Gr.E Ic/AO, Institut für Zeitgeschichte, München, Bestand Fd 14/2, 1043/53.

76. This much is suggested from even a cursory reading of the short history of the military assessments of the Greek resistance Wende wrote in the 1950s, which shows a command of the material far beyond that of a simple exegete. See Wende, "Die griechische Widerstandsbewegung."

77. Wende interview, TTDC, File 11, Part I, pp. 2, 16–17.

78. Interview of Hans Wollschläger with Richard Mitten and Felix Moreau, 23 March 1988, TTDC, File 11.

79. "Oberkommando der Wehrmacht Gruppe Ic/AO, Betr.: Festnahme von [then portions are inked out], 8.5.44." This is the report referred to by Woodhouse. I have received a photocopy of this and other documents, along with much valuable assistance in deciphering this one's nearly illegible print, from Walter Manoschek, whose help I hereby gratefully acknowledge. See Woodhouse, "A Case to Answer," p. 30. The passages from the report are cited as they appear in Woodhouse's article, with some modifications in the translation. The third paragraph of the report, which was not quoted in Woodhouse's article, has a bearing on his interpretation of the evidence.

80. Woodhouse's "a network of secret agents supported and organized by the British" is a slightly misleading translation of the German *"ein von den Engländern unterstütztes gut durchorganisiertes Agentennetz."*

81. Interview of C.W.R. Bluett with Richard Mitten and Felix Moreau, 22 April 1988. Transcript in possession of the author.

6

The Role of the World Jewish Congress

The World Jewish Congress (WJC) played by far the biggest part in the search for and disclosure of documents relating to Kurt Waldheim's past. For their efforts in 1986, WJC officials earned praise from some quarters, criticism from others. In Austria, the WJC, its secretary general Israel Singer and its president Edgar Bronfman, either individually or as a group became the objects of a relentless stream of verbal abuse which has continued unabated to this day. From literally every quarter of the Austrian public they met with hostility ranging from contemptuous dismissal to seething hatred. Then Austrian People's Party (ÖVP) General Secretary Michael Graff's taut jaw and trembling voice at a press conference given on 25 March 1986 as he reacted to presumed "threats" of the WJC with a personal version of "I'm as mad as hell and I'm not going to take this any more," revealed the depth of animosity held in the Waldheim camp towards Israel Singer. Yet even Waldheim's critics in Austria felt obliged to renounce the activities of the WJC. A photograph taken at a WJC press conference reproduced in the magazine *Profil* carried the caption "weak material, exaggerated conclusions and an unacceptable tone."[1] Daniel Charim, the designated official representative of the Austrian Jewish community, provided one of the more penetrating criticisms of the Waldheim campaign on a late evening television discussion program (*Club-2*). He, however, repeatedly stressed that he was not "the defender, not the unconditional defender of the World Jewish Congress." In the same program Erwin Ringel, leading supporter of Waldheim's opponent Steyrer, well-known psychologist and author of the book *Die österreichische Seele* [The Austrian Psyche], said he "regretted deeply the behavior of the World Jewish Congress. . . . It is aggressive behavior and partially even sadistic behavior."[2] Simon Wiesenthal even blamed the WJC for the re-emergence of antisemitism in Austria.[3] The unanimity of the enmity towards "that dishonorable lot [*ehrlose Gesellen*] from the World Jewish Congress"[4] provided fertile ground for the emergence of antisemitic stereotypes in the course of the election campaign. For some, the WJC served as a proxy for "the Jews" in general, but for virtually all as a scapegoat which could be blamed for the collapse of Austria's image abroad.[5] Driven as they were by a "blind rage," as

Peter Gnam wrote in the *Neue Kronen Zeitung* (*NKZ*), they were accused of being behind the slander campaign against Austria, of threatening the country with a worldwide economic boycott should Waldheim become president, and, with reference to the documents the WJC had uncovered and interpreted, were reproved either for negligence, tendentiousness, forgery or the suborning of witnesses. In the Austrian press, Simon Wiesenthal and other prominent Jews were repeatedly invoked to attack the WJC. Wiesenthal, for example, endorsed the widespread belief that "these people from the World Congress began at a time when they had nothing [i.e., of substance against Waldheim]."[6] Those in Austria who made such allegations against the WJC seldom specified the criteria on which they had based their judgment, nor could they produce real evidence of misdeeds which would justify the hysteria of their attacks. It therefore seems worthwhile to reconstruct the authentic practice of the WJC from sources independent of the reports in the Austrian media about its activities, in order to examine what relation this practice might have borne to the representation of it in Austrian public discourse.

The Opening Salvo

Founded in 1936, the WJC has viewed their principal role since the 1930s and 1940s as trying to raise support for Jewish communities endangered by the Nazis, assisting those forced to immigrate, to support those exiles where possible and to assist in bringing war criminals to justice.[7] Today the WJC is largely an international lobbying organization that must compete with others also claiming to represent various interests of Jews. However, from the beginning the WJC has been involved to a greater or lesser extent in trying to see that those responsible in any way for the mass murder of Jews during World War II be brought to justice for their crimes.[8] The WJC apparently first entertained concrete doubts about Waldheim's official biography only in January 1986, although they had been aware of rumors about Waldheim's past for years.[9] What aroused their interest in January 1986, as was mentioned above, was an article in the Vienna magazine *Profil* about a dispute surrounding a memorial plaque for Alexander Loehr. Loehr, it may be recalled, was the former commander of Army Group E, based in Arsakli, and was executed by Yugoslavia in 1947 for war crimes. Loehr had also founded the air force of the Austrian First Republic. The plaque in question, which was in honor of this latter achievement, had been mounted in the Vienna armory but was removed after a series of protests against it. The *Profil* article disclosed that Waldheim had served on Loehr's staff.[10] Apparently on the basis of this hint, Eli Rosenbaum, the WJC's general counsel, spent a few days in Vienna in January, in order to do some initial research. He resumed his efforts in New York, and contacted *New York Times* (*NYT*) journalist John Tagliabue. As was mentioned above, *Profil* made its first disclosures on 3 March 1986, and the *NYT* reported its findings one day later. The WJC also held their first press conference on the Waldheim affair on 4 March, where they released documents that showed that "Former U.N. Secretary-General Waldheim [had] concealed [a] Nazi past."[11] According to the WJC's press release, "Waldheim became a member of the Nazi 'Sturmabteilung' (S.A.)—the uniformed 'Brownshirts'—in 1938. Moreover, although Waldheim specifically denied in 1980 that he had ever participated in the Nazi youth movement . . . Waldheim had in fact joined the 'NS-Studentenbund' (Nazi Student Union) on April 1, 1938—less than three weeks after Austria's annexation by Germany." The "most dramatic revelations" reported on by the WJC, however, concerned the years 1942–1945. Contrary to his public claims to have been in Vienna at the time, Waldheim "was already back in military service by March 1942, serving in Yugoslavia. In July of that year the allegedly 'incapacitated' Waldheim received the 'King Zvonimir' silver medal from the Nazi puppet state of Croatia, awarded with oak leaves for 'service under enemy fire.' . . . Waldheim served on the staff of Wehrmacht General Alexander Loehr. . . . [who] was hanged in 1947 for war crimes." Documents of the Nuremberg war crimes trials showed that Loehr and "personnel under his command" supervised the deportation of the 42,000-strong Jewish community of Salonika between the middle of March and the middle of May 1943. By the end of March 1943, the WJC maintained, Waldheim was already in Salonika, "at which time Wehrmacht trains were carrying 2,000–2,500 Jews to Auschwitz nearly every day. Waldheim served on Loehr's staff at Salonika at this time."[12]

The WJC claimed that Waldheim had returned to Yugoslavia by the end of May 1943, and produced photographs of Waldheim, one of which showed him standing between high-ranking German and Italian army officers including the commander of the SS-Division "Prinz Eugen," Waffen-SS Obergruppenführer Artur Phleps. At this time, Phleps' division and the Italian, German and Croation units under him were engaged in "Operation Black," in which "the Nazis massacred thousands of civilians and burned down their villages and food supplies." Finally, the WJC made public a letter from U.S. Congressman Stephen Solarz to the then head of the CIA, Stansfield Turner, in which Turner was asked to provide information relating to Waldheim's "alleged association with the Nazi Youth Movement." Turner had replied that Waldheim had not been a member of the "Nazi Youth Movement." "Now we know better," an unnamed spokesman for the WJC was quoted as saying.[13]

The allegations raised in this first press conference held by the WJC centered on Waldheim's credibility. Edgar Bronfman's accusation that Waldheim had engaged in "one of the most elaborate deceptions of our time," was based upon two main discoveries. The first was that Waldheim had been a member of the *Sturmabteilung* (SA) and the Nazi Student Union (NSDStB) and thus had been a "Nazi." The documents offered in support of Waldheim's membership included (1) entries in Waldheim's official personnel file at the Austrian foreign ministry (the *Standesausweis mit Laufbahn*), which listed him as having been a member of the SA from 18 November 1938 to 14 August 1939; (2) Special Commission File 235, a part of Waldheim's de-Nazification procedure, according to which Waldheim had joined the SA on 18 November 1938 and the Nazi Student Union on 1 April 1938; and (3) the *Wehrstammkarte,* which *Profil* had published on 3 March 1986. Although these documents alone were not conclusive, they certainly suggested the extraordinarily high probability of Waldheim's membership.[14]

The assumption that membership in these organizations added up to a "Nazi" past, however, was more controversial. The idiom the WJC employed in their press release ("brownshirts") was strongly emotive and clearly suggested that Waldheim at least at that time had held Nazi convictions. Yet the assumption may not have been valid in Waldheim's case, and the WJC representatives do not seem to have taken much trouble to familiarize themselves with the various shades of political and ideological commitment associated with different organizations affiliated to the NSDAP. For example, they repeated the misnomer "Nazi Youth Movement" from Turner's letter to Solarz without comment. Moreover, the two organizations that Waldheim had joined as well as the circumstances under which his membership took place—after the *Anschluss*—would tend to suggest opportunism rather than conviction as the principal motive. In any case, the WJC showed little interest in such matters and would probably have thought the distinction of little relevance. The simple equation of SA membership with "Nazi" remained a fixed but possibly unwarranted assumption. It appeared in most subsequent press releases and tended to bias the interpretation of Wehrmacht documents that the WJC later discovered.[15] In order to evaluate whether the WJC was justified in claiming that Waldheim had *concealed* a "Nazi past," however, it is necessary to accept their assumption that membership in the SA and Nazi Student Union constituted a "Nazi past," whether warranted or not.

To substantiate their allegation that Waldheim had concealed his past, the WJC quoted a December 1980 letter he wrote to Congressman Stephen Solarz. Solarz had written to Waldheim after learning of an article in *The New Republic* alleging Waldheim's membership in the "Nazi Youth Movement," a puzzlingly inexact formulation Solarz, following his source's lead, repeated.[16] In his response to Solarz's letter, Waldheim wrote, "First of all, I wish to say that I was never associated in any way with the Nazi Youth Movement."[17] One can only speculate as to why Waldheim chose to repeat the formulation "Nazi Youth Movement," capitalized as though it were the name of an organization. Although the *New Republic* authors' sciolistic obfuscation probably reflected unfamiliarity with the history of Nazi Germany, it may be safely assumed that Waldheim himself was aware that such an organization did not exist, and that the formulation in his letter to Solarz was deliberately misleading. The context of the usage (he emphasized that he had never been "associated in any way") in any case implied that he was denying any sort of affiliation with National Socialist organizations, thus also the SA and the NSDStB. This latter claim of Waldheim's was completely discredited by the documents which the WJC published, even if they did not quite prove Waldheim's membership in a Nazi Youth Movement. Thus, despite the rather nondiscriminating usage, the WJC was entirely justified in charging Waldheim with having "concealed" a past they termed simply "Nazi."

According to the WJC, Waldheim had also hidden his service on the general staff of Alexander Loehr. The WJC established Waldheim's service under Loehr by citing an army personnel identification list of the staff of Army High Command 12 (later Army Group E) from June, 1942, on which Waldheim's name appeared; two contemporaneous photographs (one from May 1943, the other from December, 1944); and Waldheim's official personnel file at the Austrian foreign ministry, which listed his receipt of the Zvonimir medal and showed that he had served in the army continuously from 15 August 1939 until 11 June 1945.[18] That these documents sufficiently established the fact of Waldheim's service in the Balkans during 1942–1945 may be inferred from Waldheim's personal confirmation of this service to *NYT* journalist John Tagliabue.[19]

However, Waldheim vehemently disputed the implication that he had not been forthcoming about his military past. The WJC pressed their claims by producing an article from the *NYT* from 1981, in which Waldheim was quoted as saying, "Fortunately I didn't last long. My unit moved to the Russian front in the winter of 1942. I was badly wounded in the ankle, I couldn't walk, and they gave me a medical discharge."[20] Waldheim in fact never received a medical discharge, but soon returned to active duty (though he did not serve at the front) and remained in service until the end of the war. Waldheim's own admission of his service in the years 1942–45, combined with the evidence they produced, gave the WJC sufficient grounds to conclude that "Dr. Kurt Waldheim, the former U.N. Secretary-General, concealed for more than four decades . . . his wartime activities."

Some of the facets of Waldheim's wartime career were also presented by the WJC perhaps to suggest why they had been missing from his public biography all these years. Their efforts in this area were less successful, but whatever one may criticize about the weakness of the WJC's research or their leaders' self-confidence as to what the material they published actually proved, the WJC attempted to base their conclusions on recognized specialist literature. In order to explain the significance of the award Waldheim had won in 1942 in Yugoslavia, the King Zvonimir award, for example, Eli Rosenbaum consulted *Für Tapferkeit und Verdienst* to obtain a description of the medal, which the WJC press release repeated verbatim.[21] Gerald Reitlinger's book *The Final Solution* was the WJC's source for the role of Army Group E in the deportation of the Jews,[22] while Otto Kumm's *Vorwärts Prinz Eugen,*[23] the *Report on the Crimes of Austria and the Austrians against Yugoslavia and her Peoples*[24] und Jozo Tomasevich's *The Chetniks,*[25] all served as sources for background information on the nature of the war in German occupied Yugoslavia in general, and more particularly, for "Operation Black." All of these sources were employed to place Waldheim's wartime activities in context, and the WJC's efforts, if not always correct, were certainly warranted and laudable.

The WJC could not avoid raising questions about Waldheim's possible personal involvement, as a member of the units in question (at this time nothing specific was known about Waldheim's positions, duties, and postings, merely that he had been attached to Army Group E), in the deportation of Jews and other atrocities. The formulations in the 4 March 1986 press release intimated something foreboding. "Waldheim served on the Staff of Wehrmacht General Loehr. The WJC today made public a wartime photograph showing Waldheim, in uniform with Loehr. Loehr was hanged in 1947 for war crimes. Historian Gerald Reitlinger, in his authoritative 1953 book *The Final Solution,* states that Loehr 'was perhaps more implicated in Jewish deportations than any other Wehrmacht commander.'"[26] Although one could easily draw inferences of reprovable acts from these formulations, the WJC limited their allegations to the claims, mentioned above, that Waldheim had "concealed" his military past from 1942 to 1945, and did not accuse him of personal involvement in war crimes or other atrocities.

On the basis of the evidence from the WJC's initial press conference, it is possible to synthesize three points: (1) The specific allegations which the WJC made were justified in terms of the documents they presented. (2) The research undertaken by the WJC was, however, incomplete and in some places rather biased when it came to detailed interpretations of the evidence. The equation of memberships in the SA riding formation and the Nazi Student Union at the Consular Academy with a "Nazi past" could occasion assumptions about National Socialist ideological convictions which might not have been valid and were in any case not proven. (3) From the inception of their series of disclosures about Kurt Waldheim, spokesmen for the WJC availed themselves of a pejorative vocabulary. This usage not only conspicuously manipulated certain ambiguities in the details of Waldheim's service, but confused issues that could and ought to have been kept clear. However, despite these weaknesses, the WJC made no specific accusations that were not at least comprehensible in terms of the evidence they had discovered.

The Consolidation of the Initial Charges

After the initial press release of 4 March 1986, the WJC issued five additional in the course of the next two weeks. These five press releases contained no sensational fresh results of the WJC's own research on Waldheim. Instead, they made public material that for the most part had been uncovered by others to corroborate the WJC's allegations of Waldheim's lack of credibility. On 5 March 1986, for example, the WJC press release dealt exclusively with the Special Commission File 235, which contained the most damaging evidence suggesting Waldheim's membership in the SA and the Nazi Student Union. The following day, the WJC made public evidence which in their view showed that the "U.N. under Waldheim [had] turned down [the] United States request for Nazi archives." The WJC also presented additional material to shore up their accusation that Waldheim had also covered up aspects of his military service. A brochure from Waldheim's unsuccessful bid for the Austrian presidency in 1971 which the WJC presented, for example, claimed, "War followed and Kurt Waldheim, then a student, was called up. In 1942 Kurt Waldheim returned home wounded and resumed his studies. After his graduation in 1944, he was married and then had to return to the front."[27] The WJC also erroneously "discovered" a third Nazi organization to which Waldheim belonged, the National Socialist Riding Corps (*NS-Reiterkorps*).[28] In his personnel folder, Waldheim had listed the *NS-Reiterkorps* as an organization with which he had been marginally associated, but of which he had not been a member. This organization, however, was the successor organization to the SA-*Reiterstandarte*, and members of the latter were enrolled en masse in the new organization, the *NS-Reiterkorps*. These details as well as their significance were obviously unfamiliar to the WJC. Waldheim, in other words, had not joined a third organization, and his denial of membership in the SA-*Reiterstandarte* applied to the *NS-Reiterkorps* as well. Though few would have been in a position to argue the point at the time, this finding of the WJC in fact exposed the carelessness of the WJC's research. Taken together, these five press releases served to strengthen the earlier allegations made against Waldheim, to prove, as Elan Steinberg said to the *Washington Post*, "that Waldheim is a Nazi, a liar, and that for more than 40 years he has deceived people about his military record."[29]

On 10 March 1986, WJC vice-president Kalman Sultanik asked, exemplifying both terminological confusion as well as the extent of the WJC's accusations, "Why did he [Waldheim] conceal his 1942–1944 Nazi military service and precisely what is it about that service that he felt compelled to keep hidden?"[30] The world did not wait long for a possible answer. On 22 March 1986, the WJC published the United States Army's Central Registry of War Criminals and Security Suspects (CROWCASS), according to which Kurt Waldheim had been sought by Yugoslavia for "murder." "Both the Army and the United Nations War Crimes Commission," the statement maintained, "listed Kurt Waldheim as a suspected Nazi war criminal."[31]

The formulation "suspected war criminal," which the WJC had taken from the CROWCASS itself, corresponded precisely to Waldheim's legal status at the time, since the case against him was technically still pending. However embarassing this new information might have been for Waldheim himself, it did not represent a tendentious interpretation on the WJC's part. The same must also be said for the inaccurate information contained in the list itself, namely, that Waldheim had served as a counter-intelligence officer [*Abwehroffizier*]. The WJC's press release reported that the "listing also shows that he [Waldheim] also served as an Officer in the Abwehr, the Military Intelligence Service of the High Command of the German Armed Forces," adding that it was "the first time that Waldheim has been linked publicly to the Abwehr."[32] In fact, Waldheim never served in the *Abwehr*, the counter-intelligence section, but did serve in the "military intelligence section," which, however, was designated [Roman numeral] Ic, not *Abwehr*, as the WJC incorrectly claimed.[33] Three days later, the WJC themselves published information which showed Waldheim's actual function on the staff of Army Group E, and thereafter did not mention Waldheim in connection with the *Abwehr*.[34] What they reported on 22 March, i.e., that Waldheim was listed as an officer in the *Abwehr*, was, on the basis of the available information, reasonable and legitimate, even if mistaken. That they had acted in good faith may be inferred from the WJC's abandonment of this label *Abwehroffizier* after evidence which they published indicated that their earlier designation had been wrong. In addition to publishing the excerpt from the CROWCASS itself, the WJC also criticized the United States Army authorities for not having voluntarily provided the CROWCASS to the organization, even though the WJC had requested all "documents referring or relating to" Waldheim.

With the discovery of the CROWCASS, the discussion over Waldheim's past entered a new and far more serious phase. If, prior to 22 March, vague and above all speculative charges characterized the debate about Waldheim's wartime service in the Balkans, the listing of Waldheim as a suspected war criminal raised the stakes considerably. All the more so, as this accusation had been sanctioned—so far as the WJC knew—by two independent authorities not normally associated with judicial malfeasance.[35] In addition, the period of time during which Waldheim was supposed to have committed the acts for which he was suspected of "murder" corresponded exactly to that part of his biography which Waldheim had concealed. Finally, the WJC believed that the United States Army could have been involved in a "cover up" of Waldheim's past, which only strengthened their suspicion about Waldheim's activities.[36]

From this point on, the main elements of the WJC's own interpretive schema were firmly in place. The charges, that (1) Waldheim had been a "Nazi" (specifically, a member of 3 Nazi organizations, the SA, NSDStB and *NS-Reiterkorps*) and (2) he had concealed both this "Nazi past" as well as his wartime service in the Balkans for 40 years, were considered proven. All subsequent research undertaken by or for the WJC served to uncover and explain further details relating to Waldheim's hidden past. The suspicion that Waldheim had good reasons to suppress his years in the Balkans was significantly strengthened by the discovery of the CROWCASS. The WJC seemed to have proceeded on the assumption that there was a "smoking gun" somewhere, and saw their task as being in the forefront of those trying to find it. At the same time, however shrill their tone and questionable their conclusions, the spokesmen of the WJC did not accuse Waldheim of having committed war crimes.

25 March 1986: The Findings of Robert Herzstein

The 25th of March marked a major turning point in the Waldheim affair. At the press conference held on that day, the WJC presented the results of the research undertaken on their behalf by historian Robert Herzstein.[37] Herzstein's findings represented the first major batch of Wehrmacht documents made public that related directly to Waldheim's activities. On the basis of these, Herzstein was able to fill in many theretofore unknown details about Waldheim's duties, and, more importantly, about his knowledge of Wehrmacht policy towards partisan warfare. According to the press release distributed at the press conference, Waldheim had been "a senior intelligence officer who reported directly to the General Staff of Army Group E with responsibility for prisoner interrogation, testing of personnel for political reliability as a Nazi, and most ominously, 'special tasks'—a euphemism for distasteful operations such as assassinations, kidnappings, and deportations."[38]

According to Herzstein, Waldheim had signed reports in which "'cleansing' operations" [*Säuberungen*] as well as the "interrogation of civilians" were mentioned. In addition, Herzstein was able to relate the Zvonimir medal to the fighting between Yugoslav partisans and the Wehrmacht in the Kozara mountain range in Bosnia, described in the press release as "one of the worst atrocities carried out in the Balkans during the period." Waldheim's importance in Army Group E was also ostensibly buttressed by reference to "a sort of table of honor" on which Waldheim's name appeared.[39]

Herzstein in fact made several questionable interpretations relating to Waldheim's service in the Battle Group West Bosnia, which the WJC, trusting his judgment as an expert, repeated. For example, what Herzstein called "a sort of table of honor" for those who participated in the fighting turned out to be a list of those attending the celebration of commanding general Friedrich Stahl's 53rd birthday, held on 14 June 1942. Moreover, Herzstein's claim that Waldheim was only one of two soldiers to have received the "highly prized" King Zvonimir medal with oak leaves, awarded by by the Croation government of Ante Pavelic, was misleading. The King Zvonimir medal itself was far from being "highly prized," and Waldheim was the 916th recipient of it. It is true that Waldheim was one of two who received the silver Zvonimir with oak leaves, but this exaggerates the significance of the award. Virtually all evidence suggests that Waldheim received the award by virtue of his position in the battle group and his enjoyment of Stahl's favor, but not because of excessive "valor." Ernst Wiesinger, who served in the same Quartermasters department in Battle Group West Bosnia, also received a Zvonimir, but Waldheim's superior, Captain Plume, did not.[40]

The document on which the WJC based its claim that Waldheim had been a "senior intelligence officer"[41] was a duty roster of the general staff of Army Group E from December, 1943, as amended in February 1944.[42] Waldheim appeared as the third assistant adjutant, or O3 in the military intelligence and counter-intelligence department (Ic/AO). Waldheim did, in fact, rank third in this department's hierarchy, behind his direct superior, Lieutenant Colonel Herbert Warnstorff, the Military Intelligence Officer (Ic) and Major Wilhelm Hammer, the Counter-Intelligence Officer (AO). However, the claim that Waldheim was a "senior" officer obscures the vast distance between the Ic and AO on the one hand, and the O3 (Waldheim) on the other. For example, Hammer, the AO, substituted for the Ic, Warnstorff, in the latter's absence (he was his *Vertreter*), that means, he could issue orders and directives to subordinates, something which an O3 was never empowered to do. In terms of rank, moreover, Waldheim was not superior to others who technically worked under Waldheim's general supervision, such as First Lieutenant Helmut Poliza. Still, both Herzstein's and the WJC's interpretation of this point could refer back to a postwar study by the United States Army on the practices of military intelligence in the German army which is considered authoritative, *German Military Intelligence.*[43] Although these formulations are not found verbatim, the conclusions Herzstein reached concur with those found in this study.

In some other points of detail, Herzstein's findings were dubious, even if comprehensible. A more discriminating study of the duty roster of the general staff of Army Group E, for example, would have suggested that Waldheim's "responsibility" for interrogation of prisoners, personnel matters and special tasks could only be interpreted as a supervision of the work of others. The roster listed tasks directly under the O3, and then showed two further subordinate units, each with specific tasks and each under the direction of specifically named people. Interrogation of prisoners was listed as a duty of both sub-units, and "special tasks" [*Sonderaufgaben*] as a duty of subunit A, personnel matters under B. For example, First Lieutenant Krohne (later *Sonderführer*[44] Fischer) was responsible for "prisoner interrogation" for the areas of "Greece and border areas" and "special tasks." First Lieutenant Poliza was responsible for "prisoner interrogation" in the sub-group described as "allied areas" and for "personnel matters of the Ic/AO group." None of these tasks, however, were listed among the duties of the O3 himself. The use of the term responsibility, therefore, without specifying further what was meant by it, gave an exaggerated impression of Waldheim's actual role in the Ic/AO department.

Apart from this slightly forced interpretation of the responsibilities in the O3 sub-department itself, there were some further points that were open to dispute. There was, for example, no documentary support for the WJC's description of personnel matters as the "testing of personnel for political reliability as a Nazi," though Herzstein's statement implied as much.[45] Nor did *German Military Intelligence* suggest such an interpretation. The position in Army Group E which could be interpreted as the one ensuring the "reliability" of the soldiers was the National Socialist Leadership Officer [*Nationalsozialistischer Führungsoffizier*, or NSFO], not the O3. The NSFO in Army Group E was a Captain Pfitzer, which was clearly evident from the very document Herztein produced.[46] Herzstein was also not able to prove that the item "special tasks" (*Sonderaufgaben*) in the document in question was a "Nazi euphemism" which "usually concerned secret measures of mass terror or torture, kidnapping and execution."[47] There is no doubt that the formulation *Sonderaufgaben* could and, especially in the terminology of the SS, did serve as a euphemism for the mass murder of Jews.[48] However, simply to infer from this that this expression, used on a duty roster of a military intelligence department, must also have been such a euphemism, is unwarranted unless supported by additional evidence, which Herzstein did not provide.

The documents which the WJC published on 25 March showed conclusively that Waldheim had been informed of the most minor details of "cleansing" operations, and that he had served as an *Ordonnanzoffizier* in the military intelligence department of Army Group E. For the WJC, this represented yet another blow to Waldheim's credibility, for Waldheim was believed always to have maintained that his activities were limited to those of an interpreter. Now it turned out, according to the WJC, that he had been a "senior intelligence officer." On the basis of these discoveries, the WJC requested then Attorney General Edwin Meese to place Waldheim's name on the watch list of undesirable aliens.[49]

The WJC press release from 25 March 1986 thus contained some problematic interpretations of documents relating to Waldheim's wartime service, and the usual strong negative judgment as to his credibility: "Kurt Waldheim is a liar," the WJC said. Nonetheless, the WJC had sought expert advice before offering any evaluation of the documents themselves, and accepted Herzstein's interpretations of the evidence without exception, even when the language in the WJC's press releases was far more censorious than that in Herzstein's statement. The relevant question, therefore, would appear to be how much the documents themselves and the general state of knowledge justified the allegations the WJC advanced. However much one may criticize the WJC on scholarly or political grounds, and however judgmental and over-generalizing their own forumulations were, there was no evidence that the WJC acted in bad faith, or that they abused the expert advice which they received from Herzstein. It speaks rather to the WJC's credit that they adopted the interpretations offered by Herzstein, even when some turned out to be mistaken or misleading. The sharpness of tone, on the other hand, may be at least partly explained by the WJC's indignation over the extent of Waldheim's alleged mendacity.

The Search for the "Smoking Gun"

After the 25th of March, WJC spokesmen, emboldened by Herzstein's findings and the publication of the Yugoslav *Odluka,* became increasingly self-assured about their actions in exposing Waldheim's past. The strategy followed by the WJC, however, was in essence a continuation of the one it had pursued from the beginning, and was devoted principally: (1) to seeking out and making public more information about Waldheim's role in the Balkans, and (2) to redoubling their efforts to have Waldheim's name placed on the watch list, the case for which was only strengthened, in their view, by the documents which continued to surface.

It is not possible to mention all the details of the WJC's disclosures that followed over the next two and a half months. In most cases, the WJC's counsel Eli Rosenbaum carried out the research or research was commissioned,[50] but the WJC also frequently made documents public which had appeared elsewhere, but which were deemed of sufficient interest to warrant publication. Several set assumptions informed Rosenbaum's further research and to a certain extent led him and the other officials of the WJC to misread evidence which would have modified the interpretations they had previously made. Waldheim's "Nazi past" and its corollary implication of National Socialist ideological conviction, for example, remained a given and was mentioned in future press releases only as background information. Other such assumptions included the view that Waldheim was a compelling and important figure in the general staff of Army Group E; that Waldheim had distinguished himself in the Kozara campaign in the spring and summer of 1942, for which he had received an important award; that he must have known of the deportation of the Jews from Salonika and, corresponding to his position in the general staff, would have been involved in them; and that he most likely had been involved in planning Operation Black in Montenegro in July, 1943. For the WJC, all these assumptions had been either fully established (the "Nazi past" with the caveats mentioned above), were shared by most other researchers, or had been provided by an acknowledged expert, Robert Herzstein.

A few examples will illustrate the nature of these further disclosures. The day after the Belgrade, Yugoslavia, daily *Vercernije Novosti* published excerpts from the file on Waldheim compiled by the Yugoslav War Crimes Commission (the *Odluka*), concluding that the former U.N. Secretary General was "responsible for war crimes," the WJC issued a press release and an English translation of the file's contents.[51] On 1 April, the WJC produced further evidence that "Kurt Waldheim was on the operations staff of the military unit which carried out the 'Kozara Massacres.'"[52] Two weeks later they produced a copy of a German army document which had been "used as evidence of Nazi war crimes in Greece." This find, according to the WJC, provided "extraordinary corroboration" of the conclusions reached by Herzstein and the Yugoslav War Crimes Commission.[53] On 14 May, the WJC produced yet more documents which "support charges by Yugoslavia linking the former U.N. Secretary General to reprisal massacres against three Yugoslav villages in October 1944."[54] On 6 June they distributed documents which showed that "Waldheim conveyed to his superiors a German Army Division's request for the seizure and deportation of Greek civilians in 1943."[55]

The WJC's interpretations of the various documents they had discovered or reproduced followed similar lines. Taking the findings of the *Odluka* at face value, the WJC put a great deal of effort into locating documentary corroboration of the charges the file contained. The WJC evidently believed that the procedures followed by the Yugoslavs, the UNWCC and the United States Army had been above reproach, and in fact there was no evidence at that time that would have cast suspicion on them. Even so, not insignificant evidentiary weaknesses of the file were overlooked. For example, the only witness in the file for the massacre in October, 1944, on the road between Stip and Kocane, Captain Karl Heinz Egberts-Hilker, did not directly inculpate Waldheim in the affair. In fact, only one witness in the file, Johann Mayer, had implicated Waldheim directly in the giving of orders. The brunt of the eleven-page dossier consisted of an attempt to establish the implied complicity of Waldheim by virtue of standing orders that he would have seen or passed on or both.[56] Perhaps this is why the WJC undertook to augment the *Odluka* with documents purporting to support the Yugoslav Commission's legal reasoning. However that may be, the WJC's conviction about the simplicity of interpreting wartime documents was unwarranted, their expertise about the legal issues involved in discussing Waldheim's possible criminal role tenuous. The measured forays of the WJC and their researchers into this field indeed appear to have reinforced their policy of limiting their sometimes scathing tone to accusations on the subjects of Waldheim's credibility and his moral suitability for the job of representing the United Nations.

When they could not quote more definitive opinions of others,[57] for example, the WJC tended to be cautious in their formulations, and held back from describing Waldheim as a "war criminal" or claiming that Waldheim had been criminally complicit in war crimes. It would have been unusual in any event for WJC spokesmen to have labeled someone a war criminal who had not been convicted by a recognized competent legal authority. The presumption of innocence would normally be expressed linguistically by employing such conventions as "accused," "suspected" or "alleged" war criminal, if there were a basis for the accusation. In Waldheim's case the CROWCASS listing, the *Odluka* and the UNWCC file all justified the description of Waldheim as a suspected war criminal, and the WJC adhered to these conventions when discussing Waldheim, though sometimes just barely. In a letter to then Attorney General Edwin Meese, for example, Edgar Bronfman argued for Waldheim's inclusion on the watch list by referring to his "participation in acts of Nazi-sponsored persecution," adhering consciously, it seems, to the formulation which appeared in the Holtzman Amendment.[58] Elsewhere, the WJC spoke of Waldheim's "involvement during World War II in 'liquidation' operations in Yugoslavia,"[59] without, however, specifying this further, and on another occasion the WJC referred to Waldheim as a "participant in brutal anti-partisan campaigns in Yugoslavia."[60]

The WJC's efforts to bolster the accusations made in the Yugoslav *Odluka*, meanwhile, continued apace. On 14 April, they claimed to have found "extraordinary documentary corroboration of the conclusions reached . . . in 1947 by the Yugoslav War Crimes Commission in a decision declaring Waldheim to be a 'fugitive Nazi war criminal,'"[61] and a month later they claimed that "new documents support charges made by Yugoslavia linking the former U.N. Secretary General to reprisal massacres against three Yugoslav villages in October 1944." "Together," Bronfman was quoted as saying, "the eyewitness testimony and evidentiary documentation point a damning finger at Dr. Waldheim."[62] On 16 April, Bronfman sent a letter to then United States Secretary of State George Shultz, who shared responsibility for a watch list decision, in which he claimed that "the case against Kurt Waldheim as an accused war criminal has become prima facie with the release of the U.N. file." Waldheim, Bronfman wrote, "participated in the most cruel behavior of the National Socialists," but again neither defined participation nor identified the behavior in which Waldheim was supposed to have been involved, although the context suggests that it was his activities as O3 in the military intelligence section of Army Group E.[63]

In addition to following up the allegations contained in the *Odluka*, the WJC pursued leads of its own. On 29 April, they published documents which in their opinion demonstrated "not only that Waldheim's protestations of ignorance concerning the war-time deportations of Greek Jews are ludicrous, but also that he may well have been involved personally in their perpetration."[64] An interim balance of sorts on the previously unknown evidence on Waldheim's "hidden years" was drawn up by Eli Rosenbaum on 2 June 1986. In the press release that accompanied the report, Bronfman was quoted as calling Waldheim an "amoral and unrepentent liar," whose election as Austrian president "would be an act of symbolic amnesty for the Holocaust."[65]

The WJC's attitude towards Waldheim and the documents they uncovered or interpreted or both seemed littered with ambiguity, if not contradiction. On the one hand, WJC spokesmen always emphasized the most incriminating evidence relating to Waldheim's wartime service and frequently cited from what appeared to be highly inculpatory documents, such as the CROWCASS or the *Odluka.* Though technically there could be no objection to their quoting genuine documents, expecially from such sources, this practice blurred the lines between accusations which they were making and those they were quoting. On the other hand, the very same spokesmen repeatedly stressed that the WJC was not accusing Waldheim of being a war criminal. In an interview published on 24 March in *Profil,* Elan Steinberg stated that "Waldheim is not a war criminal, at least as far as we know now." In the same interview, Israel Singer averred that "perhaps it will turn out that Waldheim was really a harmless figure in the Wehrmacht. I would not wish to rule it out. But he lied, lied to us all [when he said] that he was in the hospital, ostensibly attending college, not in Salonika and not in Serbia, and these are only examples which we can now prove and [in which] he has confessed his lies," which clearly emphasized that the WJC's main interest was in Waldheim's lack of credibility.[66] This impression was strengthened by Singer's reference to Waldheim as a "former Nazi and a liar," not, however, as a war criminal. On 1 April, after he had seen the charges and evidence in the *Odluka,* Singer stated in an interview, parts of which were broadcast by the Austrian evening television news, "we are not carrying on a war crimes trial";[67] the WJC was merely claiming that Waldheim had not been suitable for the office of Secretary General of the United Nations. He had "dirtied" the U.N.'s good name. Austria, Singer also emphasized, should realize that it was not on trial, and neither was Waldheim, but it was legitimate to ask him why he had "such an awfully bad memory."[68] The following day Singer repeated this view in an interview in the Austrian daily *Kurier:* "It has been proven that Waldheim was in areas where horrible things occurred and that he knew about these."[69]

The WJC's hunch that Waldheim might have incurred a measure of personal criminal responsibility for acts committed while serving in the Balkans, however, was not simply a function of its trust in the official bodies which had pronounced Waldheim a suspected war criminal. Allied to this was their confidence in the legal reasoning contained in the Yugoslav file, expressed most forcefully by Eli Rosenbaum, the WJC's legal counsel. This is a line of argument which could find some support in the principles outlined in the charter of the Nuremberg war crimes trials, but which appears to have conflicted with the practice itself. Rosenbaum's attempts to buttress the meager offerings of the *Odluka,* while certainly not incogitant sophistry, turned in the end on an untenable premise.

The WJC outlined their thinking on this matter in a press release issued on 14 April. "What Waldheim did," they stated, "was identify places of partisan activity, which under orders received a year earlier, would then be subject to brutal atrocities against civilians." Since these orders must have been known to Waldheim, he must have been aware of the (criminal) consequences of his actions in identifying areas of partisan activity. He could thus have made himself criminally complicit in the massacres which followed.[70]

One piece of evidence the WJC cited, however, the 1947 Nuremberg trial against Wilhelm List and others, was especially unreliable in this connection. The defendants in that trial were, as the WJC formulated it, "charged with the mass murder of hostages and the 'reprisal' destruction of hundreds of towns and villages in the Balkans during World War II. All but two of the defendents were found guilty by the United States Military Tribunal and sent to prison."[71] In fact, the verdicts in the case militate against the WJC's interpretation of criminal complicity as it applied to Waldheim. One of those acquitted in the trial was General Hermann Foertsch. Foertsch served as the chief of staff of first the Army High Command 12 and its successor Army Group E from August 1942 until August 1943, and then as staff chief of Army Group F, to which Army Group E was subordinate, until March 1944.[72] As such, Foertsch would *ipso facto* have had to incur more criminal liability than any *Ordonnanzoffizier* like Waldheim for the transmission of orders which led to reprisal killings. Yet Foertsch was acquitted on this and every other charge at his trial.[73] As was mentioned earlier, the rulings in other Nuremberg trials also suggested that Waldheim's position as a staff officer whose function was to compile and transmit information would have protected him from criminal liability.

The thesis Rosenbaum defended, however, was identical to that offered in the *Odluka,* whose findings, as far as Rosenbaum knew, had been examined and endorsed by the UNWCC.[74] It is theoretically conceivable that a prima facie case against Waldheim could be made independent of the tainted evidence contained in the *Odluka,* if the legal reasoning had in fact accorded with the practice of the Nuremberg tribunal, and this quite irrespective of the Yugoslavs' motives in assembling the file. That war crimes had been committed in the Balkans was well known in any case. As it turned out, most of Rosenbaum's operating assumptions were unfounded, but there can be no doubt as to the seriousness with which he approached the issue. The international historians' commission concluded that such activity amounted to "consultative support for measures of repression," though it did not consider it criminal.[75] Yet Rosenbaum did not claim to have shown that Waldheim was a criminal, or even that he had made a case worthy of indictment in a court of law, though he presumably shared Bronfman's view at the time that the existence of the UNWCC file amounted to a prima facie case against Waldheim. Rosenbaum's interest appears to have been to underline Waldheim's moral obloquy in light of his dissemblance about his wartime service, and perhaps more importantly, to support the WJC's request that Waldheim should be barred from entering the United States under the terms of the Holtzman amendment. These terms, it will be recalled, require nothing more than a prima facie case in support of unspecific formulations about involvement. The arguments of the WJC seem to have been just that.

Whatever one may justifiably criticize about the WJC's research into the nature of Waldheim's "hidden" military past, be it the hyperbolic choice of words, the incomplete research, their insistent and exaggerated self-assurance or the bias of many of their assumptions, some of which have been detailed here, the substance of the allegations they made against Waldheim remain broadly confirmed, and where mistaken, nonetheless intelligible. Although they defended opinions that were controversial, the WJC attempted to base their conclusions on expert advice or specialized literature. And even where individuals drew conclusions based on unfounded assumptions, these latter were not merely tendentious nor were they beyond the realm of the imaginable. Most importantly, the evidence presented here shows that the WJC did not simply present its findings as direct involvement in war crimes, however much Waldheim and others may have portrayed the WJC's accusations as such. Yet even the more measured, if also contemptuous, remarks of Simon Wiesenthal, who stated that the WJC had begun with its disclosures "when they had nothing," are unfounded. It remains to examine just how little a dispassionate appraisal of the WJC and its accusations corresponded to the imprecatory portrayal of the WJC as malevolent, mentally disturbed slanderers in the statements of Waldheim supporters and in reports in the Austrian press.

The Drive to Have Waldheim Placed on the Watch List

After the WJC's press conference of 25 March 1986, the publication of documents detailing Waldheim's whereabouts and activities in Yugoslavia and Greece were accompanied by progressively insistent demands for the U.S. Department of Justice to act, and every suspected prevarication on the part of Attorney General Meese met with increasingly bitter criticism. On 26 March, the Attorney General's office formally requested the documents the WJC had published the previous day, in order to determine whether Waldheim should be entered on the watch list.[76] The WJC repeated this request in subsequent press releases.[77] At the end of April, the Office of Special Investigation, whose chief purpose is to enforce the provisions of the Holtzman amendment, completed a report which recommended that Waldheim be barred from entering the United States. Attorney General Meese, who considered Waldheim's case far from routine, refused to follow the OSI's recommendation immediately.[78] Meese's initial reticence merely elicited disbelief from the WJC,[79] and afterwards ever sharper condemnation. On 30 May, for example, the WJC released a statement which demanded that "Attorney General Edwin Meese should enforce the law and bar Waldheim from ever entering the United States again,"[80] and three days later they repeated the same demand even more urgently. "There is no precedent for any Attorney General to so delay implementing the findings of the Justice Department's Office of Special Investigations," the press release stated. "Any further delay would represent an obstruction of justice stemming from clear political motives."[81] In the event, Messe authorized the OSI to undertake a more thorough investigation and the decision was deferred for a year. It was finally announced in April 1987 that Waldheim was indeed to be entered on the watch list.[82] Both inside the United States and in Austria, there has been much confusion about this decision, the law on which it was based, and its legal implications. It is not possible to examine all the circumstances surrounding it in detail, but a few remarks about the decision are warranted.

Because other recent prominent cases handled by the Office of Special Investigation (OSI), such as those of Karl Linneas, John Demjanjuk and Andrija Artukovic, had led to the deportation of persons suspected of direct involvement in especially heinous crimes, the decision of the U.S. Justice Department to place Kurt Waldheim on the so-called "watch list" could be said to have led to a kind of guilt by association and does seem to have encouraged the suspicion of Waldheim's complicity in war crimes. Yet any inferences of criminal behavior drawn from the watch list decision alone would be mistaken. In a later chapter we will discuss the ways in which the arguments on the watch list decision might have colored the discussion of Waldheim's wartime past. In the present context, however, it might be helpful to explain the terms of the Holtzman amendment to the U.S. Immigration and Nationality Act as they apply to Waldheim.

The United States Department of Justice placed Kurt Waldheim, a private individual (a point it empasized), on its watch list of undesirable aliens.[83] What this means in practice is that, were Waldheim to request admittance to the United States, he would be denied an entry visa. There would appear to be some legal ambiguity as to whether Waldheim, in his capacity as the Austrian head of state, could still have been excluded under the same provisions, though the question was never tested. The relevant law, of which the paragraph affecting Waldheim, the so-called Holtzman amendment, is but a small part, is entitled the Immigration and Nationality Act.[84] The name itself gives a clue as to the procedures one might expect to be followed in executing the various provisions of the act. As a law covering immigration and not directly criminal proceedings, the act gives the attorney general or those deputed by her or him wide discretionary powers (in this the United States law is little different from immigration laws elsewhere). According to the law "the attorney general and any immigration officer . . . shall have power to administer oaths and to take and consider evidence of or from any person touching the privilege of any alien or person he believes or suspects to be an alien to enter, reenter, pass through, or reside in the United States or concerning any matter which is material and relevant to the enforcement of this Act."[85] The law thus makes a specific minister, rather than the courts, ultimately responsible for the control of immigration.

Immigration laws control who may or may not visit and reside in a particular country. They do not impose penalties for criminal violations of laws. (Once one is legally inside a country, illegal acts are, of course, punished; however, this is subsumed under the rubric of criminal law.) As such, the rules of evidence in such immigration procedures are substantially less stringent than in a criminal court proceeding. Under the provisions of the United States Immigration Act, a prima facie case suffices to exclude someone from entering the United States. If the attorney general determines that the evidence warrants one's inclusion on the list under the conditions spelled out in the law, then the person must be barred, unless he or she can dissuade the Attorney General, or another ground for exemption can be found.

Section 1182 of the act comprises, as its heading makes clear, "General Classes of Aliens Ineligible to Receive Visas and Excluded from Admission," as well as "Waivers of Inadmissibility." The provision relevant to Waldheim is Subsection (a), Paragraph (33) of Section 1182. This paragraph excludes:

> Any alien who during the period beginning on March 23, 1933, and ending on May 8, 1945, under the direction of, or in association with: (A) the Nazi government of Germany, (B) any government in any area occupied by the military forces of the Nazi government of Germany, (C) any government established with the assistance or cooperation of the Nazi government of Germany, or (D) any government which was an ally of the Nazi Government of Germany, ordered, incited, assisted, or otherwise participated in the persecution of any person because of race, religion, national origin, or political opinion.[86]

The decision of the Justice Department to place Waldheim on the watch list turns on the interpretation of the formulation ". . . assisted, or otherwise participated in the persecution of any person because of race, religion, national origin, or political opinion." Depending on how one defines the word assisted, this passage, tendentiously read, could mean anything from paper shuffling to gassings at Auschwitz.

The decision of the U.S. Attorney General (acting on recommendations of the OSI) leading to the United States' denying Waldheim an entry visa, thus did not rest on a determination of Waldheim's guilt or innocence of war crimes, but rather on the finding that he had "assisted or otherwise participated in the persecution of any person because of race, religion, national origin or political opinion," a far more elastic formulation which certainly subsumes war crimes, but also many other lesser deeds. Documents on Waldheim in the public domain, for example, showed that he had played a key role in the transfer and exchange of intelligence which was used to determine targets for "cleansing actions." Such activities fell easily under the category of having "assisted, or otherwise participated in the persecution of any person because of race, religion, national origin, or political opinion." It follows that the results of OSI investigations could not, by themselves, justify any more incriminatory inferences regarding Waldheim's actions during the war.

Waldheim's situation was indeed anomalous. Prima facie evidence of his assistance to or participation in persecution sufficed to place him on the watch list under the terms of the Holtzman amendment. The allegations made by the OSI have not been, and were not required to be, scrutinized by a court of law to determine whether they would be sufficient to indict Waldheim, much less convict him for alleged criminal behavior. There are, in fact, no provisions in United States law to try people for war crimes or crimes against humanity: those suspected of such may merely be expelled or excluded if the conditions specified in the Holtzman amendment are believed to have been met.[87]

The case of Andrija Artukovic can best illustrate this point. Artukovic was deported to Yugoslavia in 1986, not because courts in the United States had found him guilty of war crimes or crimes against humanity (for which they had no jurisdiction), but because he had violated provisions of the U.S. immigration law, among others those of the Holtzman amendment. Artukovic stood trial and was convicted of war crimes in Yugoslavia, because the Yugoslav court found the evidence, some of which the OSI had helped assemble, compelling. Kurt Waldheim was placed on the watch list because the activities he performed while stationed in the Balkans also fell under the terms of the Holtzman amendment, but not because these were found to be criminal under United States law. However, although no judicial authority has tried Waldheim, several independent bodies and some well-informed legal authorities, most notably the international historians' commission, the panel of judges involved in the Thames-HBO *Commission of Inquiry* and the British Ministry of Defense, have all examined the question of Waldheim's criminality. None of these bodies suggested that there was a criminal case for Waldheim to answer, and the depth and thoroughness of these investigations have cast serious doubts on the assumptions and reasoning underlying the OSI's deliberations.[88] It is rare, perhaps even unique, that the legal aspects of a case before the OSI should have commanded so much non-official attention. Yet even on the purely hypothetical assumption that a court in the United States competent to try him for war crimes would not convict Waldheim on the evidence, he would still be considered excludable under the provisions of law as it stands, with all the attendant ignominy this entails. It is perfectly true that being placed on the watch list carries a stigma which may not correspond to one's actual complicity in the crimes of the Nazis. Just how much journalistic license the discussion on Waldheim's wartime past engendered may be illustrated by the headline 26 March 1986 issue of the *New York Post*, which announced, reporting on a WJC news conference, that "Papers Show[ed] Waldheim was SS-Butcher." No document the WJC made public warranted such a conclusion, and the WJC press release did not even approximate this interpretation. It is to the WJC's credit that they chose not to follow the imaginative lead of such newspapers. Yet the WJC's efforts on this score were not reciprocated. In the discourse of the Waldheim camp in Austria, baseless allegations such as those contained in this *New York Post* headline were frequently amalgamated with the WJC's more considered efforts to ferret out the details of Waldheim's previously concealed past. This was not, of course, accidental. Nor was it mere chance that the WJC's ever more urgent appeals to Meese to have Waldheim placed on the watch list were presented in a way such that Meese's decision, when it came, could only be seen to have been made at the WJC's behest. In this discourse, the WJC came to embody and represent the Jews' alleged power and presumed dishonorable and vengeful character traits. The *"Feindbild 'Jud'"*—the WJC and their officials—bore little relation to the content of their allegations against Waldheim. The successful construction of the artificial image of the WJC, which even the most critical journalists in Austria (and many abroad) shared to one degree or another, was an essential prerequisite of the antisemitic turn of the 1986 election campaign.

Notes

1. *Profil*, 1 April 1986.

2. The program was broadcast on 4 April 1986. The quotations are taken from Projektteam "Sprache und Vorurteil," "'Wir sind alle unschuldige Täter!'" Studien zum antisemtischen Diskurs im Nachkriegsösterreich." Project Report, Manuscript (Vienna, 1989), p. 223. See also Ruth

Wodak, "Wie über Juden geredet wird," *Journal für Sozialforschung* Vol. 28, No. 1 (1988), pp. 117–136.

3. *Philadelphia Enquirer,* 19 May 1986.

4. Michael Graff, quoted in the *Neues Volksblatt* (*NVB*), 26 April 1986.

5. Notable exceptions among the independent daily papers included the columns by Erwin Frasl in *Kurier* on 25 March 1986 and by Gerhard Steininger in the *Salzburger Nachrichten* on 5–6 April 1986.

6. *Wochenpresse,* 1 April 1986.

7. See in general, Nahum Goldmann, *Das jüdische Paradox. Zionismus und Judentum nach Hitler* (Cologne, Frankfurt: Europäische Verlagsanstalt, 1978); Evi Beker and Eliyahu Tal eds., *World Jewish Congress. Jubilee 1936–1986* (Jerusalem: World Jewish Congress, 1986).

8. Beker and Tal, *World Jewish Congress,* pp. 23–28. See also Luc Rosenzweig and Bernard Cohen, *Waldheim* trans. Josephine Bacon (London: Robson Books, 1987), p. 123.

9. It is possible that there were other channels of information to the WJC, but the evidence is sketchy. In the event, the version of the initial impetus to investigate Waldheim further reproduced here seems entirely plausible. See *Wochenpresse,* 1 April 1986 and Rosenzweig and Cohen, *Waldheim,* pp. 141–152.

10. The details are given in *Profil,* 27 January 1986.

11. "News from World Jewish Congress" (News from WJC) 4 March 1986. Between 4 March and the second round of the election on 8 June 1986 the WJC issued press releases accompanied by documents at regular intervals. These revelations are conveniently summarized in the pamphlet *Waldheim's Nazi Past. Chronology of the Revelations* (New York: World Jewish Congress International Department of Information, 1986).

12. News from WJC, 4 March 1986. Loehr was tried and executed by the Yugoslav authorities both for his part in the bombing of civilian areas of cities during the short war which set up the German occupation, which took place in April 1941, long before Waldheim was in the Balkans, as well as his responsibility for the deaths of civilians during the partisan war, which overlapped with Waldheim's service there. There is no doubt that Loehr would have been tried for crimes at Nuremberg (Case 7), had he not previously been handed over to Yugoslavia by the Allies. See Martin Zöller and Kazimierz Leszczynski, eds., *Fall 7. Das Urteil im Geiselmordprozeß* (East Berlin: Deutscher Verlag der Wissenschaft, 1965), p. 127.

13. In the letter to Solarz Turner wrote: "You specifically mention two concerns: that he [Waldheim] may have been a member of the Nazi Youth Movement.... We believe that Waldheim was not a member of the Nazi Youth Movement." In fact, there was no such organization. Solarz appears to have used the expression "Nazi Youth Movement" as a generic category, which presumably would have included the *Hitlerjugend,* the *Bund deutscher Mädchen,* the NSDStB, and all other such organizations, though the names of these were apparently unknown to either Turner or Solarz. This corresponds to the interpretation of the WJC as well, as it suspected duplicity on Turner's part. However, since the organization specified did not in fact exist, Turner's answer to Solarz was technically correct (how could he have been a member of a non-existent organization?), but also misleading, because it is not clear whether Turner had understood the imprecision of Solarz's question. See the letter from Stansfield Turner on Stephen Solarz, 31 December 1980, attached to News from WJC, 4 March 1986.

14. Copies of these documents were attached to News from WJC, 4 March 1986. See Chapter 4.

15. News from WJC, 4 March 1986. See also, News from WJC, 5, 10 and 20 March 1986.

16. Letter from Stephen J. Solarz to Kurt Waldheim, 26 November 1980. In this letter, Solarz referred to an article from the 29 September 1980 issue of *The New Republic,* and cited an article by Martin Peretz. In fact, the original allegations that Waldheim had belonged to a "Nazi Youth Movement" had been raised by Shirley Hazzard in the 19 January 1980 issue of *The New Republic.* Neither Hazzard nor Peretz offered any evidence to support their allegations against Waldheim, and Solarz, following the lead of these two authors, asked Waldheim whether he had been a member of the "Nazi Youth Movement."

17. Letter from Kurt Waldheim to Stephen Solarz, 19 December 1980. The 31 December 1980 letter from Solarz to CIA Director Turner, quoted by the WJC in its press release, was also part of Solarz's investigation into Waldheim's past.

18. All these were attached to News from WJC, 4 March 1986.

19. *NYT,* 4 March 1986.

20. *NYT,* 13 September 1981.

21. News from WJC, 4 March 1986, and *Für Tapferkeit und Verdienst. Ein Almanach der von Deutschland und seinen Verbündeten im ersten und zweiten Weltkrieg verliehenen Orden und Ehrenzeichen* (Munich: Schild Verlag, n.d.), p. 51.

22. Gerald Reitlinger, *The Final Solution: The Attempt to Exterminate the Jews of Europe 1939–1945* (New York: A.S. Barnes, 1961).

23. Otto Kumm, *Vorwärts Prinz Eugen. Geschichte der 7. SS-Freiwilligendivision "Prinz Eugen"* (Osnabrück: Munin-Verlag, 1978), p. 76.

24. Yugoslav War Crimes Commission, ed., *Report on the Crimes of Austria and the Austrians against Yugoslavia and Her Peoples* (Belgrad: Yugoslav War Crimes Commission, 1947).

25. Jozo Tomasevich, *The Chetniks. War and Revolution in Yugoslavia, 1941–1945* (Stanford: Stanford University Press, 1975).

26. News from WJC, 4 March 1986.

27. Attached to News from WJC, 10 March 1986, translation modified.

28. News from WJC, 20 March 1986. The relevant history of these organizations is described in *Profil,* 24 March 1986.

29. *Washington Post,* 9 March 1986.

30. News from WJC, 10 March 1986.

31. News from WJC, 22 March 1986, emphasis added. According to the CROWCASS list, Waldheim had been assigned Number 79/724 of the United Nations War Crimes Commission (UNWCC) list.

32. News from WJC, 22 March 1986.

33. See Hans Kurz, James Collins, Jean Vanwelkenheuzen, Gerald Fleming, Hagen Fleischer, Jehuda Wallach and Manfred Messerschmidt, *Der Bericht der internationalen Historikerkommission,* supplement to *Profil,* 15 February 1988, pp. 8–13.

34. News from WJC, 25 March 1986.

35. The precise circumstances which had led to the establishment of the UNWCC file and the CROWCASS were at that time unknown. In fact, the Yugoslav authorities had assembled evidence against Waldheim, not because they seriously thought him personally guilty of criminal activity, but because he happened to be secretary to then Austrian Foreign Minister, Karl Gruber. Yugoslavia submitted its file on Waldheim along with many other files in a rush just before the UNWCC concluded its work in 1948. The UNWCC did not, in fact, investigate the evidence in the Yugoslav file carefully, but pronounced it sufficient to warrant prosecution. The U.S. Army list was compiled on the basis of the UNWCC file, but it did not check the evidence

either. Consequently, both the UNWCC file and the CROWCASS entry on Waldheim, which was based on it, resulted from a politically inspired but sophisticated manipulation of evidence. This could not have been known by the WJC in March 1986. For the story behind the Yugoslav *Odluka*, the UNWCC and CROWCASS as it relates to Waldheim see Robert E. Herzstein, *Waldheim. The Missing Years* (London: Grafton Books, 1988), pp. 193–217.

36. News from WJC, 22 May 1986.

37. News from WJC, 25 March 1986. See also Herzstein, *Missing,* pp. 21–23 and passim.

38. News from WJC, 25 March 1986.

39. The WJC distributed a statement by Herzstein which detailed his findings. All of them were accepted by the WJC, though not all details were mentioned in the press release. See News from WJC, 25 March 1986 and Robert Herzstein, "Prepared Statement of Prof. Robert E. Herzstein on the Wartime Activities of Kurt Waldheim," 25 March 1986.

40. News from WJC, 25 March 1986. Herzstein, "Statement," p. 5. See Hanspeter Born, *Für die Richtigkeit. Kurt Waldheim* (Munich: Schneekluth, 1987), pp. 50–51, 68–70; Walter Manoschek [Neues Österreich], ed., *Pflichterfüllung. Ein Bericht über Kurt Waldheim* (Vienna: Löcker Verlag, 1986), p. 42; Karl Gruber, Ralph Scheide and Ferdinand Trautmannsdorff, *Waldheim's Wartime Years. A Documentation* (Vienna: Carl Gerold's Sohn, 1987), pp. 171–176.

41. Herzstein had described Waldheim as a "major intelligence figure in an army of 300,000 men." Herzstein, "Statement," p. 10.

42. Attached to News from WJC, 25 March 1986. The sections of this roster relating to Waldheim's department are reproduced in Gruber, et al., *Wartime Years,* pp. 206–207.

43. Frederick, Maryland, 1984, pp. 224–225. See also Hans Kurz, James Collins, Jean Vanwelkenheuzen, Gerald Fleming, Hagen Fleischer, Jehuda Wallach and Manfred Messerschmidt, *Der Bericht der internationalen Historikerkommission,* supplement in *Profil,* 15 February 1988, pp. 8–13.

44. A *Sonderführer* had some duties akin to those of a political commissar and is described by the MOD commission as "a specialist serving with the military forces." See Ministry of Defence, United Kingdom [MOD], "Review of the results of investigations carried out by the Ministry of Defence in 1986 into the fate of British servicemen captured in Greece and the Greek Islands between October 1943 and the involvement, of any, of the then Lieutenant Waldheim" (London: Her Majesty's Stationery Office, 1989), p. 113.

45. News from WJC, 25 March 1986. Herzstein, "Statement," p. 10.

46. Military Intelligence Division, U.S. War Department, *German Military Intelligence 1939–1945,* 224–225. This document is reproduced in Gruber, et al., *Wartime Years,* p. 207. See also "Kriegsrangliste der Offiziere, Sanitätund Veterinäroffiziere und ob. Beamten des Oberkommandos Heeresgruppe," 1.7.44, Bundesarchiv-Militärarchiv, Freiburg i.B., RH 20–12/139. See also the statement of Markus Hartner, who worked in Waldheim's subdepartment, in the Yugoslav *Odluka,* reproduced in Gruber, et al., *Wartime Years,* p. 278; and Born, *Richtigkeit,* p. 172.

47. Herzstein, "Statement," p. 8.

48. See Joseph Wulf, *Aus dem Lexikon der Mörder: "Sonderbehandlung" und verwandte Worte in nationalsozialistischen Dokumenten* (Gutersloh: Sigbert Mohn, 1963), pp. 76–77, citing a communication from June, 1943, from SS-Oberführer Viktor Brack to Heinrich Himmler.

49. News from WJC, 25 March 1986.

50. After 25 March Herzstein no longer served as advisor to the WJC. See Herzstein, *Missing,* pp. 22–23.

51. News from WJC, 27 March 1986.

52. News from WJC, 1 April 1986.

53. News from WJC, 14 April 1986.

54. News from WJC, 14 May 1986.

55. News from WJC, 6 June 1986.

56. See Born, *Richtigkeit,* pp. 183–189, Kurz, et al., *Bericht,* pp. 37–39. Gruber, et al., *Wartime Years,* pp. 222–236, 281–282 and 285.

57. News from WJC, 22 March 1986: ". . . both the Army and the United Nations War Crimes Commission listed Kurt Waldheim as a suspected war criminal." See also News from WJC, from 27 March 1986: "An official decision of the Yugoslav State Commission on War Crimes concluded that Kurt Waldheim "is established by the evidence to be a war criminal," whose "extradition to the Yugoslav suthorities [sic] is mandatory."

58. News from WJC, 25 March 1986 and 26 March 1986.

59. News from WJC, 28 March 1986.

60. News from WJC, 1 April 1986.

61. News from WJC, 14 April 1986.

62. News from WJC, 14 May 1986.

63. See letter of John C. Whitehead to Edgar Bronfman, 5 May 1986, attached to News from WJC, 15 May 1986.

64. News from WJC, 29 April 1986.

65. Eli Rosenbaum, "Kurt Waldheim's Hidden Past: An Interim Report to the President," Bound Ms. (June, 1986). See also News from WJC, 2 June 1986.

66. *Profil,* 24 March 1986.

67. *Zeit im Bild 2,* Österreichischer Rundfunk (ORF), 1 April 1986.

68. The latter passages were reported in *Wiener Zeitung,* 2 April 1986.

69. *Kurier,* 3 April 1986.

70. The massacre in question took place in October 1944 on the road between Stip and Kocane. See the report of Eli M. Rosenbaum to Edgar Bronfman, "Newly-discovered Documents Linking Kurt Waldheim to October 1944 Massacres in Macedonia," 13 May 1986; News from WJC, 14 May 1986, repeated in News from WJC, 14 May 1986. See above, Chapter 4.

71. News from WJC, 14 April 1986.

72. For a detailed explanation of the command structures in the Southeast European theater, see Kurz, et al., *Bericht,* pp. 5–7; see also Herzstein, *Missing,* pp. 107–110.

73. "U.S. vs. List, et al.," in Friedman, *Laws,* Vol. II, pp. 1303–1343. Zöller and Leszczynski, eds., *Fall 7.* Foertsch's acquittal would not automatically exculpate Waldheim, among other reasons because some of the reports which were signed by Waldheim date from a period in which Foertsch was no longer chief of staff. This, however, would not alter the substantive point about Foertsch's acquittal.

74. Rosenbaum had consulted the standard work on the UNWCC, *History of the United Nations War Crimes Commission and the Development of the Laws of War.* See also News from WJC, 30 May 1986.

75. Kurz, 42. See also M. Messerschmidt in *Der Spiegel,* Nr. 9/1988.

76. News from WJC, 26 March 1986.

77. News from WJC, 28 March, 2, 9 and 18 April 1986.

78. *NYT,* 29 April 1986.

79. News from WJC, 15 May 1986.

80. News from WJC, 30 May 1986.

81. News from WJC, 2 June 1986.

82. *Wiener Zeitung,* 28 and 29 April 1987; *Kurier, Neue Kronen Zeitung, AZ,* 28 April 1987. See also *Profil,* 27 April, 4 and 11 May 1987.

83. According to the press release announcing Waldheim's placement on the watch list, "... the Department of Justice has determined that a prima facie case of excludability exists with respect to Kurt Waldheim as an individual, and his name is being placed on the 'Watchlist'"; and "Both Departments [Justice and State] emphasize that this decision deals with Mr. Waldheim as an individual for past activities." Press release issued by the Department of Justice, 27 April 1987. World Jewish Congress Commission on the Holocaust and Crimes of the Nazis, "Waldheim's Nazi Past: The Dossier," Ms. (1988), (unpaginated), Appendix.

84. Committee on the Judiciary, U.S. House of Representatives, *Immigration and Nationality Act. With Amendments and Notes on Related Laws,* 7th Edition (Washington, D.C.: U.S. Government Printing Office, 1980), pp. 38–39. For the allegations levied in the file prepared by the Office of Special Investigation (OSI) against Waldheim in support of the decision to refuse him an entry visa, see *NYT,* 28 April 1987 and *Profil,* 18 May 1987.

85. Committee on the Judiciary, House of Representatives, *Immigration and Nationality Act,* p. 53.

86. Ibid., pp. 38–39.

87. It is theoretically conceivable that the United States could pass a war crimes law similar to that recently adopted by the British House of Commons (over the opposition of the House of Lords). Such a law would provide criminal penalties under United States law for those suspected of having committed war crimes or crimes against humanity during the Nazi period. However, the legal and constitutional issues which the debate in Britain highlighted would make such a law's passage in the United States exceedingly unlikely. The crimes involved, for which the alleged criminals may be held accountable under the British law, for example, were neither committed against British citizens nor on British soil, and were thus not offenses against English law. Moreover, the retroactivity of the legislation—some of the crimes in question were not criminal under English law when they were committed—would seem to all but exclude the introduction of legal remedies in the United States beyond the power to exclude or deport.

88. The best discussion of the weaknesses of the OSI allegations is in to be found in Hubertus Czernin, "Waldheims Balkanjahre," *Profil,* Nos. 49–52, 1987, and 1–4, 1988; and *Profil,* 18 May 1987.

7

The Waldheim Affair in the United States

On Sunday, 9 March 1986, speaking on the television news program *Pressestunde,* Austria's answer to *Face the Nation,* Waldheim expressed his irritation at those fellow citizens unwilling to take his word on faith alone. "But you must also understand," his long monologue began, "that I am getting tired of being accused uninterruptedly of things which are not true, and of the fact that one is more ready to believe others, for example the *New York Times,* which has spread the most grotesque things about me, than the man who has loyally served his homeland for forty years."[1] Hugo Portisch, as television commentator and co-producer of two multi-part historical documentaries *Austria I* and *Austria II* somewhat akin to Austria's historian laureate, and not normally noted for unseemly outbursts, also had some rather unkind words for the peccant ways of this exemplar of American newspaper journalism. In a talk show discussion in September, 1986, after Waldheim's election victory, he declared that the *New York Times* wanted to make Waldheim into a "Nazi hangman." "One has to say that antisemitism is horrible," he continued, "but what appears in the *New York Times* is also mendacious and vile."[2]

Vehement negative judgments on the quality of the *Times'* reporting thus reached far beyond the Waldheim faithful. Even in Austrian newspapers that made earnest efforts to avoid partisan reporting, misconceptions about the paper and what it had printed abounded, which effectively hindered readers dependent on these media for their information in forming an opinion not heavily influenced by the Waldheimian optic. The *Wiener Zeitung* (*WZ*), truly not a mouthpiece of the Waldheim campaign organization, reported in its 6 March 1986 issue that "the *New York Times* had . . . reproached [*vorgeworfen*] Waldheim for being a member of various Nazi organizations."[3] Likewise on 30 March, the headline in the *WZ* reported "New Reproaches of the NYT against Waldheim."[4]

These examples, representing a broad spectrum of opinion in contemporary Austrian political culture, all shared a common assumption which pervaded virtually all reporting in Austria on the Waldheim affair's reception in the United States, namely, that anything and everything which appeared in print in the *NYT* somehow represented its editorial line, or at least conveyed the opinion of the newspaper. Both Waldheim and the *Wiener Zeitung* were incontestably referring to news reports which the *NYT* had published[5] and not editorials, or, for that matter, even opinion columns. With Portisch, it is unclear to what he is referring, but his nescient amalgamation was as preposterous as Waldheim's.

To explain the media attention, particularly that of the *New York Times*, given to Kurt Waldheim as a centrally organized "defamation campaign" in the face of potentially conflicting evidence required an assumption that there was a uniform editorial "line" of the *NYT* or even of "the American media" which embraced all news reports, editorials and opinion columns published on the Waldheim affair. Though most consistently propounded in Austria by Waldheim and his supporters, this assumption was far more widespread. In fact, it distorted the writing (and presumably the thinking) of otherwise more cautious journalists. Such internalized assumptions helped determine, during the Waldheim campaign, the discursive possibilities of how one was able to think of the Waldheim affair, or what Noam Chomsky has called the "bounds of thinkable thought," though ironically it was the *Times* Chomsky chided (in the context he cited, rightly) for itself being instrumental in establishing these boundaries.[6] Facts which in principle could have occasioned a critical rethinking of such assumptions were either ignored or incorporated into the propaganda and interpretation patterns which the Waldheim camp had successfully erected, and in which many in the Austrian press were willfully or passively complicit. Even neutral or not obviously biased statements were at the mercy of the preconceived notions, stereotyped images and simple prejudice within which the Waldheim affair was largely debated in Austria. The distortion of reality, here as with the World Jewish Congress (WJC), helped reinforce certain ancillary prejudices about Jewish power, especially in the media, while the image of the *NYT* waging a "campaign" against Waldheim and "Austria" at the side of, if not on the instructions of, the WJC, provided those for whom the Jewish world conspiracy offered a convenient explicatory nostrum just the pretext required.

The *New York Times* and the Waldheim Affair: Making the News Fit to Print

Between 4 March and 15 June 1986, the *NYT* printed a total of 129 individual items which either explicitly dealt with Kurt Waldheim and the controversy over his past or the presidential campaign in Austria, or in which the Waldheim affair was mentioned in some connection. These 129 broke down into:

1. News Reports: The 107 news reports comprised 77 longer and 30 shorter texts. The great majority of the longer articles (63) were written by *Times* journalists, others were dispatches of the new agencies Reuters, Associated Press (AP) or United Press International (UPI). The shorter news items were either from the *NYT* itself (or from a source which could not be identified

[Special to the New York Times]), frequently, however, from Reuters, AP and UPI. Included in this group were the short summary items in the Sunday *Times's* "The Week in Review" section. Of these 107 news reports, ten were devoted predominantly to—or contained information that relied chiefly on—press conferences or press releases of the WJC.[7]

2. Editorials: Between 4 March and 15 June (one week after Waldheim's election) the *NYT* published three editorial opinions on various aspects of the Waldheim Affair: 19 April, 12 May and 10 June.
3. Opinion Columns: The "Op-Ed" side of the *Times* contained two types of opinion columns: Of those five commentaries from columnists on the *NYT* staff mentioning Waldheim or the Waldheim affair during the period in question, two were by Anthony Lewis ("Abroad At Home"); one by Flora Lewis ("Foreign Affairs"); and two by William Safire ("Essay"). Opinion columns by authors not on the staff of the *Times* are normally accepted by virtue of some specific social or political function these authors exercise, because they are leading personalities or opinion leaders, because they possess particular expertise to comment on a given subject, or because they are either directly affected by an issue or have some special interest in it. These criteria, of course, are not mutually exclusive. Such articles are generally longer, more systematic and far more prominent than letters to the editor, though they serve a similar function. The *NYT* published seven such personal opinion columns on Waldheim, among others from Robert Herzstein, Kurt's son Gerhard Waldheim and Edgar Bronfman.
4. Letters to the editor: A total of seven.

Specific discursive, rhetorical or argumentative strategies correspond to each type of newspaper text, among other reasons because the declared objective of a news report is to inform, that of an opinion column to persuade.

This brief description of the kinds of items published by the *NYT* (and by other papers following its general pattern) exposes the speciousness of such remarks as "The 'New York Times' *reproached* . . . Waldheim" when a news article must have been the reference. The careless usage of the Austrian *Wiener Zeitung,* however, was taken over and magnified by less conscientious editors and journalists, and served to elide important distinctions, with the result that the *NYT* was represented largely as the propaganda arm of the World Jewish Congress. As for the usage itself, what the *Wiener Zeitung* could only have meant was that the *NYT* had reported that documents the paper had received from the WJC and from *Profil* suggested Waldheim's membership in two Nazi organizations. It is everyone's privilege to reject the conclusions which John Tagliabue, the journalist in question, drew from these documents (i.e., that they did not suggest Waldheim's membership), as well as any other aspects of the report. That, however, is not the same as accusing the *NYT* of having "reproached" Waldheim merely because the paper reported something it deemed newsworthy. The most that could have been said about the editors of the paper in relation to this article was that they judged Tagliabue's work competent and free enough from bias to let it appear in the paper as a report.[8]

In order to evaluate certain aspects of the reporting in the *NYT*, it is important to keep a couple of characteristics of news articles in mind. The first is the writing technique known as the "inverted triangle." According to this model, which is used above all to give editors more flexibility in making cuts to news items, the contents of the article are stated very generally in the intial two or three paragraphs, after which details relating to the story are given in descending order of importance (the idea being that cuts should be made to less significant material). Apart from techniques employed to determine the authenticity of documents or the accuracy of allegations, in news articles themselves reporters for newspapers such as the *Times* also rely on certain journalistic conventions in order to maintain the balance of news reports or at least to reduce their bias. These include allowing adequate space to those personally affected by reports to deny or refute them, attempting to provide a context to the report itself, and employing formulations which indicate clearly that an opinion is being reported rather than endorsed.[9] As we will see below, the use of these techniques and conventions did not always have the intended result. It would therefore repay critically evaluating what the *New York Times'* journalists actually reported, what the paper's editors opined, and what its columnists averred, to indicate some of the errors (both of omission and commission) that were made and how these came to be made. Such gaps in the *Times'* reporting and the paper's perceived "tilt" against Waldheim could offer his supporters a confirmation of sorts of essential components of the *Feindbild 'Jud'* in 1986. For if accurate reporting by the *New York Times* of information that was merely inconvenient for or embarassing to Waldheim could be successfully portrayed as part of a hostile international "campaign" against him or Austria, how much more easily could genuine errors of interpretation, mistaken assumptions, etc., on the part of *Times* reporters lend themselves to manipulation as verification of the Waldheim camp's assumption of media animus.

The First Report

The character of the *NYT's* reporting may be illustrated by examining its first report on the Waldheim affair. As was mentioned above, the occasion for the *Times's* initial report was that it had received documents relating to Kurt Waldheim's past from the WJC. These contained evidence that Waldheim had omitted details about his past, namely, membership in two Nazi organizations and military service under a General who was executed as a war criminal after the war. It is self-evident that such information about a former secretary general of the United Nations would be considered newsworthy, and this independently of Waldheim's candidacy for the Austrian presidency. John Tagliabue, the journalist assigned to the story, first confirmed the authenticity of the documents he had been shown, then contacted Waldheim. On Sunday, 2 March 1986, Tagliabue discussed his evidence with Waldheim. On the same evening the magazine *Profil* appeared with its report. Tagliabue filed his report on 3

March 1986, and it appeared on the following day with the headline: "Files Show Kurt Waldheim Served Under War Criminal." The article began with the following summary: "Kurt Waldheim, former Secretary General of the United Nations, was attached to a German Army command in World War II that fought brutal campaigns against Yugoslav partisans and engaged in mass deportations of Greek Jews, according to official documents made available here" [i.e., Vienna]. "The documents also show," the report continued, "that, as a young man, he was enrolled in two Nazi Party organizations."[10] Immediately following this passage, Tagliabue noted the source of the various documents on which he had based his report, and gave background information to help explain the disclosures, for example, that between 1938 and 1945 Austria had been a part of Nazi Germany.

The report then explained why these documents were of interest: "In authorized biographies and in a recent autobiography, Mr. Waldheim does not discuss his activities during the years involved, 1942 and 1943. Mr. Waldheim . . . acknowledged in an interview Sunday that he had served in the units in question. But he said he had played a minor role and knew of no war crimes or atrocities ascribed to the units." Waldheim, moreover, "said it was the first time that he had heard of mass deportations of Greek Jews from Salonika." After mentioning Waldheim's current candidacy for president of Austria, the report carried Waldheim's initial response: "He [Waldheim] accused his opponents of using the information about the war years to damage him politically. "The timing of it is perfect," he said. "For 40 years these things have rested." Mr. Waldheim belittled his membership in the Nazi groups, saying that his activities were intended to shield him and his family, who were known as opponents of the Nazis." It should be noted here that Waldheim's denial, his interpretation of the documents, as well as his explanation of the reasons behind the disclosures, were given a prominent place in the article. At the same time, Tagliabue appears to have assumed Waldheim's membership in these organizations, something which Waldheim flatly denied.

Tagliabue then provided more details about the various documents he had received and those which had appeared in *Profil,* all of which had been "corroborated independently." There had been, wrote Tagliabue, accusations in the past relating to Waldheim's alleged Nazi past, but "Mr. Waldheim has said on each occasion that he never was a member of a Nazi organization or a Nazi-affiliated organization." In the more comprehensive discussion of the content of the documents themselves and their significance, Tagliabue reached conclusions similar to those of Hubertus Czernin from *Profil* and the WJC:

> The documents show that in July 1942, after a campaign against Yugoslav partisans, Mr. Waldheim was awarded a high military decoration of the Nazi puppet state of Croatia, the Order of the Crown of King Zvonimir. . . . Mr. Waldheim, as a 20-year-old student at the Consular Academy here, was enrolled April 1, 1938, in the Nazi student union, about three weeks after the Anschluss. The following Nov. 18, he was enrolled in a mounted unit of the Sturmabteilung, or SA, the paramilitary Nazi organization known as the

> Brownshirts. He remained a member until he entered military service on Aug. 15, 1939. . . . Mr. Waldheim was assigned to German Army Command 12, based in Salonika, Greece, on March 14, 1942, and was sent to Belgrade where he apparently served as an Italian-German interpreter in Yugoslavia and Albania in 1942 and 1943.

Waldheim's own specific explanation followed each of these allegations. For example, referring to Waldheim's alleged membership in the SA and the Nazi Student Union, Tagliabue reported: "Mr. Waldheim said he became aware after the war that he had been enrolled in the SA,[11] but that he had not considered himself, at the time, a member of that organization or of the Nazi student union. The two groups, he said, had been established by 'one or two students' and were used for 'social gatherings, coffee parties and things like that. . . .'" Tagliabue also reported that Waldheim's "basic motive for taking part in the gatherings was to shield himself and his family from political harassment, a common enough motive at the time."

In addition to Waldheim's own denial, Tagliabue quoted an evaluation of Kurt Waldheim's political affiliations by the district leader of the NSDAP (*Gauleiter Niederdonau*), which, the paper wrote, "revealed lingering distrust" of young Kurt by the Nazis. He again quoted Waldheim and reported that an investigation of Waldheim by the Austrian authorities in 1946 had cleared him of any suspicious Nazi affiliations. The article then quoted what seems to have been Waldheim's second line of defense, should his categorical denials have proved unconvincing, namely, that even if he had been a member of these organizations, "it would still not be a sign of Nazi thinking."

Tagliabue's treatment of Waldheim's military service followed the same pattern. He mentioned that the years 1942–1943 were "potentially" embarassing because Waldheim had served in the staff of General Loehr, "at a time of military operations against Yugoslav partisans and mass deportations of Greek Jews." In spite of Waldheim's repeated insistence that he had been discharged from the Wehrmacht in 1942 after his leg injury, the report continued, the former Secretary General had in fact served in the AOK 12 under Loehr.

Because the documentary evidence relating to Waldheim's service in the Balkans at the time of Tagliabue's report was so scant, there were several major gaps: all he could report with certainty was that Waldheim had served on Loehr's staff, that he had apparently been assigned to serve in Yugoslavia, and that he had received the King Zvonimir award from the puppet state of Croatia. Tagliabue did not report anything more. Waldheim confirmed each point, but could or would not offer any information to help explain them or explain how they related to one another. On the contrary, Waldheim's principal strategy was to anticipate possible inferences and dismiss them out of hand. For example, asked about the Zvonimir decoration and the photograph of him at the Podgorica airport together with SS-General Artur Phleps, among others, Waldheim replied that it was "'absolutely absurd' [to think] that he was in any way involved in atrocities. He described his role as that of an interpreter in discussions between Italian and German commanders." As for the award itself, "Mr.

Waldheim acknowledged having received the Zvonimir medal, but said it was given to virtually all staff members 'as a matter of routine.'" Though Tagliabue appears not to have suggested it, Waldheim added that "'someone with bad intentions might conclude, because partisans were there, Waldheim must have committed war crimes,'" which would be "'pure nonsense. I committed no crime in the whole time. I sat there and the German command gave orders to the Italian units and they needed an interpreter. I was not chief of the liaison staff. There was a whole group of interpreters.'"

Tagliabue consulted the work of two recognized experts for background information about the deportations from Salonika, historians Raul Hilberg and Gerald Reitlinger. If Reitlinger's claim, which Tagliabue quoted, that Loehr was "perhaps more implicated in Jewish deportations than any other Wehrmacht commander," was accepted, and Waldheim himself conceded having served under him, then it required no hostile predisposition on Tagliabue's part merely to ask what Waldheim knew of these deportations and what his role in Loehr's staff had been. Waldheim's responses, which were confusing when not tergiversating, were reported extensively and neutrally. For example, "Mr. Waldheim acknowledged that he had been serving on General Loehr's staff in Salonika, but he said his activity consisted in analyzing reports on enemy troop movements. He denied knowing anything of the deportations." Tagliabue also wrote that Waldheim was "visibly shaken" when told of the deportations, and quoted his denial extensively. Likewise Waldheim's answer to his inquiry as to why he had not referred to this part of his military career in the past: "'This is not a book of memoirs in the ordinary sense, nor is it a comprehensive account of events during my term of office as Secretary General of the United Nations.' He said he never considered his later wartime experiences as worthy of comment." The final item which made it into the report was a brief reference to the correspondence between Waldheim and Stephen Solarz, and Solarz and the CIA, over Waldheim's past.

This first news report on Waldheim exemplified the techniques and conventions referred to above in a number of ways. Firstly, Tagliabue presented as "fact" (as they applied to Waldheim)[12] only those items which could be supported by documentary evidence and which Waldheim personally confirmed or which could be verified independently (such as the correspondence between Solarz and Waldheim or Solarz and the CIA). Waldheim conceded several details about his military service in Army Group E which documents obtained from the WJC had suggested. Tagliabue also believed that Waldheim confirmed a prewar membership in the SA. Waldheim's book was in the public domain in any case. No allegations implying Waldheim's personal involvement in criminal activities were made or quoted in Tagliabue's article. Secondly, Waldheim was confronted by Tagliabue with every piece of evidence which he introduced in his article, and Waldheim's explanations, denials or comments on them were quoted or reported at length. Waldheim consistently attempted to deflect any suggestion that he might have been associated with criminal activity. Although he had not raised the issue himself, Tagliabue reported Waldheim's protestations of innocence and even quoted unnamed "political commentators" who maintained that "the most serious accusation against him may ultimately turn out to be that he was not forthcoming about his past." In addition, Tagliabue on at least one other occasion employed a phrase—writing "a common enough motive at the time" to describe Waldheim's claim that he had participated in riding exercises of the SA in order to protect his family from political persecution—which cast a positive light on the credibility of Waldheim's explanation. Finally, there were several gaps in the picture presented of Waldheim's past in Tagliabue's article. These can be explained partly by incomplete, mistaken or misleading statements which Waldheim made about his past, by misunderstandings, but above all by the limited amount of documentation available. These gaps cannot, however, be explained by unwarranted bias on Tagliabue's part.

The Barriers to Clarity

Although no serious critic would claim that the *NYT* printed a tendentious report, it does not follow that the *Times's* journalists' efforts were beyond reproach. It is important to avoid unfairly using the advantages of hindsight to score cheap debating points. Still, it is possible to indicate some inferences that were drawn too hastily, and to point to journalists' insufficiently questioning their own assumptions about the evidence they were evaluating. This was less a problem of inadequate information than of a want of critical thought. Taken as a whole, the *NYT* reporting tended to rectify most serious mistakes of this kind, but certain assumptions, made for whatever reason (and here Waldheim's own contribution to the confusion was a major one), helped define the terms of the debate in the United States, and on at least one occasion may have contributed to conveying a misleading impression of a claim Waldheim was alleged to have made. Retracing some of these assumptions in the first reports published by the *NYT* will assist in explaining the way in which the Waldheim affair "played" in the country as a whole.

The ambiguities surrounding Waldheim's years at the Consular Academy were not clarified any further in the *NYT* report. Tagliabue, like the WJC and Solarz before him, did not recognize the imprecision of the term "Nazi Youth Movement" in the correspondence between Solarz and Waldheim, and did not question Waldheim about it. Waldheim, for his part, did not enlighten Tagliabue about these distinctions. At the same time, Tagliabue, unlike the WJC, made no reference to a "Nazi past," but concerned himself exclusively with documents which suggested Waldheim's membership in the two National Socialist organizations.

The discrepancies in Waldheim's role and function during his Wehrmacht service in the Balkans in 1942 and 1943—the documents the *NYT* cited related only to these years—also remained, and Waldheim did little to resolve them. The evidence cited by the *NYT* on 4 March 1986 in fact applied to at least three distinct functions during this period of Waldheim's service: as second *Ordonnanzoffizier* (O2) in the quartermaster's department in Battle Group West Bosnia (Zvonimir); as interpreter in the German-Italian liaison staff assigned to the 9th Italian Army (Podgorica photo); and as third *Ordonnanzoffizier* (O3) on the general staff of Army Group E. Such details were not known to Tagliabue or anyone else at this time. Possibly not even Waldheim remembered exactly the various capacities in which he had served, but he contributed little to help explain them.

Prior to his service with Battle Group West Bosnia, Waldheim had been assigned to a liaison staff with the Italian 5th Mountain Division (Pusteria). At the time of Tagliabue's article, and for some days afterwards, Waldheim seems to have confused these two assignments from spring and summer 1942. Otherwise his response to Tagliabue's inquiry about the Zvonimir medal, "I sat there and the German command gave orders to the Italian units and the Italians gave messages back, and they needed an interpreter," made no sense. Waldheim had received the award after troops of the Battle Group West Bosnia had "cleansed" the Kozara mountains, an action they undertook without Italian support.[13] Waldheim, moreover, had not served as an interpreter with Battle Group West Bosnia, but as the second *Ordonnanzoffizier,* and it was for this role that he received the award. His erroneous statement, however, appears to have been the source of much confusion. Authors of several reports in the *NYT* assumed that Waldheim had always claimed only to have served as an interpreter in Army Group E. This assumption, repeated in press reports as background information, also affected the content and to some extent the tone of the controversy over Waldheim's past.

On the assumption, for example, which the WJC shared, conceivably based at least partly on *NYT* reports, that Waldheim had always said that he had only been an interpreter in Army Group E, then the discovery that he had also served as the third *Ordonnanzoffizier* in the military intelligence section (Ic/AO) of Army Group E would do additional damage to his already declining credibility. In fact, Waldheim's statements were themselves contradictory. Apart from the faulty recollection about the nature of his role in this one instance, he never explicitly conceded that he had served in any other role.[14] Waldheim did describe the nature of his duties as O3 to the Ic/AO, for example, that his "activity consisted in analyzing reports on enemy troop movements," but did not mention that that had been a different assignment, and Tagliabue was presumably not certain that the duties of an interpreter on the general staff did not include this. However, it is highly improbable that Waldheim could remember details about the duties he had performed as O3, but not the designation of the position he had had. Thus, the primary source of this confusion was Waldheim himself.

Tagliabue's article also reinforced another assumption about Waldheim's army career which had first appeared in *Profil* and which had far-reaching consequences, namely, that Waldheim had been present in Salonika during the deportations of the Jews. The article in the *NYT* noted correctly that "the potentially most embarassing disclosures concern Mr. Waldheim's presence in Salonika in the spring of 1943, after the Yugoslav campaign." Citing Raul Hilberg's work, Tagliabue noted that the deportations had occurred between March and May 1943, "part of which time Mr. Waldheim was in Salonika." As we have seen, Waldheim was away from Army Group E headquarters for most of the time of the deportations, but this became known only in

April 1986. The formulation in the article apparently attempted to reconcile the dates of the deportations with the photograph from 22 May 1943 which showed Waldheim at the Podgorica airport. Two things in this article, however, could have been pursued further.

Since Tagliabue was unaware of the details of the various formations which were subordinate to the High Command of Army Group E, it seems fair to assume that the precise connection of the SS Division "Prinz Eugen" to Army Group E was also unknown to him. Tagliabue had himself written that Waldheim had served under Alexander Loehr. Should Waldheim's photo with an SS-General of another army division not have appeared as confusing or even contradictory, and at least occasioned further questions? If Waldheim, moreover, according to Tagliabue's own report, had been 200 kilometers away from Salonika (in Podgorica) in May, 1943, then it would seem obvious to query whether and when Waldheim had also been present in Salonika during the remaining weeks of the Jewish deportations.

Tagliabue's lapses were venial, because Waldheim contributed nothing to help clarify such gaps in the documentary evidence. He claimed, for example, that he had seen the SS General Phleps only this one time (at the Podgorica airport), but could offer no additional information of the circumstances of the meeting. Moreover, Waldheim never contested that he had been in Salonika during these weeks; he merely disputed vehemently that he had known (or knew) that deportations had taken place. Indeed, Waldheim himself neglected to mention either that he had not actually been stationed in Salonika, but in a village 5 kilometers away, or that he had not, with the exception of a few days, been in Greece during the period in question.

Tagliabue also appears to be the source of another formulation which quickly became a fixed assumption in the *NYT* reporting. Waldheim, according to this view, is supposed to have claimed not to have heard of any atrocities which units attached to Army Group E had committed. In the 4 March 1986 article, Tagliabue wrote that Waldheim had "acknowledged in an interview Sunday that he had served in the units in question. But he said he had played a minor role and knew of no war crimes or atrocities ascribed to the units. In the interview, he said it was the first time that he had heard of mass deportations of Greek Jews from Salonika." The context of the quotation did not make clear of exactly which "war crimes or atrocities" Waldheim here claimed ignorance. The passage which followed, however, strongly suggested that he could only have meant the deportations of Jews, not atrocities in general: "Mr. Waldheim called it 'absolutely absurd' that he was in any way involved in atrocities. He described his role as that of an interpreter in discussions between Italian and German Commanders. . . 'Someone with bad intentions might conclude, because partisans were there, Waldheim must have committed war crimes,' he said. 'That is pure nonsense.'" Here Waldheim did not deny knowledge of atrocities (it is clear from the context that he was alluding to mass shootings, the destruction of villages, etc.), but rather his personal participation in such acts.

It is possible that the word atrocity meant different things to Waldheim and Tagliabue. Waldheim was fully aware of the measures taken by the Wehrmacht against Yugoslav and Greek partisans. If, however, he did not consider these atrocities,[15] then he could have said without contradiction that he "knew of no war crimes or atrocities ascribed to the units" in which he had served, as Tagliabue reported.[16] If Tagliabue, on the other hand, held such measures indeed to be atrocities, then Waldheim's statement that he knew of no atrocities could appear to be equivalent to a claim that he was unaware of the fighting against the partisans itself, which would have been entirely without credibility.[17] Although the evidence tends to support this interpretation of the origin of the misunderstanding, it cannot be known for certain. What remains beyond doubt is that this unclarity or misunderstanding was the basis of two fixed assumptions relating to Waldheim's knowledge of the deportation of the Jews from Salonika and of Wehrmacht reprisal policy, each of which fed convictions from both Waldheim and his critics that the other was dealing in bad faith.

For several weeks, it was a given that Waldheim had claimed not to have known of atrocities (understood in the sense of reprisal killings, etc.) committed by units of Army Group E. This opinion was repeated as background information in *NYT* reports, and was mentioned in several WJC press releases. Indeed, *Times* journalist James M. Markham reported in an article published on 17 April 1986 that Waldheim had "conceded for the first time that as a lieutenant in the German Army he was aware of atrocities committed against Yugoslav partisans." When documents with Waldheim's initial proving his intimate knowledge of reprisal measures against partisans were discovered, his statement that he had not known of these atrocities appeared as mendacious or at least implausible. Assuming, of course, that Waldheim had made such a statement in this form. In any case, at least one journalist of the *NYT* abandoned this assumption by mid-May at the latest. In an article published on 15 May 1986, Elaine Sciolino wrote that "Mr. Waldheim has never denied knowing about massacres against partisans, but has stated repeatedly that he neither ordered nor took part in any massacres."[18]

A convenient and easily understandable reference point for certain aspects of Waldheim's wartime career was offered by the deportation proceedings in the United States against Andrija Artukovic, former interior minister in the "independent" state of Croatia, which had been completed shortly before the disclosures about Waldheim's wartime service by the *NYT*. It could, however, conjure up infelicitous associations which Waldheim almost certainly would rather have avoided. In order to make Waldheim's King Zvonimir decoration comprehensible to his readers, *NYT* journalist John Tagliabue needed to refer to the Pavelic government of Croatia which had awarded it. How better explain this than by referring to the proceedings against this government's former minister of the interior? "The documents show," the relevant passage began, "that in July 1942, after a campaign against Yugoslav partisans, Mr. Waldheim was awarded a high military decoration of the Nazi puppet state of Croatia, the Order of the Crown of King Zvonimir." This state, Tagliabue continued, "was known for persecuting Jews, Serbs and gypsies through deportations, forced labor and mass murders. A former Cabinet minister of that state, Andrija Artukovic, was recently extradited by the United States to Yugoslavia to stand trial on war crimes charges." Tagliabue used the reference to Artukovic exclusively as background and suggested no other connections between the two. Other factors, independent of Tagliabue's own article, may have served to strengthen associations between these two. In any case, there seems to have been no good reason not to have made this reference.

During the following three weeks, the *NYT* reported only intermittently on Waldheim. The content of these articles ranged from the reactions of Jewish organizations in the United States to the disclosures about Waldheim[19] to new disclosures which had been published in other newspapers,[20] to the saga of the disappearance and rediscovery of Waldheim's personnel file in the Austrian Foreign Ministry.[21] Both Waldheim's denials and his counteraccusations were given much space in these articles. For example, on 6 March, John T. McQuiston reported on Waldheim's appearance on the CBS *Morning News.*[22] In this article, McQuiston related Waldheim's belief that the accusations against him were motivated by electoral considerations and Simon Wiesenthal's opinion that, although he did not believe that Waldheim had been a member of the NSDAP, he doubted that he could not have known of the deportations of Jews from Salonika. McQuisten also quoted Hagen Fleischer, an expert on the German occupation of Greece between 1941 and 1945 and later a member of the international historians' commission, that Waldheim had "had nothing to do with Greek Jewry." In addition, McQuiston reported that the WJC had denied Waldheim's accusation that the disclosures were timed to coincide with the Austrian elections. On 8 March, Ronald Smothers reported on a telex from Waldheim to Edgar Bronfman of the WJC in which he claimed to have been "deliberately misinterpreted" and quoted Waldheim's denials once again. A Reuters dispatch from Vienna on Waldheim's appearance on the Austrian TV *Pressestunde* was published on 10 March under the headline "It's A 'Smear,' Waldheim Says."[23] During this period, two letters to the editor were published. The first, from Joseph M. Segel, former head of the United Nations Association of the USA, was clearly pro-Waldheim, the second, from Abraham Foxman, Associate Director of the Anti-Defamation League of B'nai B'rith, was just as clearly anti-Waldheim. This period also witnessed the reinforcement of several assumptions about Waldheim and his past, which appear traceable either to misunderstandings or to incomplete, misleading or false statements from Waldheim himself, but which in any case circumscribed the conceptual framework within which the discussion on his past took place. Waldheim himself, however, never challenged these assumptions as such, merely offered another version of their meaning. The *NYT,* therefore, continued its reporting along the same lines as before, confronting new evidence or new accusations with Waldheim's denials or explanations of them, without, however, altering the framework of the debate.

One early example of how assumptions relating to Waldheim's membership in the SA and the Nazi Student Union could affect reporting on his military career was an unsigned article in the *NYT* on 5 March 1986 describing the anger of Jewish organizations when they learned of Waldheim's past. In summarizing Waldheim's denials the article stated that "Mr. Waldheim, who had previously said he had never had anything to do with Nazi groups, acknowledged that he had served in the military units in question. But he said he had played a minor role in their activities and knew of no atrocities. He also acknowledged being enrolled in two Nazi organizations in college."[24] The clear association of "Nazi groups" with "military units" could easily harden the assumption that Waldheim's military service represented a continuation of a "Nazi past," unless the SA and SNDStB were themselves the "military units" mentioned. In general, the reports in the *NYT* tended to conflate the two. Although it is in general legitimate to refer to the Wehrmacht as the "Nazi military command" or something similar,[25] this is an over-simplification which does not clarify much about either the Nazis or the Wehrmacht. Moreover, if Waldheim's membership in the SA and student union did not automatically imply firm National Socialist convictions, it is doubtful whether one could draw any worthwhile inferences about his military activities from his "Nazi past."

By 9 March, however, Waldheim's membership in these two Nazi organizations was considered proven. Although the information contained in the documents released by *Profil* and the WJC (especially the SK-235 file) played a role, the decisive point for the *NYT* seems to have been Waldheim's verbal acknowledgment of his membership in the 2 March 1986 interview with John Tagliabue. Waldheim's contention that he had been misquoted was rejected after the transcript had been checked, and was not even reported after 9 March. The "Week in Review" section of the Sunday *Times* stated, for example, that "the former Secretary General of the United Nations acknowledged that he had joined a Nazi student union and a unit of the Nazi paramilitary SA, or Brownshirts, in 1938."[26] From this point there was no doubt as to his membership.

The *NYT* continued to report Waldheim's claim that he had only served as an interpreter, but missed an opportunity to obtain a more precise picture of Waldheim's true responsibilities. Part of the confusion related to generalizations the *NYT's* journalists extrapolated from specific answers Waldheim provided them about his wartime activities. For example, while it is virtually certain that Waldheim only interpreted between "Italian and German commanders" at the meeting at Podgorica airport (shown on the photograph), and that Waldheim's description of his duties here as elsewhere was uninformative, *NYT* reporters' inattentiveness also played a role. For example, on 8 March, Waldheim was quoted as saying that ". . . independent sources have confirmed that my services as an interpreter and staff officer were completely unrelated to such tragic and deplorable events." Waldheim thus appeared to be referring to at least two distinct positions, but only if one knew that interpreters were not also staff officers. Yet even this vague allusion is incomplete, because it subsumes under the generic category "staff officer" not only his service as *Ordonnanzoffizier* in the military intelligence department of Army Group E, but also his role as first *Ordonnanzoffizier* in the German liaison staff with the Italian 11th Army and as second *Ordonnanzoffizier* in the quartermaster's department of Battle Group West Bosnia.[27]

CROWCASS and After in the *New York Times*

Although the WJC published a part of the CROWCASS list on 22 March, the *NYT* did not report on this explosive document ("Waldheim Figures in 1948 List") until three days later, and then only on page five. Waldheim, Stephen Engelberg wrote, "was identified as a suspected war criminal on lists kept by the United States Army, according to a document in the National Archives." The formulations used by Engelberg in the article reflected the incompleteness of the information available. He reported, but did not endorse, the contents of the list: "According to the List Mr. Waldheim served as a staff intelligence officer from April 1944 to May 1945 with Army Group E, a force that occupied Yugoslavia and waged a campaign against its partisan forces." Engelberg also reported that the CROWCASS listing made reference to a UNWCC file on Waldheim, and that Waldheim's name appeared only on the 1948 CROWCASS, but not earlier ones. Apart from Waldheim's categorical denial of involvement in war crimes, the report also quoted Alan Ryan, former head of the Office of Special Investigation, as saying that "the names on the list were often based on unverified accusations," clearly mitigating any negative inferences which might be drawn from the list.[28]

In addition to the main article, the *Times* published a Reuters dispatch reporting on a press conference with Simon Wiesenthal in Vienna, at which he also downplayed the significance of the listing. According to Reuters, Wiesenthal emphasized the importance of whether the published list was an interim or the final one, on which Waldheim's name may no longer have appeared. It was possible, Wiesenthal said, that Waldheim's name was dropped from an earlier list because of lack of evidence. In the event, he added, frequently the names of all soldiers of a given unit were entered on this list.[29] As it turned out, few of the mitigating assumptions advanced by Wiesenthal applied to Waldheim's case.[30] Yet the overall impact of the *NYT's* reports on the CROWCASS listing was not at all unfavorable to Waldheim.

The New York Times *and the World Jewish Congress*

One of the allegations most consistently circulated by the Waldheim camp and its media supporters in 1986, and a necessary assumption for the conspiracy explanation of the Waldheim controversy, was that the World Jewish Congress was waging a "slander campaign" against the former U.N. Secretary General in tandem with the *NYT.* The belief in the collusion of an international Jewish organization with the premier opinion-leading newspaper in the United States found many adherents in Austria in 1986, and has since then shown few signs of abating. As one of the truest of the "scholarly" believers in the theory, Esther Schollum, wrote, "In looking through the reports of the *New York Times* on the subject of Waldheim in March of this year [1986], one is struck by their exact chronological correspondence to the 'disclosures' of the WJC." Leaving aside the banality of this remark—why should the reports of the *New York Times* not have corresponded chronologically to the WJC's disclosures, if these latter were deemed newsworthy—Schollum's judgment, which is factually mistaken in any case, offered little more than belated scholarly cover for the Waldheim camp's propaganda invention.[31] John Tagliabue's initial report, even with its weaknesses, belied the claim of a concerted "slander campaign" against Waldheim, on both counts. If one examines the *Times*'s reporting of events, disclosures, criticism, etc., in which the WJC was directly involved, this charge becomes even less tenable. Not only did the *NYT* conduct their own analyses of documents independently of the WJC, the paper frequently reported divergences between its own reporters' conclusions and those of the WJC. At all times, *NYT* journalists kept a critical distance from the WJC's allegations.

This can best be illustrated by the coverage of the WJC's press conference of 25 March 1986, at which the results of Robert Herzstein's research were presented. The *Times* article, written by Elaine Sciolino and published on 26 March, carried the headline "Jewish Group Offers Documents It Contends Implicate Waldheim." The title alone suggests the *NYT's* distance from the Jewish organization's allegations. In the report itself, Sciolino employed similar formulations. The WJC had made documents public, she wrote, "that it said showed that Kurt Waldheim, as an intelligence officer in the German Army took part in campaigns against Yugoslav partisans in World War II." Whenever interpretations of documents by the WJC or by Herzstein were mentioned, Sciolino used the same devices: "At a news conference, the American Jewish Congress said that Mr. Waldheim . . . "; documents "bear a signature that the World Jewish Congress asserts is Mr. Waldheim's"; "Mr. Waldheim became sole head of the intelligence unit in the second half of 1944, according to Dr. Herzstein's interpretation of the documents," etc.

Sciolino reported Waldheim's claim that he had served only as a German-Italian interpreter, as well as the WJC's claim that the documents it was publishing exposed this as untrue. The WJC, she reported, alleged "that Mr. Waldheim, while serving as a first lieutenant in the Balkans, had responsibility for the interrogation of Allied prisoners, for making sure his fellow intelligence officers were loyal, and for unspecified special assignments." She also provided more details about the documents the WJC presented, including Herzstein's interpretations, which were summarized in language nearly identical to that of his statement. The same neutral style applied to reporting on WJC President Bronfman's request of Attorney General Meese to place Waldheim on the watch list. Waldheim's own position was quoted extensively. The charges, he was quoted as saying, were "pure lies and malicious acts." He had only acted as an interpreter and "had not taken part in fighting against Yugoslav partisans." The somewhat perfunctory character of these quotations here appears to reflect more Waldheim's unwillingness or inability to contribute details which could help clarify the significance of the documents than Sciolino's journalistic indolence. Waldheim merely recited what had become the ritual response to the publication of documents on his past: the whole thing was nothing other than "malicious" slander, virtually unworthy of comment.[32]

The skepticism of *NYT* journalists towards the WJC's interpretation of documents seems to have increased as time wore on. The WJC was repeatedly mentioned in the background information as the source of documents relating to Waldheim's past,[33] but the documents which the WJC published assumed a less prominent place in the reporting. Later, in April and May, the *NYT* frequently presented the results of research undertaken independently of the WJC, above all by Robert Herzstein, after he had severed his ties with the Jewish organization. Sciolino even seemed to have developed heightened reservations as to the reliability of the information the WJC provided.

In a summary article for the Sunday paper, for example, Sciolino wrote that "the World Jewish Congress released documents that, it said, identified him [Waldheim] as an intelligence officer with responsibility for questioning Allied prisoners and checking the loyalty of fellow intelligence officers." The same detachment was shown towards the Yugoslav daily *Vercernije Novosti*: "A Belgrade newspaper said Yugoslav War Crimes Commission documents listed Mr. Waldheim as a war criminal wanted in connection with 'murder, slaughter, shooting of hostages and ravaging of property by burning of settlements.'"[34] In another article which reported that Israel would get access to Waldheim's UNWCC file she wrote that "the World Jewish Congress said the documents showed that Mr. Waldheim was an intelligence officer."[35]

Similarly, in an article which appeared on 8 April, Sciolino reported that "the World Jewish Congress today made public a new set of documents that it said showed that the army group to which Mr. Waldheim was attached ordered deportations of Jews from Greece in 1944," but in the same piece pointed out that "the documents, found in the National Archives, do not contain any reference to Mr. Waldheim, who was a staff officer in Army Group E."[36] She was equally meticulous about a document which had served as a piece of evidence at the Nuremberg war crimes trials: this situation report from 1 August 1944 "carried what the Jewish group said was Mr. Waldheim's signature, although the Nuremberg translation termed the signature illegible."[37] As it happened, the initial on this document was indeed Waldheim's, but Sciolino's usage exemplified her critical distance from the interpretations the WJC had offered. Moreover, the context of the article itself indicated that for her, the document, if genuine, would only raise doubts about Waldheim's ostensible remark that he "took part in or knew of atrocities or deportations," not, however, that it represented a "corroboration" of the Yugoslav War Crimes Commission finding, as the WJC had claimed.[38]

Sciolino's most forceful exception to the WJC's reading of documents came in an article from 15 May on the press release of the WJC from the previous day, "New Papers Issued in Waldheim Case."[39] According to Sciolino, the documents "contribute to a growing body of evidence that he not only misrepresented his war record for 40 years, but also continues to issue statements that are at best misleading. But they do not prove that he either ordered or took part in the massacres."[40] Sciolino neglected to mention that the WJC had not claimed that Waldheim had taken part in any massacre, merely that the evidence thus far assembled would suffice to justify his indictment as an accessory to murder, should Yugoslavia choose to make its War Crimes Commission file on Waldheim public.[41] Instead, she quoted what she apparently thought was the contrary opinion of Robert Herzstein, who had previously been known above all as the expert which the WJC had consulted. "Other experts," Sciolino wrote, "said the documents did not bring Mr. Waldheim any closer to war criminality. 'He supplied the information on which the massacres were based,' said Robert E. Herzstein, professor of history at the University of South Carolina. 'He didn't order them. He didn't kill them himself.'" It was in this article that Sciolino abandoned what had until then been an *ideé fixe* of the *NYT's* coverage. "Mr. Waldheim has never denied knowing about massacres against Partisans," she wrote, "but has stated repreatedly that he neither ordered nor took part in any massacres."[42]

NYT journalists also reported (sometimes unfounded) criticism of the WJC's methods and its allegedly exaggerated accusations. Waldheim's own denials and dismissals of the WJC's charges were regularly reported, but sources not obviously partisan towards Waldheim were also quoted generously. For example, on 9 April Sciolino reported the opinions of unnamed "U.N. officials" who had criticized the WJC for revealing its documents in a piecemeal fashion in order to gain maximum publicity. Naturally, the WJC's explanation of why the documents were only published in batches was also reported, which conformed to the normal practice of offering space to those affected by criticism to counter it, and this irrespective whether it was Waldheim or his critics.[43] In an article published on 11 April, *NYT* journalist John Tagliabue quoted Ivan Hacker, head of the Jewish community organization in Vienna, who criticized the "form" of the WJC's investigation and disclosures. According to Hacker, the WJC had raised serious accusations without being able to prove that Waldheim had been involved in war crimes or atrocities.[44] Such criticisms, along with the WJC's reply, were also recorded in an unsigned article summarizing "unanswered questions" in the Waldheim case.[45]

Finally, Simon Wiesenthal's bitter and massive objections to the WJC were the subject of a long article. The famed Nazi hunter had previously figured prominently in an article in which he took pains to say that he was not defending Waldheim.[46] This time, however, wrote James M. Markham, Wiesenthal "accused the World Jewish Congress today of stirring antisemitic sentiment in his country through its campaign against Kurt Waldheim." Although he continued to criticize Waldheim, the article continued, "the 77-year-old Mr. Wiesenthal said Mr. Singer and the executive director of the World Jewish Congress, Elan Steinberg, had undone years of patient work for reconciling young Austrians and Jews by aggressively mixing in Austria's internal politics."[47] Markham also quoted Wiesenthal and Hacker, who both attacked the WJC for the same interview, and repeated without comment Wiesenthal's opinion that the *NYT* appeared to be "following the conclusions of the World Jewish Congress" that Waldheim was a war criminal, an opinion whose premise and conclusion were both false. Wiesenthal's views were balanced, not by Tagliabue's commentary, but by the reactions to Wiesenthal's charges of several prominent Jewish figures, such as Elie Wiesel and Henry Seligman of the American Jewish Congress, contained in an article which the *NYT* printed on the same page. However, no representative of the WJC was quoted in either article. Thus, on this occasion, when the *Times* coverage deviated somewhat from the normal practice of allowing those criticized a chance to answer, the benefit fell to the WJC's critics.[48]

The Accusations and the Evidence

In addition to the evaluations of documents and interpretations presented by the WJC, the *NYT* strove periodically to provide its readers with an overview of the various charges made against Waldheim, and the evidence on which they were based. On 11 April, for example, the *Times* published such a summary article by Elaine Sciolino entitled "Waldheim Uproar: Where It Stands." The article was written after Sciolino had read the so-called memorandum, "Dr. Kurt Waldheim on Recent Allegations Levied Against Him," which Waldheim's son Gerhard had circulated to the press,[49] which meant that she was in possession of the most up-to-date version of Waldheim's defense. The article itself took the form of a series of questions followed by answers she felt the evidence merited.

She introduced the piece by reporting that Waldheim had represented his military service as ending after his leg injury in 1941 in his previous biographies. Documents which the WJC had published showed, on the contrary, that he had served as a staff officer in an army unit "that fought brutal campaigns against Yugoslav partisans and took part in a large scale deportation of Greek Jews." Her stated point of departure was one even Waldheim himself would later come to acknowledge, namely, that he had not been completely forthcoming about his military past.[50] The first question she posed was whether Waldheim had been "a member of the Nazi Party?" "No evidence has come to light that he ever joined the Nazi Party," she answered. "But according to documents found in the Austrian archives, as a 20-year-old student at the Consular Academy in Vienna, Mr. Waldheim was enrolled on April 1, 1938, in the Nazi student union, about three weeks after Hitler annexed Austria. On Nov. 18, 1938, Mr. Waldheim was enrolled in a mounted unit of the SA, the paramilitary Nazi organization known as the Brownshirts." Sciolino reported that Waldheim had "acknowledged that he was enrolled in these two groups," but stated that he did not consider himself an active member.

After summarizing the version of his biography Waldheim had publicly presented until March 1986, Sciolino then asked, "What are the charges against Mr. Waldheim?" "The first charge," she answered, "is that Mr. Waldheim was not completely candid about his past. The second charge is that after the war Mr. Waldheim was wanted by Yugoslavia as a war criminal for taking part in reprisals against civilians." The formulation of the first allegation is charitable, the second beyond dispute, unless one claims that the Yugoslav War Crimes Commission file itself was a forgery. Then followed a summary of the state of knowledge at the time of writing:

> According to German war documents found by the World Jewish Congress, from 1942 to 1945 Mr. Waldheim was a first lieutenant in the Balkans, including duty with Army

> Group E, where he was responsible for various intelligence duties. His duties included appraisals of the enemy, reports concerning operations, the questioning of prisoners and personnel matters. An intelligence report signed by Mr. Waldheim on July 2, 1944, says that "after the burning down of numerous houses, in the face of our forces, the bandits," a name for partisans, withdrew, although it does not specify who set the houses afire. Other German army documents show that Mr. Waldheim was present at high-level staff meetings, where he is repeatedly described as a lead-off speaker concerning the situation in the Balkans. The context suggests that under these circumstances, he would have been conversant with at least the broad lines of Army Group E's many operations.

As an example, Sciolino referred to a document from 9 August 1944, in which Waldheim reported on the success of "Operation Viper." Apart from some insubstantial errors,[51] Sciolino's summary conforms to the state of knowledge at that time, and she at no time made any charges which could not muster some documentary support.

Army Group E, she wrote, which was "under the command of Gen. Alexander Loehr, an Austrian who was executed as a war criminal," "committed brutal reprisals against civilians after German soldiers were killed by Yugoslav guerillas" and "took part in the mass deportation of Greek Jews and burned villages." Her separation of what was known about the atrocities committed by Army Group E and the charges against Waldheim suggests that Sciolino wished to avoid amalgamating the two. Although she mentioned Waldheim's King Zvonimir medal (which she mistakenly reported as his only decoration during the war),[52] there was no implication of Waldheim's personal involvement (other than his knowledge of them) in the measures attributed to Army Group E. Indeed, she failed to mention the campaign in which Waldheim had been awarded the Zvonimir decoration (in western Bosnia, around the Kozara mountain range), in which thousands of civilians were killed or deported.

In answering the question, "What does Mr. Waldheim say to the recent charges?" Sciolino offered an extensive synopsis of the "Memorandum" which Waldheim himself had commissioned. "Mr. Waldheim now acknowledges that he served with the German Army in Yugoslavia and Greece from April 1942 to the end of the war in 1945," she wrote. "He has revised his official biography to include that information." Later, she reported that Waldheim had "denied that he took part in atrocities against Yugoslav partisans or directed the questioning of prisoners, [and] repeated that all of his duties were as a noncombatant staff officer. He said he largely functioned as a German-Italian interpreter, although he acknowledged that he compiled data submitted by the operational commands and occasionally took part in daily staff meetings where these matters were discussed. He said he was unaware of the deportations of Jews from Greece."[53] She also quoted Gerhard Waldheim's dismissal of the credibility of the chief witness in the Yugoslav file, Johann Mayer, "an Austrian clerk who worked with Mr. Waldheim in Army Group E." Rather than offering an opinion on whether Waldheim was a war criminal, Sciolino described the origins of the charges against Waldheim and the authorities who had made them:

> Mr. Waldheim was wanted as a war criminal by the Yugoslav War Crimes Commission after the war. According to Yugoslav documents, Mr. Waldheim was wanted in connection with "murder, slaughter, shooting of hostages and ravaging of property by burning of settlements." It described Mr. Waldheim as "in hiding" and his extradition as "mandatory." Yugoslavia sent a copy of its report, dated Dec. 25, 1947, to the 17-member United Nations War Crimes Commission. That commission reviewed the evidence and concluded that Mr. Waldheim should be accused of "murder, putting to death of hostages." He was given an "A" listing, which was reserved for those war criminals against whom the commission believed prima facie evidence had been presented and whom it believed should be delivered for trial.

This passage presents the history of the Yugoslav file as accurately as it could have been at that time. Waldheim's own "Memorandum," for example, had no better explanation of it. The one really problematic formulation in this passage has to do with Sciolino's description of category "A" listings. Persons against whom there is prima facie evidence of criminal activity are, until an acknowledged legal authority pronounces them guilty or innocent, merely suspected of having committed war crimes. Describing suspects with an "A" listing simply as "those war criminals," as Sciolino did, dissolves precisely the distinction between between alleged and convicted which ought under all circumstances to be maintained. The linguistic imprecision which Sciolino exhibited, however, seems to have been taken over from the *Odluka,* the CROWCASS and the UNWCC files themselves.[54] Finally, Sciolino mentioned that Yugoslavia had never pursued Waldheim as a suspected war criminal after the war, and that the current government had not given any explanation of the circumstances of the file. She considered it a "mystery" why the documents about Waldheim's past had surfaced just now, but suggested that it was probably related to the race for the Austrian presidency. The article closed with Waldheim's reiteration that the initial charges were the doings of people who opposed his candidacy.[55]

This report from 11 April indicated the quality and the general tone of the later *NYT* coverage of the Waldheim affair. Sciolino cleared Waldheim of association with the NSDAP, but correctly mentioned evidence which suggested his membership in the SA and the Nazi Student Union. The first "charge," that Waldheim had omitted significant parts of his biography, related to his credibility, and was substantiated by comparisons of Waldheim's public stance with documents which suggested otherwise, as well as by Waldheim's own revision of his public curriculum vitae. The accuracy of the second "charge," merely that Waldheim had been sought by Yugoslavia after the war as a suspected war criminal and was as a consequence listed with the UNWCC and in the CROWCASS, cannot be doubted. Not even Waldheim disputed the fact, merely the credibility of the principal witness against him, Johann Mayer, which Sciolino duly reported.[56] In addition, she mentioned evidence which significantly weakened the significance of the Yugoslav file itself. With hindsight it is possible to notice several mistaken assumptions or errors of fact in Sciolino's reporting. Judged by the standards of what was then known, however, this report is essentially accurate and as balanced as could have been expected.

Related Aspects of the Waldheim Affair in the *New York Times*

Between the WJC's press conference on 25 March and the second round of the election in Austria, the *NYT* reported far more frequently on the Waldheim affair. The main points of interest seem to have been Waldheim's past and the effects this might have had on his activities as secretary general of the United Nations.[57] The newspaper described newly discovered documents[58] and commissioned historians to investigate Waldheim's wartime service.[59] The *Times* also reported on the controversy surrounding the publication of Waldheim's UNWCC file[60] and on the investigation of the OSI in the Justice Department and OSI-head Neal Sher's recommendation to place Waldheim's name on the watch list.[61] Waldheim's denials and counter-attacks received the *Times's* attention,[62] as did his later concessions, apologies and the alterations in his biography.[63] In addition to Waldheim himself, the *NYT* also gave ample space to the public efforts of defenders of Waldheim (such as the former Austrian Foreign Minister Karl Gruber and Waldheim's son Gerhard) to counter the accusations made against the former U.N. Secretary General.[64] The paper also exhibited a growing interest in the election campaign in Austria as the first round approached.[65]

Austria and Its Past

An article written by John Tagliabue in April, "A Tense Time Now for Jews of Vienna,"[66] dealt with the effects the discussion over Waldheim's past was having on the Viennese Jewish community. He described the intensification of the election campaign after the first disclosures and added that "the charges and countercharges have opened old wounds and renewed bitter discussions. The terms used now are whether Mr. Waldheim, in glossing over his wartime past, was not somehow representative of a generation of Austrians who passed from subservience to the Nazis to postwar posterity [sic] with what appeared to be little introspection or regret." Tagliabue's formulation of this issue reads like a paraphrase of the statement, which he quotes, from Fritz Molden, prominent member of the Austrian resistance, former agent of the Office of Strategic Services, and, in the spring of 1986, a well-known supporter of Waldheim. "There was a disadvantage," Molden had told Tagliabue, for "while the Germans were forced to face the past, and there was Nuremberg, the Austrians immediately felt themselves as liberated . . . [the Allies] laid a cloak over all Austria. . . . It's clear to me that it was a grave misfortune, because we were never forced, as the Germans were, to face up to ourselves." Other aspects of Austria's postwar history that Tagliabue mentioned in his article, such as the 500,000 former Nazi party members who were initially disenfranchised and then reintegrated into the republic and all political parties and the former Nazis in the first government of Bruno Kreisky, etc., are commonplaces of political debate in Austria, and Tagliabue's source for this could easily have been Molden as well, though any one of dozens of historians or journalists would have said the same.

Molden was also a source for other articles dealing with the subject "coming to terms with the past." In Molden's opinion, as he told Elaine Sciolino in a telephone interview, Waldheim was part of a wartime generation in Austria which had "subconsciously misled themselves and their own children and the world by pushing a lot of things that happened 40 years ago under the nearest carpet." "In that era," he continued, "that was considered the honorable thing to do. . . . In a way, we are guilty for not cleaning up the mess in 1945."[67]

Similar formulations were also to be found in an article by James M. Markham published the following day for the Sunday edition. In this report, Markham described his impressions of the election campaign in light of Austrian history. "Mr. Waldheim's grudging acknowledgment of his role as a German staff officer—and the angry, xenophobic reaction of many of his compatriots—have illuminated a reluctance among Austrians to accept their historical responsibilities," he wrote. "Many Austrians share an interest in forgetting. Because of its 'first victim' status, enshrined in the Allies' Moscow Declaration of 1943, Austria was spared reparations and paid little to Jews and other Nazi victims. 'De-Nazification' was perfunctory and truncated by the advent of cold war. By 1949," he concluded, both "the People's Party and Socialists were wooing former Nazis, who founded their own organization, which became the Freedom Party, now a junior partner in the Socialist-led Government."[68] In another article, Markham quoted Waldheim's view that "this congress [WJC] tries to ruin the reputation of a whole generation. . . . We were not doing anything but our duty as decent soldiers. We were not criminals but decent men who faced a terrible fate."[69]

Reference to the historical symbolism of Waldheim's candidacy was not the product of any journalist's imagination at the *NYT,* but to a large extent had been promoted by Waldheim himself. It remains anyone's privilege to criticize or even reject the synoptic version of Austrian history presented in these articles. However, the interpretation appears to have been based for the most part on the statements of Austrians themselves, and the most frequently quoted source was Fritz Molden. At the same time, Waldheim's own interpretation of the historical dimension of his candidacy was clearly and prominently represented. In the main, the *NYT* reporters who wrote about Austrian history avoided crude generalizations, but the vocabulary they employed, ascribing to the collective "Austrians" characteristics which "a people" could only metaphorically possess, was not without its problems. Yet this does not stand out as a special attribute of the *NYT* reports on the Waldheim affair, but is merely an unfortunate element of much contemporary political discourse.

The Austrian Presidential Election Campaign

This tension in the *NYT's* reporters' assumptions about politics in general and Austrian political culture in particular tended to be reflected in their handling of the electoral campaign itself. On the one hand, the emphasis in the reports was on the putative impact of the international controversy over Waldheim's past on his electoral chances. It would also have been surprising if the slogan of the Waldheim campaign, "We Austrians will elect whom *we* want!" had not found a corresponding echo in the *Times's* reports on the election. At the same time, however, the Austrian internal political aspect of the electoral contest was not neglected, as the articles by James Markham illustrated.

Markham reported, for example, that Waldheim owed part of his advantage over his principal opponent, the Socialist former health minister Kurt Steyrer, to the defiant reaction of "the Austrians" to the presumed "threats" of Israel Singer and Elan Steinberg of the WJC. As Waldheim himself was quoted as saying, "To tell the Austrians if you elect Waldheim you will have six difficult years—this is interference in the domestic affairs of a country."[70] Two weeks later, shortly before the first round of the election, Markham wrote that "the conservative People's Party has consistently portrayed Mr. Waldheim as the victim of a 'campaign' nourished by the Socialist Party and supported by the World Jewish Congress." But, he added, "although fresh documents about Mr. Waldheim's war record receive considerable attention in the United States, they have recently had a much smaller impact in Austria."[71]

In his windup report on the first round, moreover, Markham emphasized that in Austria, the Waldheim affair was an essentially different matter than in the United States, Western Europe and Israel. For many in these countries, he wrote, "the election has become something like a moral referendum on how Austrians weigh the accusations that Mr. Waldheim hid his service as a German Army staff officer in Greece and the Balkans and dissembled about what he knew of the deportations of Jews and the execution of anti-Nazi partisans." Markham also pointed out that in Austria, where partisan allegiances are stronger, the election had "a second dimension. For Mr. Mock's People's Party, the election of Mr. Waldheim is seen as a major step toward ending 16 years of socialist domination of Austrian politics and bringing about the kind of shift to the right that occurred in West Germany in 1982 when Chancellor Helmut Kohl came to power." Thus, it was also "the high political stakes riding on the election" which had "sharpened the passions unleashed by the swirl of accusations around Mr. Waldheim."[72]

Although Markham clearly saw the internal dimension as secondary, his report on the first round also underlined that "Waldheim's strong showing today marked a further erosion of the Socialist Party's hold on the country, which it has politically dominated for 16 years. The party, which now leads the coalition Government of chancellor Sinowatz, has been plagued by scandal and lackluster leadership." In this context, he wrote, "the accusations against him brought out a feisty streak, and he turned the issue of 'meddling in Austrian politics' to his domestic advantage."[73] This theme, that Waldheim's election was not merely a referendum over his past or an act of defiance against a foreign (Jewish) enemy, but represented a political contest with much riding on its outcome, as well as the view that this aspect was too little understood in the United States, was found consistently in Markham's reports.[74] Exactly how little Markham's reports were heeded may be seen by examining the *Times'* own editorials on the affair.

The OSI and the Watch List

The efforts of the WJC to have Waldheim placed on the Attorney General's watch list, which dated from 25 March 1986, received considerable attention in the *NYT*. The paper reported Bronfman's initial request, the OSI's decision to begin an investigation, as well as the U.S. government's request for access to Waldheim's UNWCC file. In this latter article, Elaine Sciolino described the role of the OSI as being "to track down, investigate and deport Nazi war criminals." The relevant law requires, she continued, that "anyone who assisted the Nazis in persecuting people because of their race, religion or political opinions can be denied a visa or deported."[75] Nearly identical formulations about the function of the OSI and legal framework for a watch list decision appeared in other articles.[76] Yet virtually every one of these was imprecise and misleading. As we have seen, the provisions of the Holtzman amendment do not require that the commission of crimes be proved to exclude or deport someone; prima facie evidence which supports the suspicion that someone was involved in the persecution of people "because of their race, religion or political opinions" suffices. No one can be brought to trial in the United States for suspected war crimes not committed on United States territory. Those who fall under the provisions specified in this amendment, however, may be denied entry visas to the United States, or, if they had fraudulently entered the country or had become naturalized citizens or both, may be stripped of this citizenship and deported.

The descriptions offered in several *NYT* reports, however, confuse most of these points. In the first place, it is slightly misleading to assert that one "can" be denied a visa or deported, since, apart from special exceptions for "national security" reasons, those who fall under the conditions spelled out are required to be excluded. Moreover, Elaine Sciolino's phrase that the purpose of the OSI is "to track down, investigate and deport Nazi war criminals," obscures significant evidentiary distinctions and assumes a trial procedure by a recognized court at which someone suspected of crimes had been convicted. Yet precisely such a procedure cannot, under existing laws, take place in the United States, while the evidentiary requirements of the Holtzman amendment are significantly, one might say qualitatively, less stringent. Sciolino's usage, if taken literally, would in effect abolish the presumption of innocence for anyone placed on the watch list under the terms of the Holtzman amendment. This would be inadvisable, for while it is certainly true that all convicted war criminals would fall under the stipulations of the Holtzman amendment, not all who appear on the watch list under the terms of this law must be war criminals.

The contrasting cases of Kurt Waldheim and Andrija Artukovic again illustrate this point. Artukovic was, under the provisions contained in the immigation law, deported to Yugoslavia, where he stood trial and was convicted of war crimes. It is, however, technically only on the basis of the judgment of the Yugoslav court that one may properly refer to Artukovic as a "war criminal" (as opposed to suspected, alleged, etc.). Kurt Waldheim, on the contrary, has been tried by no judicial authority. He was investigated by the OSI and on its recommendation was placed on the watch list because the OSI found that his activities while stationed in the Balkans amounted to assistance to or participation as defined in the Holtzman amendment, not, however, because he was a "war criminal," as Sciolino's wording would imply.

That Sciolino's failing was not an isolated aberrance is confirmed by an article written by Philip Shenon on OSI-head Neal Sher's initial recommendation to place Waldheim on the watch list. "Mr. Sher's office," Shenon wrote, "is responsible for tracking down and deporting Nazi war criminals."[77] In addition to the difficulties with this formulation mentioned above, however, Shenon compounded his error by introducing an additional irrelevant point: the OSI's ostensible function, to "deport war criminals," had absolutely no bearing on Waldheim, who would have to be barred from entering. Shenon also recorded the OSI's reasoning: "Mr. Sher asserted that war records showed Mr. Waldheim was a 'special missions staff officer in the Intelligence and Counterintelligence branch' of the German Army's Group E, which was involved in reprisals against civilians in the Balkans." It is impossible to tell from Shenon's article whether Sher actually meant that Waldheim's mere membership to the Ic/AO department of Army Group E sufficed to place him on the watch list, and Sher gave a second reason, that the photograph of Waldheim at Podgorica airport "contradicted" his claim "that he was not involved in Operation Black,"[78] though Sher did not specify the nature of the participation. In any event, the OSI had far sounder reasons one year later when the decision to place Waldheim on the list was taken.[79] Be that as it may, if one assumed that the task of the OSI was to track down "Nazi war criminals," then would it not follow that by his recommendation, Sher had merely been carrying out this obligation, namely, that he had "tracked down" a "Nazi war criminal?" Sher, of course, made no such claim, but Shenon's phrasing strongly suggested just such a conclusion, which in Waldheim's case would have been without foundation.

At the same time, corresponding to the normal practice, Shenon quoted contrary or qualifying opinions, such as Waldheim's denial that he had served in the *Abwehr* (counter-intelligence) section.[80] He also reported that the Austrian President, Rudolf Kirchschläger, had concluded that the documents he had been shown would not justify an indictment of Waldheim on war crimes charges. Finally, a spokesman for the Justice Department was quoted as saying that Sher's recommendation "certainly does not represent department policy." In other articles, moreover, the Attorney General's office indicated its official distance from Sher's report even more strongly.[81] It is difficult to assess the effect of such an article on a reader. Even if one accepted the implied equivalence between entry on the watch list and "Nazi war criminal," the very insistence of Justice Department spokespeople that Sher's proposal had not been adopted could have partially annulled Sher's conclusions.

In its reporting on the OSI investigation, the *NYT* failed to report accurately the legal framework within which such a decision would be taken, as well as what counted as evidence. In addition, it failed to employ formulations which would have avoided any conflation of watch list and "Nazi war criminal." Finally, it neglected to submit Sher's report and the conclusions he reached to scrutiny by experts competent to do so. Consequently, although in other places *Times* reporters took steps to counter hasty inferences about Waldheim's possible criminal conduct, these reporters must bear some of the responsibility if their readers drew such inferences on the basis of the information they received from the *NYT* on the Justice Department investigation.

Waldheim's United Nations War Crimes Commission File

From the moment that it learned of its existence,[82] the *NYT* reported regularly and extensively on the efforts of various governments to obtain Waldheim's UNWCC file or to have it made public. The circumstances surrounding Waldheim's file were both exceptional and ironic: a dossier believed to contain information on possible criminal activities of a former U.N. Secretary General was stored in an archive which the United Nations administered and access to which was strictly controlled. This fortuity alone would have occasioned great interest in its publication. There was, however, some confusion in the United States about which authority was entitled to do what with the UNWCC files. The reporting of the *NYT* thus must be seen in light of these factors and judged according to the light it shed on them. Here the paper's journalists acquitted themselves well.

In his initial article, Stephen Engelberg reported both that a UNWCC file must exist and quoted Alan Ryan, former head of the OSI, to the effect that the United Nations had refused access to Justice Department investigators, which the United Nations disputed.[83] In an article published on 2 April, Elaine Sciolino mentioned that several politicians in the United States had demanded the immediate publication of Waldheim's file, but added, citing the official history of the UNWCC, that under the terms of the agreement by which the United Nations had agreed to house these files, they "may be inspected and used only for official United Nations purposes."[84] Only three such files had been delivered since 1948: those of Adolf Eichmann, Klaus Barbie and Josef Mengele. Francois Guiliani, spokesman for U.N. Secretary General Perez de Cuellar, was quoted as saying, "only governments can request access to the files, and no government has requested access to Mr. Waldheim's file since revelations about his war record first came to light several weeks ago."[85]

In this article, therefore, the demands of various United States senators and members of the House of Representatives, among others, were shown to be impermissible, not because of any conspiracy to protect Waldheim, but by the provisions contained in the agreement giving the United Nations administrative control over the files. Similarly, the claim that the United States had been unable to inspect the files was "balanced" by the U.N.'s flat denial. The mention of Eichmann, Barbie and Mengele served merely to underline the U.N.'s desire to avoid fishing expeditions, not, however, to draw any comparisons between these three and Waldheim. That Waldheim was only the fourth person, after such notorious cases as Eichmann, Barbie or Mengele, whose past could be clarified by his UNWCC file, appears to have been a complete coincidence. The evidence strongly suggests that it was attributable either to ignorance of the archive in which these documents were stored or to lack of sustained interest on the part of the relevant governments to investigate suspected war criminals.[86] Of course, this was small consolation for Waldheim, who could not prevent his being mentioned in connection first with Eichmann, Barbie and Mengele and later with Alois Brunner and Hermann Klenner (GDR member of the U.N. Human Rights Commission whom Israel suspected of having a shady past). The point which they had in common, however, related exclusively to the accident that they all had or might have had UNWCC files.

The conditions under which the UNWCC files may be examined, as well as the history of the War Crimes Commission itself, were covered in two longer articles. Elaine Sciolino, who wrote them, relied heavily on the official history of the UNWCC. The Commission existed from 1943 to 1948 in London, she reported in an article published on 10 April 1986, in order to collect evidence from governments of member states of war crimes, to scrutinize the allegations made by these governments against those suspected of having committed these crimes, and then to inform the governments "where the material available appeared to disclose a prima facie case." The Committee on Facts and Evidence examined, according to the history cited by Sciolino, "whether there appeared to be sufficient evidence to warrant the listing of the persons charged as war criminals in order that they might be detained and prosecuted by the member governments." Waldheim's case, she continued, was given an "A" designation, which "was reserved for those war criminals . . . whom the committee believed should be delivered up for trial." Waldheim's UNWCC file was based on documents assembled by the Yugoslav War Crimes Commission, which "said Kurt Waldheim was wanted for 'murder, slaughter, shooting of hostages and ravaging of property by burning of settlements.'" She stressed, however, that "Waldheim was never detained, or prosecuted as a war criminal." Apart from providing several new details on the history of the UNWCC, Sciolino's article goes some way to explaining why Waldheim's UNWCC file *ceteris paribus* should have cast such suspicion on the former secretary general. Sciolino assumed that the Committee on Facts and Evidence (a body whose work was not self-evidently suspect) had examined both the accusations and the evidence against Waldheim collected by the Yugoslavs. On the basis of this check, it recommended that Waldheim be listed in the "A" category, reserved for those suspects who "should be delivered up for trial." As the research of Robert Herzstein has shown, however, the UNWCC did not follow this procedure rigorously in Waldheim's case, and the Yugoslav War Crimes Commission itself seems not to have acted in good faith in assembling evidence.[87] At the time Sciolino was writing, however, there was no reason to have doubted that the procedure described in the official history had been followed with Waldheim's file. Given that the charges in the UNWCC file related to precisely the period of his military service which Waldheim had kept hidden for forty years, it should have come as no surprise that the story was seen as potentially explosive, and that the mere existence of such a file would cast Waldheim in a somewhat unfavorable light. The passages Sciolino quoted from the UNWCC file and the Yugoslav finding also confirm that the careless usage of the words "war criminal" to describe those who were really only suspected of criminal activity originated in the United Nations and Yugoslav documents themselves, rather than in the minds of the *NYT's* journalists.

Two days later, Sciolino reported again on the background of the UNWCC file.[88] She summarized both the allegations and the evidence against Waldheim in the Yugoslav Odluka. This latter consisted primarily of the testimony of Johann Mayer, Karl Heinz Egberts-Hilker, and Marcus Hartner, three of the principal witnesses who provided testimony in Waldheim's file.[89] The only passage Sciolino quoted from this testimony was Hartner's opinion that Waldheim "rejected National Socialism more because of religious and conservative reasons than because of social or scientific reasons." Immediately after quoting Hartner's statement, Sciolino summarized Waldheim's explanation of the Stip-Kocane events contained in "Memorandum," as well as his contentions that Egberts-Hilker was unknown to any surviving staff officer of Army Group E and that Mayer had not served in the Ic/AO department.[90] Thus, apart from the sloppy wording which could obscure the boundaries between "suspected war criminal" and "war criminal" per se, the reporting of the *NYT* on the *Odluka* and the UNWCC file contained no evidence of inordinate bias against Waldheim. On the contrary, Sciolino cited not only Waldheim's own statements, but also exculpatory evidence contained in the *Odluka* itself.

Waldheim and Israeli Politicians

It seems obvious that the Israeli government would have shown a great deal of interest in the possible criminal past of someone who had served under Alexander Loehr, believed to have been the German Army general most involved in the deportation of Jews. Israeli officials' efforts, reported in the *Times,*[91] were directed predominantly towards gaining access to Waldheim's UNWCC file, although various Israeli politicians also commented on different aspects of the Waldheim affair. Shimon Peres, for example, then prime minister, demanded that the United Nations make the Waldheim file public.[92] Since only governments were allowed access to such files and no other government had until then requested the file, Peres said, the Israeli government had demanded the file.[93] Peres justified his government's action partially because of the large amount of interest in the United States, but Benjamin Netanyahu, then Israel's ambassador to the United Nations, emphasized the intrinsic seriousness of the matter. "On the basis of this file," he was quoted as saying, "there is no way this matter can be put to rest. . . . There is clear need for further comprehensive investigation."[94]

On 3 May, the *NYT* reported the remarks of the then Israeli Foreign Minister Yitzhak Shamir at a press conference he held while passing through New York. Shamir declared that Waldheim's election as president would be a "real tragedy," but refused to be drawn on the question whether he would be reluctant to visit Austria if Waldheim won. In his opinion, Waldheim would never have been elected secretary general of the United Nations had his past been known, and he said Israel's priority was to discover whether "all these suspicions" were true. Although not a judge himself, Shamir said, "you can't deny that all the indications and all the information we are getting every day are leading in one direction: the direction of accusing him of being in the Nazi camp." Elaine Sciolino, who filed the report, wrote that Israel was itself investigating Waldheim's wartime service and that it had called on the United Nations to make all UNWCC files public. On 5 May, the *NYT* published an AP dispatch from Tel Aviv, which was attached to the main article reporting on the results of the first round of the presidential election, in which Waldheim fell just short of an absolute majority. Israel's deputy foreign minister, Moshe Ahrens was, according to AP, "shocked" by the outcome. "It has been 40 years since the Holocaust," he was quoted as saying, "and we had believed that the German and Austrian nations were making a very serious effort to rehabilitate themselves. [The results were] shocking, not just for every Jew but for every civilized person." The placement of this article suggests that Ahrens's statement—the only from an Israeli politician—was viewed by the *Times* editors as just one more comment from an interested party.

Three weeks later, the *NYT* carried a short report on Israeli Justice Minister Yitzhak Modai's statement that enough evidence had been assembled against Waldheim to indict him as an accessory to Nazi war crimes under Israeli law. Modai added that he had not seen any proof that Waldheim had been personally involved in criminal activity, "but we have enough proof that he, in his capacity as an intelligence officer in the German Army in the Balkans, would pass on information [that would] lead to liquidation actions," in other words, the identical grounds contained in the *Odluka*. Modai's remark was dismissed by a Waldheim aide as a "witchhunt."[95] It was not clear from this brief piece in the "Around the World" section how broadly the term "accessory to Nazi war crimes" was to be interpreted, but the position of the report indicates that, although the item possessed news value, it was not deemed worthy of a full report itself.

A far more prominent position was given to another article about Modai on 5 June, three days prior to the second round of the election, which carried the headline, "Israeli Aide Lacks Waldheim Proof," and the subtitle, "Justice Minister Says He Has No Firm Evidence Austrian Committed Atrocities." This article, by Thomas L. Friedman, could be read as a refutation of Modai by Modai himself. "The Israeli Justice Minister said today," the report began, "that the Government had been unable to turn up any firm evidence that Kurt Waldheim . . . personally took part in atrocities while he was an officer in the German army in World War II." Modai's remarks, according to Friedman, "were the first official confirmation that Israel, in its own research, had not been able to produce any evidence linking Mr. Waldheim personally to specific Nazi war crimes." Friedman's belief that this was the "first official confirmation" that there was no proof of Waldheim's personal involvement in war crimes, of course, contradicted the report of 23 May, in which Modai had stated that he had sufficient evidence to indict Waldheim as an accessory to war crimes, but no proof of his personal involvement. Friedman also quoted "political circles" who complained that Modai's admission could damage Israel's case against Waldheim only four days before the election, and referred to members of the Israeli government who were concerned about the lack of coordination in the response to the Waldheim affair. While Shamir called upon the Austrians not to elect the former Secretary General, Friedman continued, Shimon Peres was more reserved, apparently based on the belief (as it turned out, probably justified) that Waldheim's electoral chances could only improve if Israel were seen to be exerting pressure.

On the assumption that statements of Israeli politicians on Waldheim and the Waldheim affair were considered legitimate news items, there was no identifiable partiality against Waldheim in the reporting. If anything, the contrast of the two articles about Modai would appear to have tilted the balance in Waldheim's favor. Although the 5 June item contained nothing which had not already been reported on 23 May, if one did not read these two articles carefully, one could easily have concluded that the Israeli government had exonerated Waldheim from involvement in war crimes.

The Opinions of the *New York Times*

As was mentioned above, and is clear to its regular readers, the *NYT* observes recognizable boundaries in the structure and appearance, even if not always in the content itself, between news reports and editorial opinion. Indeed, it takes an effort not to notice these differences, because editorials always appear in the same place.[96] Editorials, moreover, do not conform to the rules and conventions which apply to news reports, for they openly and explicitly present the opinion of the editor(s) of the paper. They often attempt to provide a broader view of an issue beyond the day-to-day political wrangle, and equally frequently offer specific proposals for action (such as a new law or a candidate in an election). As might be expected, explicit argumentative strategies are employed in editorials which theoretically have no place in news articles themselves.

Between 4 March and 10 June 1986, the *NYT* published three editorials relating to Waldheim. The first appeared on 19 April, fully six weeks after the paper had first reported on the former secretary general's past. The title and first sentence of this editorial suggested that the immediate occasion for it was an article of 17 April. In this report, James M. Markham had written that Waldheim had "conceded for the first time that as a lieutenant in the German Army he was aware of atrocities committed against Yugoslav partisans, but he insisted that he had not been implicated in them." As we have seen, Markham's contention that Waldheim had never before conceded knowing of "atrocities" depended upon how one defined them. The editors, however, in this instance apparently based their own remarks on the contents of Markham's article, which stated that Waldheim had just then made the concession referred to in the editorial. The editorial carried the title "Kurt Waldheim Remembers," and addressed the question of Waldheim's damaged credibility and the consequences the editors believed Waldheim should draw from it.

> Kurt Waldheim now remembers that yes, he did prepare battlefield reports while serving as a German Army lieutenant in the Balkans. And yes, he was aware of atrocities

> and heard about measures against Jews; he knew Jews were taken to an unknown fate, but "I didn't know it was such a mass affair." World War II was a "nasty, dirty" conflict—German soldiers, too, were seized as hostages and executed. If Mr. Waldheim's memory is improving, his reputation is not.

After presenting its opinion that there were grounds for criticizing Waldheim independently of any direct interest in the Austrian presidential election itself, the editors wrote:

> By all accounts he retains a good chance to be elected president of Austria on May 4, notwithstanding his admission that he has long misrepresented his wartime role. But the people of Austria should understand the widespread concern. If Mr. Waldheim is not guilty of war crimes—and no one has proved that he is—why did he cover up the simplest biographical facts for all these years? Probably because he thought the world would never have him as Secretary General of the United Nations. But now mendacity, too, is indelibly part of his record.

The editorial emphasized that Waldheim was not guilty of war crimes, but considered his "mendacity" to be an ineffaceable stain on his reputation. But although they did not suggest that Waldheim remained silent to cover up a criminal past, the reason the editors advanced as to why Waldheim should have hidden his past "all these years" was imaginative indeed. Could the editors seriously have thought that Waldheim would have been planning his duplicity immediately after the war (for that is when it began) with an eye on a future candidacy for the post of U.N. Secretary General? The editorial conceded that Waldheim himself claimed to have a clear conscience, to have been an opponent of the Nazis and to have committed no war crimes, but considered it understandable why he would have found his service in the Balkans embarrassing. The brutality of the war in the Balkans, which was surpassed only by the mass murder of the Jews, the editors argued, would offer grounds enough. Finally, the *NYT* criticized the way in which Waldheim only acknowledged details of his past bit by bit. "Uglier even than Mr. Waldheim's deceptions," they concluded, "are his new attempts to portray conquerer and conquered as guilty of equal crimes. Mr. Waldheim has every right to try to rescue honor from the emerging record. But he can hardly blame the world for wishing he would go off and do it in private."[97]

The three accusations against Waldheim were, according to the editors of the *Times,* (1) that he had hidden his past, principally his service in the Balkans, for forty years; (2) that even now he had not come completely clean about this past, and only admitted things after documentary evidence made it impossible to deny them; and (3) that Waldheim had attempted to ameliorate his own situation by reversing the roles of victim and victimizer. This editorial explicitly rejected the idea that Waldheim was a war criminal, even though the existence of the Yugoslav and UNWCC files was known. These three criticisms sufficed, in the opinion of the *NYT* editors, to disqualify Waldheim for the office of Austrian president. Although they considered

Waldheim's honor severely compromised, they implicitly acknowledged the possibility of his reestablishing it.

It was not unusual for the *NYT* to offer an opinion on events in a foreign country, or even to express a preference for the outcomes of elections. However, the interest of the *NYT* in Waldheim was not dictated by its desire to endorse one of Waldheim's opponents. It is even probable that this was the first time the *NYT* ever published an editorial on a candidate in an Austrian presidential election. The context made clear that the significance of the Waldheim affair lay in the role Waldheim played in the international arena, as a former secretary general of the United Nations. It would have been rather unusual if the *NYT* had not offered an editorial opinion on an issue of this sort.

The *Times* printed two other editorials on Waldheim-related matters. The first of these, "Open the Waldheim File," published one week after the first round of the Austrian election, dealt with Waldheim's UNWCC file, which the editors wanted the United Nations to make public. By then, however, the editors had shifted away from the relative indifference towards the election they had exhibited in the first editorial. The main reason for opening Waldheim's file, they argued, was to assist Austrian voters in determining Waldheim's suitability for office. "Enough Austrian voters apparently were troubled by doubts about Kurt Waldheim's fitness to serve as their president to deny him his predicted majority in a first-round election." Austria thus has time "to ponder war-crimes charges against him, and crucial to any final judgment is hostile testimony contained in long-buried files kept at the United Nations."[98]

Austrian President Kirchschläger, the editors suggested, himself had found nothing incriminating in the documents shown him, and wished to leave the ultimate judgment to the Austrian voters. The UNWCC file, argued the *NYT,* could help them make this evaluation. Consequently, the *NYT* called on the United Nations to make the file public on its own initiative, and if they did not, then the U.S. government itself should do so. In order to protect persons still living who might be mentioned in the file from possible embarrassment, the *Times* proposed that a panel of jurists examine the file prior to its publication. "Opening these files," the editorial concluded, "would help Austrians make the symbolically fateful choice Mr. Waldheim's candidacy represents. It might also prod memories in a nation that was too quick to bury its complicities in Nazi aggressions and brutalities. Mr. Waldheim now admits to having lied to the United Nations about the extent of his services in Hitler's army. Inadvertently, he now offers the world organization a chance to reclaim the truth."[99]

This editorial assumed both that Austrians necessarily viewed the election exclusively as a moral referendum on Waldheim's past, and that their votes for or against Waldheim would represent a corresponding stand on this issue. It is true that Waldheim and the ÖVP both strove to reduce the election to these terms, though based on value judgments very different from those imagined by the *Times* editors. Yet the evidence suggests that these assumptions, which the editors of the *NYT* did not bother to demonstrate, were little more than wishful thinking. The election analysis of their own reporter James M. Markham offered little support to these beliefs.[100] In underlining their belief that Waldheim's candidacy had, after the results of the first round of the election were known, assumed a new symbolic significance, the *Times* editors employed an idiomatic shorthand which treated Austria as an undifferentiated whole, capable of acting (or not) as an historical subject. Although such a perception is common enough, its usage signified a specific ideological notion of politics and, moreover, was merely the mirror image of the Waldheim camp's own efforts to portray the criticism of Waldheim as a criticism of "Austria."

The third editorial dealing with the Waldheim affair within the timespan of this study, "Dutiful in Austria," appeared on 10 June 1986. It addressed the results of the Waldheim's election and its consequences. "Like Kurt Waldheim during Hitler's war," the article began, "a majority of Austrian voters have done what they took to be their patriotic duty. By a margin of 54 to 46, they elected Mr. Waldheim President, as if to exonerate all Austria of complicity in Nazi atrocities." Although the *Times's* own reporter James Markham had stressed that in Austria perhaps other factors might have been instrumental in deciding voting preferences,[101] for the editors the only relevant consideration was the idea that the election necessarily was (rather than ought to have been) a referendum on "Austria's" Nazi past. The editorial did concede that the office of president is "mainly symbolic," but criticized the Austrians for having "put a conspicuously flawed figure on their highest pedestal."[102]

The editorial summarized the *Times's* criticism of Waldheim. The editors believed that although no war crimes had been proved against him, Waldheim's suppression of his service in the Balkans and the alibis he offered in justification of it were detestable enough. However, they added, "Service in Hitler's army is not the issue; to think it is would impose the same doctrine of collective guilt the Nazis imposed on their victims." They cited the example of President Richard von Weizsäcker of the Federal Republic of Germany to show that it was not necessary for those burdened with the Nazi legacy to remain silent: Weizsäcker had found "moving, necessary words" to express his country's historical responsibility. "At no point in his charmed career," the editors argued, "has Mr. Waldheim, a former Secretary General of the United Nations, attained those moral heights. For all his eminence, he remains what he was in the Balkans, an adapting subaltern. That should not affect his eligibility to visit the United States, whose doors ought to remain open to all political figures. But it will certainly affect his welcome."

In this passage, the editors of the *NYT* seemed to suggest that Waldheim's principal failing was his inability to find the appropriate words to express the repentance which falls to Austria's lot. In any event, the editors plainly had no wish to identify themselves with those accusing Waldheim of war crimes: here, as in the earlier editorials, the issues were Waldheim's credibility and his moral aptness to serve as the president of Austria. In addition, they argued explicitly against preventing Waldheim from visiting the United States, what must be seen as an implicit riposte to those demanding that Waldheim be placed on the watch list.[103]

The "Op-Ed" Page: Columns on the Waldheim Affair

The columns which appeared on the "Op-Ed" page represented by definition the views of the author. Consequently, opinions expressed in these commentaries do not properly belong in any analysis of *NYT* editorial policy, except insofar as it might be reflected through the publishing of a disproportionate number of authors representing one position in a dispute to the detriment of others. As we have seen, in Austria during the election campaign little or no distinction was drawn between the various types of texts which the *NYT* printed: whatever appeared in the *Times* was ascribed to the paper's editorial line, and this, according to one prominent personality, was both "mendacious and vile." However hostile or contemptuous the tone of some authors critical of Waldheim (the overwhelming majority), none of them accused Waldheim of individual involvement in war crimes, and several emphasized the contrary. The moral outrage of those writing was perhaps selective or even hypocritical. Yet they did not overstep the boundaries of criticism which public figures in the United States normally face. Moreover, the longest such column, by Kurt Waldheim's son Gerhard, exhibited as little regard for accuracy or balance as those of the former secretary general's critics. This is, of course, an everyday experience for reflective readers of the Op-Ed page, but the systematic distortion by Waldheim and his supporters in Austria of this modest form of pluralism was all the more effective because they could portray the content of these colums as part of a *NYT* "campaign" against him.

Three of the columnists who write regularly to the *Times* contributed pieces mentioning or dealing with the Waldheim affair. Of the three, William Safire, Flora Lewis and Anthony Lewis, only Safire bears discussing in any detail, principally because he was frequently invoked as the example most illustrative of the distorted reporting in the *NYT*.[104] Safire, former speech writer for Richard Nixon, has long been known and admired or detested as a conservative columnist at the *Times* with a cultivated penchant for verbal overkill in unmasking perceived error in others. It was doubtless Safire's refined political and ethical percipience which placed Nixon's speeches on the cutting edge of moral good sense during his tenure in the White House, and has served Safire well since then. Safire also has a sensitive appreciation of the uses and abuses of the English language. But while his "On Language" features in the *Sunday New York Times Magazine* are nearly always informative and frequently entertaining, his regular "Essay" pieces are more likely to enrage (or inspire, according to taste) rather than to enlighten. His column, "Waldheim's Secret Life,"[105] was little different. Safire argued, fairly enough, that "Kurt Waldheim's entire postwar life has been a lie. For 40 years, including a decade undermining Israel as the United Nations' top official, he has pretended to be doing something else in another place when Nazis were shipping Jews to Auschwitz for extermination and murdering Yugoslav partisan hostages." Yet for Safire this seemed less important than which "nations knew of his [Waldheim's] past during his rise to power" or whether Waldheim had been "subject to blackmail." He offered some evidence which he believed suggested that the Yugoslavs or Soviets might have exercised influence on Waldheim, but left it at that.

Safire next asked whether it had been "wise" for the WJC to break the Waldheim story, since it could "play into anti-Semitic hands—and encourage bigots and long-time Nazi sympathizers to elect the man whom they now see as one of their own." His answer was no, because "sometimes practicality asks too much. The Waldheim candidacy is an outrage to Western values and a sickening referendum on nostalgia for Nazism." As remedies, Safire proposed a general boycott of the Salzburg Festival or banning Waldheim from visiting the United States. For Waldheim himself, Safire accorded no hope: had he been an honorable man, he would not have lived this lie. The Austrians themselves, on the other hand, could still redeem themselves. "They can resist the temptation to bait the Jews and please the Russians and stick it to the West. Or the nation that brought the world Adolf Hitler can, through the election of one of his secret followers, say to the world that it is proud of its most infamous son."[106]

In this column, Safire lived up to the reputation for subtlety of mind and depth of vision for which he has become famous. His colleagues on the *Times,* Flora Lewis and Anthony Lewis, did not quite conceive of the Waldheim election as a test of the mettle of western civilization, but both did stress the symbolic nature of the Waldheim candidacy. Anthony Lewis's two "Abroad at Home" columns[107] as well as Flora Lewis's "Foreign Affairs" piece[108] did not diverge notably from the position argued by the editorials in the *NYT,* and both shared the assumption that the issue in the election was for or against the Nazi past, even if they, unlike Safire, did not view Waldheim as a mere stalking horse for Adolf Hitler. Anthony Lewis, in his second column, "Austria, Look at Yourself," written after Waldheim's election victory, also proposed measures of protest to express individuals' "moral revulsion at the Austrians' choice."[109] Neither, however, went beyond the general framework which the *Times* editorials had outlined.

All three of the regular columnists for the *NYT,* then, found words to express their dislike of Waldheim ranging from the merely harsh to the objurgatory. In Safire's case explicitly, in the others more indirectly, this criticism of Waldheim elided with either a premonitory or *post factum* condemnation of "Austrian voters" or even "the Austrians" themselves. Despite the severity of their verbal assaults, however, none of them stated or implied that Waldheim had been involved in war crimes. Flora Lewis, in fact, referred to Waldheim as an insignificant figure, while Anthony Lewis expressly stated that there was no evidence that Waldheim had personally participated in atrocities.

The columns on the Op-Ed page included a variety of shades of opinion within a fairly circumscribed conceptual framework. Altogether, there were seven such guest columns, of which five were critical of Waldheim or "Austria," one favorable to Waldheim, and one addressed a procedural side issue. As with the columns by Safire and Flora and Anthony Lewis, opinions expressed in such contributions were not, or not necessarily, those of the paper's editors. Editorials, of course, can express similar or identical opinions to those offered on the Op-Ed page, but this would not alter the point.

The first such commentary to appear was entitled "Questions About Waldheim," by Robert Herzstein.[110] Herzstein, it will be recalled, was a recognized expert on the Wehrmacht and on war crimes,[111] had been employed as research consultant by the WJC prior to 25 March, and was responsible for the first significant find of documents relating to Waldheim's military career. His unique competence at that time would have assured him space on the Op-Ed page in any case. Herzstein's contribution posed three questions about the Waldheim affair, the most significant of which was the latter's possible relation with U.S. intelligence after the war.

Two articles appeared on the Op-Ed page on 15 May, and were presented as two individual views as to the implications of a Waldheim election victory. The first was co-authored by Marvin Hier and Abraham Cooper, both officials of the Simon Wiesenthal Center in Los Angeles. They recommended that Waldheim be barred from entering the United States, even though this might be seen as a "slap in the face" of a friendly country. What concerned them was not only Waldheim's untruths but also "the implication that they are accepted by his countrymen. Such acceptance suggests an indifference to the clearest manifestation of evil in the history of mankind—the Third Reich. Furthermore, it brings into focus the doctrine that seeks to heap the Nazis' crimes on the same pile with all wars of history while blurring the distinction between perpetrator and victim." By barring Waldheim, "the United States would signal the world on the eve of the 40th anniversary of the Nuremberg War Crimes Tribunal that, just as it will never be an advocate of collective guilt, it will never join forces with those whose arrogance promotes collective innocence." Since Hier and Cooper apparently equated head of state, country and people and inferred the possibility of moral action by this collective, it is not clear why they considered the United States, whose president Ronald Reagan had visited the Bitburg cemetery in West Germany accompanied by Chancellor Helmut Kohl, to be a superior moral authority. The idiom they employed, though common enough, was particularly ironic because one of Waldheim's "countrymen" who apparently accepted Waldheim's untruths was Simon Wiesenthal.

The accompanying article, by Amos Perlmutter, professor of political science and sociology at the American University, attempted to discuss the Waldheim campaign in light of Austrian history, especially antisemitism, but in the process he confused as much as he clarified. "Austria," he wrote, "may be one of the most consistently anti-Semitic countries in Europe. As much as music, gemütlichkeit and coffee cakes, anti-Semitism is a part of Austrian culture and it has been since the Hapsburg Empire, between the wars, in the Hitler era and the postwar years." He discussed the history of antisemitism in Austria, with particular focus on the figures Schönerer, Lueger, Hitler, the Austrian Heimwehr, the contribution of Austrians to the "Nazi war," etc. "The Waldheim affair," he argued, "has reopened these wounds and stirred up virulent anti-Semitism in Austria. It was as if the Austrian people, in seeing Kurt Waldheim accused, felt themselves accused along with him. Their reaction—their support for him and the hundreds of hate letters sent to Austrian Jews—was in itself a verdict of sorts." No one, least of all Perlmutter, "will be surprised if Mr. Waldheim is elected next month. His spirit clearly prospers in Austria."

Though it was important to call attention to this aspect of the Waldheim affair, Perlmutter's history lesson contained some errors and many over-generalizations (this is particularly true of his discussion of the Heimwehr), though such subtlety is not always possible in a short piece. Still, the logical acrobatics he performed cannot be explained by problems of space. The syllogism runs: In Austrian history there have been various kinds of antisemitism. The Jewish Community has received several hate letters. Ergo: "Austria may be one of the most consistently anti-Semitic countries in Europe." Perlmutter, however, curiously omitted the Catholic antisemitic tradition in his survey of antisemitism in Austria. Moreover, he seemed neither to have recognized any differences in the ways in which antisemitic beliefs had been or might be realized politically prior to and after 1945, nor to have accepted that these differences might have limited the political possibilities for carrying out anti-Jewish acts openly in contemporary Austria. Finally, his undifferentiated view of "the Austrian people," which "felt themselves accused along with him," could, at the time of his writing, at most have represented just under fifty percent of eligible voters, and then only on the condition that his assumptions about voting behavior were true. In sum, Perlmutter offered little more than an inversion of the Trapp family mythology, and, though less insidious, did not really assist in understanding the nature of appeals to antisemitic prejudice in a country where such attitudes are, at least officially, proscribed.[112]

The next contribution came from Harvard law professor Alan M. Derschowitz.[113] He did not deal directly with Waldheim's past, but merely proposed a way to ensure that Austrians could get the truth out about his past, namely, that Austrian voters "should demand that he submit to vigorous cross-examination by an independent counsel before the election." On 6 June, the *NYT* published two articles dealing with the Waldheim controversy. The longer of the two, indeed, the longest of any such contribution, "What Did Waldheim Do In The War? Why the Critics Are Unfair," was by Gerhard Waldheim. In this contribution, Gerhard Waldheim attempted to refute the most important accusations made against his father, but his article continued the strategy which had been pursued by the senior Waldheim of exaggerating or distorting the accusations of his unnamed "critics," introducing irrelevant points, and providing incomplete or misleading information. For example, Gerhard Waldheim argued that even Waldheim senior's "critics have had to admit that he was not involved personally in war crimes" and cited Simon Wiesenthal in support, but neglected to mention that the unnamed "critics" need not retract something they had not previously alleged. In the first instance, therefore, Waldheim junior "refuted" a charge not raised against his father from any serious quarter.

After disposing of the first issue, he set his sights on the two allegedly remaining: that Waldheim "was less than forthcoming about his wartime record, and the guilt-by-association charges—what did he know and what could he have done about it?" Gerhard Waldheim adduced misleading material that he believed supported his father's claims to openness about his past, but had no comment on evidence to the contrary. One example was Waldheim's official personnel form and official curriculum vitae in the Austrian foreign ministry. These, claimed Gerhard Waldheim, proved that his father had not suppressed his wartime service in Yugoslavia and Greece. What he neglected to add was that these documents were only made public, by his father, in March 1986, when they were shown to selected journalists in Vienna. Until then, these documents had not been accessible to the public. Since no one could have known what Waldheim had left out of a confidential questionnaire, no one had ever accused him of having denied his past in such documents. What others, among them the WJC, did claim, was that Waldheim had deliberately suppressed his Balkan service in the version of his past he had presented publicly. Thus, the evidence purporting to substantiate Waldheim senior's credibility turned out to be proof of very nearly the contrary.

Gerhard Waldheim was on slightly more solid ground in citing a passage of the German edition of his father's book *In the Eye of the Storm.* The German version mentioned that Waldheim was recalled to active duty, and that he was near Trieste when the war ended. For Gerhard Waldheim, Trieste was a clear reference to the "southeastern front," while the mention of Waldheim's service at the end of the war showed that his father had not intended to hide his later wartime service. In a certain respect Gerhard Waldheim was right: even though the reference was elliptical, Kurt Waldheim's public mention of his service at the end of the war, because it contradicted most other public versions of his past, could have been the stimulus for further investigation, and it was really not Waldheim's fault that no one followed up this hint with the necessary research until 1986.[114] At the same time, the correspondence with U.S. Congressman Stephen Solarz proved that Waldheim had attempted to mislead interested parties about his past. In a letter dated 26 November 1980, for example, Solarz wrote Waldheim asking for, among other things, "the names and numbers of the units you served in during the years 1939–1945? What were your specific responsibilities as an officer with these units?" Waldheim's reply of 19 December 1980 mentioned his service with the "45th Aufklärungsabteilung of the Wehrmacht" (i.e., reconnaissance unit), and then wrote "I myself was wounded on the eastern front and, being incapacitated for further service on the front, resumed my law studies at Vienna University where I graduated in 1944." No mention here of Trieste or the "southeastern front," no mention of any service in Army Group E, etc. It is curious that in his book Kurt Waldheim should have mentioned an area in Italy which he never in fact reached, but omitted places in Greece and Yugoslavia such as Arsakli, Pljevlja, Banja Luka, and Athens, where he was stationed for months at a time.

Gerhard Waldheim, even at this late date, failed to give a complete account of his father's various assignments. During the war, he wrote, his father "was an interpreter and was sometimes used in a liaison function to the Italian Army. He had no powers of command, no combat role of any kind, nor was he present at or in any way involved in atrocities against partisans or civilians." Absent from this description was the position which Waldheim exercised for the longest period of time, that of third *Ordon-*

nanzoffizier in the military intelligence department of Army Group E, a fact which had been established beyond doubt on 25 March 1986. Gerhard Waldheim challenged the credibility of Johann Mayer, the principal witness of the Yugoslav Odluka, attacked unnamed "researchers who were not military historians, who were unable to interpret military documents properly," but mentioned neither whom he meant nor which interpretations of what documents he was challenging. He ended by expressing regret at the "bad feelings" which had developed in the Jewish community because of the controversy surrounding his father, and quoted a platitudinous but troubling appeal from the former secretary general about the need to "learn from history" and to guard against a second Auschwitz by striving, "in the spirit of toleration and reconciliation, to forgive—but never to forget," a formulation which merely begged the question as to who is to be tolerant to whom and who should forgive whom for what.

The pendant to Gerhard Waldheim's piece was an article by Menachem Rosensaft, founder of the International Network of Children of Jewish Holocaust Survivors. If the former believed that his father's past had been above reproach, and had shown his "active support for the Jewish people" in word and deed, Rosensaft reached nearly opposite conclusions. In his contribution, "He Can't Be Exonerated Of His Guilt," Rosensaft contended that Waldheim's guilt was not personal involvement in crimes (as, for example, it would be with Adolf Eichmann, Josef Mengele or Klaus Barbie). "Kurt Waldheim belongs in a different category altogether, and he may or may not in fact have been a war criminal. But that hardly exonerates him of guilt for his participation in the absolute evil of the Hitler era." As a "willing and apparently enthusiastic servant" of Hitler and the Third Reich, moreover, even though not necessarily a war criminal, "he certainly was a Nazi soldier who—both by his actions and by his failure to protest even a single atrocity—endorsed all the reprehensible policies of the Hitler regime. As a result, he is no more a desirable member of society than were Mengele or Eichmann."

Rosensaft's judgment was a severe one. Since in history "there is virtually no such thing as simple or clear-cut responsibility," he argued, "Kurt Waldheim and everyone else who participated in any way in implementing the Nazi ideology are collectively responsible for the Third Reich's crimes against humanity. In matters of historical responsibility, no one is only a little bit guilty."

Rosensaft propounded a thesis of collective guilt (or responsibility, as he used the terms interchangeably) whose limits he himself seemed not fully to understand. At first he exempted Waldheim from personal guilt for crimes, naming Eichmann and Barbie as counter-examples, but went on to argue, on the basis of his conception of collective responsibility, that Waldheim was no less guilty than either of these. It is laudable that Rosensaft wished to contest every attempt to render the crimes of the Third Reich harmless and even understandable that he saw Waldheim's personal biography as symptomatic of the danger that the memory of the crimes against the Jews was being slowly erased. Yet his amalgamation of personal and collective guilt and his inability even to acknowledge the category "opportunist," made it exceedingly difficult to take seriously his moral injunction against anyone "who participated in any way in implementing the Nazi ideology."

The final article from the Op-Ed page was by Edgar Bronfman, and appeared on 15 June with the title "Shame on Austria."[115] Bronfman also saw Waldheim's election as a "symbolic amnesty for the Holocaust" on the part of the Austrians, but immediately qualified this statement by noting that forty-six percent of the voters did not vote for Waldheim. Repeating the accusations against Waldheim, Bronfman rehearsed the series of "lies" Waldheim had told. "Yes, it is a fact that for 40 years he lied about his past . . . about his status in Hitler's Army . . . about where he served during World War II—with an army group in the Balkans that conducted murderous reprisals against Yugoslav partisans and civilians and that sent thousands of Greek Jews to their deaths in Nazi camps . . . [and] about what functions he performed during his military service." He was careful, however, not to identify the WJC itself with charges of criminal behavior. "It is not the World Jewish Congress that has accused Mr. Waldheim of war crimes; it is the United Nations War Crimes Commission that has done so."

After discussing the background to the UNWCC file, Bronfman mentioned some of the more disquieting features of the election campaign, especially the antisemitic tone which was struck, and defended the role of the WJC as having ensured that the Austrians confront the Nazi era. The Moscow declaration, which had characterized Austria as a victim of rather than willing participant in National Socialism, was regrettable and meant that "there was never a wholehearted de-Nazification program there. The world might well conclude that had such a program been in effect, the Austrian people would never have been presented with a Waldheim candidacy." It is, of course, open to question whether the absence of an effective de-Nazification is traceable solely to a formulation in the Moscow declaration, and it is misleading to assert that a more thorough de-Nazification would have discovered Waldheim's "Nazi past" and thereby precluded his candidacy for the Austrian presidency. As we have seen, Waldheim was investigated and cleared by the de-Nazification authorities after the war, who obviously had a very different understanding of "Nazi" than did Bronfman. At the same time, although he made sometimes inapposite generalizations about "Austria," Bronfman took pains to distinguish between Austrians who had voted for and those who had voted against Waldheim.

"Balance" in the *New York Times*

The self-inspired objectives of the *NYT* to provide a balanced version of "all the news that's fit to print," are never absolute and must always be seen in relation to the self-imposed determinants of legitimate or reasonable debate which characterize the editorial policies of major U.S. newspapers and magazines. It was not our objective to examine all items of the *NYT* on the Waldheim affair for all possible biases they might contain, but merely to investigate the broader intellectual framework of the paper's reporting and editorial policy. Certain assumptions in the *Times's* reporting and in its editorials helped mold the debate on Waldheim by defining its terms and norms. Our main concern was to investigate whether and to what extent an additional element of bias existed, and how far this might have been traceable to factors external to the intrinsic difficulties which the story itself presented, i.e., whether and to what extent these terms and norms represented merely so many constricting presumptions. Having examined the news reporting and editorials in detail, it is possible to draw a balance of the *Times's* "balance."

We should first recall exactly what confronted reporters without rigid preconceived notions about Waldheim's "Nazi" and "criminal" past. Documents on various aspects of Waldheim's past were being made public piecemeal and unsystematically. Under the best of circumstances, any competent interpretation of them would have demanded extensive background knowledge of the Nazi state and party structures, the various paths of command of the German Army in the Balkan theater and the theory and practice of the Nuremberg War Crimes Tribunal. Waldheim himself labelled every attempt to verify independently bits of information about his previously hidden past a "slander," while his own counterinterpretations were at best confusing, and frequently disingenuous.

A comprehensive overview of the material on Waldheim was nearly impossible. Consequently, journalists were left to their own devices, to inform themselves of the issues and relevant background information, and, if they were so inclined, to guard against any overt biases. Within the conceptual framework in which the Waldheim affair came to be debated (with Waldheim's own tacit consent), the *NYT* reporters by and large adhered to the conventions of balance to which newspapers in the United States aspire. While the *Times's* reporters frequently missed opportunities to reach beyond the merely competent, their stories were not tendentiously anti-Waldheim. In the course of the three months of intense reporting, journalists writing on Waldheim became gradually more informed, though they remained hampered by certain assumptions which had emerged at the beginning of the controversy. (For example, the assumption that Waldheim had been in Salonika during the deportations was never really abandoned, although the evidence clarifying it was available from mid-April, 1986.) The reporting on the election campaign itself showed a sophisticated appreciation of the situation in Austria which, though not faultless, provided enough information for a balanced judgment of the domestic political significance of the electoral contest.

Allegations from all quarters were independently confirmed, expert advice was sought, and contrary opinions were cited. Reports on Waldheim's Nazi affiliations were formulated primarily as membership in organizations, not simply as a "Nazi past." Moreover, neither John Tagliabue, Elaine Sciolino nor James Markham implied Waldheim's personal involvement in war crimes or "atrocities," but in fact underlined the absence of such evidence, especially when discussing the Yugoslav and UNWCC files. The principal failing related to the loose usage of "war criminal" when discussing these documents and the Office of Special Investigation. Though the impact of this laxity is difficult to assess, it certainly cannot have helped clarify the legal issues surrounding the watch list proceeding.

In addition to these features, which were internal to the text, the *NYT* also accorded space to articles portraying Waldheim's views. Headlines such as "Waldheim Says His Past Was Misrepresented,"[116] "Waldheim Says Reports Are 'Unfounded',"[117] "It's A 'Smear,' Waldheim Says,"[118] "Waldheim Charges 'Conspiracy' Against Him,"[119] "Waldheim Says Papers Shed No Light on Career,"[120] "Waldheim Condemns Bigotry,"[121] show that the *NYT* gave ample prominence to Waldheim's own defense against his critics. Stand-in figures such as his son Gerhard or former Austrian Foreign Minister Karl Gruber were also cited extensively, as well as Waldheim's "Memorandum," though without any corresponding rebuttal by the WJC. The *NYT* also printed articles detailing how "Waldheim's Son Seeks To Counter a 'Manhunt,'"[122] and reported Simon Wiesenthal's attacks on the WJC and Helmut Kohl's spirited defense of Waldheim.[123] It would be mistaken to infer from the headlines cited above any sort of editorial policy, as these must be seen alongside other headlines such as "Waldheim Called a 'Liar' By Jewish Leader."[124] More important, in the reports where Waldheim's version of events remained the principal topic, the conventions of balance required that space also be given to those who took exception to this view. The reporters working on the Waldheim story tended to follow this pattern, but when they did not, it could redound to Waldheim's benefit.

The editorials themselves, although they came out expressly against a possible move to bar Waldheim from visiting the United States, contained a fairly narrow view of the political axes of the Austrian election campaign, seeing it essentially as a moral referendum on Waldheim's mendacity or on "Austria's" Nazi past. The editors appear not to have examined critically the assumptions on which this view was based. James Markham's reporting, which exhibited a far more subtle understanding of Austrian political culture, could be read as a corrective.

The selection of columns on the Op-Ed page, though the content was in no way representative of an editorial policy, showed no inordinate bias, and in all likelihood represented the proportion of pro- and anti-Waldheim contributions which the *Times* received.

The Reporting of Other Papers

As one might expect, the spectrum of reportorial quality and editorial opinion in papers other than the *NYT* was fairly broad. Several assumptions which informed the reporting in the *Times* were also to be found in the reports of other newspapers. Here it is only possible to give a few examples which illustrate this variety, and which indicate the tenor and focus of the debate over Waldheim in U.S. newspapers.

After the initial publication of the documents by the WJC and the report in the *NYT*, a fairly broad consensus formed that a "Nazi past" had been established beyond doubt. For many, this seemed to be the most important question, because it functioned as an over-arching concept from which all else regarding Waldheim's wartime service followed. This was most obviously the case with the tabloid dailies, and predictably the *New York Post* served as a pioneer. Headlines such as "Another Ex-Nazi

Vies for U.N. Post";[125] "If de Cuellar doesn't open U.N. files, he becomes part of the Nazi coverup";[126] or, as the *New York Daily News* headed its editorial on Waldheim's election, "Heil to the Chief!"[127] all exemplify the tendency. The *Post* referred to Waldheim early on as a "true believer,"[128] while the *Los Angeles Times* published a cartoon depicting Waldheim as Hitler in a brown shirt.[129] Such images fade slowly, and every new discovery about Waldheim's wartime service seemed to confirm them. Yet this could be so only on the dubious assumption that National Socialist ideological conviction was a prerequisite of military duty in the German Army.

Examples of both measured and nearly fraudulent editorial practices could also be found in the reporting on Waldheim's military career. To begin with the latter, the *Post* reported on 26 March 1986 on documents revealed at the WJC's press conference of the previous day with the headline, "Papers Show Waldheim was SS-Butcher,"[130] although neither the WJC, Robert Herzstein nor any document presented at the press conference offered the slightest bit of evidence for such a claim. On 15 May, the headline "'Waldheim Signed Death Warrant for 114 Yugoslavs,'" referred to Deborah Orin's article on documents the WJC had previously published. The article itself, which reported, among other things, that "newly discovered documents signed by Kurt Waldheim directly tie the former U.N. chief to the World War II massacre of 114 Yugoslavs, the World Jewish Congress charged yesterday,"[131] and paraphrased more or less what was contained in the WJC's press release, was far less dramatic than the headline would imply. To drive home the point, however, this article was placed next to a large photograph of Andrija Artukovic, the "Butcher of the Balkans," who had just been sentenced to death in a Belgrade court.[132]

On the other hand, the descriptions of the significance of the documents in the quality newspapers were far more discriminating. In an article by Joseph C. Harsch in the *Christian Science Monitor*, for example, the critical element referred specifically to Waldheim's suppression of details about his past, not to possible criminal activity. "The question of Waldheim's guilt or innocence turns on how much he may have known about the war crimes committed under the Loehr command, and what he might have done about them had he known," he wrote, a forumulation which appeared almost verbatim in the defense Gerhard Waldheim wrote for the Op-Ed page of the *NYT*. "Knowledge of a misdeed," Harsch warned, "is not necessarily complicity. With knowledge he might have protested, or joined an anti-Nazi underground, or fled the country. But like many Austrians, Waldheim did none of these. He served in the German Army to the end of the war." He concluded by writing that "Waldheim is not a proven or even accused war criminal. He is guilty of concealing that part of his past which is now an embarassment to him."[133] Harsch was technically incorrect that Waldheim was not an "accused war criminal," since the proceedings of the Yugoslavs were never officially terminated, but he drew no unwarranted conclusions about Waldheim's military career.

The handling of Austria's past was also a theme of quality papers, and, although the same assumptions about national collectives appear here as in the *NYT*, there is no evidence that this is specific to reporting on Austria. For example, the *Washing-*

ton Post published a background article on the election by William Drozdiak, "Austria Confronts Its Nazi Past." Drozdiak described "Austria's" role in the the Third Reich, recalled the historical tradition of antisemitism and the insufficient process of "coming to terms with the past." "The controversy over allegations of war crimes by former U.N. secretary general Kurt Waldheim," he wrote, ". . . has grown beyond one man's concealed past to expose a whole nation's tortured conscience about Nazi sympathies and antisemitism." It is not entirely clear from this passage whence the allegations had come, nor whether Waldheim himself was suspected of war crimes or whether he had accused someone else. Moreover, Drozdiak, like most other writers in the United States, ascribed psychological categories to the Austrian "nation," without specifying the mechanisms through which such afflictions are manifested. As for the analysis itself, the very sources he quoted for his article (Oliver Rathkolb, an historian, Hilde Weiss, a sociologist, Peter M. Lingens, then editor of *Profil,* and Ivan Hacker, then president of the Jewish Community organization in Vienna), all Austrians, show that he was concerned to show "another" Austria.[134] In a later report on the election, Drozdiak emphasized the importance of the "historical" factor far less than, say Markham of the *Times.*[135] A similar approach may be seen in other reports in the *Washington Post,* where the theme of Austria's past appeared.[136] Jim Mulvaney from *Newsday,* on the other hand, played up the domestic party political component in his analysis of the elections. "Waldheim's victory over Socialist Party candidate Kurt Steyrer," he wrote, "was a measure of a growing conservative trend in Austria, as well as a nationalist backlash against international criticism of the Nazi war record of Waldheim and indeed, of the whole nation."[137]

Whatever tendencies might have existed in news reports to portray the election as a referendum on Waldheim's and Austria's past were reinforced by editorials, for virtually without exception those examined took this view. A few representative examples must suffice, for the similarity of arguments was striking. The *Arizona Republic* had strong words for an Austria which "has yet to come to grips with its past." "That a majority of its citizens could vote for a revealed liar with a shadowy past steeped in the darkness of one of the blackest chapters in human history," the editors continued, "ought to unsettle the Austrian national conscience." The portrait of Austria, "if not the most . . . certainly one of the most antisemitic countries in the world," was not flattering: "Adolf Hitler learned his antisemitic lessons in Vienna; proportionally more Austrians than Germans joined the Nazi Party; fewer Austrian than German Jews survived the Holocaust; according to Simon Wiesenthal, Austria was responsible for at least half of the Jewish dead in the extermination camps; and thousands of Austrians participated in the genocide at all levels of the Nazi killing machine," the paper recalled.[138]

Similarly, an editorial in the *Washington Post* from the end of April suggested that this view had established itself rather early.[139] Among the questions which arose out of the research into Waldheim's past, the *Post* editors believed, were whether "Mr. Waldheim, who has now admitted concealment of his 1942–1945 war service, [was] also concealing participation in the gross war crimes for which his commanding officer, among others, was tried and convicted." "Why was it," the editorial continued, "that Yugoslavia, who at one point had classified him too as deserving prosecution for murder and killing hostages, did not prosecute him and held silence on the charges thereafter?" The main questions, the editors believed, involved Waldheim's integrity, but there were others, such as whether Waldheim was "acting out a certain characteristic story of Austria, the one that many Austrians have perhaps desperately wanted to believe and tell, in which they were the victims of Hitler, not his supporters and accomplices?" The election (they were referring to the first round) was, they concluded, "a nation-defining choice of whether to confront its past, ugly as some of it unquestionably was, or to stay with Kurt Waldheim in a mode of forgetting and denial."[140]

The *Christian Science Monitor* shared this view of the election. Although many Austrians considered the presidential election an internal affair, the editors claimed, for them "to elect a man to such a high office, amid controversy over an unacceptable Nazi past, would indicate a willful disregard of international standards of decency." "The Austrians," the paper argued, "declared early on by the Allies to have been among Nazism's first victims, have not had to come to terms with this chapter of their history, as the Germans have. The Waldheim drama may prove to be the catalyst for some needed soul-searching by Austrians."[141] In this respect, moreover, the "quality newspapers" were little different than the tabloids, although the rhetorical style of the latter was frequently more caustic. The *New York Daily News,* for example, wrote of the international impact of the election: "When Austrians go to the polls, they should ask themselves if a brazen liar is fit to be their president. And what they'll be telling the world if the answer is yes."[142] Unlike the reports, which did occasionally mention that other factors played a role in the election, the editorials either took no note of these, or considered them irrelevant to the broader issue as they defined it.

If the editorials exhibited a monotonous affinity in their perceptions of the issues at hand, the variety of opinion expressed in columns did not. For example, if Alan Ryan, former head of the OSI, could in all seriousness write that "Waldheim may be innocent, but why is he acting like so many Nazi war criminals have,"[143] Lars-Erik Nelson, writing in the *New York Daily News,* castigated what he viewed as hypocrisy in the Waldheim affair. "What he [Waldheim] is guilty of is selective memory, a common European and American disease. To call it 'Waldheimer's disease' is a good joke, but it is far more widespread than Kurt Waldheim." Nelson recalled other national "nightmares," such as collaboration in France, the Hungarian and Romanian troops who fought for Hitler, the terrorist past of Israeli Prime Minister Yitzhak Shamir, the shooting of German civilians by allied soldiers in Dresden, the interning of United States citizens of Japanese heritage during the second World War, and the welcome shown by U.S. authorities to former war criminals merely because they could help combat communism. "None of these Western crimes compare with the crimes of the Nazis," he argued in conclusion, "but the forgetting of them compares exactly with Waldheim's crime."[144]

An analogous divergence could be seen in the evaluations of Waldheim as an individual. Richard Cohen, writing in the *Washington Post,* saw portentous implications in Waldheim's personal failings. Though "it is barely acceptable for him to say he was oblivious to mass murder when he was a junior officer[,] it is not acceptable for him to say he spent a life that way." Cohen's conception of duty was also some distance from Waldheim's: "As a man and as a political leader, it was his obligation to find out what happened during the war, to see what, in his modest way he made possible—to know and, in the telling phrase of Arthur Koestler, 'to be haunted by his knowledge.'" Waldheim, however, did not feel haunted. "He proclaims his innocence by confessing ignorance. But what it really comes down to is indifference—an inadvertent confession of guilt. It is what made the Holocaust possible."[145]

For Smith Hempstone, writing in the *Washington Times,* on the contrary, Waldheim's was an all too human fate. It is true, he asserted, that "Mr. Waldheim for 40 years clearly was something less than candid when he led the world to believe that his military career ended in 1941." Yet "to date there is no convincing evidence . . . that he was involved in reprisals against Yugoslav partisans and that he somehow participated in the deportation of 43,00 [sic, i.e., 43,000] Greek Jews from Salonika. . . ." Moreover, "from what is known of the Waldheim family, it is not illogical to believe that the young lieutenant did not have much use for the Nazis. It is equally clear that he, like millions of other men, not unnaturally hoped to survive the war and to make a decent life for himself afterward. That he felt he had to conceal the truth about his war service is a personal tragedy; it is not a crime."[146]

Understanding for both Waldheim's personal plight and the predicament of the Austrians was shown by former Congressman Otis Pike, in a piece he wrote for *Newsday.* "How would we feel," he asked, "if the news media of some major power–France, say—kept up a running attack on a candidate for the presidency of the United States for a period of six months before the election? We wouldn't like it. Neither did the Austrians." President Waldheim, he admitted, "has lied about his war record. So, apparently, has a guy who is running for governor of Massachusetts. So did a guy who ran against me once. It is the sort of thing that might impel one to vote against a person, but doesn't disqualify him from running." In closing, Pike reiterated that, whatever Waldheim's sins, the election was for the Austrians to decide. "So there he sits, president of Austria. Ex-member of the German army? Certainly. Ex-Nazi? Maybe. Guilty of war crimes? Possibly. But until someone comes up with a lot better evidence than anyone has come up with thus far, we would be wise to put ourselves in the shoes of the Austrians and get off his case."[147]

Concluding Remarks

These few examples indicate the variety of opinion, editorial style and reportorial merit which characterized newspaper coverage of the Waldheim affair in the United States. The idea of an organized "campaign" with the common objectives of defaming Waldheim and "Austria," which was habitually reported or assumed by even respected Austrian newspapers, appears even less plausible in light of the above evidence than it normally would. Which is not to say that this view was not repeatedly reported in Austria during the presidential election campaign. Characteristically, the journalists of the *Neue Kronen Zeitung* led the way in first inventing, then reinforcing this myth. On 15 March 1986, Kurt Seinitz wrote:

> America's mass media, above all the *New York Times* and the three major TV networks CBS, ABC and NBC, have made the Waldheim "disclosures" into the biggest Nazi campaign since "Bitburg". . . . Israel's mass media also reported critically on both occasions, but without the subjective hysteria which overcomes Jewish journalists and Jewish politicians in the U.S.A. when dealing with the Nazi period. . . . America's large media wage an especially peculiar battle in this connection, in the form of regular attacks of hysteria, whenever a genuine or allegedly crypto-Nazism or antisemitism is discovered anew.[148]

On the contrary, apart from the nearly unanimous belief that the election did or ought to represent a referrendum on Austria's Nazi past, it was difficult to distinguish even an accidental convergence of opinion among the various papers in the detailed presentation of Waldheim's past and its significance. Although several assumptions were shared, the terms of the debate per se were never questioned by Waldheim himself. In this context, the Waldheim affair appears structurally to have been not dissimilar to any number of media events since the exposure of the Watergate scandal.

The initial news value of Waldheim had little or nothing to do with tactical electoral considerations, but rested almost exclusively on his prominence as former head of the United Nations. It was, moreover, predictable that Waldheim's own past would be seen as a surrogate for the Austrian *Lebenslüge,* once it became clear that the evidence uncovered about his past had not caused him to forfeit electoral support. It was all the more to be expected, given the predominance of a political discourse which ascribed even psychological categories to some fictive person, be it a nation or state. Such a discursive Procrustean bed limited the types of questions which were asked, just as the failure to question the assumptions common to both Waldheim and the reporters covering the story ensured that the discourse would not change. At the same time, because Waldheim portrayed his own past as unblemished and his character unimpeachable, he provided editorial writers in the United States with an easy symbolic target for settling accounts only indirectly related to Waldheim himself. Put bluntly, swimming with the current of moral abuse directed at Waldheim and "Austria" obviated the search for culprits closer to home and more threatening to cherished ideological assumptions about the nature of American politics, and the entire foundation of the post-World War II western political settlement.

There were, however, also features of the Waldheim affair which would have taxed the efforts of the most critically minded of journalists working for daily papers. The majority of newspapers in the United States were dependent for their information on the WJC. Very few papers employed their own researchers or consulted their own experts, and as a consequence, the interpretations of the WJC came to dominate the news items. Since the language of the WJC spokesmen was frequently exaggerated and at best ambiguous, the room for interpretive imagination was quite large. The *New York Post* is but one example of just how wide the scope was.

With all these caveats, nonetheless, the overall coverage of the disclosures by "opinion leaders" such as the *New York Times* and *Washington Post* consisted largely of reports which followed closely texts of documents themselves, and offered tentative and qualified conclusions. Where they lacked expertise themselves (virtually the entire time), reporters sought independent confirmation from experts and offered space to Waldheim's contrasting interpretations. Moreover, in at least one case, *NYT* reporters abandoned earlier conclusions when these proved no longer tenable. And at no time did the *NYT* openly accuse Waldheim of having been involved in war crimes. The tabloids, on the other had, discovered the "smoking gun" at regular intervals.

We might ask, to return to Seinitz's fantasies, where exactly he hoped to find "the American media" of which he spoke, and whether the "subjective hysteria" did not lay rather in his own projection of a media conspiracy against Waldheim and "Austria?"

Notes

1. *Pressestunde,* Österreichischer Rundfunk (ORF), 9 March 1986.

2. "Man muss sagen, der Antisemitismus ist schreklich, aber was in der *New York Times* steht ist auch verlogen and gemein." Club 2: *Glücklich ist, wer vergisst,* ORF 16 September 1986.

3. *Wiener Zeitung* (*WZ*), 6 March 1986.

4. *WZ,* 30 March 1986.

5. The first editorial in the *New York Times* (*NYT*) on Waldheim appeared on 19 April 1986, long after both these reports had appeared.

6. See, among others, Noam Chomsky, "The Bounds of Thinkable Thought," *The Progressive,* October 1985, pp. 28-31; idem, *American Power and the New Mandarins* (London: Penguin, 1967); compare Edward S. Herman and Noam Chomsky, *Manufacturing Consent. The Political Economy of the Mass Media* (New York: Pantheon, 1988). Over the past several years Chomsky and Herman, either separately or together, have painstakingly exposed various biases encountered in the established opinion leaders, particularly the *New York Times.* Although I would not endorse all their interpretations or their explanation of how these "bounds" are imposed in the mass media in the United States, I consider their work to be of high quality and of enormous heuristic value. The results of my own research have yielded far fewer egregious assaults on accuracy in the columns of the *Times's* reporting on the Waldheim affair than those catalogued by Chomsky and Herman regarding stories more intimately bound up with United States foreign policy and/or corporate interests. I cannot offer an explanation of this divergence, but perhaps the Waldheim affair's lack of very direct proximity to the real affairs of state may offer a clue. In the event, I have applied Chomsky's notion of the "bounds of thinkable thought" here to press reports in Austria on the WJC and the *NYT.*

7. Articles on 4, 6, 25 and 26 March; 3, 5 and 22 April; 15 and 16 May, 1986, referred to information which the *NYT* received directly from the WJC. Often the same information was pub-

lished simultaneously by the WJC and the paper, but it in these cases the material would not necessarily have come from the WJC (one example was the copy of a telex Waldheim sent to Edgar Bronfman, a copy of which Waldheim sent directly to the *NYT*). There were other instances when the *NYT* had received documents from the WJC but only reported on them in detail later. For example, the *NYT* had received a copy of the SK-235 from the WJC at the latest by 5 March 1986, but only reported on it days later, and then they cited the Austrian magazine *Profil.* See News from WJC, 4 and 5 March 1986; *NYT,* 8 and 9 March 1986.

8. This is not to say that I believe either Tagliabue's initial report or any other report in the *NYT* to be free from bias. The relevant question is how scrupulous he or other reporters were in evaluating the material at hand and how "balanced" it was under the normal criteria applied by the *NYT.*

9. The guidelines which journalists are conventionally expected to follow in writing news reports are stated generally in the "Statement of Principles" adopted in 1975 by the American Society of Newspaper Editors. This is reprinted as Appendix IV of in John Hohenberg, *The Professional Journalist. A Guide to the Practices and Principles of the News Media* (New York, etc.: Holt, Rinehart and Winston, 1978), pp. 575–582. See also ibid., pp. 100–124, 319–337.

10. *NYT,* 4 March 1986. All references in this section, unless otherwise indicated, are taken from this article. Remarks, etc., in brackets are mine.

11. This passage, according to which Waldheim learned after the war that he had been enrolled as a member of the SA, was later the occasion for the Waldheim camp's claim that he had been misquoted. On 5 March 1986, Waldheim denied having made this concession to Taliabue. The following day the *NYT* reported that its editor, Warren Hoge, had confirmed the accuracy of the quotation against the recorded interview. In Austria, several newspapers carried Waldheim's claim that the *NYT* had misquoted him, but only one, the independent *Salzburger Nachrichten* (*SN*), published the details of the interview transcript, which confirmed Tagliabue's initial report. See *NYT,* 6 March 1986, *SN,* 8/9 March 1986.

12. The quotation marks are used here to indicate that some facts are more "factual" (or, as the colloquial redundancy would have it, "truer") than others. Some of the points about his wartime service which Waldheim here confirmed, such as the nature of his duties in Army Group E, and which Tagliabue repeated in good faith, turned out to be either incomplete or false. Our interest here, however, is not only how close Tagliabue came to nailing down the "real" story on 3 March, but rather the degree of bias and balance which his article exhibited on the basis of information which he could have been expected to know or find out. It goes without saying that certain statements which were held to be facts could and did erect barriers to thought, which hindered some reporters in fitting the disparate pieces of Waldheim's wartime past together into a comprehensive picture. For this reason I speak here not of facts, but of "facts."

13. See Walter Manoschek [Neues Österreich] (ed.), *Pflichterfüllung. Ein Bericht über Kurt Waldheim* (Vienna: Löcker Verlag, 1986), pp. 11–19.

14. Indeed, Waldheim compounded the mistake by emphasizing, as he told CBS, "all I did was to interpret between Italian and German commanders." See *NYT,* 6 March 1986.

15. Waldheim frequently refused to describe the reprisal measures carried out by the Wehrmacht against civilians as atrocities. In place of these he spoke of "hard conflicts" or brutal "struggles" against the enemy, but not in this first *NYT* article. See, for example, Waldheim's remarks in an interview with Rudolf Nagillar in the Austrian news program *Zeit in Bild I,* ORF 25 March 1986.

16. *NYT,* 4 March 1986.

17. Even if Waldheim had not made such a statement to Tagliabue, he did state on at least one occasion that he was unaware of Wehrmacht reprisal policy. In an interview published on 10 March 1986 Waldheim was asked whether he was aware that "at that time the order was to shoot suspected partisans?" His reply: "I never saw such an order. I had nothing to do with these things." Waldheim's statement is untrue. He kept the war diary of the German liaison staff to the High Command of the Italian 11th Army between 19 July and 21 August 1943. On 8 August 1943 Waldheim recorded an order from Hitler which ordered the shooting of members of the "bandits" [*Banditen*] taken prisoner in battle. BundesarchivMilitärarchiv Freiburg im Breisgau, RH 31 x/1.

18. *NYT,* 15 May 1986. As we have seen, it is not true that Waldheim "never denied knowing about massacres," but Sciolino corrected the impression given by most previous articles in the *NYT.*

19. *NYT,* 5 March 1986.

20. *NYT,* 7 March 1986 and 9 March 1986.

21. *NYT* 15 March 1986 and 20 March 1986.

22. *NYT,* 6 March 1986.

23. *NYT,* 10 March 1986. This dispatch reported Waldheim's remark that the *NYT* had "spread the most grotesque things about me."

24. *NYT,* 5 March 1986.

25. Ibid. Although it is fully correct and necessary to distinguish between the Nazi party apparatus and the Hitler regime on the one hand and the German Army command on the other, in the final analysis the Wehrmacht was the military power of Nazi Germany and dutifully carried out its policies, including mass murder and the deportation of Jews. However, it bears repeating that in the absence of any other evidence, it would be unjustified to infer any Nazi conviction out of mere service in the army. See, in this connection Manfred Messerschmidt, *Die Wehrmacht im NS-Staat: Zeit der Indoktrination* (Hamburg: Decker, 1969); Manfred Messerschmidt and Fritz Wüllner, *Die Wehrmachtjustiz im Dienste des Nationalsozialismus: Zerstörung einer Legende* (Baden-Baden: Nomos Verlagsgesellschaft, 1987); Manfred Messerschmidt, "Harte Sühne and Judentum: Befehlslage und Wissen in der deutschen Wehrmacht," in Jörg Wollenberg, ed., *"Niemand war dabei und keiner hat's gewusst"* (Munich: Fischer, 1988); Hans Safrian, "Wiener Täter, Wiener Methode: Die Deportationen der Juden aus Saloniki," in Walter Manoschek, Hans Safrian, Florian Freund, Pertrand Pelz and Rubina Möhring, "Der Balkankrieg im Zweiten Weltkrieg als Teil der österreichischen Zeitgeschichte," Ms. (Vienna, 1989) pp. 140–195; Walter Manoschek and Hans Safrian, "Genocid und Kriegsverbrechen am Balkan," in Walter Manoschek, Hans Safrian, Florian Freund, Pertrand Pelz and Rubina Möhring, "Der Balkankrieg im Zweiten Weltkrieg als Teil der österreichischen Zeitgeschichte," Ms. (Vienna, 1989), pp. 19–32.

26. *NYT,* 9 March 1986.

27. See *NYT,* 6, 8 and 9 March 1986.

28. *NYT,* 25 March 1986.

29. Ibid.

30. This does not, of course, mean that Waldheim is necessarily any more incriminated, but it does mean that the reasons the CROWCASS listing is not as serious as it at first appears are different from those suggested by Wiesenthal. See Herzstein, *Missing,* pp. 193–217.

31. Esther Schollum, "Die 'Waldheim-Kampagne' in den österreichischen und internatinalen Medien," in Andreas Khol, Theodor Faulhaber and Gunther Ofner, eds., *Die Kampagne. Kurt Waldheim—Opfer oder Täter? Hintergründe und Szenen eines Falles von Medienjustiz* (Mu-

nich and Berlin: Herbig, 1987), p. 48. In the press release distributed at the press conference announcing the book the study is described as the "first scholarly assessment of the campaign against Kurt Waldheim."

32. *NYT,* 26 March 1986.

33. See for example, *NYT,* 11 and 27 April 1986.

34. *NYT,* 30 March 1986.

35. *NYT,* 5 April 1986.

36. *NYT,* 8 April 1986. Sciolino's statement that the WJC published this document on 7 April, the date she filed the article, presents something of a problem. The WJC published no press release on this date, and the brochure "Waldheim's Nazi Past," in which all the disclosures the WJC made are listed, shows only references to press releases from 2 and 9 April, but not 7 April. The document to which she refers in her article, however, was only published on 29 April, according to WJC records. See News from WJC, 2, 9, and 29 April 1986; "Waldheim's Nazi Past," 8–10.

37. *NYT,* 14 April 1986.

38. *NYT,* 14 April 1986; News from WJC, 14 April 1986.

39. *NYT,* 15 May 1986. The caption under the headline read "World Jewish Congress Says Documents Back Charges by Yugoslavs in 1940s." See News from WJC, 14 May 1986.

40. *NYT,* 15 May 1986.

41. See News from WJC, 14 May 1986.

42. *NYT,* 15 May 1986.

43. *NYT,* 9 April 1986.

44. *NYT,* 11 April 1986.

45. *NYT,* 15 May 1986.

46. *NYT,* 22 April 1986.

47. Wiesenthal was alluding to an interview in *Profil,* on 24 March 1986.

48. *NYT,* 17 May 1986. The main article bore the headline, "Wiesenthal Faults Jewish Congress on Waldheim."

49. "Dr. Kurt Waldheim on recent allegations levied against him," 14 April 1986. Gerhard Waldheim had given this memorandum to the United States Department of Justice on 6 April.

50. This much may be inferred from the fact that Waldheim felt forced to revise his official biography on file with the Austrian Foreign Ministry, as reported in the *NYT,* 9 April 1986, as well as from his remarks on CBS News's *60 Minutes,* "I do apologise to all my friends in the United States and here that I didn't mention this," quoted in *NYT,* 14 April 1986.

51. For example, that one of Waldheim's duties in the staff of Army Group E was the interrogation of prisoners, or that the German word "Banden" refers to "bandits" (it means "bands"). It has not been proved that Waldheim himself ever carried out an interrogation, although there is no doubt that he processed the intelligence received from the interrogations.

52. According to his personnel file in the Austrian Foreign Ministry, Waldheim received three other awards during his military career in addition to the Zvonimir medal. A copy of this document is reproduced in Manoschek, *Pflichterfüllung,* p. 40.

53. *NYT,* 9 April 1986.

54. The Odluka and the UNWCC files are reproduced and translated in Gruber, et al., *Wartime Years,* pp. 212–248. CROWCASS is attached to the WJC press release, News from WJC, 22 March 1986.

55. *NYT,* 11 April 1986.

56. Johann Mayer was a personnel clerk in department IIa (Adjutancy and Personnel relations for Officers) of Army Group E from July, 1944. He was stationed in Salonika itself, and not in Arsakli. After the war, Mayer was imprisoned in the Yugoslav POW camp in Kocevje. His testimony, which was included in the *Odluka,* deeply incriminated Waldheim, but was itself internally contradictory. Mayer's credibility as a witness was questioned by several fellow veterans who had been interned with him. See Gruber, et al., *Wartime Years,* pp. 230–233, 241; and the affidavit from Mayer's predecessor as personnel clerk, Franz Kaupe, in ibid., pp. 253–255; See also *Profil,* 7 April 1986; Herzstein, *Missing,* p. 198.

57. See *NYT,* 30 March 1986; 25 April 1986.

58. See *NYT,* 28 March 1986; 3 and 10 April 1986; 2, 13, 14, 15 and 19 May 1986; 4, 5, 6, 7 and 10 June 1986.

59. *NYT,* 2 and 13 April 1986; 2, 13 and 19 May 1986; 4, 5, 6 and 7 June 1986.

60. See *NYT,* 2, 3, 5, 8, 9, 10, 12, and 14 April 1986.

61. See *NYT,* 26 March 1986, 9, 12, 25, and 29 April 1986; 16 May 1986; 3, 5 and 7 June 1986.

62. See *NYT,* 28 March 1986 and 3 April 1986.

63. See *NYT,* 9, 13 and 14 April 1986.

64. See *NYT,* 23, 25 and 26 April 1986.

65. See *NYT,* 4, 11, 17, 23 (on the speech of then Austrian president Rudolf Kirchschläger), and 27 April 1986; 3, 4, 5, 11, 22, and 25 May 1986; 7, 8, 9, 10, 12 and 15 June 1986.

66. *NYT,* 11 April 1986.

67. *NYT,* 26 April 1986.

68. *NYT,* 27 April 1986.

69. *NYT,* 1 May 1986.

70. *NYT,* 17 April 1986. Waldheim's reference is to an interview in *Profil,* 24 March 1986.

71. *NYT,* 3 May 1986.

72. *NYT,* 4 May 1986.

73. *NYT,* 5 May 1986.

74. See *NYT,* 7, 8, 9, and 15 June 1986.

75. See *NYT,* 26 and 17 March, 2 and 9 April 1986.

76. See, for example, *NYT,* 29 April 1986 and 3 June 1986.

77. *NYT,* 25 April 1986.

78. Waldheim served as an interpreter during this meeting at the airport, and the historians' commission has established conclusively that the plans for the operation had been made prior to this meeting. See Kurz, et al., *Bericht,* pp. 37–39. Robert Herzstein has provided important additional details of this meeting, and his conclusions were also different from Sher's. See Herzstein, *Missing,* pp. 88–90.

79. See *NYT,* 28 April 1987; *Profil,* 18 May 1987.

80. Sher himself did not claim that Waldheim had served in the *Abwehr* in the passages quoted by Shenon. The formulation "Intelligence and Counterintelligence branch" is merely the accurate translation of the designation Ic/AO.

81. For example, *NYT,* 29 April 1986.

82. News from WJC, 22 March 1986; *NYT,* 25 March 1986.

83. *NYT,* 25 March 1986.

84. See United Nations War Crimes Commission, *History of the United Nations War Crimes Commission and the Development of the Laws of War.* London, 1948.

85. *NYT,* 2 April 1986.

86. See *NYT,* 3 and 5 April 1986; 2 and 25 May 1986. In this connection see Palumbo, *Waldheim File,* passim. That the interest in the UNWCC archives was not restricted to Waldheim is suggested by the fact that soon after this archive was rediscovered as a consequence of the Waldheim affair, the Israeli government delivered up a request for the UNWCC files of several people whom they wished to investigate. *NYT,* 12 April 1986; 8 June 1986.

87. See Herzstein, *Missing,* pp. 159–264.

88. *NYT,* 12 April 1986.

89. Captain Egberts-Hilker was the commander of the 122nd reconnaissance unit of the 22nd Infantry Division, which was under the overall command of Army Group E. Egberts-Hilker's unit burned three Macedonian villages along the road between Stip and Kocane in October, 1944. According to his testimony in the Yugoslav file, Egberts-Hilker's unit carried out the action because of standing orders "which said that in case of an attack on our unit by armed citizens-civilians, the dwellings these civilians lived in were to be burned, and the entire male population from 16–60 years was to be killed." In this file, Waldheim was implicated in this massacre because his activities as 03 in the military intelligence branch of Army Group E included the transmission of such orders, not because of his direct participation in the event Egberts-Hilker described. Indeed, in his testimony, Egberts-Hilker did not mention Waldheim by name, and in a statement he made shortly before his execution, he accepted "the entire responsibility" for the action. Waldheim's name is not mentioned in this statement either. Markus Hartner was a cartographer in the Ic branch of Army Group E and the author of a very detailed chart diagramming the various areas of responsibility in the unit, as well as a description of his colleagues in the military intelligence department, both of which were also contained in the Odluka. The translation of Egbert-Hilker's statement is from Gruber, et al., *Wartime Years,* p. 233; his 1947 statement is quoted on p. 55, note 32. The complete testimony of Hartner is reproduced, and the portions of it relating to Waldheim are translated, in ibid., pp. 272–282. See also Herzstein, *Missing,* pp. 193–202.

90. *NYT,* 12 April 1986.

91. See *NYT,* 2, 3, 5 and 10 April 1986.

92. *NYT,* 3 April 1986.

93. *NYT,* 5 April 1986.

94. *NYT,* 10 April 1986.

95. *NYT,* 23 May 1986.

96. Of course, this does not mean that such distinctions are not overlooked, even by scholars who should know better. See Schollum, "Waldheim-Kampagne," p. 49; M. Gottschlich and K. Obermair, "Medienreaktionen des Auslands auf die Bundespräsidentschaftsund Nationalratswahlen 1986" (Vienna: Institut für Publizistik and Kommunikationswissenschaft, Universität Wien, 1986). See also Gottschlich and Obermair, "Der 'Fall Waldheim' als Medienereignis. Antisemitismus in österreichischen Medien" (Vienna: Institut für Publizistik and Kommunikationswissenschaft, Universität Wien, 1987). Though their work should not be confused with the partisan diatribes of Esther Schollum, the "content analysis" they undertook also obscures this essential distinction.

97. *NYT,* 19 April 1986.

98. *NYT,* 12 May 1986.

99. *NYT,* 12 May 1986.

100. See *NYT,* 5 May 1986; further, Ernst Gehmacher, Franz Birk and Günther Orgis, "Die Waldheim-Wahl. Eine erste Analyse" *Journal für Sozialforschung* Vol. 26, No. 3 (1986), 319–331.

101. See *NYT,* 9 June 1986.

102. *NYT,* 10 June 1986.

103. The editors of the *NYT* had altered their opinion on this issue by April 1987. See the editorial "Mr. Meese vs. the Nazis," *NYT,* 29 April 1987.

104. See, for example, the column of Viktor Reimann in the *NKZ,* 26 April 1986, and the remarks of Fritz Molden in the television discussion program *Club 2,* ORF 4 June 1987.

105. *NYT,* 21 April 1986.

106. Ibid. Safire also mentioned Waldheim in a column "Vidal, Waldheim, Grant." The principal target of Safire's attack was Gore Vidal, author of, among other books, *Lincoln.* Waldheim figured only peripherally in this essay, and Safire used the reference to him merely to discredit Vidal. *NYT,* 19 May 1986.

107. *NYT,* 1 May and 12 June 1986.

108. *NYT,* 24 April 1986.

109. The concrete example he suggested was that James Levine should boycott the Salzburger Festspiele in protest against Waldheim's election. See *NYT,* 12 June 1986. For a detailed discussion of these and all the opinion columns mentioned in this section, see Richard Mitten, "Szenen aus dem Präsidentschaftswahlkampf 1986: Die Entstehung eines Feindbildes," in Projektteam "Sprach und Vorurteil," "Unschuldige Täter," Vol. 2, pp. 100–111.

110. *NYT,* 8 April 1986.

111. He had been called as an expert witness at deportation proceedings by the OSI. See Herzstein, "Statement," pp. 1–2.

112. *NYT,* 2 June 1986. Just how vulnerable such overgeneralizations are may be seen in the two letters to the editor referring to Perlmutter's article. One was by Thomas Klestil, then Austrian ambassador to the United States, the other from Lilly B. Freed. See *NYT,* 2 June 1986.

113. *NYT,* 25 May 1986.

114. See the brochure from Waldheim's 1971 presidential election campaign, attached to News from WJC, 10 March 1986.

115. *NYT,* 10 June 1986. The same article was published as "The Digging Into Waldheim's Past Will Continue," in the *International Herald Tribune,* 11 June 1986; and "Kurt Waldheim and Moral Amnesia," *World Jewish Congress News & Views,* April–June 1986.

116. *NYT,* 6 March 1986.

117. *NYT,* 8 March 1986.

118. *NYT,* 10 March 1986.

119. *NYT,* 28 March 1986.

120. *NYT,* 3 April 1986.

121. *NYT,* 22 May 1986.

122. *NYT,* 23 April 1986. See *NYT,* 25 April 1986, in which excerpts from a long interview with Karl Gruber were published. See also *NYT,* 12, 13 and 17 April 1986.

123. *NYT,* 17 May and 27 April 1986. In a radio interview broadcast in Austria, Kohl had praised Waldheim as a "great patriot" and dismissed the "arrogance" of those born after the war.

124. *NYT,* 19 April 1986.

125. *New York Post,* 13 May 1986.

126. *New York Post,* 6 May 1986.

127. *New York Daily News,* 9 June 1986.

128. *New York Post,* 11 March 1986.

129. *Los Angeles Times,* 10 June 1986.

130. *New York Post*, 26 March 1986; see also News from WJC, 25 March 1986. Cf. *New York Post*, 7 June 1986: "Waldheim Clubbed Man To Death—Israelis."

131. *New York Post*, 15 May 1986.

132. *New York Post*, 15 May 1986. See also News from WJC, 14 May 1986.

133. *Christian Science Monitor*, 8 May 1986.

134. *Washington Post*, 3 May 1986.

135. *Washington Post*, 5 May 1986.

136. See *Washington Post*, 3 May 1986, 5 May 1986 and 25 May 1986.

137. *Newsday*, 9 June 1986.

138. *The Arizona Republic*, 10 June 1986.

139. *Washington Post*, 27 April 1986.

140. *Washington Post*, 4 May 1986.

141. *Christian Science Monitor*, 6 May 1986.

142. *New York Daily News*, 6 June 1986.

143. *Washington Post*, 27 April 1986.

144. *New York Daily News*, 14 May 1986.

145. *Washington Post*, 9 March 1986.

146. *Washington Times*, 30 April 1986. See also *Newsday*, 11 June 1986, "Waldheim Case has Parallels in Other Nations," by Arnold J. Lapiner.

147. *Newsday*, 11 June 1986.

148. *Neue Kronen Zeitung*, 15 March 1986.

8

The "Campaign" Against Waldheim and the Emergence of the *Feindbild*

The Contenders for Conspiracy

In principle it is possible to ascribe to nearly any designated agent the power to organize and carry out a major conspiracy. The political, intellectual and ideological traditions of a given culture, however, would tend to privilege some candidates over others. Theories whose remote and usually spurious factual basis could not claim at least some tenability, moreover, would tend either to find too little resonance among those in a position to influence public opinion or would be in danger of being replaced by others considered more compelling. Consequently, we should expect both the broad outlines of the nature of the conspiracy as well as those individuals or groups capable of assuming the role of conspirators against Waldheim to be intelligible to Austrians historically and culturally, and to possess sufficient explanatory power to account for further developments within this preferred interpretive framework.[1]

The available possibilities for explaining a "campaign" that ostensibly had been initiated by socialists, led by an organization called the World Jewish Congress and promoted by the *New York Times* were thus somewhat limited.[2] Conspiracy theories of the modern age have tended to attribute events of international significance whose agent or agents are not otherwise easily identified to international communism or international Jewry, frequently both (or some appropriate substitute such as international Freemasonry).[3] They were, moreover, seldom able to point to a specific program of action the conspirators were following, the Protocols of the Elders of Zion being rather the exception. This very vagueness, however, promoted the flexibility necessary to amalgamate otherwise contradictory aspects of reality without endangering the basic beliefs. Both the unbroken tradition of antisemitic prejudice in Austria, the re-educational policies (not) pursued by successive postwar governments, and the general non-confrontational approach of Austria's political elite towards troubling ideological legacies, would all suggest that a Jewish conspiracy theory, even though articulated in a "post-Auschwitz" idiom, would have good chances of being passively accepted if not actively embraced. And even for those disinclined towards such simplified interpretations, it was at least comprehensible. It was, in any case, there for the taking.

In the hands of the Nazis, the conflation of the international Bolshevik and Jewish conspiracy was complete. Hitler argued in *Mein Kampf,* for example, that "in Russian Bolshevism we can see the attempt of Judaism in the twentieth century to acquire world domination."[4] *Der Stürmer,* which published articles such as "Bolshevism and Synagogue," considered Bolshevism "radical Jewish domination."[5] The linking of socialism and Jewry was not, however, a German import. The Austrian Farmers' League opposed socialism in Austria less because of political differences than because "predominantly Jewish elements are active in the leadership."[6] The belief that the press is dominated by the Jews has important antecedents in Austrian antisemitic political culture,[7] but find contemporary expression as well.[8] On the assumption that many Austrians also share corresponding prejudices about Jewish power and influence, which all the available evidence suggests,[9] then the probability that the Jews would be seen as the author of and power behind such a "campaign" rises. The mere constellation of the "facts" of the disclosures about Waldheim along with the limited reservoir of apposite explanatory frameworks would seem, in the Austrian context, to favor a Jewish conspiracy theory even without any explicit references.

Some Austrian newspapers, however, did their part to firm up ambiguities. In the *Neue Kronen Zeitung* (*NKZ*), which functioned during the election campaign as a sort of self-appointed pro-Waldheim journalistic hit squad, Peter Gnam wrote as early as 6 March 1986: "Exactly two months prior to the presidential election, reports on the ostensibly previously secret Nazi past of Kurt Waldheim appeared in *Profil* and the *New York Times,* and, in order to make the timing perfect, the World Jewish Congress attacked the 'liar Waldheim.'" Gnam's colleague Ernst Trost, for his part, assailed the "poisoners" working "to destroy [Waldheim's] reputation. They were active in Austria and New York, the center of the western news. The *New York Times* was fed a story according to the motto: it matters not whether the charges are accurate, something will stick."[10] Outside Vienna the picture looked similar. Willi Sauberer wrote in the Carinthian *Volkszeitung* on 25 March that "everyone involved in politics knows the channels through which reporters—from *Profil* to the *New York Times*—can be fed material to make certain it is published. Just as one knows what [kind of] power the World Jewish Congress represents, especially in the press sector."[11] Viktor Reimann, also of the *NKZ,* frequently alluded to the "World Jewish Congress and its minions in the mass media" [*ihm hörigen Massenmedien*].[12] In April, 1986, he asked what Israel Singer had hoped to achieve with the "threats" he made against "Austria" in an interview and answered: "Either he greatly overestimated himself or his congress or he wanted to show the world that Jewish influence, above all in the U.S.A., is so powerful that all have to dance to his tune, even when the attacks prove to be unjustified and way below the belt."[13]

The variations on the *"Feindbild 'Jud'"* which could be found in sections of the Austrian media in 1986 were neither wholly explicit nor even fully elaborated. The explanatory model advanced by the Waldheim spokespersons and articulated by his supporters in the press, ultimately grounded in a Jewish conspiracy theory, did possess a certain logic, which enabled those embracing it to make the revisions necessary to accommodate discrepant facts, but which, like all such models, was immune to falsification proper.[14] One would in any case seek in vain for a systematic exposition of the theory: to claim publicly that "the Jews" were behind the Waldheim affair, or that there was an "international Jewish conspiracy" which controlled the international press, would ordinarily meet with official public censure, while the expression of too openly derisory attitudes towards Jews sometimes even has temporary political consequences in Austria.[15] Many who aided in the construction of the negative stereotypes which emerged in 1986 would protest vehemently their innocence of antisemitic prejudice, and in some cases not obviously insincerely.[16] The point is not to ascribe conscious antisemitic hostility to the politicians and journalists involved, much less to imply that their actions or words reflected antisemitic prejudice in any unmediated sense. It is nevertheless possible to suggest that some journalists and politicians actively participated in, while several others exhibited a studied indifference towards, the construction of this new antisemitic *Feindbild* in Austrian political discourse, since sufficient evidence existed to expose as contrived several of the assumptions of the Waldheim camp's explanation of the controversy surrounding his past. In this chapter we will attempt to reconstruct the various pieces of the mosaic which formed what might be termed the suppositional fundament of an international conspiracy theory. To a certain extent, the discourse about the "campaign" necessarily presupposed notions of a conspiracy. As the "campaign" against Waldheim became causally connected with Jewish organizations, the *New York Times* and the state of Israel, the way was opened for a battery of auxiliary anti-Jewish prejudices which both reinforced each other and ostensibly confirmed the initial premise.

The existence of a directed international "campaign" against Kurt Waldheim, later against Austria, as an explanation of the disclosures about his past, was an assumption which became a fixed point in the Austrian media. As a consequence, the hunt for those responsible for this "campaign" acquired a new significance. Initially, the SPÖ was seen as the initiator, and although it reappeared periodically as a mysterious ancillary power behind the disclosures, the WJC became the primary target of abuse.[17] In the face of numerous indications that a "campaign" of this sort had never existed (and could not possibly exist), this assumption persisted, and was rarely questioned.

According to this Waldheimian view, moreover, this was not merely a "campaign," but a "slander campaign." If the allegations made against Waldheim by the WJC were untrue, then they were by definition slanders. Those who raised them, and *a fortiori* those who continued to repeat them, could only be perpetrators of a "slander campaign." A number of strategies were employed by the Waldheim camp to make this corollary assumption persuasive. Most allegations were categorically denied. For some of those remaining, Waldheim and his supporters offered reasonable sounding explanations, but far more frequently the points raised by the WJC and others (who usually remained unnamed) were systematically inflated or otherwise distorted, so as to be able more easily to dismiss or refute them. The information which could be inferred independently from the documents the WJC published was also amalgamated with the WJC's own interpretations of the documents or its related moral judgments on Waldheim, again in order to show that the criticisms were slanderous. With embarrassing if not necessarily inculpatory documents surfacing nearly daily, but with few authorities around who could reliably interpret what they meant, Waldheim's own carefully selected exculpatory details helped reinforce the impression that the WJC and the *NYT* were making charges which were self-evidently false. Yet Waldheim and his press supporters were also able to embrace figures like Simon Wiesenthal and Bruno Kreisky, authorities whose statements could be used to discredit the WJC while providing a kind of "Jewish" cover for those who reiterate them. Such a strategy was all the more effective when these Jewish authorities disputed accusations the WJC had not made. Similarly, through a bit of academic legerdemain, some prominent Austrian scholars were able to offer a certain respectability to Waldheim's claim that the allegations against him made by the WJC were exaggerated, unsupported by evidence, merely untrue or mendacious.

Once in place, this pattern of interpretation heavily influenced the attitude towards any further disclosures by the WJC or the *NYT*. In the first place, so the argument went, those who vilified an innocent man placed themselves beyond the pale of reasoned debate. Additional charges they might make could only be new slanders and therefore unworthy of discussion. The words "documents" and "disclosures," for example, were frequently written inside quotation marks, as though there were some doubt that the WJC were disclosing documents. These were coupled with the by then ritualized categorical denial or the invocation of the word slander or both.[18] After 24 March 1986, moreover, when an interview with representatives of the WJC became known, which contained passages perceived by many as "threats" against Austria, the "slanders" against Waldheim were portrayed as having been coupled with an attempt to intimidate the Austrian people.

No reasonable person, according to the conception described here, would raise unsubstantiated charges against someone of Waldheim's integrity, and would certainly not persist in them after everything had been cleared up. That the WJC continued its investigation into Waldheim's past, however, showed that its interest in Waldheim was somehow not rational. Thus the search for the "real" motives which could explain the WJC's behavior. The WJC's spokesmen were described as dishonorable by some, mentally unbalanced by others. Above all, however, their actions were explained by their thirst for revenge. This, as we will see, dominated the discussion of Israel Singer's alleged "threats" in the Austrian media. The fear of the power of the WJC at the head of the international "campaign," without which the "threats" against Austria could at most be a risible, if unpleasant, irrelevance, was also coupled with attempts to debase the organization and its significance. This apparent antinomy, however, was only apparent, for such a combined strategy enabled one to disparage the WJC for waging a "slander campaign," while erecting another pre-emptive defense against the charge of antisemitism. (Following the theory that one cannot fear an international Jewish conspiracy if one holds the supposed head of it to be so unimportant.)

All the while, of course, the behavior of the WJC was contrasted with various "good Jews" who were not criticizing Waldheim or who were attacking the WJC. The very fact, however, that other Jews were invoked to isolate the WJC suggests the prejudiced nature of these arguments. If the WJC had been seen merely as a "small private organization," as was claimed, and its being Jewish had been immaterial, why call upon other Jews to condemn them? The idiom used to explain the actions of Israel Singer often assumed him to be representative of Jews in general, or of at least unreconcilable Jews, and blurred distinctions between the WJC, world Jewry and "those outside Austria" (*das Ausland*).

Three days before the second round of the presidential election, Alois Mock, then chairman of the People's Party and later Austrian foreign minister in the grand coalition, appeared on the evening news program of the Austrian broadcasting service. He assailed "that guy Singer [who] travels all over the world and demands, with the pressure of the international media, that documents be examined in archives to which there has been public access for forty years. Some say, okay, we can look at them. We don't want to risk the pressure and the conflict with those men who were also able to count on the services of large international media in their unprecedented man hunt [*Menschenhatz*]."[19] Mock's comments were a fitting conclusion to the propaganda war with and against "the campaign" which he and his party had so successfully waged. It remains for us to show how he got there.

The Reification of the "Campaign"

As we have seen, the expressions "slander campaign" and "trash can campaign" had been employed as electoral propaganda by the Waldheim camp prior to the disclosures about his past. Although the SPÖ had made similar attempts to cast attacks on Kurt Steyrer in the same mold, these were slogans to which the ÖVP would lay exclusive claim. Inherent in the notion of "slander campaign," of course, is the assumption that there is a centrally directed effort with specific aims, or a "campaign," and need not imply any particular qualifying adjective. That such a vocabulary was readily available may have facilitated its widespread adoption after 3 March. Far more important was the compelling nature of such an explanation: the nearly simultaneous publication of previously unknown but nearly identical documents about Waldheim's past in Austria and the United States presumably could only have been possible by means of an internationally coordinated "campaign" against him. Once adopted, this convenient and not wholly inconceivable interpretive model was never abandoned, and determined the subsequent political debate in Austria on the Waldheim affair.

Die Presse, for example, wrote as early as 5 March 1986 about the "campaign" against Waldheim which the *NYT* had joined.[20] After several foreign newspapers had taken up the subject of Waldheim, the definition of the "campaign" altered. As long as the "slanders," whether about Waldheim's role in 1968 or about his possible Nazi affiliations were published in Austria (at least as the original source), it was to be expected that the ÖVP would ascribe them to the Socialists. They, after all, had fielded Waldheim's major opponent. This was echoed in several newspapers. Richard Nimmerrichter, one of the most widely read columnists in Austria, by making "certain campaign helpers of the candidate Steyrer" responsible for the disclosures,[21] continued this line of argument even after it was known that the *NYT* had reported on Waldheim's past. On the whole, however, after the *NYT* itself had apparently joined this "campaign," such an explanation became increasingly less convincing. Even the most paranoid foe of the SPÖ could not seriously believe that the *NYT* acted at the behest of the Socialist Party central office.

Two days after the first article in the *NYT, Die Presse* reported on what it termed the "witch hunt [*Kesseltreiben*] against Kurt Waldheim." An article by Hans Wilhelm Vahlefeld on the same page carried the headline "Material Came from the World Jewish Congress." This news report clearly implied that the disclosures were part of a plan. "On Monday of this week, as reported, *Profil* brought Kurt Waldheim's *Wehrstammkarte* . . . on Tuesday, the *New York Times* published reports on Waldheim's presence in Salonika as a Wehrmacht soldier. . . . The ÖVP can no longer believe this is mere coincidence."[22] Vahlefeld did not concede the possibility that *Profil* and the *NYT* had carried out their investigations independently, but thought it relevant to report on the "lightning fast" transmission of news reports and photos about Waldheim to other U.S. and international newspapers. In an age of mass electronic telecommunications (which makes the statement trivial), emphasizing such a thing can only have reinforced the impression that the action was highly coordinated. In the event, for both the editors and Vahlefeld the "campaign" was a given, while the mention of the WJC as the source of the documents which the *NYT* published as part of a "witch hunt" against Waldheim suggested something sinister.

Two versions of the origins of the "campaign" were formed in the initial reactions to the *NYT* report. The first view saw the SPÖ as author, the WJC merely as the SPÖ's accomplice. Peter Gnam of the *NKZ* wrote of unidentified sources "in Austria" who had given "tips and hints" to unnamed persons abroad.[23] Undisputed was that it was a joint "campaign," organized in Austria. Gnam's aside that the role of the WJC was to provide "the corresponding [media] amplification," assumed that the organization was in a position to make such a contribution: Jewish power in the service of the Socialist presidential candidate Kurt Steyrer. Parallel to this version of the international "campaign" was the view that the SPÖ had probably instigated it, but in the final analysis was merely willing to utilize the "campaign," which it did not lead or control, for its own candidate's advantage. The *Wiener Zeitung,* for example, reported that the ÖVP caucus of the national and federal assemblies had voted unanimously and "filled with rage" to condemn the "campaign of defamation and slander against Dr. Kurt Waldheim" and had demanded that the SPÖ disavow it, which at least implied that the "campaign" was independent of the Socialists.[24]

Peter Gnam of the *NKZ* entitled his column of 7 March simply "The Campaign." The ÖVP was out to catch whoever had "instigated the Waldheim campaign," which sounds absurd only in translation (The ÖVP, of course, had instigated Waldheim's election campaign [*Wahlkampf*], but was hunting those behind "the campaign" [*die Kampagne*]). Those responsible remained unnamed, for Kurt Bergmann, ÖVP member of parliament and self-appointed chief detective, had no proof, merely an explanation: "In such a matter," he was quoted as saying, "it is enough to light a single match."[25] The existence of the campaign was also not questioned by *Die Presse* when it reported on the same day that "the Yugoslav daily *Vjesnik* [had] joined the campaign against Waldheim."[26] Or on the following day, when it reported on the "Further Discussion about Waldheim and the Campaign." The paper quoted the second president of the National Assembly, Marga Hubinek, about rumors that Socialist Party officials had been involved in the disclosures, while reporters from *Die Presse* had undertaken their own research and discovered close connections between Herbert Lackner, journalist for the Socialist daily *AZ*, and the *NYT*. "Lackner," it was reported, had "worked as a waiter near New York during the first half of the 1970s."[27]

At this point, Waldheim presented himself as a victim of a "campaign" but refused to be pinned down on the specific names of those responsible. Asked by a journalist of the *Salzburger Nachrichten* whether he thought the discussion over his past would harm his chances he replied, "Certainly not. On the contrary, it will improve them. The Austrians will know how to distinguish between an election and a mud-slinging campaign [*Schmutzkampagne*]. And this is a mud-slinging campaign, which has been in preparation for some time. That we know." He was shown a leaflet which named the SPÖ as the orchestrator of the affair, and stated that although he was unaware of the leaflet, he knew "who is behind the campaign. I will not name names."[28] By downplaying the role of the Socialists, of course, Waldheim had in effect named the WJC as the instigator of the "campaign" against him.

The results of an opinion poll commissioned by the *NKZ* suggested that the Waldheim camp had gotten its message across. Under the headline "Majority of Voters Defend Waldheim," the paper reported on 9 March that 71% of those asked responded to the question, "Do you consider it a coincidence that these allegations were raised in the midst of an election campaign," not unexpectedly "No."[29] Though the very formulation of the question was bound to elicit the desired response, this poll did suggest that reporting which took the existence of a planned and coordinated campaign for granted articulated a widely held assumption. The same issue of the paper reported on the connections between Austrians and the *NYT*. Georg Tidl, historian and employee of the Austrian broadcasting company, but not an official of the SPÖ, was named as the source of the documents the *NYT* had published, though this conflicted with the *Times's* own version as well as other newspaper reports. In addition, the *NKZ* noted that ÖVP party chief Alois Mock had been indirectly warned, by Tidl, that he possessed embarrassing material about Waldheim. These bits of information, which at least should have suggested caution in inferring the existence of a "campaign" of the nature previously reported, had no bearing on the journalists writing for the *NKZ.* Indeed, ÖVP party secretary Michael Graff was quoted afterwards, without any passages qualifying the assumptions of fact in his statement, that "the swine [*Schmutzfinke*] in the SPÖ are deceiving themselves. The trash can campaign is going to blow up in their faces."[30]

In his first major television appearance after the disclosures, Waldheim continued his strategy of making allusions to knowing who was behind the "greatest slander campaign in the republic since 1945," but again refused to be more specific. He emphasized that he did not blame the SPÖ for the "campaign" against him, but would not identify the real culprits. In the context, this anonym could only be the WJC and the *NYT,* which his outburst about the *New York Times* quoted above clearly indicates.[31]

If Waldheim knew the culprits, most other Austrian papers did not, and the search for the miscreants behind the disclosures went forward. The weekly *Wochenpresse, Profil's* principal competitor, dedicated its 11 March 1986 issue to the "story behind the story." The *Wochenpresse* journalists discovered several possible candidates for the person who really supplied whom with what.[32] The essential point here is that such an earnest search for those behind a "campaign" must necessarily assume its existence. This belief, moreover, was shared by reporters who attempted to write balanced reports. The *Oberösterreichischen Nachrichten,* for example, reported Kurt Bergmann's accusation that Hans Pusch, an official in the chancellor's office, was the person behind the "slander campaign," as well as then Chancellor Fred Sinowatz's denial. That there was such a "campaign," of course, was never doubted.[33]

The Waldheim camp appears to have pursued a dual strategy in the affair, in order to cover all bases. On the one hand, ÖVP point man Kurt Bergmann, under the cover of the virtually unconditional immunity enjoyed by Austrian members of parliament, continued to accuse Cabinet Secretary Hans Pusch.[34] He published a dossier of the evidence against Pusch and the SPÖ, and in the midday radio news program declared that "for me it is clear that the Chancellor's office is in control [*Fäden zusammenlaufen*] and that the cabinet secretary [i.e., Pusch] is pulling the strings." Asked for concrete evidence that this "campaign was begun with the knowledge of [SPÖ] general secretary [Peter] Schieder," Bergmann became a bit vague. "For us, it is beyond doubt, and there is evidence from SPÖ circles, that in several strategy sessions . . . [it was said] that one must ignite this material."[35] What is remarkable about this exchange is less Bergmann's allegations than the questions put to him by radio journalist Fritz Pesata. Pesata never once asked whether talk of a "campaign" was perhaps misleading. Indeed, although Pesata himself retained a skeptical distance to Bergmann's allegations, based as they were on very meager evidence, he conceded the essential point, namely that the various disclosures and interest in Waldheim's past were all part of a "campaign."

Mock and Waldheim, however, took some distance from this view. Mock, also quoted on the news program, believed he possessed "genuine indications that this campaign is being sustained in SP circles,"[36] which indicated that the "campaign" had an independent existence. On the same day, Mock declared that the new evidence of Waldheim's membership in the *NS-Reiterstandarte*[37] would not affect his party's support for him. Rather, "we will stay with Waldheim until the very end [*mit allen Konsequenzen durchtragen*]. Someone wants to destroy him with this campaign, but we will prevent it."[38] Waldheim also "regretted" some of the more crude formulations of Bergmann, and said that he held himself aloof from such things.[39] This did not prevent him, however, from deploring the "malicious allegations" of the WJC, or describing the disclosure of the Central Registry of War Criminals and Security Suspects (CROWCASS) as "a new high point of the dirty campaign."[40]

On 20 March 1986, Waldheim invited a few selected journalists to a private briefing, called as part of a media offensive to counter the suspicion regarding his membership in the SA and NSDStB. At the meeting, Waldheim showed those present (no one was allowed to photocopy it) his own personnel file from the foreign ministry. No definitive conclusions can be made about Waldheim's possible Nazi affiliations on the basis of these documents alone, but *Profil* described it as showing with virtual certainty that Waldheim had been "a member of the SA and the [Nazi] Student Union."[41] For Waldheim, and for the majority of the journalists invited, however, this document showed conclusively, as the *Neues Volksblatt* (*NVB*) wrote, that the allegations about a Nazi affiliation had "collapsed."[42] "Thank God the file was located," Waldheim is reported to have said. "There it states in black and white that I was not in the SA and the [Nazi] Student Union."[43] Dieter Kindermann from the *NKZ* repeated the official Waldheim line,[44] ditto the *Oberösterreichische Nachrichten*[45] and *Die Presse.*[46] Even Hans Rauscher, columnist for *Kurier,* who in general maintained a skeptical attitude towards Waldheim, professed his conversion. He "believe[d] Kurt Waldheim" when he said that he had never been a member of any Nazi organization.[47] The Socialist Party paper *Neue AZ/Tagblatt* (*AZ*), which had not been invited to the rendezvous, reported, not unexpectedly, that Waldheim had "refuted himself."[48]

By 22 March, a broad consensus had formed among important sections of the Austrian press that ambiguities and suspicions surrounding Waldheim's Nazi affiliations had been conclusively refuted. (By this time in the United States, it will be recalled, the consensus was that they had been conclusively proven.) Apart from *Profil,* which could be dismissed as a maverick publication, the SPÖ paper *AZ,* which had its own partisan interests in criticizing Waldheim, and the *Salzburger Nachrichten,* which was not so easily dismissed, there was virtual unanimity that documentary evidence proved that he had been a member neither of the SA nor of the NSDStB. As such, the "campaign" presumably had, or ought to have, collapsed for lack of evidence. Anyone who continued to accuse Waldheim of having a "Nazi past," therefore, could only be acting disingenuously, if not simply out of malice. The date is also significant, for at precisely the moment when Waldheim and his supporters were celebrating their public relations triumph, the WJC was holding a press conference in New York at which it released a copy of the CROWCASS, which listed Waldheim as a suspected war criminal.

Just how important this consensus was for the Waldheim camp may be seen by its reaction to a column by Karl Heinz Ritschel, editor of *Salzburger Nachrichten,* a provincial paper whose editorial line has traditionally been close to the People's Party. Ritschel had been a thorn in Waldheim's side for some time. In the week following the first article in the *New York Times,* his paper published a transcript of Waldheim's remarks to *Times* journalist John Tagliabue, in which the former conceded that he could have been a candidate member of the SA.[49] Two days later, it reported that Waldheim's wife Elisabeth "Sissy" Waldheim had left the Catholic church in 1938 (the year of the *Anschluss*) and only rejoined just prior to their marriage.[50] Neither of these disclosures had endeared Ritschel to Waldheim supporters. His column on 22 March 1986, entitled "the candidacy of one without credibility," however, written in the immediate aftermath of the press briefing of 20 March, unleashed a fury of damage limitation activity on the part of Waldheim and his supporters and showed that any talk of a uniform press support for Waldheim in Austria would be mistaken. "The issue in the 'Waldheim case,'" Ritschel wrote, "is the credibility of a man who wants to be president. Waldheim has said that he swears never to have been anywhere; he gave his word of honor—he lied to all of Austria." By his actions, Waldheim had "disqualified himself—by behaving in a frightening, yes, even childish way." "Who can still believe and trust him?" he queried rhetorically, and concluded that Waldheim's loss of credibility was "an irredeemable debt."[51]

An Austrian newspaper which could not be accused of having any party political interest in Waldheim's defeat published a searing criticism of Waldheim's credibility whose tone and content were not essentially different from the "slanders" expressed by the WJC (or, later, the *NYT*). The danger which such a situation posed to a propaganda line which argued that Austria was under attack from a foreign enemy was apparent, and the reactions tended to mirror this.

In a letter to the *Salzburger Nachrichten,* for example, Waldheim referred to the "various pieces of evidence for the truth" of his statements and added that "not even the research of my slanderers in the central archives was able to turn up any basis for my ostensible membership [i.e., in two Nazi organizations]."[52] Michael Graff of the ÖVP claimed to be "disappointed that such a respected editor could be so wide of the mark."[53] Richard Nimmerrichter of the *NKZ* considered Ritschel's article "the absolute zenith of the great Waldheim cannibal feast." Ritschel, "self-styled editor-in-chief of the *Salzburger Nachrichten,* has fired off a broadside compared to which even the attacks of the World Jewish Congress appear as harmless curiosities."[54] The SPÖ apparently viewed Ritschel's article as a sign that support for Waldheim within the "*bürgerlich*" camp was crumbling, and hoped to use it to drive a wedge between the pro- and anti-Waldheim factions.[55]

Whatever effects Ritschel's arguments might have had on People's Party supporters who might still have had open minds[56] were rendered irrelevant by the events of the next several days. These events, or, more properly, the reception of these events, which could not have been foreseen, shifted the emphasis and vehemence of the "campaign" discourse in Austria. Although at tactically important moments individual figures in the SPÖ continued to be blamed for the "campaign," and though it is even possible for such a campaign to be dicephalous, the WJC increasingly became the principal villain, while the SPÖ assumed a subsidiary role. But that there was a "slander campaign" about, was never placed in doubt.

The "Slanders" and Their Function

The antisemitic *Feindbild* which emerged in the course of the Waldheim election found a convenient target in the WJC, quite in the manner of the traditional scapegoat. At the head of an international "campaign" against Waldheim and Austria, so the argument went, was an organization which was not beneath slander, mendacity, suborning witnesses and assorted other real or imagined sins. One of the constituent elements in the demonization of the WJC was to portray its continual disclosures of documents themselves as "defamation," and either disregard or contemn the allegations they raised. In early April, 1986, for example, Peter Klar, columnist for the official ÖVP daily *NVB,* offered a particularly graphic example of this view. Although Klar amalgamated all Waldheim's critics, his description of the "strategy" they employed indicated clearly the subject he had in mind:

> The authors of this trash can campaign against Kurt Waldheim could have been taught by Josef Goebbels. He is known for his recipe: one makes slanderous assertions and supports them with documents which can raise suspicion but which prove nothing. These accusations are not made all at once, but are produced again and again as new "disclosures." Now since the energy of the opponent is bound up with the need to disprove all the suspicions and accusations, the ever-changing group of accusors maintain tension and a climate of impurity until the entire contrived edifice of lies collapses. Then it is too late for the one affected, because a decision based on the propaganda has already been taken.[57]

Apart from strongly implying that the WJC were no better than the Nazis, Klar also illustrated one of the most compelling weapons in the Waldheim propaganda arsenal, namely, the assertion of the self-evident absurdity of the allegations against him. The explanation of Waldheim's alleged Nazi past was relatively easy. Not only could Waldheim produce his own documents that "proved" he was not a member of the SA, he could also rely upon the consensus of his fellow citizens that, even had he been a member of these organizations, the charge that he was a "Nazi" was indubitably false. Waldheim's service in the Wehrmacht, on the other hand, was far less tractable, in light of the streams of documents which were appearing regularly in several different newspapers as well as at WJC news conferences. The Waldheim camp was able to set the terms for the debate of these issues by itself pre-emptively introducing the question of criminality, ascribing this allegation to the WJC, and then demonstrating that the WJC could not sustain this "charge" with any evidence. The WJC refused to give up its campaign, it was argued, and carried it on with the most vile slander, namely, by accusing Waldheim of being a war criminal. This approach also helped cement the corollary accusation that the WJC was attacking Austria: If Waldheim was a war criminal, then all Austrians who served as soldiers in the Wehrmacht would be as well.

One of the few uncontested assumptions in Austria during the presidential election campaign was that the WJC had branded Waldheim a war criminal. Scarcely a newspaper, not even *Profil* or the *Salzburger Nachrichten,* can be exempted on this score.[58] In Chapter 6, we were able to show how the WJC dealt with the war criminal charge, and established that, whatever ambiguities might have been involved in their choice of words, and however much certain newspapers in both the United States and abroad may have extrapolated on the basis of these, the WJC never actually accused Waldheim of personal involvement in war crimes. It did endorse the reasoning contained in the Yugoslav *Odluka,* and gathered documentary evidence which it believed corroborated it, but on several occasions the WJC explicitly refused to refer to Waldheim as a war criminal. In addition, we have shown that the issue of criminality was introduced before the WJC had released a single document about Waldheim. Campaign press spokesman Gerold Christian refuted thereby a charge that the WJC could not have made, and that Hubertus Czernin of *Profil* had also not introduced.[59] The issue of possible criminality was a legitimate one, since Waldheim had been suspected of war crimes by both Yugoslavia and the UNWCC. The point is that this question had no necessary connection to the WJC, and at no time did the organization or its spokesmen accuse Waldheim of complicity in war crimes.

Still, this assumption persisted. The speech given by then Austrian President Kirchschläger on 22 April 1986 was constructed in a way which not only clearly accepted this premise, but also defined the issues so narrowly that any further disclosures of documents could be easily portrayed as yet another slander against Waldheim.[60] The perpetuation of the notion that the WJC was making accusations it could not prove was sustained above all by systematically distorting the accusations themselves, conflating evidence and accusations, and enlisting the support of experts, especially the Jewish ones, and witnesses to Waldheim's character and army service. From the very beginning of the debate on Waldheim's past, inexplicable "errors" appeared in the reporting, even among papers whose efforts seem to have been sincere.

A report in *Die Presse* on the first press conference of the WJC, for example, took some linguistic and journalistic liberties which in the end served unjustifiably to discredit the WJC. The report by "ett." of a UPI agency dispatch transformed the statement of Eli Rosenbaum, then legal counsel of the WJC, that Army Group E had "supervised the 1943 deportation" of the Jews of Salonika into a statement that the unit in which he had served had "sent" them to Auschwitz.[61] It was, of course, of little consequence to the Jews of Salonika whether Army Group E had actually organized or "merely" arranged transport, even if the latter would represent participation in a crime against humanity.[62] Rosenbaum's remarks need not have been as nuanced as they were, but the rendering in *Die Presse* article suggested a level of involvement which was not part of the WJC's allegation.

In the same paragraph, "ett." reported that "on the other hand, the president of the Central Jewish Council in Greece, Joseph Lovinger, confirmed that Waldheim's name had never been mentioned in connection with National Socialists who persecuted the Jewish community."[63] Lovinger's statement that Waldheim was not mentioned "in connection with National Socialists," however, is germane to this issue on the assumption that only National Socialists were involved in the persecution of Jews, which, even if Lovinger had believed it, would still not be accurate. The passage in the WJC press release itself concerned the involvement of the Wehrmacht in the deportations of Jews, a fact which was not contested. It might have been of significance to ask how Waldheim could have served in Army Group E (which he confirmed) without having heard of atrocities and crimes against humanity which units under the command of Army Group E had committed. Instead, "ett." quoted a statement which was largely irrelevant to the issue and, by using the formulation "on the other hand [*hingegen*]," implied that Lovinger's statement refuted Rosenbaum's, in other words, a "charge" of a kind of involvement in the deportations that the WJC had not made.

On the following day, *Die Presse* published a report in which Simon Wiesenthal was quoted extensively. Among other things, the report emphasized Wiesenthal's information that it was not Waldheim's unit which had carried out the deportations. Since the WJC had not made this accusation, Wiesenthal's statement represented a clarification or refutation, not of an allegation of the WJC, but of a position ascribed to it by *Die Presse.*[64] A report by Peter Gnam in the *NKZ* had much the same effect. Gnam spoke of the "wild sense of outrage" over the "campaign against Waldheim," and presented his version of the background:

> The *New York Times* had asserted that during the war Kurt Waldheim belonged to an army group which committed war crimes in Greece and Yugoslavia. Yugoslav partisans and Greek Jews [according to the *Times*] were liquidated. Waldheim has given assurances that he had never participated in such activities and also knew nothing about them. Thereupon, the head of the World Jewish Congress, Bronfman, spoke of Waldheim as "one of the greatest disappointments of our time, because he has denied all of this for forty years." Waldheim considers this "foul and deceitful." He was an interpreter during the time in question.[65]

Gnam's distortion of the *NYT* report was too extensive to have been accidental. His formulation, "the *New York Times* asserted" misleadingly implied that the newspaper was doing something other than printing its reporter's findings. This consorted well with the portrayal of the report as part of a "campaign." The usage also implied that there was some uncertainty as to whether Waldheim had served in the unit, or that troops of this unit had committed war crimes. Yet Waldheim personally conceded that he had served with Army Group E, and never denied that troops under its command had committed war crimes. He merely contested his involvement or knowledge of them or both. Gnam's usage could only obscure these distinctions.

Moreover, both the statement Gnam attributed to Edgar Bronfman as well as the context in which it had been made were Gnam's inventions. Bronfman's alleged statement that "Waldheim was one of the greatest disappointments of our time, because he has denied all of this for forty years," could not be found in any of the available materials. The *NYT* article does not contain this statement. Though the quotation in this form did not appear anywhere else to my knowledge, the context clearly suggested that it had been taken from the WJC's press release. There Bronfman was quoted as saying, not that Waldheim was a "disappointment" (though for Bronfman he clearly was that), but that he had engaged in "one of the most elaborate deceptions of our time."[66] Far more serious than attributing the wrong word to Bronfman, however, was the impression that the placing of the quotation gave. Bronfman's statement, correctly or incorrectly rendered, did not refer to Waldheim's statement that he had "never participated in such actions," as Gnam's introductory adverb "thereupon [*daraufhin*]"[67] implied, but rather to Waldheim's (wanting) credibility, i.e., that he had concealed his Nazi affiliations and military service for 40 years. Anyone reading Gnam's article, however, could only have concluded that Bronfman had implicitly or explicitly accused Waldheim of involvement in war crimes. The manifold inaccuracies that this article contained followed a pattern: they inflated the nature of the WJC's criticism of Waldheim and in doing so linked it to accusations of involvment in war crimes which they had not made. From such information it is but a short step to the conclusion that the WJC was slandering Waldheim with exaggerated and utterly unfounded charges, and was being seconded by the *NYT.*

If papers like *Die Presse* and the *NKZ* were relatively unabashed in the journalistic assistance they provided to the Waldheim propaganda strategy, distortions of a similar nature befell reporters who by all appearances attempted to approach the questions without preconceived notions about what their investigations would show. Two journalists who then worked for the independent daily *Kurier* interviewed Johann Auf, a Wehrmacht veteran who had served with Waldheim in Arsakli. According to the headline, this one witness was able to explain "which attacks . . . are true and which are false." Apart from making unwarrantedly immodest claims, *Kurier's* headline had been formulated in such a way that virtually anything which Auf related about his experience in Greece could be considered a refutation of a "false" attack. In point of fact, Auf did help clarify some details about Waldheim's service in Arsakli: he was the first to mention that the headquarters of the Army Group E general staff were located in Arsakli rather than Salonika, that Waldheim had been in the Ic department and that his immediate superior officer had been Lieutenant Colonel Herbert Warnstorff, not Alexander Loehr. On 4 March, the WJC presented documents which showed that Waldheim had served in Army Group E, and it alleged that he had concealed this service from the public for forty years. Merely producing documents which showed or suggested that Waldheim had served under Loehr in Army Group E cannot be considered "allegations," however, unless the documents themselves are not held to be genuine. Not even Waldheim questioned the authenticity of the documents the WJC presented. The failure of the *Kurier* reporters to clarify this point could only have suggested that Auf's statement had rectified an in fact non-existent false assertion.

Auf's opinion that Waldheim "did not have a function which was even militarily relevant" was simply false, but no evidence of this was in the article. Moreover, the introduction of Auf's story about the partisans cutting off the genitals of a live captured German prisoner, even if true, in the context could only have been read as neutralizing or cancelling out the atrocities committed by the Wehrmacht.[68] At the time of this initial interview, there was not enough information freely available to have enabled these journalists to check Auf's statement thoroughly for accuracy. At the same time, the lack of virtually any critical distance to the details Auf provided, combined with the newspaper's unjustified pretensions as to what the article showed and the fact that the article addressed not a single actual allegation the WJC had made, could not but have reinforced the impression that the charges against Waldheim were untrue. And those who make untrue statements about someone are slanderers.

The distortions of the allegations made against Waldheim and the employment of tendentious labels to describe undisputed facts which we have examined here all took place during the first week of the Waldheim affair. The quality of the reporting in Austria, however, in general did not improve. This can best be seen by examining the round of disclosures and their reception between the 22nd and 28th of March. During this week, the construction of the *Feindbild* was able to record a major advance: now fear and resentment engendered by the "threats" made by the WJC against "Austria" were added to the dynamic of exaggerating and otherwise distorting its "allegations" or "attacks," in order to expose them as groundless and their authors as shameless vilifiers. Again, with few exceptions, prominent politicians and representatives of several non-party newspapers helped the Waldheim camp promulgate its view, which in its broad outlines posited that Austria was under attack by a powerful international Jewish conspiracy, spearheaded by the WJC, against which only a united front of all Austrians behind Waldheim could succeed. Just as the original "campaign" discourse could not emerge *ex nihilio,* so too did the imprecation of a conspiracy theory require the assistance of a series of coincidences which could be portrayed as confirming notions associated with an international "campaign" against Waldheim. Here it is possible to see how such a meta-reality was both a condition and guarantor of the explanations of the "campaign" against Waldheim.

On Saturday, 22 March 1986, the WJC held a press conference in New York, at which it made available to journalists the CROWCASS of 1948. This list, it will be recalled, recorded that Waldheim was being sought by Yugoslavia for crimes allegedly committed during his service in the Balkans. The first reactions in Austria to this press conference came the following Monday. The ÖVP paper *NVB* led the way. The WJC, it claimed, had accused Waldheim of "having been suspected by Yugoslav authorities of having been involved in war crimes in 1948."[69] The *NVB* saw the significance of this "disgusting witch hunt" against Waldheim, which was becoming "dirtier" by the day, as confirmation of the suspicion of a coordinated attack. After high SPÖ officials had charged Waldheim with unspecified "memberships during the Nazi period," the paper wrote, "at the weekend the World Jewish Congress pounced: Waldheim was sought, 'suspected of participation in murder.' Waldheim's response: 'A new high point of the mud-slinging campaign!'" According to Waldheim's press spokesman, Gerold Christian, the allegations were "insinuations sucked out of thin air," and clearly contradicted "the clear and objective statements of Simon Wiesenthal, Gideon Rafael and Schlomo Avineri, former general directors of the Israeli Foreign Ministry as well as Israel's former U.N. ambassador, Jehuda Blum."[70] It apparently bothered neither Christian nor the *NVB* editors that, of the four Jews summoned forth in Waldheim's defense, only Wiesenthal to my knowledge ever made a statement about the CROWCASS, and he only on 24 March, i.e., after this article had appeared.

As the *NVB* had done in its report, the headline in *Die Presse,* "World Jewish Congress on Waldheim: Suspected War Criminal in 1948"[71] also misleadingly signalled doubt as to whether Yugoslavia had suspected Waldheim. The WJC had published the CROWCASS, which contained Waldheim's name. However, to have written, as did the *NVB,* that the WJC, and not the U.S. Army (which had compiled the list), had "reproached" Waldheim for having been on a list, could only make sense if the list itself were not genuine. Yet neither the *NVB* nor *Die Presse* explicitly challenged the authenticity of the document itself, nor do these papers appear to have examined the details of the list, what this implied about Waldheim's earlier claims that he had only served as an interpreter, etc., all of which had been discussed in the WJC's press release.[72] In fact, no formulation in the WJC's press release is factually inaccurate on the basis of the information they had at the time. The usage in both papers, but not only these,[73] implied that the WJC had once again slandered Waldheim by accusing him of war crimes, as the rubric in the article in *Die Presse,* "The Witch Hunt Against VP [People's Party] Candidate Continues" indicated. The *NKZ* reported that the publication of the CROWCASS indicated that "the campaign about the alleged NS-Past of Kurt Waldheim had reached a new negative high point," in one fell swoop linking this controversy about Waldheim's war service to the debate over his former Nazi affiliations and positing the absurdity of both. The paper concluded its coverage by quoting Waldheim as saying that he "would not be bullied by this psycho-terror."[74]

The Austrian daily *Kurier* did report the contents of the CROWCASS, and distinguished its contents from the WJC's own allegations. However, the emphasis in the reporting was more on Waldheim's personal political response than on the possible legal implications of the list. The banner headline of the 24 March 1986 edition of the paper read "Waldheim: 'I'm not giving up!'" and mentioned in smaller print both that Yugoslavia had placed him on a list of war criminals and that Waldheim suspected that all officers of his unit had been placed on the list en masse.[75] On page two, Hans Rauscher wrote an article with the headline, "Waldheim Placed on War Criminals List in 1948—Significance Unclear,"[76] to which was added, "Document published in New York." In this report, Rauscher explained the background of the CROWCASS list. His description of the list was by and large accurate, although he stated as fact that "in 1944/45 [Waldheim] had served as a staff officer in the Ic (Abwehr) department of the general staff of Army Group E," which was not entirely accurate. What was noteworthy about this article was Rauscher's effortless endorsement of Waldheim's own line of argument under the guise of independent reporting.

It will be recalled that the headline in *Kurier* noted that Waldheim had suspected that all officers of his unit had been placed on the list. Rauscher wrote that "it is, however, questionable whether this registration on a list means anything. It is entirely possible that the Yugoslavs simply entered all officers of Loehr's staff or even other Wehrmacht units as a group on a list of those sought and then gave it to the Americans or the U.N. . . . Waldheim himself also considers this a possible explanation." Rauscher's guess, portrayed here as an independent opinion with which Waldheim agreed, could have been checked easily enough. Since *Kurier* itself knew of at least one other officer on the general staff, Waldheim's immediate superior Herbert Warnstorff,[77] a quick glance at the CROWCASS under the letter "W" (the names were listed alphabetically) could have determined whether indeed all officers had been placed wholesale on the list. Warnstorff's name was not on it.

In the end, the only point Rauscher considered relevant was one which repeated Waldheim's own view. Yet if Rauscher's diminution of the significance of this listing was based upon a surmise which could be (and in this case turned out to be) false, then presumably the charges themselves would have to be taken far more seriously. Rauscher did not concede the possibility that his guess could be checked and thereby be completely wrong,[78] nor did he examine any of the charges made in the document itself. These journalistic lapses and *Kurier's* implicit endorsement of Waldheim's claim that the charges were "absurd" made forming an opinion on the issues independently of the Waldheim explanation virtually impossible. All the more, in the same issue *Kurier* published an interview with Waldheim in which his remarks "what the World Jewish Congress is doing is absurd, an effrontery, groundless, it is impudence now to want to brand me as a war criminal," were presented without any kind of qualifying remarks, although it was clear from *Kurier's* own report that Waldheim's attack on the WJC was groundless.[79] ÖVP politicians also assisted in the amalgamation of charges made in a U.S. Army document, whose authenticity was not questioned, with the WJC's publication of the document itself. Then party head Alois Mock was quoted as saying, with reference to the disclosure of the documents, that "the defamation campaign against Waldheim has assumed the character of a man hunt."[80] Michael Graff had gone on the offensive early. Appearing on the televised *Pressestunde* on Sunday, 23 March, Graff denounced the "over-agitated attacks" of the WJC and warned that their behavior "could release emotions in Austria which no one wants," an implied threat that if the WJC did not stop, it must reckon with a wave of antisemitism in Austria. Apart from his assumption that the behavior of individual Jews could be responsible for antisemitism (without it Graff's remarks made no sense), his statement in effect meant that the Austrian Jewish Community was being held hostage for the good behavior of the WJC.[81]

Some journalists did question the authenticity of the Yugoslav charges. Walter Zeiner wrote a comment in the *Neue Voralberger Tageszeitung* on the publication of the CROWCASS. The WJC, he stated, now accused Waldheim of having participated in murder during the Second World War. Zeiner's claim is untrue, but he was consistent enough to imply that the document was not genuine. Yugoslavia would never have voted for Waldheim as U.N. Secretary General, he wrote, if he "had appeared on a list of war criminals." "The question remains," he concluded, "what does the campaign fomented by the World Jewish Congress want?"[82]

The belief that it had not been the U.S. Army or Yugoslavia, but the WJC which had "attacked" or "accused" Waldheim of war crimes during World War II, was, then, a fairly widespread one. Most reporters did not examine the documents or even the WJC's statement, much less discuss them seriously. Even when the documents themselves and their presentation were not so obviously distorted, the interpretation was either misleading or it accorded with the Waldheim camp line. Even the *Wiener Zeitung,* which had accurately and dispassionately described the documents and their contents, referred to the publication of the documents as "accusations" of the WJC.[83]

On 24 March, Simon Wiesenthal invited reporters to a briefing at which, among other things, he discussed the CROWCASS listing. In Wiesenthal's view, the fact that Waldheim's name was on the list would not incriminate him without additional evidence. Moreover, he argued, there had been several such lists, and it could be that Waldheim had appeared on one list but was deleted from subsequent versions if the Yugoslav authorities later detemined that the evidence was insufficient to sustain an indictment.[84] Wiesenthal also rejected the accusation that he had assumed the role of and "exculpatory witness" for Waldheim. Wiesenthal said he doubted that Waldheim had been personally involved in war crimes but could not believe he could have been unaware of the deportations of Jews from Salonika. "That must have been the main topic of discussion then, and therefore I do not believe him," he was quoted as saying.[85] Finally, Wiesenthal confirmed that persons "from Austria" had come to him in the Autumn of 1985 in search of incriminating material against Waldheim.[86]

The tendency in reporting on this briefing depended roughly on how one viewed the Waldheim affair, for Wiesenthal's punctiliously balanced views offered solace to both Waldheim's supporters and his critics. The *Neue Zeit,* the SPÖ paper in Graz, emphasized Wiesenthal's repudiation of the allegation that he was exonerating Waldheim,[87] while the *Südost Tagespost* countered with a headline stating Wiesenthal's ostensible opposition to the anti-Waldheim "agitation."[88] In several papers in which Wiesenthal was mentioned in connection with the CROWCASS, moreover, the authenticity of the document itself was called into question.[89] An article in *Die Presse* will illustrate the point. The headline over an article by "HWS" read "Wiesenthal Doubts Waldheim's Guilt." According to the report, Wiesenthal had expressed his doubts as to whether Yugoslavia had even placed Waldheim's name on a war crimes list, which is a very subtle, but immensely significant, "misunderstanding" of what Wiesenthal actually said.[90] This belief, however, died a slow death. On 1 April, for example, Peter Gnam reported on a statement from the Yugoslav government according to which Waldheim's extradition had not been pursued. This, Gnam argued, "confirmed speculation that, as a member of the staff under General Loehr, Waldheim, like all officers, was initially automatically placed on this list by the Yugoslavs, without having done anything wrong."[91] Even papers not following the Waldheim line subserviently questioned the CROWCASS's authenticity implicitly or explicitly, and this with the apparent imprimatur of Simon Wiesenthal. Because most derivative reports distorted Wiesenthal's remarks, they cannot but have further undermined the WJC's claims to legitimacy as a participant in the Waldheim debate. If it is possible that Yugoslavia had never suspected Waldheim of being a war criminal, which is what these doubts would logically imply, then the enormity of the slander raised by the WJC would increase nearly exponentially, and the conspiracy against Waldheim would also have to include the U.S. Army. The use and abuse of Simon Wiesenthal's statement served, whether consciously or not, to reinforce the claim, as the *NVB* put it, that the WJC was continuing its "Witch Hunt against Waldheim with New Lies."[92]

The "Threats" of the World Jewish Congress

Between the WJC's publication of the CROWCASS and the press conference they held on 25 March, the Austrian magazine *Profil* printed an interview with Israel Singer and Elan Steinberg, general secretary and executive secretary of the WJC, respectively. We have shown above that the existence of an international "campaign" against Kurt Waldheim led by the WJC and supported by the international press, above all the *NYT,* had become a fixed assumption in Austrian public discourse. Moreover, as we have just seen, the belief that the WJC had accused Waldheim of being involved in war crimes, perhaps even on the basis of forged documents, had also been widely circulated in Austrian papers. It is important to recall this context once again in order to understand the change the dynamic of the debate on Waldheim's past underwent during this week. Below are a few passages out of this interview, which in Austria has become nearly legendary:

> Singer: The Austrian population should be clear that the next six years will be no bed of roses for them if Waldheim is elected. If he does not ruthlessly and completely lay bare his past before the election, this will come to haunt him and every Austrian for the next six years. Bitburg was bad enough, but it only lasted for one day. The actions against Waldheim will last six years.
>
> Profil: Aren't you exaggerating your influence?
>
> Singer: It hasn't been a question merely of the work of the WJC for some time now. Jewish and expecially non-Jewish organizations all over the world will prepare a proper reception for Waldheim in whichever country he travels to as Austria's representative. . . .
>
> Steinberg: . . . We have received inquiries about Waldheim for several years. But Waldheim is not a war criminal—at least so far as we know now. . . .
>
> Singer: . . . Perhaps it will turn out that Waldheim was really a harmless figure in the Wehrmacht. I would not wish to exclude this [possibility]. But he lied, lied to us all [when he said] that he was ostensibly in the hospital, ostensibly at the university, not in Salonika and not in Serbia, and these are only the examples we are already able to prove and where he has confessed his lies.

> Profil: In some Austrian newspapers one could read that by your actions you have become a tool of a [political] party. [And] that the current government and the [consular] representatives here in New York gave you the first hints and provided you with the documents.
>
> Steinberg: That is absolute nonsense and [shows that someone is merely] looking for an easy fall guy [*Haltet den Dieb-Mentalität*] which is unworthy of the Austrians. We don't care who wins the election, from which party he is . . . .
>
> Profil: What do you plan to do if Waldheim is elected?
>
> Singer: We aren't planning anything. It then becomes a problem of the Austrians. They have to try to live with it. As far as I know, Austria tries hard to present itself all over the world and especially in the U.S.A. as a tourist spot, a country of technical and cultural exports and as an ideal country for foreign industrial investment. Who do you think will want to have anything to do with this country, whose representative has been exposed as a liar in front of the whole world?
>
> Profil: Will there be a boycott of Austrian goods?
>
> Singer: We are not talking of measures against Austrians. The Austrians set the conditions, they create the facts. They elect a representative, we don't. And it will be perhaps the most important election since 1945. It will show the world whether there is a new Austria, one which has freed itself from the past. The Austrians must bear the consequences and I can tell you, the next six years with Waldheim will not be easy.
>
> Profil: What do you mean concretely?
>
> Steinberg: What do you think? Do you think we are going to pull back after Waldheim's election? It will naturally continue. We will continue to search. And specialists from the U.S.A., Germany, Yugoslavia, the Soviet Union and Austria will be joining us. Up to now it has been an affair of Waldheim's. But then it will be one of all of Austria. Then the entire world will say that a former Nazi and liar is Austria's representative. Everyone with an Austrian passport will be travelling with this cloud of uncertainty. I can't imagine that the Austrians want such a thing.[93]

The interview itself contains several contradictory passages. Singer and Steinberg deny any interest in the Austrian elections, yet they made their preferences for the outcome unmistakably clear. Singer claimed that the WJC would do "nothing at all" if Waldheim were elected, while Steinberg asked rhetorically, "Do you think we are going to give up after the election?" Finally, Steinberg stated quite clearly that Waldheim "is not a war criminal," but then added, "as far as we know up to now." The passage where Singer asserted (or predicted) that, if the Austrians elected Waldheim, the six years of his presidency would be "no bed of roses" for them, could be interpreted semantically as a threat, were one so inclined. Both Singer and Steinberg, however, diluted the purely "Jewish" element of the "danger" by emphasizing the "non-Jewish organizations all over the world" who were interested in the Waldheim case and especially non-Jewish American politicians who had "no interest in [who wins] the Austrian presidential election," and "certainly not that a socialist [should] win it," but who would find it outrageous that "a former Nazi and liar [could become] Austria's representative."

There are thus passages in this interview which could be perceived as threats against Austria. Peter Sichrovsky, who conducted the interview, appears to have understood the "bed of roses" passage as such. Moreover, other papers, such as the West German *Süddeutsche Zeitung,* whose reporting on the Waldheim affair was of high quality, apparently also saw it this way. It published an AP dispatch from Vienna with the headline "Jews Warn Austrians Against Waldheim's Election."[94] As late as November, 1986, Simon Wiesenthal could complain that the WJC's "collective threats against all Austrians have provided resentment against all Jews."[95] However, Singer's and Steinberg's statements could only in fact be seriously considered threatening if the WJC in fact possessed the power and influence necessary to effect all those measures they had ostensibly threatened. Underlying this belief, however it may be expressed, is a prior assumption about the international power of Jews, in short, the hoary but apparently atavistic notion of the world Jewish conspiracy, which in the course of the Waldheim affair enjoyed something of a revival.[96] It was above all this cluster of assumptions and associations, rooted in prejudice, fear and hostility, and condensed in the attacks on the WJC, which determined the antisemitic character of the pro-Waldheim political discourse, whether from the mouths of party officials or the pens of sympathetic journalists.

The intensity of the reaction to this interview and the "threats" it contained can scarcely be exaggerated and may be illustrated by an almost arbitrary selection of press reports. The headline of the ÖVP paper *NVB,* "Violent [*heftig*] Threats against Austria because of Waldheim," was emblematic. In the accompanying article, it wrote that the representatives of the WJC had "gone so far as to warn Austria against making a 'Liar' and 'Nazi' president." Michael Graff was quoted as saying that the ÖVP would not allow an Austrian to be destroyed this way and repeated his own implied threat about the "emotions which no one wants."[97] The *Neue Vorarlberger Tageszeitung,* which supported Waldheim in the election, exhibited unusual virulence and a particularly evocative idiom. In its headline the paper complained that "Jewish Council wants Collective Liability. Everyone must Bear the Consequences." The accompanying unsigned article argued that "with a sort of collective liability in the event of Kurt Waldheim's election as president, the World Jewish Congress has threatened [that] actions against Waldheim would pursue him and every Austrian for the next six years."[98]

In *Die Presse,* a paper with pretensions to possession of broad vision,[99] Ilse Leitenberger availed herself of similar literary techniques, but with vague allusions to the commonality of interests between old Nazis and the WJC. She asks what "prompted the World Jewish Congress—which has entirely different tasks to accomplish—to zero in on a man who has not the slightest thing to do with the affairs of world Jewry?" The WJC, moreover, though it made accusations itself, "considers itself above criticism, but has always been a willing tool of a handful of diehard reactionaries who never miss a chance to trade in a dark past. It is namely they who already bear a considerable amount of blame for the fact that a new antisemitism, whose escalation we cannot yet conceive, can no longer be denied." Implied is the hypocrisy of the WJC, which attempted to make Waldheim into a Nazi while itself being in league with the genuine old Nazis (the term *"Ewiggestriger"* can only be a reference to these). In any event, the members of the WJC, and the joint interest they have in trading in the "dark past"—the ambiguity of this allusion makes it unclear what is meant precisely—are responsible for the re-emergence of a potentially virulent antisemitism, whose existence Leitenberger did not dispute. The vague innuendo and indistinct language give Leitenberger's piece a somewhat ethereal quality. What is clear is the message that the WJC had no moral right to criticize Waldheim, since this was not an affair concerning "world Jewry" and it should not complain about antisemitism in Austria, for it was responsible for its re-emergence.[100]

As Leitenberger's article implied, the antisemitic ambience in Austria was becoming increasingly difficult to deny. *Die Furche,* a weekly which may be broadly characterized as a liberal Catholic paper and whose journalists in the past have taken uncompromising stands against antisemitism,[101] publishes a regular column by Herbert Feichtelbauer called "Klipp und klar" (roughly "short and to the point"). In the first issue of *Die Furche* to appear after this interview, Feichtelbauer, as all others who blamed antisemitic prejudice in Austria on the WJC, warned the WJC not to tempt fate by misbehaving:

> But just as Auschwitz should never again be, because it should never again be allowed to be, our Jewish friends must see the writing on the wall. What is happening these days begets new evil, where only reconciliation can heal. Whoever fears what is most frightful deep down in the Austrian soul, should not rouse it with wild actions [*berserkend*]!. . . If the representatives of the World Jewish Congress today concede privately that they do not believe Waldheim to be a war criminal, but that he must be taught a lesson for his shilly-shallying, they are playing with fire. If they threaten Austria with a diplomatic, travel, trade and tourist boycott if Waldheim is elected, then they become complicit in the consequences which we dread.[102]

Simon Wiesenthal himself later also added his voice to those blaming the WJC for "reviving antisemitism" in Austria. "It is not their [WJC] revelations about Waldheims's past" which was the cause, but rather "an interview by Israel Singer . . . telling Austrians that Bitburg was one bitter day for President Reagan and that if Austrians elect Waldheim, the population of Austria is going to get six years of Bitburg." "This," Wiesenthal concluded, "makes antisemites of young people—and 70 percent of the population was born after the war."[103]

Wiesenthal's words found a wide echo in many Austrian newspapers. Viktor Reimann, columnist for the *NKZ,* was one of many who cited Jewish authorities to attack the WJC: he mobilized not only Wiesenthal, but Nahum Goldmann, former president of the WJC, against Singer. In a piece published on 25 May, Reimann wrote, "Simon Wiesenthal . . . criticized Israel Singer for having given new sustenance to antisemitism in our country with his threats against Austria. Singer arrogantly stated that antisemitism only stems from antisemites, although he could have learned otherwise . . . from Nahum Goldmann."[104]

It had been open season on the WJC for several weeks, but Wiesenthal's remarks lent a new legitimacy to an old idea, widespread in Austria,[105] that Jews themselves were responsible for antisemitism. Wiesenthal's endorsement of it, however, did not make it any less prejudicial, for underlying the belief that the actions of any one individual Jew could be the *cause* of antisemitism is an assumption projecting the presumed personal traits of one member of a group onto the group as a whole. This assumption lies at the heart of all ethnic prejudice.[106] If Singer's statement had actually been the *occasion* for renewed hostility towards Jews in Austria (which is scarcely to be doubted), this would merely confirm the prior existence of the imputative assumption among those making this claim about the WJC.

Both the Austrian Press Agency (APA) and *Die Presse* reported on 25 March that former chancellor Bruno Kreisky had condemned the "disgusting meddling" and "colossal vileness" of the WJC,[107] and his statement, as was usual in Austria, found a significant response in the papers.[108] In this context, however, Kreisky's statement seems to have served predominantly to reinforce the allegation against the WJC that its charges were all "slander," and this by a prominent Jew. This seems at least indirectly confirmed by the reports of newspapers which suddenly found something to applaud in a remark of Kreisky's. The *Tiroler Tageszeitung,* the paper of the Tiroler Farmers' Association, for example, not normally given to showing Kreisky in a favorable light, quoted him extensively in an article headlined "Kreisky to Jewish Congress: Improper": "It is absolutely improper to talk this way. Until now, at least, such threats were not common among serious people in the West. And against a state which alone declared its willingness to provide a transit route for Russian Jews."[109]

More surprising still is the treatment Kreisky received in the ÖVP's *NVB.* The headline announced simply "Kreisky: Improper Intervention of Jewish Circles." In the remarks quoted, the former chancellor seemed offended that the WJC had criticized Waldheim, and not Kreisky himself: "The anti-Waldheim campaign of the World Jewish Congress is an exceedingly stupid intervention in our election. Yet what is being done with Waldheim is nothing. If I had run for president, they would have attacked me much more severely."[110] Kreisky cannot seriously have believed that the words of two officials of the WJC constituted an improper intervention in the internal affairs of Austria, because he always prided himself for his views of and solutions to international affairs, which not even the most strident patriot could consider internal to Austria. Moreover, Kreisky did not accord the WJC any possible interest in Waldheim other than hostility to Austrian politicians as Austrians. Apart from any personal motives he might have had, Kreisky's remarks appear to have been related more to his fear that the attacks of the WJC would redound to Waldheim's advantage, and his wish to deny him this patriotic trump. Whatever his reasons, the attacks on the WJC—phrased as his attacks on other Jewish opponents frequently were[111]—provided just the kind of Jewish cover for others with perhaps less subtle dialectical skills. As in the case of Wiesenthal, Kreisky's statement helped legitimate and thereby positively reinforce the main lines of assault on the WJC and its right to participate in the debate about Waldheim's past. The insinuation that the WJC might have had tactical political interest in the outcome of the Austrian presidential election was a mere coda to the outpouring of scarcely concealed rage following their interview in *Profil.* A new crescendo, however, was already in the making, even as the reactions to the WJC's "threats" and "meddling" had not yet abated. The ensuing debate over the WJC's disclosures on 25 March indicated that any new act the WJC committed could be, and was, interpreted as a confirmation of the Jewish conspiracy against Waldheim and Austria. As Klaus Emmerich, Washington correspondent for the Austrian Broadcasting Company's news department, stated, "Now, of course, the campaign comprises not only the Waldheim case, . . . but rather in the meantime also [comprises] the case of Austria."[112]

As we saw above, on the basis of information contained in the CROWCASS, the WJC reported in its press release of 22 March that Waldheim had been listed as an *Abwehroffizier.*[113] This claim was an accurate rendering of the information contained in the CROWCASS, but nevertheless mistaken. However, the WJC mentioned this connection only this once, and for a very simple reason: at their press conference on 25 March, the WJC made public a new set of German army documents which proved conclusively that Waldheim had served as the third assistant adjutant in the military intelligence section of Army Group E, but not as the counter-intelligence officer, as the CROWCASS had claimed.[114]

This latter press conference took place at 10:00 a.m. New York time, which is 4:00 p.m. in Vienna, on 25 March 1986. The noontime radio news program, Mittagsjournal, broadcast from noon to 1:00 p.m. on the 25th, carried a number of items on the topic of Waldheim and presented opinions on "accusations" which the WJC had not yet even made (and some of which they never made). The general tone of the program was set in the introductory remarks of the moderator: "the announcement by representatives of the WJC . . . that they would raise further serious charges against the ex-secretary general," he said, "has ushered in a new phase in the discussion."[115] Although the press conference was to take place in four hours' time, the moderator himself already anticipated the debate, and linked it to the recent attacks on the WJC resulting from the *Profil* interview: "Now, on the one hand, there is the question of Waldheim's alleged involvement, but the discussion has already focused on the question to what extent the WJC has quasi-intervened in internal Austrian affairs."

The moderator could not have known what the WJC would say in its press conference, and thus made vague allusions to "involvement," careful, however, to distance himself from any possible association by utilizing the word "alleged." This is a proper journalistic convention to guard against excessive bias. However, this convention was abandoned in the second half of the statement, in which the moderator identified fully with the wave of hostility among Austrian politicians and in most newspapers. By choosing the formulation "to what extent" the WJC might be intervening, the moderator had conceded the point that the WJC were intervening. On the basis of the same known facts, the question could just as easily have been why politicians and journalists in Austria viewed the publication of genuine documents about a former head of the United Nations as intervention in the internal affairs of Austria. This, however, would have required a more consistent maintenance of journalistic skepticism, which apparently came more easily when dealing with the WJC.

Extensive research on the reporting of the Waldheim affair has shown that, although there were significant exceptions, the Austrian state-owned broadcasting company was on the whole simply not up to the task.[116] This failing was particularly striking on 25 March, because the news departments were "reporting" on events yet to occur. For example, then ÖVP general secretary Michael Graff's remarks on the unseen documents and on the discussion as a whole were allowed to stand, without any hint that they contained false or disputed facts and assumptions. Graff, the moderator stated, "is completely convinced that Waldheim had nothing to do with war crimes. And the documents announced for this afternoon in New York can only serve as a continuation of the obscene campaign [*Sudelkampagne*]."[117] Graff was not asked on what he based his judgment that Waldheim had had "nothing to do with war crimes." From Austrian newspapers, however, it was known that at least two different bodies specifically established to prosecute alleged war criminals suspected otherwise.[118] Moreover, Graff's own transparent strategy was to link the WJC to allegations that Waldheim was a war criminal, and to use this inflated (and untrue) assertion to discredit whatever charges the WJC might actually have raised (they had not yet said anything) at the press conference. The reporter neither rectified Graff's factual errors nor attempted to relativize Graff's statement as a contested opinion. Yet this information was freely available.[119] In this radio program, not only was the WJC not asked for a statement, but listeners were provided no competing or contrasting interpretive framework for the documents the WJC was to publish.

The press conference did in fact begin at 4:00 p.m. central European time. The WJC, or, more specifically, Robert E. Herzstein, the historian they had commissioned to look into Waldheim's past, produced and interpreted documents which, among other things, proved beyond any doubt that Waldheim's claim only to have served as an interpreter in Army Group E was false.[120] Waldheim had, the documents showed, also served as a staff officer in military intelligence section of the general staff. This was the only point revealed by the WJC and Herzstein relevant to Waldheim's *position* in Army Group E. Neither Herzstein's prepared statement nor the WJC's press release made any reference to Waldheim as an *Abwehroffizier*.

This appears not to have hindered Austrian broadcasting service (ORF) journalist Edgar Sterbenz from claiming, in his report on the press conference broadcast on the evening news program. "Yes, the documents just published by the World Jewish Congress show that in Yugoslavia during World War II, Kurt Waldheim served not only as an interpreter, but also as an interrogation officer of the *Abwehr*."[121] Radio reporter Fritz Pesata summarized the "charges": the WJC believed that the allegations that Waldheim "was a Nazi," that he "had lied for forty years" and that he had "*known about war crimes* and personally taken part in partisan activities" had all been proved (emphasis added). Asked to comment, Waldheim initially repeated his standard perfunctory denial and, without having seen any of the documents themselves, felt in a position to affirm that there would be nothing in the documents that "would be dishonorable or prove any crimes whatsoever." Although Pesata's summary of the "charges" was not entirely accurate, Waldheim's statement was a denial of a charge which the WJC (according to Pesata himself) had not raised.[122] Knowledge of war crimes is not participation. Pesata's silence on this point left the impression that the WJC had accused Waldheim of involvement in war crimes, a charge Waldheim effortlessly "refuted." Shortly thereafter, Pesata repeated Sterbenz's error about the press conference. "According to these photocopies of documents presented today you were not only an interpreter but also, and this is new, interrogation officer of the *Abwehr.* Is that correct?"[123] To which Waldheim replied, "Now, that's not right. I was not an *Abwehroffizier.* There was a separate *Abwehroffizier.*" Once again, accusations which the WJC had not made were introduced into the discussion, while the substantive elements of the documents they produced went virtually unmentioned. Waldheim was thereby offered the opportunity not only to "disprove" the WJC's "charges" (the documents the WJC published proved that Waldheim was not the *Abwehroffizier* of Army Group E), but also (and this with the full complicity of the ORF radio journalist) to portray the WJC as the purveyor of easily discredited allegations, in other words, as "slanderers."

Austrian newspapers in general fared little better, and were able to call once again on the support of Simon Wiesenthal. Dieter Kindermann of the *NKZ* wrote a report on these disclosures which carried the title, "Wiesenthal: Just Hot Air!"[124] Wiesenthal appears to have read neither the WJC's press release nor Herzstein's prepared statement which contained his interpretations of the documents. He was quoted by Kindermann as saying, "Over there are people who have not learned to read German military documents. There was no differentiation between the counter-intelligence and the intelligence department, which existed in every division." Wiesenthal's claim about the differentiation of the intelligence (Ic) and counter-intelligence (*Abwehr*) departments is confusing at the very least. According to the *Handbook for General Staffs in Wartime,* the duties of the Ic and the Abwehr were combined (i.e., there was no separate *Abwehroffizier*) in military units subordinate to the command level of "Army," but in Army groups (such as that in which Waldheim served) the Ic was separate from the *Abwehr.*[125] There is no indication from Kindermann's article what exactly Wiesenthal had been referring to, and the point is recondite in any case. Ironically, although it was technically incorrect, Wiesenthal's statement, if interpreted literally, would have confirmed the charge, falsely attributed to the WJC, that Waldheim had been an "interrogation officer of the *Abwehr.*" The point is this: if there was no differentiation between the intelligence section and the counter-intelligence section, as Wiesenthal claimed, then why should one object to referring to Waldheim as an "interrogation officer of the *Abwehr*?" It is not a question whether the WJC or Herzstein interpreted all the documents correctly. Wiesenthal's claim, that these "people" had not learned to read documents, appears to have been referring to an "error" that the WJC had not made. The authority of Simon Wiesenthal was used once again to underpin the belief that the WJC was making wild accusations they could not prove. Paired with Wiesenthal's blanket condemnation of the WJC interpretations, and no corrections from Kindermann, Waldheim's statement that he had never been an "*Abwehroffizier*, a member of the Nazi secret service and certainly [not] a war criminal," appeared not only irrefutable but also an accurate portrayal of the accusations made against him.[126]

Waldheim campaign officials also did their part in constructing the image of the WJC as slanderers. Heribert Steinbauer, Waldheim's campaign manager, considered the "most disgraceful aspect" of the documents published was that "war crimes with personal liability" had been construed out of mere service in the Wehrmacht.[127] The *Tiroler Tageszeitung,* on the other hand, reported on the "charges which had been leveled against him [Waldheim] in the recent past of ostensible membership in NS organizations and participation in war crimes as well as the deportation of Jews."[128]

Neither ORF journalists nor the other papers cited above attempted to deal with the content of the disclosures the WJC made on 25 March. Some journalists, however, did.[129] The documents which the WJC presented at its 25 March press conference provided both an opportunity and, since the documents and the related press materials were freely available, something of a litmus test. On 28 March, three days after the press conference, *Kurier* devoted two major articles and a guest commentary to them. Hans Rauscher was the author of one of the articles.[130] He wrote: "The conclusions which Robert Herzstein, the historian from the University of South Carolina engaged by the World Jewish Congress, drew from the documents are unacceptable." It is Rauscher's privilege to claim this, but he apparently based his statement simply on the interpretation of another historian, Erwin Schmidl. Schmidl is the author, among other things, of a recent study on the *Anschluss,* but there is no obvious reason, and Rauscher did not offer any additional ones, why Schmidl's opinion should be accorded more credibility than Herzstein's, except, perhaps, that Herzstein was from South Carolina, and Schmidl from Vienna. "But the documents which Hersztein presented and which bear Waldheim's signature," Rauscher continued, "show that he compiled and passed on incoming *reports* on interrogations, 'cleansing actions' and 'those shot in punishment.' He must have known of atrocities, but these do not show that he personally took part" (emphasis in original).

Rauscher had once again trained his polemical sights on the wrong target. He stated that Herzstein had accused Waldheim of participation in atrocities, whereas in fact the documents showed only that he gathered and transmitted information about them. What did Herzstein actually say? The statement which Herzstein read at the press conference, and which was distributed to those present, contained a great deal about Waldheim's activities. "A few days later," Herzstein said in one passage, describing a document he had discovered, "Lt. Waldheim compiled a report for his commander and his chief describing 'mopping up' operations north of Tripolis. On July 18, Waldheim reported on more Zervas interrogations. By this time he was responsible for drafting these vital reports; his role had expanded beyond verifying this textual accuracy on behalf of his superior." Later on Herzstein mentioned that "1st Lt. Waldheim continued to report on the enemy situation in a broad arc, stretching from the Balkans to the Mediterranean, from Italy to France . . . Waldheim continued to assist Lt. Col. Warnstorff in preparing high-level briefing reports for the General Staff, concerning 'mopping up' operations and related matters."[131]

Neither Herzstein in his statement, nor the WJC in its remarks (which did not diverge from Herzstein's findings), alleged that Waldheim had "taken part" in the activities on which he reported. Rauscher, and Schmidl, insofar as his advice influenced Rauscher, simply erected a straw man: "unacceptable" interpretations, which Herzstein had never made, were ascribed to him and then "refuted" with the very interpretations Herzstein had himself given. The title of Rauscher's article was, incidentally, "WJC in Need of Evidence."

In the same issue, *Kurier* published an interview with Herbert Warnstorff, Waldheim's superior in the military intelligence department of Army Group E's general staff, with the headline "Former Superior Exculpates Kurt Waldheim."[132] This was true enough, but it was due far more to Rauscher's interview technique and lack of preparation than to the intrinsic merits of the case he presented. For example, merely the fact that Waldheim was, as Warnstorff emphasized, only a "desk soldier" [*Schreibtischsoldat*] and not engaged in combat, need not have exculpated Waldheim in the slightest, as the verdicts of the Nuremberg Tribunal after the war demonstrated. Warnstorff's claim that during his tenure in Arsakli he had "never learned anything about the deportation of Jews" was even less reliable. Warnstorff had said earlier in the interview that he had worked with Waldheim only in the period between spring 1944 and spring 1945,[133] that is, approximately six months after the deportations of Salonika's Jews had been completed. At the time this article appeared, the dispute about Jewish deportations revolved around the question of whether Waldheim could have been unaware of the deportations of tens of thousands of Jews from Salonika when he was stationed a mere 3 miles away, in the village of Arsakli, the site of the general staff headquarters. These deportations took place between 15 March and 7 August 1943. In March, 1986, everyone involved (including Waldheim himself) assumed that he had been in Arsakli (or in Salonika, since the usage was not very precise) this entire time. Later, as we have seen, it was learned that Waldheim had been away from the area for all but a few days of the period in question. Journalists who had been exceptionally well informed might also have known about the deportations of the Jews from the areas formerly occupied by Italy, and which took place after Italy's capitulation. Warnstorff himself must have been aware of these latter deportations, as the documentary evidence unequivocally shows. Still, it is not this latter point which shows extreme indulgence on Rauscher's part, but the lack of attention to the presumed dates of Waldheim's presence in Salonika. The question everyone was asking Waldheim was how it was possible for him to have been stationed in Arsakli but not have noticed these deportations between March and August 1943? And it is this question which Warnstorff was personally unable to answer, since according to the interview itself, Warnstorff only came to Arsakli in 1944. Yet not only did the interviewer fail to address this problem, he also missed the most obvious of all. Nowhere is it suggested that Warnstorff, as Waldheim's direct superior, could not implicate Waldheim in deportations or other atrocities without thereby incriminating himself. Taken as a whole, these errors of fact and judgment made the exonerative character of this interview a foregone conclusion. The informative value of this issue of *Kurier* was less than none, for the interpretive schema which guided his research made the information Rauscher turned up highly suspect. The only possible contribution which it and the above article could make to a discussion of the "charges" against Waldheim was to reinforce, with the assistance of superficially impressive evidence, scholarly advice and an eyewitness, the notion that the WJC was recklessly raising baseless accusations.[134]

The manipulative deprecation of the WJC and its research undertakings was also able to enlist scholarly support. In April 1986 Erika Weinzierl, Gerald Stourzh, Horst Haselsteiner, Arnold Suppan, Maximilian Liebmann, Roman Sandgruber, Robert Kriechbaumer and Franz Horner, all established scholars at prominent Austrian universities, took part in an intellectually dishonest attempt to impugn Herzstein's reputation. They issued a "declaration" under the aegis of the Karl von Vogelsang Institute, which could be described as a People's Party think tank, "On the Interpretation by Prof. Robert E. Herzstein of the Documents Relating to Dr. Kurt Waldheim Published by the World Jewish Congress." Among other things, the authors criticized Herzstein's "interpretations, according to which Dr. Kurt Waldheim was a war criminal and had been entrusted with 'special tasks' [*"Spezialaufgaben"*] which included executions, imprisonment [*Festnahmen*] and deportations." Herzstein's interpretations were not in their opinion "inferable from the documents." Whatever one may think of Herzstein's assessment of these materials, the claims advanced by these scholars are specious on at least two counts. Firstly, the authors' citation technique was remarkably careless. The Wehrmacht duty roster Herzstein presented contained the entry *"Sonderaufgaben,"* which Herzstein correctly translated as "special tasks." Herzstein claimed further, in my opinion erroneously, that the term "special tasks" was a euphemism similar to "special handling" (*Sonderbehandlung*), which "usually concerned secret measures of mass terror or torture, kidnapping and execution." The authors of this declaration, however, who quote the term *"Spezialaufgaben,"* apparently amalgamated the latter part of the German compound noun *Sonderaufgaben* with Herzstein's English translation of the first part. To my knowledge the term *"Spezialaufgaben"* appeared on no document discussed by Herzstein, and certainly not the duty roster to which these authors were alluding. Whether or not one agreed with his interpretation of this term, however, Herzstein rendered it into faultless English. Secondly, and far more serious, was the claim by these scholars that Herzstein had called Waldheim a war criminal. This was simply a crude invention. These scholars did not mention any specific evidence (or even the grounds) on which they based their judgment, nor did they cite a single document to support their counter-interpretations. One can only speculate about the motives of historians who criticized a colleague for being unable to support his interpretations with documentary evidence, while in the very declaration, in which their indictment appears, they themselves misquoted an important document and offered not a single source to substantiate their own evaluation. It was, of course, better for them to do so: they could not have produced any such document where Herzstein had ever claimed that Waldheim was a "war criminal" or that he "had been involved in criminal activities according to the Hague Convention on Land Warfare."[135] These scholars' use of highly questionable methods to peremptorily malign a colleague are grounds for grave concern in themselves. More fatefully, their efforts *nolens volens* lent academic respectability to the more overtly political portrayal of the WJC as an organization raising slanderous and unsupported allegations against Waldheim. Michael Graff, for example, adduced this "expert opinion" offered by "nine well-known scholars" as evidence that the traducing WJC was repeating, in his redundant phrase, "groundless falsehoods."[136]

A "Dishonorable Lot"?

One of the inferences educed from the basic premise that the WJC was making exaggerated allegations against Waldheim unsupported by any evidence was the ancillary proposition that the WJC, a "mafia of slanderers," as Michael Graff described them,[137] would stop at nothing to get Waldheim. Though the charge of dishonor against Jews has a long history in Austria,[138] the allegation in 1986 that the WJC was "dishonorable" appears traceable to the idea that the WJC had reneged on the terms of an agreement made with the then Austrian ambassador to the United States Thomas Klestil or with Austrian President Kirchschläger. On 5 April, George Possanner of *Die Presse* mentioned an "offer" the WJC had ostensibly made. Possanner gave no sources for his report, but claimed that Israel Singer and Edgar Bronfman had agreed to end the WJC's "publicity campaign" against Waldheim if President Kirchschläger would consent to inspect all the available documents (including the UNWCC file) relating to Waldheim's wartime past. This deal, reported Possanner, was allegedly struck at the WJC's fiftieth anniversary celebration.[139] Five days later, on 10 April, the *NVB* quoted Michael Graff's reactions to a press conference the WJC had held in London. "Singer's new attacks, which cannot be supported by any evidence, are considered to be dishonorable and slanderous in Austria." They were dishonorable, he went on, because they violated the agreement made between President Kirchschläger and Edgar Bronfman, according to which the WJC had consented not to make any further attacks on Waldheim.[140] On the same day, Peter Gnam wrote a column for the *NKZ* in which he claimed, among other things, "One can without hesitation forget about the documents of the World Jewish Congress. For Israel Singer in an interview has again dismissed Waldheim as having known of war crimes even though he had earlier agreed to acknowledge Kirchschläger as an arbitrator and not to interfere any more." These new attacks, Gnam concluded, "both disqualify him and devalue the ostensibly compromising material against Waldheim."[141] Gnam's opinion that the motivation of anyone could or should vitiate the significance of evidence which can be independently verified and interpreted, suggested that his primary interest lay not in evaluating the information about Waldheim's past. A month later, Gnam's colleague at the *NKZ*, Richard Nimmerrichter, repeated the same charge, but Nimmerrichter was not certain who had made and broken the agreement with Kirchschläger. The WJC would be presenting new "documents" against Waldheim, Nimmerrichter wrote, "although this private organization, which is completely without authority vis-à-vis the still sovereign state of Austria, announced solemnly that it would cease making public material in a piecemeal fashion after it had given a mound of documents to the incumbent President Kirchschläger."[142]

By 26 April, the opinions about the WJC had consolidated to such an extent that Michael Graff had coined a new descriptive phrase incorporating them. He condemned, he said, the "disgraceful [*infam*] attacks of that dishonorable lot from the World Jewish Congress."[143] Graff's opinion was endorsed two days later by then party chairman Alois Mock, who was quoted as saying that "one must call things by their right names."[144] The belief that the WJC, apart from resorting to slander against Waldheim, had also acted dishonorably in still other ways, remained uncontested, because it appeared to be based on a legitimate grievance. However, the evidence for the allegation that the WJC violated an agreement is suspiciously thin, while the charge of "dishonor" appears to have been a reflex reaction based on pre-existent prejudices.

Official Austria only really became interested in the documents of the WJC after they had published the CROWCASS on 22 March, which made reference to a file on Waldheim lodged in the archives of the UNWCC. On 26 March 1986, the Yugoslav daily *Vercernje Novosti* published excerpts from Waldheim's *Odluka*, which had been compiled by the Yugoslav war crimes commission and on which the UNWCC file was based.[145] According to the *NYT* of 2 April, Francois Guiliani, advisor to U.N. Secretary General Perez de Cuellar, stated that only governments could request UNWCC files and that up to that time no government had requested the document.[146] The following day Reuters reported that "Mr. Waldheim . . . welcomed a decision he said the Jewish group [WJC] has made to send documents to the current Austrian President, Rudolf Kirchschläger, as a sign that the organization would not in the future interfere in Austria's internal affairs."[147] There was no mention here of any fixed agreement, merely of a "sign," and the pejorative way in which it was expressed suggested that Waldheim's remark expressed his personal wish.

The Israeli government then requested access to the file and on 4 April it received assurance from the United Nations that this would be granted.[148] On 8 April the *NYT* reported that Austria had also requested permission to inspect the file and that its request had been approved.[149] Both Wolfgang Petritsch from the Austrian embassy and Karl Fischer, Austria's ambassador to the United Nations, were quoted in the article, but neither mentioned any agreement between the WJC and the Austrian ambassador. Rather, both emphasized that the embassy had only requested the documents with Waldheim's approval. Also on this date, the Vienna daily *Wiener Zeitung* published a report in which then Austrian Foreign Minister Leopold Gratz recounted the background to the decision to request the file, but did not mention any agreement. According to the paper, Gratz had empowered Klestil to receive the documents from the WJC. Gratz also recalled that the WJC had expressed to Klestil their complete confidence in Kirchschläger's objective judgment of the documents. The only condition which either side placed on this "agreement," i.e., that the WJC would provide documents to Kirchschläger was, according to Gratz's version as reported, the WJC's insistence that the documents include the UNWCC file.[150]

On 9 April, the WJC distributed a press release, "Austrian Government Receives WJC Evidence on Waldheim."[151] The press release mentioned that Ambassador Klestil[152] and Fischer had been received in the WJC's offices, where they were given the documents to hand on to President Kirchschläger. In the letter he sent accompanying the documents, Israel Singer wrote, "We are hereby transmitting to you, as a man we trust, the documents we have so far found in open United States archives and ask you to understand our deep concern in this affair. We shall continue our search for as much information as we can. We consider this our duty, since so many have been lax."[153] Not only did Singer not mention any agreement to stop publishing documents on Waldheim, he announced that the WJC would continue its search. In the press release which told of the Austrians' receipt of the documents, moreover, the WJC announced a further press conference at which they would release more documents.[154] The activities of the WJC would thus appear to preclude their having made such an agreement. It also seems unlikely that the Austrian delegation would have accepted the documents in the face of such a flagrant violation.

What about Kirchschläger? In his letter of 23 April to Israel Singer, Kirchschläger stated that Klestil had been his intermediary in contacts with Edgar Bronfman, and underlined that he himself had given the reasons for receiving and evaluating the documents.[155] It seems reasonable to assume, therefore, that Kirchschläger would have been informed of any possible agreements which Klestil had arranged with Bronfman. In his televised address on 23 April, Kirchschläger had explained the two reasons alluded to in his letter to Singer:

> [By agreeing to take the documents] I wanted to bring some calm to the massive international attention of the mass media, which encompassed the whole of the western and even parts of the third world . . . I have only partially achieved the goal of calming things down. The wave of news reports has assumed a life of its own which is difficult to contain. At least the press conferences of the World Jewish Congress in New York, which were taking place daily or every other day, have stopped. That, in turn, helped realize the second hope I had entertained when I agreed to accept the documents. The tension which had arisen because of a reaction to actions which are being interpreted as an external interference in the presidential election campaign and necessarily had their effect on our Jewish fellow citizens, has tapered off.[156]

There was no mention here that Kirchschläger had had reason to expect the WJC to end their press conferences. Indeed, his formulation "at least" [*immerhin*], indicated that the greater distance between press conferences was a welcome, but certainly not self-evident, consequence of his decision to inspect the documents. Kirchschläger's speech contained at least one implicit criticism of the WJC, which suggests that he was not being excessively charitable to the organization. Moreover, he described his reasoning for receiving the documents in considerable detail. It is difficult to imagine that he would not at least have made some reference to a promise which had not been kept.

There is, then, not a single piece of hard evidence that a commitment by the WJC to end their disclosures had ever been given. This appears a rather meager evidentiary basis upon which to accuse the WJC of having acted dishonorably. Yet neither Michael Graff nor any of the Austrian journalists who had made the claim bothered to check into it. It became yet another apodictic assertion enlisted to support the authentic defamation of the alleged "slanderers" from the WJC.

This interpretive schema stuck, and resurfaced in a far more virulent form shortly before the second round of the election. The news weekly *Wochenpresse* reported in the first week of June that a "contact man" of the WJC had offered someone named Sokratis Chatzisvangelis $150,000 if he would make a perjured statement incriminating Waldheim.[157] Apart from Chatzisvangelis's statement itself, there was no evidence for this allegation, which the WJC vehemently denied. Though the accusation could not be proved in any case, in the context of June 1986 it appeared highly implausible, even assuming the basest motives of the WJC. On 29 May 1986, the Zurich *Weltwoche* published an article by Hanspeter Born which retold the story of Jesoua Matza. Matza, 61 years old and living in Israel, was a native Greek Jew who had managed to escape the fate of most other Greek Jews from his hometown of Ioannina by fleeing. Matza, his cousin Michael Matza, Moshe Mioni and Nahum Negrin, all originally from Ioannina, believed they had recognized (from a contemporaneous photograph they saw in 1986) Waldheim as the young German officer who had overseen the collection of the valuables of the Ioannina Jews and, Jesoua Matza believed, the officer who had struck him with his stick. The details of this story are of only marginal relevance here, and Waldheim has up to now had an airtight alibi for the period in question.[158] Here it only bears mentioning that, apart from any other considerations, witnesses claiming to have evidence of Waldheim's involvement in heinous crimes had already voluntarily come forward and their accusations were in the public domain. The WJC, moreover, had based their investigation from the very beginning entirely on documentary sources. Why, when the WJC's officials were confident that their case against Waldheim had been established, should they contemplate an act which would discredit all the work they had previously undertaken?

The answer to this question offered by the Waldheim camp was not hard to guess. Again, Michael Graff showed the way. The text of the telegram he sent to Edgar Bronfman and made public two days prior to the second round of the election, provided a succinct summary of the points made here and requires no additional comment:

> Although I am used to your organization's [making] untrue and slanderous accusations against Kurt Waldheim, which cannot in the least be corroborated by ostensible docu-

> mentary evidence, I would never have assumed that you would go so far. . . . I had expected the World Jewish Congress to issue an immediate denial of the report in the *Wochenpresse* and to initiate legal action against Chatzisvangelis, but I have not heard of any such efforts [on your part]. . . . If I do not receive a satisfactory explanation within a reasonable period of time, I will have to assume that the World Jewish Congress actually attempted to bribe a witness. The Austrian people will draw the appropriate conclusions.[159]

What Motives Could "They" Have?

Everyone seeks explanations of social phenomena, and utilizes available interpretive schema for doing so. Those who accepted the elements of the *Feindbild* we have described here were no different. Once the "what" and "how" of the WJC's "trash can campaign" against Kurt Waldheim had been established, it was natural to inquire as to the "why." In this case, the question read, what possibly could have motivated the WJC to wage a campaign of lies and slanders, to threaten Austrians with six years of strife should they dare to elect Waldheim, and to persevere in the face of such obvious failure? Since any reasonable person could see that all the allegations were untrue, so this line of argument went, there could be no rational grounds for investigating the concealed past of a former secretary general of the United Nations who might have had Nazi affiliations and might have known of atrocities committed by the Wehrmacht units in which he had served. Yet the WJC persisted in their "slander campaign" against Waldheim, and commanded not only the international press, but the Israeli government as well. What could be the reasons?

The common denominator in all the explanations on offer was the thirst for revenge. One frequently mentioned candidate for the WJC's revenge was Waldheim's policies towards the Middle East while at the United Nations. "The same group," as the *NVB* formulated it, made "Waldheim responsible for the Middle East policies of the United Nations during his service as Secretary General."[160] Waldheim himself offered this as an explanation,[161] and there were variants. For example, Gerfried Sperl, then writing for the *Süd-Ost Tageszeitung,* believed Arafat's visit to the United Nations to be "without doubt one of the roots of the attacks of the 'World Jewish Congress.'" It wanted simply to avenge this deed.[162] Far more frequent, however, were references to personal revenge or other irrational motives. Michael Graff, as might be expected, had a fitting response. The henchmen of the WJC in Israel, he said via the ÖVP press office, were motivated by "hatred and a craving for recognition."[163] The WJC, reported the *NKZ* shortly before the second round of the election, "was becoming ever more dogged" in its slander campaign. It "is smearing and slandering more wickedly than ever, [and] international socialism pours oil on the fire."[164] Kurt Vorhofer from the *Kleine Zeitung* believed he had located the reason in the psychic imbalance of the Jews after Auschwitz. "Even if one emphatically rejects the methods employed against Kurt Waldheim and Austria," he wrote, "one should say in these Jewish functionaries' favor that we are dealing with people who, like so many other

Jews, have been psychically severely damaged."[165] Kurt Seinitz of the *NKZ* explained on 28 March 1986, as the headline over his article says, "Why the World Jewish Congress and Israel Singer are so Angry." The reason, he suggested, was the personal revenge of Israel Singer. "Singer's father," Seinitz wrote, "had to 'clean' the streets of Vienna with a toothbrush in 1938."[166] Less charitable was Seinitz's colleague Peter Gnam. The "attacks of the World Jewish Congress on Waldheim," he wrote, were the result simply of "hatred and blind rage."[167] Even psychologist Erwin Ringel, a prominent opponent of Waldheim, characterized the behavior of the WJC as "sadistic."[168]

The World Jewish Congress as Political Synecdoche

Public discourse about Jews or things Jewish in Austria since the end of the Second World War has been conditioned by the public taboo against open expressions of antisemitic prejudice. Though, as we have seen, these taboos have not prevented such beliefs finding periodic public expression, usage which recalls the period prior to 1945 has generally been subject to negative sanctions. As a consequence, the expression of overtly defamatory statements against "the Jews" or the invocation of explicit motifs a là *Stürmer* are relatively rare, and seldom occur outside situations where the consent of the audience is presumed (for example, neo-Nazi or some veterans' organizations or in closed groups of like-minded individuals, so-called *Stammtischgespräche*) or where anonymity obviates personal responsibility and thereby accords speakers a measure of license otherwise wanting.[169] It also means that protestations of the many Jewish friends one has,[170] how strongly one supports Israel, or that one's attack was limited to the World Jewish Congress, a small private organization, may, and frequently did, disguise unspoken (and perhaps even unconscious) prejudice.[171] In the debate over Waldheim's past, those who assailed the WJC most vigorously were often those who protested their innocence of antisemitic prejudice most vociferously. Michael Graff of the People's Party represented a sort of textbook example of this phenomenon in official Austrian political culture. Graff's lengthiest opportunity to answer charges that he had pandered to antisemitic prejudice came in an interview in the late night news program in Austrian television. He was responding to criticisms raised by representatives of the Austrian Jewish community against the ÖVP. Graff's response was first to establish his party's credentials as one which was "founded in the year 1945 by men who had come out of the concentration camps and prisons of the Nazi regime." He then offered his own personal defense in a somewhat rambling fashion:

> I always used these expressions [such as "dishonorable lot"] in a context. I always added [that] I meant these officials of the World Jewish Congress, who had broken their word to the Austrian president; who—although they knew otherwise—because they repeatedly came up with the same documents, which do not prove anything other than that Dr. Waldheim was a first lieutenant in the Wehrmacht—[I] always added [that] to it.

In the very next line, however, Graff added, attempting to be funny, "I am not demanding that you show Israel Singer now. Then I would really accelerate antisemitism in Austria."[172] This was clearly something Graff had not thought through, but it exposed what he had up to then so well concealed: the existence of strong antisemitic prejudice which could be exploited for political ends. The assumption to which Graff's aside alluded was that the behavior of one single Jew, however offensive it might be felt to be, somehow reflected on Jews as a whole. And the readiness to manipulate this assumption (whether or not Graff believed it himself is immaterial; its political potential was for him a given) informed not only Graff's own actions in the campaign. The appeal to it, primarily the systematic demonization of the WJC, became a set piece in the Waldheim camp's propaganda repertoire. It has been shown above that merely feeling threatened by the interview with two officials of the WJC necessarily presumed beliefs about the power of international Jewry, whether these were articulated openly or not. There were, however, more direct associations made which suggested that the WJC had assumed a representative function, what I have termed political synecdoche, for both the Jews as a whole and for the more nebulous but equally evocative German expression for "abroad" (*das Ausland*).

The discursive manifestations of this idea were varied and could be more or less explicit. Kurt Vorhofer, for example, wrote "Of course it was necessary to answer the monstrous attacks which came from the Jewish side." Since the WJC were by consensus the principal authors of the "monstrous attacks," Vorhofer's description left little doubt that it was conceptually interchangeable with the Jews.[173] After the first round of the election, the SPÖ paper in Carinthia asked, as its banner headline proclaimed, "Is Waldheim Beholden to World Jewry?"[174] In the context of the election campaign, and the frequently expressed hopes of the ÖVP for a knee-jerk electoral reaction of defiance toward the WJC's attacks, the implication of the headline, even though (or perhaps because) it had come from a Carinthian paper which opposed Waldheim, was unmistakable. In a similar vein, Kurt Markaritzer of the *Neue Volkszeitung Kärnten Osttirol* wrote, "Now it is not easy to counter Jewish attacks. Spokesmen of this people have a right to excessive tolerance, in light of the frightful horrors of the Nazi period. One need not and should not take what they say too literally."[175]

Similar examples could be found of the direct and explicit association of the WJC with world Jewry or simply Jewry, but it is probably not accidental that they tended to be found in provincial newspapers, where familiarity with the preferred forms of linguistic etiquette might have been less developed. In fact, the WJC also came to stand for the forces from "abroad," as head of an international campaign against Austria. The Waldheim camp deployed this theme skillfully in its electoral propaganda, and in appealing to Austrians to unite against the foreign (Jewish) danger it could call upon equally potent sources of national identity such as Austria's being the perpetual victim of international *Diktat.* The amalgamation of the WJC with *"das Ausland"* gave rise to a kind of coded language, in which the eschewing of attacks from "abroad" could become synonymous with the rejection of criticisms "from the Jewish side."

In the event, the German *Ausland* lent itself particularly easily to such an amalgamation.[176] A phrase for which there is no exact equivalent in English, *das Ausland* is a singular noun describing everything which lies outside the boundaries which define the country. In some usages, the word *Ausland* could connote an idea of "those out there," but the normal translation as "foreign countries" implies a plurality of subjects which the singular *das Ausland* simply obliterates. In the debate on the Waldheim affair, *das Ausland* was frequently described as though it possessed capacities of action normally associated with more differentiated individual units, but which in this case could only have helped forge the link between *das Ausland* and the WJC. For example, Dieter Lenhardt of *Die Presse,* alluding to the *Profil* interview with Israel Singer and Elan Steinberg, and the disclosures the WJC had made, wrote of the "now completely unvarnished foreign intervention in the Austrian presidential election."[177] More concretely, a spokesperson of Waldheim's campaign office referred to the disclosure of documents as the "meddling of *das Ausland.*"[178] This statement not only assumed that *das Ausland* was capable of intervening in the election (the phrase was not "from abroad" [*aus dem Ausland*], but simply "of abroad"' [*des Auslands*]), it connected an amorphous and undefined group with actions which, according to general agreement, the WJC had been carrying out.

Other references to *das Ausland* or some variant which, in the context, could only have been referring to the WJC, also helped forge the chain of associations. The then second president of the National Assembly, Marge Hubinek of the ÖVP, asked rhetorically "whether it is, then, still necessary . . . to elect the president by popular vote, if some few foreign [*ausländisch*] functionaries believe that they can decide who will become Austrian president."[179] The only "functionaries" who were mentioned in connection with Waldheim and influence on the election, it hardly need be said, were those from the WJC. The *NVB* wrote an article headlined "Agitators in New York in the Final Push against Waldheim." In the article itself, Michael Graff was quoted as denouncing "the hectic activities of the lobby of the World Jewish Congress," which not only made the WJC into so important an organization that it required its own lobby, but also signalled to those listening the relevant coded allusions: "The stronger the foreign interventions become, the more the second round becomes an act of patriotism and Austrian self-respect."[180] "The fact remains," concurred Walter Salzmann one week later, "that *das Ausland,* and especially the World Jewish Congress, was consciously engaged in this campaign and has unfortunately not understood that they [could] not have done their organization and thereby the Jewish fellow citizens in Austria a greater disservice than to have taken over and to continue leading the chase [*Jagd*] after Kurt Waldheim."[181]

On one occasion, Viktor Reimann of the *NKZ* felt obliged to defend his journalistic honor, and in so doing identified clearly against whom he was protecting it. "What we did, and what the sense of journalistic decency required of us, was to defend a fellow citizen, who had certainly not brought disgrace upon our country, from infamous accusations from outside, [which were] possibly initiated in Austria [*Inland*]. What the World Jewish Congress and the part of the American mass media under its influence [have done], will simply not do any longer."[182] A leaflet published by the "Youth for Waldheim" initiative condemned in a similar bellicose manner "the foreign organizations" who wanted to determine the outcome of the Austrian presidential election by duress.[183]

Perhaps the most compelling evidence of the explicit association of the WJC with Jewry as a whole, however, was visual. In its 1 April 1986 issue, the weekly news magazine *Wochenpresse* carried a long background article on the WJC and an interview with Simon Wiesenthal, in which he expressed sharp criticisms of the organization's handling of the Waldheim affair. The article on the WJC was not in itself excessively tendentious. Moreover, the editors of the magazine were apparently conscious of the perils of publishing an article on this subject. After much consideration they decided to run it, but were determined to avoid, as Gerald Freihofner wrote, "in any way providing ammunition for latent antisemitism, which is still widespread in the Austrian population."[184] The cover story, entitled "Waldheim's Adversaries: The World Jewish Congress," was accompanied, as such stories are, by a photograph, whose semiotic significance is so obvious that Freihofner's protestations in the magazine could almost be seen as an April fool's joke. This photograph showed a male bust figure from the rear, with a yarmulka on his head. In the middle of the yarmulka was an embroidered Star of David. An anonymous male figure with a yarmulka could be related to the WJC alone, however, only if it were an identifying feature of the organization or its members. In the popular imagination, of course, a yarmulka is the characteristic which marks off, not the WJC, but "the Jews." The message this cover photo conveyed was a simple but powerful one: when we say World Jewish Congress, we mean the Jews.

Every new disclosure of documents in New York confirmed the Waldheimian prognoses and increased the hatred against the WJC. An organization which did not shrink from slander and whose general secretary thirsted for revenge, had truly earned a corresponding reaction. And the WJC received it. That the supporters of Waldheim in the ÖVP and among sympathetic journalists, by joining the crusade against the WJC, fomented real hatred and psychological terror, was taken in stride. This made the question whether their efforts were subtle or coarse, open or adumbrative, intentional or accidental, passionate or merely indifferent, largely irrelevant. They did little to combat the trend. Perhaps some had an inkling of the hatred which ensued. At least for the leading politicians of the ÖVP, the perceived political stakes overrode any qualms which they might otherwise have entertained.[185] They could not have wished for a more appropriate tool than the WJC.

One of Waldheim's election campaign brochures carried the headline "This is How They Wanted to Destroy Kurt Waldheim!" Though out of context the anonymous references might be thought to suggest sciamachy, appearances deceive. "They" were indeed not explicitly defined, and the contradictory references in the brochure to the SPÖ members involved in the "campaign" merely broadened, but did not alter, the principal reference point. The *Feindbild 'Jud'* which had been constructed around the WJC made such details superfluous. For those who had "understood" the events until then had no trouble making the necessary associations and, as Graff put it, drawing "the appropriate conclusions." Richard Nimmerrichter, columnist for the *NKZ*, captured the essence of the matter accurately, but he defined the audience receptive to such appeals (most of whom were readers of his own column) far too narrowly: "For incorrigible Nazis, the World Jewish Congress came as an unexpected windfall, for [in the WJC] they saw the muddled ideas of Rosenberg and Goebbels on the international Jewish conspiracy confirmed in their minds in a way they never would have expected."[186]

Notes

1. See Teun van Dijk, *Prejudice in Discourse. An Analysis of Ethnic Prejudice in Cognition and Conversation* (Amsterdam/Philadelphia: Benjamins, 1984), pp. 13–41.

2. For the various usages of the word "campaign" see Chapter 3, note 82.

3. See Norman Cohn, *Warrant for Genocide. The Myth of the Jewish world-conspiracy and the Protocols of the Elders of Zion* (Chico, California: Scholars Press, 1981 [reprint of 1969 edition]); Johann Rogall von Bieberstein, *Die These von der Verschwörung: Philosophen, Freimauer, Juden, Liberale und Sozialisten als Verschwörer gegen die Sozialordnung* (Frankfurt am Main and Bern: Peter Lang, 1978). The Bishop of Linz, Gföllner, issued a pastoral letter a few days before Hitler was appointed chancellor in Germany in which it states: "Degenerate Judaism [*Judentum*], in league with world free masonery is also the bearer of mammon capitalism and dominant founder and apostle of socialism and communism, the forerunner and pacemaker of bolshevism." Quoted in Anton Pelinka, *Stand oder Klasse? Die christliche Arbeiterbewegung Österreichs 1933-38* (Vienna: Europaverlag, 1972), p. 216.

4. Cited in Kurt Schubert, "Der Weg zur Katastrophe," *Studia Judaica Austriaca* Vol. V. (1977), p. 57.

5. Ibid.

6. *Volkswohl* (1919), cited in Jonny Moser, "Die Katastrophe," p. 83. See also Leopold Spira, *Feindbild 'Jud'* (Vienna: Löcker Verlag, 1981), pp. 15–68.

7. The "international Jew press" was a frequent theme of the Christian Social party. See, for example, *Reichspost*, 10 November 1987; 18 November 1897, 12 January 1898, and 15 January 1989. See Sigurd Paul Scheichl, "The Contexts and Nuances of Anti-Jewish Language: Were all the 'Antisemites' Antisemites?" in Ivar Oxaal, Michael Pollak and Gerhard Botz, eds., *Jews, Antisemitism and Culture in Vienna* (London and New York: Routledge & Kegan Paul, 1987), p. 91. See also Rudolf de Cillia, Richard Mitten and Ruth Wodak, "Von der Kunst, antisemitisch zu sein," in Karl Albrecht-Weinberger and Felicitas Heimann-Jelinek, eds., *Judentum in Wien. Sammlung Max Berger* (Vienna: Historisches Museum der Stadt Wien, 1987), pp. 94–107.

8. In response to a question from *Le Monde* journalist Claire Tréan, Waldheim replied that the international press "is dominated by the World Jewish Congress. That is well known!" *Le Monde*, 3 May 1986.

9. Hilde Weiss's 1983 study on antisemitic prejudice showed that many Austrians continue to believe that Jews possess a great deal of power and influence. Weiss did not, of course, ask her respondents whether they thought the Jews controlled the international press. However, a poll conducted by Gallup in 1980 showed that nearly 50% of those questioned responded to the statement "The Jews control world politics" with either "agree" or "tend to agree." Respondents to a

questionnaire prepared by Weiss (she conducted the investigation in 1976) expressed similar assent to the statement that the influence of the Jews is underestimated. At the same time, Weiss was able to gather opinions about characteristics traditionally considered typically Jewish, such as solidarity and diligence, using statements such as "Jewish solidarity is exemplary." In this context it is of secondary interest whether these characteristics were considered positive or negative. The principal goal was to establish the extent to which generalization and stereotyping about Jews along traditional lines has persisted. Our interest in these data is to determine whether statements of politicians or newspaper articles in Austria during the presidential election of 1986 could have suggested, promoted, encouraged or would not have actively combatted a Jewish conspiracy theory. An ancillary interest is, naturally, what kind of (cognitive) responses such allusions could be expected to elicit. Hilde Weiss, *Antisemitische Vorurteile in Österreich. Theoretische und empirische Analysen* (Vienna: Wilhelm Braumüller, 1987); Wodak, et al., *Unschuldige Täter*, passim.

10. *Neue Kronen Zeitung* (*NKZ*), 6 March 1986.

11. *Volkszeitung*, 25 March 1986.

12. *NKZ*, 3 May 1986; 4 May 1986.

13. *NKZ*, 13 April 1986.

14. On this general characteristic of conspiracy theories see Allport, *Prejudice*, pp. 165–177; 395–409.

15. In November, 1987, Michael Graff gave an interview to *L'Express* journalist Michèle Georges. In response to a question about the then upcoming historians' commission, Graff replied, "As long as it is not proven that he [Waldheim] singlehandedly strangled six Jews, then there is no problem." See *L'Express*, 13 November 1987. As a result of the uproar over these remarks after they had become known in Austria, Graff was forced to resign as ÖVP Secretary General. Graff today is the official party spokesman for judicial affairs, and for all intents and purposes has been "rehabilitated." Former Foreign Minister Karl Gruber, who was known as a leader of anti-Nazi resistance in Tyrol, remarked in February 1988, also in an interview with a foreign journalist, that the report of the international historians' commission was critical of Waldheim because "one [member] was a socialist and three were of Jewish background." Given the chance to withdraw his remark over the next several days, Gruber stood by his judgment and protested that he had many Jewish friends. His remark was condemned by Austrian Chancellor Franz Vranitzky, who personally sent apologies to every member of the historians' commission, and even Waldheim was forced to disclaim Gruber's remarks. This public expression of fairly crude antisemitic prejudice did not hinder the ÖVP top brass from celebrating Gruber's eightieth birthday several months later, nor the Austrian broadcasting company from featuring it on the evening news. Gruber's remarks in the original interview were broadcast on the *Zeit im Bild I* news program. See Ruth Wodak, "The Waldheim Affair and Antisemitic Prejudice in Austrian Public Discourse," *Patterns of Prejudice* Vol. 24, Nos. 2–4 (1990), pp. 18–33; Projektteam "Sprache und Vorurteil," "Unschuldige Täter," Vol. 1, pp. 235–241.

16. In a televised interview in June 1986, in which he responded to charges made the Austrian Jewish Community that he had enlisted antisemitism in the election campaign, Michael Graff stated that his party "was founded in 1945 by men who had come out of the concentration camps and prisons of the Nazi regime. . . [and that the ÖVP] had always known what a poison antisemitism is . . . and always condemned it." Apart from being untrue, Graff's remarks strike one as particularly affected in light of his later remarks. See Projektteam "Sprache und Vorurteil," "Unschudige Täter," Vol. 1, Appendix III.

17. On the attribution of responsibility for the "campaign" in the Austrian newspapers *Die Presse* and the *NKZ,* see Projektteam "Sprache und Vorurteile," *Unschuldige Täter,* Vol. 2, Part II, pp. 174–76.

18. See, for example, *NKZ,* 12 April and 6 May 1986.

19. Österreichische Rundfunk (ORF), *Zeit im Bild I,* 5 June 1986.

20. *Die Presse,* 5 March 1986.

21. *NKZ,* 5 March 1986.

22. *Die Presse,* 6 March 1986.

23. *NKZ,* 6 March 1986.

24. *Wiener Zeitung* (*WZ*), 6 March 1986; The resolution is printed in full in *Neue Zeit,* 22 March 1986.

25. *NKZ,* 7 March 1986.

26. *Die Presse,* 7 March 1986.

27. *Die Presse,* 8 March 1986.

28. *Salzburger Nachrichten* (*SN*), 8 March 1986.

29. *NKZ,* 9 March 1986.

30. *NKZ,* 8 March 1986.

31. *Pressestunde,* ORF, 9 March 1986, quoted in Chapter 6. See also the reports on Waldheim's appearance in *Kleine Zeitung, Kurier, Die Presse, NKZ,* 10 March 1986; Compare *Süd-Ost Tageszeitung,* 11 March 1986; *WZ,* 11 March 1986.

32. *Wochenpresse,* 11 March 1986.

33. *Oberösterreichische Nachrichten,* 22 March 1986.

34. This line of argument was also supported by the ÖVP paper *Neues Volksblatt* (*NVB*), which designated Pusch and SPÖ General Secretary Peter Schieder as "Wire-pullers of the Waldheim Campaign." *NVB,* 22 March 1986.

35. *Mittagsjournal,* ORF, 21 March 1986.

36. Ibid.

37. From the date of this statement, it is clear that Mock was referring to the NS-*Reiterkorps,* not the SA *Reiterstandarte,* but the point is relevant only to show how easily a document could be employed to "disprove" any number of allegations.

38. *Kurier,* 22 March 1986.

39. *Kurier,* 23 March 1986.

40. *Kurier,* 24 March 1986.

41. *Profil,* 24 March 1986.

42. *NVB,* 22 March 1986.

43. *Oberösterreichische Nachrichten,* 22 March 1986.

44. *NKZ,* 22 March 1986.

45. *Oberösterreichische Nachrichten,* 22 March 1986.

46. *Die Presse,* 22 March 1986.

47. *Kurier,* 22 March 1986.

48. *Neue AZ/Tagblatt* (*AZ*), 21 and 22 March 1986. See also *Neue Zeit,* 22 March 1986.

49. *Salzburger Nachrichten* (*SN*), 8–9 March 1986.

50. *SN,* 11 March 1986.

51. *SN,* 22 March 1986.

52. *SN,* 28 March 1986. It is not clear which "slanderers" Waldheim meant, nor which archives were involved, but in any case his statement was palpably false. See *Profil,* 24 March 1986.

53. ORF, *Pressestunde,* 23 March 1986, cited in *WZ,* 25 March 1986.

54. *NKZ,* 26 March 1986.

55. *Kurier,* 23 March 1986; *WZ,* 23 March 1986 and 24 March 1986. See also *NVB,* 24 March 1986 and *NVB,* 25 March 1986.

56. Whether such disaffection would have had any concrete result is another matter. Waldheim told *Kurier* on 23 March, "I am not considering giving up my candidacy. *Kurier,* 23 March 1986. Michael Graff was quoted as saying that "We [ÖVP] are not considering giving up [on Waldheim]. Out motto is 'Now More Than Ever!'" *NKZ,* 29 March 1986.

57. *NVB,* 12 April 1986.

58. *SN,* 23 April 1986 and especially 1 April 1986; *Profil,* 24 March 1986.

59. *WZ,* 4 March 1986. See above, Chapter 3.

60. The text of this speech is reprinted in *WZ,* 23 April 1986. See also Projektteam "Sprache und Vorurteil," "'Wir sind alle unschuldige Täter!' Studien zum antisemtischen Diskurs im Nachkriegsösterreich." Project Report, Manuscript (Vienna, 1989), pp. 207–213.

61. *Die Presse,* 5 March 1986.

62. The distinction is that the formulation "sent" implied an organizational role and command authority which Army Group E did not possess in this question.

63. *Die Presse,* 5 March 1986.

64. *Die Presse,* 6 March 1986.

65. *NKZ,* 6 March 1986.

66. "News From World Jewish Congress" (News from WJC), 4 March 1986: "Bronfman said that Waldheim had engaged in 'one of the most elaborate deceptions of our time.'" The error possibly relates to the morphological similarities between the German words for disappointment (*Enttäuschung*) and deception (*Täuschung*), though this is not certain.

67. According to Langenscheidts German-English dictionary "daraufhin" can also mean "after that," "as a result," "on the strength of it," "therefore," "in answer to it," and "in response." I have chosen the meaning which suggests the weakest causal relation, but all would confirm the point I am making. See Heinz Messinger and the Langenscheidt-Redaktion, *Langenscheidts Grosswörterbuch der englischen und deutschen Sprache* (Berlin, Munich, Vienna and Zurich: Langenscheidt, 1982), p. 259.

68. *Kurier,* 6 March 1986.

69. *NVB,* 24 March 1986. The German sentence itself makes it unclear when Waldheim was supposed to have committed the crimes listed or when Yugoslavia had accused him: *von jugoslawischen Stellen, im Jahre 1948 an Kriegsverbrechen beteiligt gewesen zu sein.*

70. Ibid.

71. *Die Presse,* 24 March 1986.

72. See News from WJC, 22 March 1986.

73. See, for example, *Tiroler Tageszeitung,* 24 March 1986.

74. *NKZ,* 24 March 1986.

75. *Kurier,* 24 March 1986.

76. This was a boxed report. Above it, on the same page, was another headline on the story. The rubric stated "Ex-U.N. [Secretary] General shaken over the 'new absurd effronteries [*Frechheiten*]" and the headline itself, "Waldheim Emphatically: 'Have a Clear Conscience!'"

77. See *Kurier,* 6 March 1986.

78. In fact, this listing was far less significant than it would appear. However, this had nothing to do with the objections Rauscher raised.

79. *Kurier,* 24 March 1986.

80. *WZ,* 25 March 1986.

81. *Pressestunde,* ORF, 23 March 1986.

82. *Voralberger Tageszeitung,* 25 March 1986.

83. *WZ,* 25 March 1986.

84. *WZ,* 25 March 1986. The CROWCASS combined accused war criminals from various national lists. At the time of this press conference, the Yugoslav file which served as the ultimate source of the allegations which landed Waldheim on the CROWCASS had not yet been made public. Thus Wiesenthal's wholly justified question about the sequence of Yugoslav lists.

85. *Tiroler Tageszeitung,* 25 March 1986.

86. Ibid. This, however, was apparently in connection with Waldheim's service under Pannwitz, not with his service under Loehr. See *Profil,* 24 August 1987.

87. *Neue Zeit,* 25 March 1986.

88. *Südost Tagespost,* 25 March 1986.

89. See *WZ,* 25 March 1986; *Neue Vorarlberger Tageszeitung,* 25 March 1986; *SN,* 25 March 1986.

90. *Die Presse,* 25 March 1986.

91. *NKZ,* 30 March 1986.

92. *NVB,* 26 March 1986.

93. *Profil,* 24 March 1986. The interview was conducted in English in New York by Peter Sichrovsky. The original transcript of the interview is not available. The above passages are a translation of the German text as it appeared in *Profil.*

94. *Süddeutsche Zeitung,* 25 March 1986; 1 April 1986. See, however, the column by Anthony Lewis on 12 June 1986. In this piece, Lewis wrote, among other things, "Those of us who think there is an eternal obligation to remember what Nazism meant are free to express our moral revulsion at the Austrian's choice. The opportunity to do so, and the responsibility, lie especially with those in the public eye whose acts may have an impact on the Austrian imagination." What Lewis saw as an individual's duty to protest one's disfavor at Waldheim's election, of course, could also be interpreted as a "threat" against Austria, but only under certain assumptions. In any case, there is more than one interpretive possibility for such statements.

95. Quoted in *International Herald Tribune,* 4 November 1986.

96. See in this connection the interview with Kurt Schubert, Professor of Judaic Studies at the University of Vienna, in the *SN,* 15 April 1986.

97. *NVB,* 25 March 1986.

98. *Neue Vorarlberger Tageszeitung,* 25 March 1986. It is difficult to convey the real flavor of this passage in English. The word *"Judenrat"* is, in Germany and Austria, very reminiscent of usage from the Nazi era. "Jewish Council" is in fact a major edulcoration. The German *"Sippenhaftung,"* a much stronger word than guilt by association would normally imply, describes a situation in which all members of a group (a family, for example), are held collectively responsible for the behavior of any individual member. What made this passage particulary unsavory is that this sort of collective liability is known to most Austrians because of its application to families of political opponents or deserters by the Nazis. Normally it functions as one explanation why there was so little active and passive resistance to Nazi rule, and as such is convincing. However, in this context, because it is such an uncommon word, its usage suggested parallels between the Nazis and the WJC.

99. *Die Presse* advertises itself as "the broad horizon [*der grosse Horizont*]."

100. *Die Presse,* 25 March 1986. I have translated the WJC as "it" rather than "they," which I otherwise prefer, to avoid causing confusion in tracing the referents to the pronouns in this exceptionally convoluted passage. Not even Leitenberger's turgidity, however, can explain Helmut Gruber's misreading of her as arguing that "the Jews trade in a dark past" [*"Die Juden machen Geschäft aus ihrer Vergangenheit"*]; Gruber's interpretation can be excluded on simple grammatical grounds. See Helmut Gruber, *Antisemitismus im Mediendiskurs. Die Affäre "Waldheim" in der Tagespresse* (Wiesbaden: Deutscher Universitäts-Verlag, 1991), pp. 215–217, 253–254.

101. See *Die Furche,* 31 July 1971, quoted in Spira, *Feindbild,* p. 136.

102. *Die Furche,* 28 March 1986.

103. *Philadelphia Enquirer,* 19 May 1986. See also *New York Daily News,* 16 May 1986 and *NYT,* 17 May 1986.

104. *NKZ,* 25 May 1986.

105. But by no means unanimous. Gerhard Steininger of the *Salzburger Nachrichten,* for example, wrote that "We have latent and acute antisemitism among us once again. Heaven forbid that we should have anything against our Jewish fellow citizens, just against those 'certain Jewish circles,' best exemplified by Israel Singer. Is antisemitism thereby even a trace more harmless if it conjures up only one or a few scapegoats?" *SN,* 5/6 April 1986.

106. See Allport, *Prejudice,* pp. 9ff.

107. Austria Presseagentur (APA)-dispatch 25 March 1986; *Die Presse,* 25 March 1986.

108. *NKZ,* 26 March 1986; *Kurier,* 26 March 1986; *AZ,* 25 March 1986, among others.

109. *Tiroler Tageszeitung,* 25 March 1986. In February, 1980, the then editor of this paper, Rupert Kerer, wrote an article on the relationship between the Catholic Church and antisemitism. In this commentary, Kerer wrote: "The destruction of taboos by Jewish minds [*Geister*] has become fateful for humanity; laws, without which humanity would sink back into anarchy and its primitive nature." Kerer then catalogued the Jewish culprits, who (counting the honorary Jews as well) included Freud and Marx and Engels, Oppenheimer and Adorno, Brecht and Marcuse. "The 'Lexicon of Judaism' counts among its many steps forward for humanity, many which were actually steps backward into barbarity. The Jews will not enjoy reflecting on this role in world history, but it is here that the roots of antisemitism are to be sought." Quoted in Spira, *Feindbild,* p. 29.

110. *NKZ,* 26 March 1986.

111. For this aspect of Kreisky's politics, see Martin van Amerongen, *Bruno Kreisky und seine unbewältigte Gegenwart* (Graz: Styria Verlag, 1977), passim; Spira, *Feindbild,* pp. 133–153; Robert Wistrich, "The Strange Case of Bruno Kreisky," *Encounter* (May, 1979) pp. 78–85; and Ruth Wodak, Peter Nowak, Helmut Gruber, Johanna Pelikan, Rudolf de Cillia and Richard Mitten, *"Wir sind alle unschuldige Täter!" Diskurshistorische Studien zum Nachkriegsantisemitismus* (Frankfurt am Main: Suhrkamp, 1990), pp. 282–299.

112. *Zeit im Bild I,* ORF, 25 March 1986, cited in Wodak, et al., *Unschuldige Täter,* p. 180.

113. News from WJC, 22 March 1986. The point is significant in that the counter-intelligence section of Army Group E was *ceteris paribus* more likely to be involved in activities judged to be criminal. On the *Abwehr* in Army Group E, see Hans Kurz, James Collins, Jean Vanwelkenheuzen, Gerald Fleming, Hagen Fleischer, Jehuda Wallach and Manfred Messerschmidt, *Der Bericht der internationalen Historikerkommission,* Manuscript, 202 pp. plus addenda, Vienna, 1988. The report was printed as supplement in *Profil,* 15 February 1988, pp. 8–11.

114. News from WJC, 25 March 1986.

115. *Mittagjournal,* ORF, 25 March 1986. This broadcast is analyzed in greater detail in Projektteam "Sprache und Vorurteil," "Unschuldige Täter," Vol. 1, pp. 323–333.

116. See Projektteam "Sprache und Vorurteil," "Unschuldige Täter," Vol. 1, pp. 182–206.

117. *Mittagjournal,* ORF, 25 March 1986.

118. See, for example, *Kurier,* 24 March 1986.

119. In my opinion, false or misleading statements made by a journalist cannot be excused merely because he or she has not taken the trouble to research an issue. In point of fact, however, not only the press release of the WJC on 22 March 1986, but also *Kurier* contained all the information one needed to expose Graff's statement as crass and fallacious political propaganda. I cite the Austrian source(s) here principally to erode possible objections that the WJC's press releases were too difficult for Austrian journalists to come by. This is a rather flimsy excuse, but the point stands *a fortiori* when the information was easily accessible in one of the major Austrian daily papers which every ORF journalist reads. See News from WJC, 22 March 1986 and *Kurier,* 24 March 1986.

120. As we have seen, there is room for dispute as to how consistently Waldheim had maintained this position, but it was widely believed at the time that Waldheim had indeed made this claim.

121. *Abendjournal,* ORF, 25 March 1986. The "headlines" of the main evening television news program repeated the identical formulation "interrogation officer of the counterintelligence section." *Zeit im Bild I,* ORF, 25 March 1986.

122. Unless, of course, Pesata considered all "partisan activities" to be war crimes, which in the context seems unlikely.

123. One need only look at this duty roster to see that the formulation "interrogation officer of the *Abwehr*" is nonsense. "Interrogation" appears only in the sections describing the duties of the military intelligence section (Ic), but is not listed as a task of the counter-intelligence section (*Abwehr*). Moreover, the duties of the *Abwehr* section appear on a separate page altogether. Neither the WJC nor Herzstein had claimed that Waldheim was an "interrogation officer of the Abwehr." See News from WJC, 25 March 1986; Robert Herzstein, "Prepared Statment of Prof. Robert E. Herzstein on the Wartime Activities of Kurt Waldheim," 25 March 1986. The two relevant portions of this duty roster are reproduced in Karl Gruber, Ralph Scheide and Ferdinand Trautmannsdorff, *Waldheim's Wartime Years. A Documentation* (Vienna: Carl Gerold's Sohn, 1987), pp. 190–191.

124. *NKZ,* 26 March 1986.

125. *Handbuch für den Generalstabsdienst im Kriege,* cited in Kurz, et al., *Bericht,* p. 8.

126. *NKZ,* 26 March 1986; see also *Kurier,* 3 April 1986.

127. APA-dispatch, 27 March 1986. Steinbauer employs the passive, but the internal evidence leaves no doubt as to who was doing the construing.

128. *Tiroler Tageszeitung,* 5–6 April 1986.

129. In this connection it must be recalled that our analysis here concerns predominantly daily newspapers. *Profil* journalist Hubertus Czernin, who first broke the Waldheim story, provided high quality weekly analyses of the documents which were appearing. Writing for a weekly magazine is not the same as meeting daily deadlines, and one should not set unrealistic standards for the latter. However, the reports of *Profil* belie any notion that the astoundingly low quality of the reporting on the Waldheim affair in Austria was due to lack of sufficient information.

130. *Kurier,* 28 March 1986.

131. Herzstein, "Prepared Statement of Prof. Robert E. Herzstein on the Wartime Activities of Kurt Waldheim," 25 March 1986, pp. 8, 9–10.

132. *Kurier,* 28 March 1986.

133. This statement is inaccurate. Warnstorff became Ic in August 1943, while Waldheim was serving in Athens, and was Waldheim's superior from October, 1943, after he had returned to Arsakli from his temporary assignment in Athens. See Hanspeter Born, *Für die Richtigkeit. Kurt Waldheim* (Munich: Schneekluth, 1987), p. 102.

134. Rauscher's efforts were, as far as can be ascertained, undertaken in good faith, and other articles of his showed that he was capable of serious critical journalism. The point here is that in the situation we have described, any such lack of critical scrutiny contributed to the construction or reinforcement of the *Feindbild.* See *Kurier,* 7 May 1986.

135. The declaration is reproduced in Andreas Khol, Theodor Faulhaber and Gunther Ofner, eds., *Die Kampagne. Kurt Waldheim—Opfer oder Täter? Hintergründe und Szenen eines Falles von Medienjustiz* (Munich and Berlin: Herbig, 1987), between pages 160–161; see Herzstein, "Statement," p. 8.

136. See the APA dispatch 22 April 1986 and *NVB,* 23 April 1986. To her credit, Professor Weinzierl has since repudiated the use to which the declaration was put.

137. *NVB,* 2 June 1986.

138. To cite but two examples: The empress Maria Theresa rejected an application of a Jew for a residency permit for Vienna with the words, "I know of no more wicked plague for the state that this nation [which] drives people into poverty by means of fraud, usury and financial transactions and all other unpleasant activities, before which an honorable man would recoil in disgust." Quoted in Nikolaus Vielmetti, "Vom Begin der Neuzeit bis zur Toleranz," in Anna Drabek, Wolfgang Häusler, Kurt Schubert, Karl Stuhlpfarrer and Nikolaus Vielmetti, *Das österreichische Judentum. Voraussetzungen und Geschichte* (Vienna and Munich: Jugend und Volk, 1974), pp. 59–82, here p. 81. In 1902, the Austrian duelling fraternities passed a resolution at a meeting in Waidhofen which established the eponymous principle, according to which duelling with Jews was proscribed because, being dishonorable, one could not achieve "satisfaction" from them. The resolution is quoted in Dirk van Arkel, "Antisemitism in Austria." Dissertation, University of Leyden, 1966, p. 176.

139. *Die Presse,* 5 April 1986.

140. *NVB,* 10 April 1986.

141. *NKZ,* 10 April 1986.

142. *NKZ,* 6 May 1986.

143. *NVB,* 26 April 1986.

144. *WZ,* 29 April 1986.

145. *Kurier,* 26 and 27 March 1986; News from WJC, 27 March 1986; *NYT,* 27 March 1986.

146. *NYT,* 2 April 1986.

147. *NYT,* 3 April 1986.

148. *NYT,* 5 April 1986.

149. *NYT,* 8 April 1986.

150. *WZ,* 8 April 1986.

151. News from WJC, 9 April 1986.

152. The WJC press release does not mention Petritsch, which suggests that either the *NYT* reporter or the WJC was mistaken.

153. Letter from Israel Singer to President Rudolf Kirchschläger, 8 April 1986. attached to News from WJC, 9 April 1986.

154. News from WJC, 9 April 1986.

155. Letter from Kirchschläger to Israel Singer, 23 April 1986.

156. *WZ,* 23 April 1986. See Projektteam "Sprache und Vorurteil" *Unschuldige Täter,* Vol. I, pp. 207-213.

157. *Wochenpresse,* 3 June 1986.

158. See *Weltwoche,* 29 May 1986. For the evidence for and against Matza's allegations, see Born, *Richtigkeit,* pp. 9–13.

159. Quoted in *NVB,* 6 June 1986.

160. *NVB,* 24 March 1986.

161. See, for example, APA-dispatch, 25 March 1986.

162. *Süd-Ost Tagespost,* 27 March 1986.

163. ÖVP press release: "Graff: Israels Justizminister soll auf seinen Staatspraesidenten hoeren." 22 May 1986.

164. *NKZ,* 31 May 1986.

165. *Kleine Zeitung,* 27 March 1986.

166. *NKZ,* 28 March 1986. At an exhibition of photographs of Viennese Jews, which ran during the meeting of the WJC in Vienna in 1985, Singer recognized his father in a photograph of Jews being forced to scrub the streets by gangs of SA members.

167. *NKZ,* 28 March 1986.

168. *Club 2,* "Unser Wahlkampf," ORF, 3 April 1986. See Ruth Wodak, "Wie über Juden geredet wird," *Journal für Sozialforschung* Vol. 28, No. 1 (1988), p. 128.

169. See Projektteam "Sprache und Vorurteil," *Unschuldige Täter,* Vol. 1, pp. 53–60; 86–111; and especially pp. 214–293.

170. Or variations like the following from Waldheim: "I am on very congenial terms with the president of the Jewish community organization [*Kultusgemeinde*] and with a number of prominent Jewish fellow citizens, and I would regret it deeply if such [i.e., antisemitic] feelings were aroused." Quoted in *Wochenpresse,* 29 April 1986.

171. Gordon Allport called attention to what he called a "refencing device," which enables people to hold to pre-judgments even in the face of contradictory evidence. According to this view, by making exceptions for a few favored cases, the negative rubric may be retained intact for others. See Allport, *Prejudice,* pp. 23–24.

172. This interview is analyzed in depth in Projektteam "Sprache und Vorurteil," "Unschuldige Täter," pp. 201–206. The transcript of the interview is attached as Appendix III. Alois Mock had offered a similar line of argument in *Mittagsjournal,* ORF, 26 May 1986.

173. *Neue Voralberger Tageszeitung,* 13 May 1986.

174. *Kärntner Tageszeitung,* 13 May 1986.

175. *Neue Volkszeitung Kärnlen Osttirol,* 28 May 1986.

176. The German dyad *Inland/Ausland* is similar in function to the English interior/exterior, but the latter is not automatically associated with political or cultural units. Since there is no real expression which conveys its meaning, I will employ the German *das Ausland* when nothing else will do, without, however, artifically declining for case variations which do not exist in English.

177. *Die Presse,* 27 March 1986.

178. *SN,* 27 March 1986.

179. APA-dispatch, 27 March 1986.

180. *NVB,* 22 May 1986.

181. *NVB,* 29 April 1986.

182. *NKZ,* 3 May 1986.

183. Leaflet (no date), "Jugend für Waldheim," File "Waldheim" VIII, Dokumentationsarchiv des österreichischen Widerstandes, Vienna.

184. *Wochenpresse,* 1 April 1986.

185. Austrian Jewish community representatives held a press conference on 25 March 1986, at which their spokespersons characterized the appeal not to arouse "feelings which no one wants" as "a warning, which we can only interpret as a threat." *AZ,* 26 March 1986. On the following day Alois Mock appeared on the noontime radio news program *Mittagsjournal* and said, "... and I also appeal to the rational forces inside the World Jewish Congress to consider stopping this campaign and not [thereby] arouse feelings which none of us want." *Mittagsjournal,* ORF, 26 March 1986.

186. *NKZ,* 27 March 1986.

9

When "The Past" Catches Up

The accommodations to antisemitic prejudice on the part of Kurt Waldheim, but far more strikingly on the part of his supporters, undoubtedly brought him some votes he would not otherwise have polled. If the historically conditioned induration of the majority of Austrian voters towards this kind of politics did not cost Waldheim the election, Waldheim's mere invocation of a slander campaign does not appear to have won it for him, either. The image of Waldheim and Austria as the victims of a coordinated international Jewish conspiracy was so firmly established by the end of April that after the first round of the election in May, the debate on Waldheim's past inside Austria ebbed, even as interest abroad in Waldheim and the Austrian connection was just beginning to flow.

The traditional May Day festivities in Vienna in 1986, which the Socialists hoped would give their candidate Steyrer one last major public exposure, took place (literally) under the radioactive cloud of the world's worst nuclear disaster at Chernobyl. As the full extent of the accident gradually became known, Austrians, like all other Europeans, were forced to direct their attention to the implications this would have on their lives. The pundits, if not the psephologists, attributed Waldheim's failure to win an outright majority in the first round, one week after Chernobyl, to the last-minute surge of support for the Green candidate Freda Meissner-Blau, in turn traceable principally to the heightened concern with environmental issues.

Whatever actually determined Austrian voting behavior is open to a great deal of speculation,[1] but it may be safely ruled out that the result was in any significant way influenced by a negative backlash against the Waldheim camp's antisemitic wager. Waldheim's performance in the first round on 4 May 1986 (he received 49.7% of the valid cast ballots) made it abundantly clear to the Socialists that no votes were to be won by calling inordinate attention to Waldheim's desperate standing abroad. The Socialists, of course, had known all along that taking too unambiguous a stance against the construction of the *Feindbild 'Jud'* would be a loser at the polls. After the first round, the SPÖ altered its tactics and attempted to stress Steyrer's ability to reconcile a divided nation, but, barring an unforeseen debacle, the result of the second round was a foregone conclusion. The election came, and Waldheim won it handily: his 53.9 percent of the votes was the best result of its kind (i.e., when not running against an incumbent) in the history of the Second Republic.

The leaders of the People's Party had reason to celebrate. They had been able to capitalize on the disaffection of voters with the government for any number of reasons and defeat the Socialists in a national election for the first time in sixteen years. Waldheim's victory, they hoped, would inaugurate a conservative turn in Austrian politics, and the new president would be their key to the chancellor's office. The hoped-for turn came, all right, but in an unexpected guise. The day after Waldheim's election, then Chancellor Fred Sinowatz resigned and ceded his place to the Socialist banker, Franz Vranitzky. Telegenic and astute where the pyknic Sinowatz was merely clumsy and frequently pathetic, Vranitzky exuded technocratic competence and hastily abandoned a number of shibboleths of Socialist economic policy that he had defended as finance minister until the very day he became chancellor. And if the leader of the ÖVP, Alois Mock, might have had a fighting chance to appear a serious contender for leadership against Fred Sinowatz, in a political and electoral culture becoming increasingly "Americanized"—i.e., in which poignant media images and their accompanying platitudes were being substituted for less glamorous but more informative programmatic debates on issues—he was no match for Vranitzky's projection of cool efficiency.

Meanwhile, things were looking rather dismal for the leader of the FPÖ, Norbert Steger, vice-chancellor in the small coalition with the Socialists. Under attack from several sides, Steger was unseated as party leader at a conference in September, 1986, by Jörg Haider, by all accounts the comer in Austrian politics. Haider's main power base is in Carinthia, and he has possessed an impressive knack for appealing both to old Nazis and the Austrian equivalent of Yuppies. It was Haider's cultivation of the former which cost the FPÖ its seats in the cabinet, for Vranitzky declared himself unwilling to govern jointly with a party under Haider's leadership. The breakup of the national coalition brought new elections to the National Assembly, but the ÖVP's hopes of riding the Waldheim bandwagon to the chancellory proved misplaced. Indeed, if anyone benefitted from the residual effects of the "Waldheim phenomenon" it was the Haider FPÖ, and in the November 1986 elections his party scored its biggest success ever (not counting the 1949 elections; the FPÖ was founded in 1954).[2] No party in parliament received an absolute majority, but the Socialists under Vranitzky were able to win a plurality of seats and thus retain the position of chancellor. They and the ÖVP formed a grand coalition, the first since 1966, with Franz Vranitzky serving as chancellor and Alois Mock as vice-chancellor and foreign minister.

Together, the two major parties were forced to confront both the domestic legacy of the Kreisky era and the international fallout of the Waldheim affair. Apart from the inconvenience of having to travel outside Vienna to meet visiting foreign government officials, as protocol would otherwise have required the latter to pay a courtesy call on Waldheim (though the reticence of such officials to make such visits tapered off significantly as his term progressed), or the embarrassment of having to exclude the president of the Republic from ceremonies marking the fiftieth anniversary of the

Anschluss in 1988, the burdens the government was forced to bear were in fact rather few. Life with Waldheim in the Hofburg, while not without its awkward moments, became all the more easy to tolerate because Austrian politicians could reckon with the short and selective memories of the main players on the international stage. It bears emphasizing that the ignominity into which Waldheim personally had so visibly fallen has witnessed no corresponding international concern for the Waldheim phenomenon in Austria itself. It was hardly to be expected that Waldheim would be invited to any country in western Europe, though the pilgrimage of the good and the great of the continent to Hirohito's funeral in Japan suggests that the primary considerations here were not moral. Yet no one has evinced the slightest hesitation in receiving Alois Mock in his many travels abroad, either as foreign minister or as leader of the International Democratic Union (an informal umbrella organization of conservative parties bringing together the likes of, among others, Helmut Kohl, Margaret Thatcher and George Bush) even though, as this study shows, Mock and his party were arguably more responsible than Waldheim himself for the revival of antisemitic prejudice as a political tool in contemporary Austria.

Mock seems to have drawn the appropriate conclusions from this positive reinforcement. As recently as May, 1990, for example, he offered his views on the situation in the Middle East in the wake of the killing of seven Palestinians in Rishon-le-Zion by the Israeli Ami Popper, and added his voice to intensified (pre-Gulf war) international calls for the Israeli government to engage more seriously in the "peace process." Such demands made on Israel are frequent, if somewhat inconsistent, and may be defended on any number of grounds. Foreign Minister Mock, however, went one better: he stated that the climate of violence and hatred in the occupied territories might not only promote desperate acts of deranged individuals; it also, in Mock's words, provided a "fertile ground for the desecration of Jewish cemeteries,"[3] a clear reference to the contemporaneous events in Carpentras, France and elsewhere. Mock's public pronouncement illustrated in a particularly graphic way that a heightened historical consciousness about the Nazi period, which the surfeit of commemorative occasions in 1988 surely encouraged, offered no safeguards against anti-Jewish hostility when a political point was to be scored: the Jews were still responsible for acts of antisemitic violence. More generally, Mock's unrepentant remark confirmed the Janus-faced nature of antisemitic prejudice in post-Auschwitz Austrian political culture.

The initial years of Waldheim's term in office were dominated by the debate on the historians' commission report and the series of memorial services during the year 1988, all of which were followed with interest by the international media, and all of which Waldheim endured and survived. In a relatively short period of time, Austria came in for large doses of *Vergangenheitsbewältigung* ("coming to terms with the past"). We have suggested above the ways in which certain cultural traditions of antisemitic prejudice as well as particularly evocative images out of the Austrian past both fostered the emergence of specific lines of argument about Waldheim and the "campaign" against him as well as offered a distinctive idiom of precedents, allusions and metaphors which set limits to what was perceptible or even thinkable in the debate itself. It is both the cluster of beliefs, prejudices, moral conviction and knowledge about Jews as well as the willingness and ability to realize this antisemitic potential in an apposite post-Auschwitz discursive and political form that may be labelled the Waldheim phenomenon proper. Although the attention of the international media intermittently focussed the eyes of the world on the problems Austria had in "coming to terms" with "its past," this intersection of past and present in the Waldheim affair was merely the specific Austrian variant of a much broader problem. The Waldheim affair may soon be forgotten, but the Waldheim phenomenon will simply not go away.

"Coming to Terms with the Past"

The German compound noun *Vergangenheitsbewältigung,* which the English expressions "coming to terms with" or "mastering" the past attempt to approximate,[4] has been bandied about a great deal in Austria since the Waldheim affair, and, as a new central European buzz-word far more frequently invoked than understood, has received a renewed currency since the changes in the former Soviet Union and the fall of the Communist regimes in central and eastern Europe. In fact the term appears to be a post-Second World War coinage,[5] and perhaps emerged partly because conventional expressions were felt inadequate to deal intellectually, psychologically or even morally with the very magnitude of the Nazi crimes—the "past" it was suggested be "mastered"—or perhaps a new term was needed because the Nazi period was felt too discrepant with the values the post-Nazi German elites believed Germanic culture ought to have embodied. Though the term itself, and the discussions it symbolizes, are more familiar in their West German context, because of the so-called *"Historikerstreit,"* the dispute on the relation of the Nazi period to German history and political culture, the theoretical issues involved in the process of *Vergangenheitsbewältigung* apply equally to Austria.[6]

Critics of the concept *Vergangenheitsbewältigung* frequently find fault with the idea of mastering or coming to terms with the past. There is some justice to this complaint, for it is not entirely clear what mastering would mean in practice and the abstract quality of the German word leaves open exactly who or what is to come to terms with the past. However, even if one could settle on a common definition of "mastering" (*Bewältigung*), one would still be saddled with defining what is to be mastered, and "the past" is no less problematic. Indeed, the former difficulty seems less intellectually disturbing than the latter, because virtually everyone who has discussed this issue has assumed in one form or another that there is "a past" to be mastered. But that is precisely the point which in my view ought to be contested. However one may define it, "the past" has been and is continually being "mastered," "confronted," or "conquered" inasmuch as this past serves to confirm explicit or implicit political objectives, buttresses a specific geneological or teleological account of history for a given cultural unit over time, or simply reinforces the common values or assumptions of a dominant political culture. Every such "mastering" of "the past," moreover, must simultaneously presuppose a "mastering" of the present. In the same way, to articulate political goals presumes an attempt to "master" a specific "past." The assumption which thus seems unreliable is that there is such a thing as "the past," which one need merely recognize and thereby master, in whatever way one proposes. On the contrary, the past comprises a number of possible interpretations of things which have gone before, of which one comes to be seen as the preferred and designated bearer of the label "the past."

This is not the place to embark upon a full-scale discussion of the possibilities of historical knowledge. However, a couple of assumptions that have informed this work on the Waldheim phenomenon ought to be made explicit. In dealing with the problem of *Vergangenheitsbewältigung,* I have found Richard Rorty's pragmatic conception that all knowledge is opinion plus a reasonable justification immensely suggestive, even if somewhat unsettling. As I understand this view, one's claims to historical knowledge would imply simply that one had been able to demonstrate that a specific knowledge claim conformed to the intersubjective beliefs that the audience to which the claim was addressed had no reason to doubt at the time it was given. It would be impossible to test these intersubjective beliefs themselves, because there is no prior set of "objective" background beliefs that could guarantee any more secure knowledge, in other words, no beliefs in terms of which we could evaluate the content of our own knowledge claim.[7] As applied to the problem of history, this idea would seem to suggest in addition that what might count as the criteria for determining the quality and coherency of an historical explanation could only be conventions which could not be further tested independently of those (or other) conventions themselves. Any claim to ultimately rational foundations for history would thus be precarious, because there is no independent language of rational explanation in terms of which we could assess the conventions one employs in historical explanations, for no language of rational explanation itself possesses conventions which have themselves been grounded independently of these very conventions.[8]

In fact, even though historians lack an Archimedian point from which they can ultimately judge the worth of competing historical explanations, they work as though these conventions were rationally grounded, and the products of their efforts merit assent or dissent according to conventions which the profession itself accepts as valid. I do not wish to pronounce on the worth of this epistemological compromise in itself, though I think it important to recognize that it is a compromise. What this seems to imply for the concept of "coming to terms with the past" is that there are structural barriers to an "objective" historical knowledge inherent in the practice of historical scholarship itself and *a fortiori* in the dissemination of this information to a wider public. It follows that the discussion of *Vergangenheitsbewältigung* must transcend the question of how people might best learn about "the past," and instead address the problem of how the ways in which these people receive information foster the idea that there is "a" past and abet a specific conception of what "the past" is.

In other words, how do obstacles to knowledge tend to promote an idea of the past, and what effects might this have on the way people view contemporary events?

We are, in fact, able to "know" about the past only by virtue of that which is conveyed to us as the past. We can never have more than indirect access to what has occurred in the past. We form a conception of it through what is handed down to us as history, that is, as various accounts of these events, be it through books, magazines, personal recollections, or other media. The version of history which comes broadly to be considered as "the past" predominates because it is the one to which we have the most frequent, even if not exclusive, access.

The Metaphor of the Mozartkugel

The ways in which barriers to the free exercise of critical intelligence in the construction of historical consciousness are erected might perhaps be best illustrated by a metaphor and an example. Because of its ironic suitability in a discussion of the Waldheim phenomenon in Austria, I have chosen a Mozartkugel as the metaphor. The Mozartkugel contains four concentric layers of confection. At the center is the pistachio creme, which here represents original source materials with which the historian works. These documents are neither necessarily complete nor unproblematic. Under the most favorable of circumstances, these documents could not yield an account of the past, in Ranke's words, "as it really was."

If we take our culinary historiographical critique further, we come to the marzipan, which in our model stands for specialized historians. These scholars possess a variety of interests, ideological viewpoints, personal histories and degrees of intellectual honesty and scholarly competence. Neither the historical questions they attempt to answer, nor the criteria which determine the worth of their contributions to historical scholarship, moreover, are uninfluenced by the values of a culture. One would thus expect a corresponding range of interpretations of the documents available to them. When one adds to this the institutions which can influence or determine the diffusion of a specific historiography and also the political and social powers which can prescribe the direction, if not the results, of research, then it is not difficult to imagine that a national history which tended to articulate with favored cultural values would emerge in a predominant position.

The nougat creme is our next destination, and in this metaphor it represents non-specialist intellectuals. In fact, it is this layer of the intelligentsia which teaches the population as a whole the history it learns. But where have they learned their history? These teachers, journalists, writers and other non-historian scholars must rely on those books which have been written by specialists or by popularizers of specialist works. We have already questioned the potential biases of these professional historians. The intelligentsia in the marzipan layer would represent yet another filter of beliefs and assumptions about culture and society which would make the version of history they represent even more dependent on the published sources favoring the dominant view or views, and would likely adapt its own conception of the past to this dominant one, if for no other reason than lack of access to competing ones.

Finally, we have arrived at the outer layer of chocolate, in our example the population not included in the previous two layers. The ideas which they have of history are dependent almost exclusively upon oral accounts from family or friends, things they were taught in school, what they take in of newspapers or the electronic media, and from books about history that they may occasionally read. These people would probably be less used to the kind of intellectual disputes which lead one to question her or his presuppositions, and would be at least as subject to the pressures to conform and accept dominant cultural values as the historians and non-specialist intelligentsia. If we recall the dependence of this layer on the intelligentsia, of the intelligentsia on specialist historians, and of these on their own ability to evaluate critically sources which are not themselves self-evidently intepretable, then is it really surprising that it is only with the greatest of efforts that people are able to establish and maintain a skeptical distance to the version of "the past" which conformed most closely to the assumptions of their political culture itself, or, in other words, is it difficult to see how "the past" passes so easily over our lips? Michael Stürmer, one of the leading protagonists in the *Historikerstreit,* wrote "in a land without history [he was speaking of West Germany], he wins the future who provides the memory, forms the concepts and interprets the past."[9] Although historian Ian Kershaw, in his thoughtful book on the historiography of Nazi Germany, described Stürmer's remarks as "almost Orwellian,"[10] Stürmer has in my view landed on the central issue in dispute. Although from a purely scholarly (one might even say antiquarian) standpoint the *Historikerstreit,* in Kershaw's words, may have "resulted in no new lasting insights into a deep understanding of the Third Reich,"[11] it does not follow, as Richard Evans has written, that the debate "has little to offer anyone with a serious scholarly interest in the German past,"[12] for this overlooks the point which Stürmer has grasped completely and arguably was the main reason for the heat of the debate, namely, that every "seriously scholarly interest in the German past" must necessarily be concerned with the German present and future. If there is no certain point which allows us to determine what "the past" actually was, what counts as "the past" can only have meaning in relation to values with contemporary political relevance. And serious scholars neglect this aspect of history at their peril.

The situation is not really so bleakly rigid as the metaphor of the Mozartkugel would imply, for at every stage in the acquisition of historical knowledge it is possible for one's critical intelligence to engage one's ideational environment, and in many societies there is enough material available to form alternative conceptions to the commanding one. To stretch the metaphor a bit, everyone is able to eat and digest the whole Mozartkugel. Yet the limits to exercising this theoretical freedom are real and the various institutions and professional and political rituals within a given culture tend to restrict, rather than expand, the possibilities of mounting fundamental intellectual challenges to the values or interpretations at hand. The Waldheim affair offered many such examples of the limits to critical thought imposed by certain preconceptions about Austrian history. I would like to end this theoretical discourse with the story of the fate of a single document relating to Waldheim's past and the pitfalls one must avoid on the road to historical knowledge.

Let us begin in the center of the Mozartkugel, with the original sources themselves. The document in question was a report from 25 May 1944 prepared by the military intelligence section of Army Group E, in which Waldheim served. The original of this report, which is stored in a German archive, was initialled, it has been consensually established, by Waldheim, then the section's third *Ordonnanzoffizier.* This report, which surveyed the general military situation, contained the following passage relating to the effectiveness of reprisals against partisans: "exaggerated reprisal measures undertaken without a more precise examination of the objective situation have only caused embitterment and have been useful to the bands." The significance of this document, of course, only becomes apparent in a particular context. But here there is no consensus. In his book on Waldheim, Robert Herzstein wrote that "the agreeable young lieutenant who had worked so hard to prove his political reliability to his Nazi masters became one of the first—indeed one of the only—Wehrmacht officers to put his doubts on record."[13] Herzstein based this judgment on his study of "thousands of similar documents" and had found "few stronger protests of this kind, and then only from the pens of far more powerful men." Herzstein described this unique protest of Waldheim's as "moral in inspiration" even if not "couched in moral terms," and added that "there is no evidence that Waldheim ever openly criticized or otherwise protested against Nazi brutality on any other occasion,"[14] but Herzstein's interpretation made clear that this was a protest of German military policy on Waldheim's part.

This same report was examined by Hanspeter Born, also author of a book on Waldheim's wartime past. Born also viewed it as a "revision" in Waldheim's thinking about the effectiveness of these measures, but he appeared to want to minimize the significance of what would seem to be a fairly straightforward criticism. Born emphasized, for example, that there was no evidence that anyone in the command staff of Army Group E "ever had any moral scruples about the employment of 'punishment' [Sühnemassnahmen]."[15]

It is possible to view the significance of this report of 25 May 1944 in terms of Waldheim's personal role in Army Group E in yet a third way. On 9 December 1943, then Army Group E Chief of Staff August Winter delivered remarks to an afternoon briefing of the general staff. Among other things, Winter opined that "unfortunately, we are not able to behead everybody. However, whenever one exacts punishment, one must restrict it to the truly guilty and hostages, not flatten areas which were completely uninvolved. This only leads to the growth of band activity."[16] It was thus clear at the highest levels of Army Group E from as early as December 1943 that the "punishment"of the partisans was not having the intended effect. In April 1944, the Ic/AO department's specialist on Greece, Hans Wende, was sent to Athens to assess public attitudes towards the Germans, and gather what intelligence he could about the various resistance organizations. In the report he filed upon his return, Wende was candid about the efficacy of reprisals: "The punishment [meted out] . . . has stiffened and increased hostility towards the Germans. There is enormous bitterness over the hanging of 5 Communist hostages in the city. . . . The actions of the Germans are not seen as the justified punishment of a crime, but rather arbitrariness against innocents, since the shooting of hostages does not deter those actually guilty. . . ." Nearly equally important in this context are the handwritten marginal comments. Alexander Loehr, the commanding general of Army Group E, wrote "Good Report!" at the top, and Herbert Warnstorff, the Ic, wrote, next to Wende's comments on the shooting of hostages, "there is, however, no other solution." Seen in the context of Winter's own reservations about the efficacy of reprisal policy and the corresponding change in that policy by the Wehrmacht command itself, and the evidence that suggested that by May 1944 such doubts about the deterrent effects of reprisal shootings were more or less conventional wisdom, Waldheim's ostensible protest appears in a somewhat different light. Waldheim, in other words, would have written this report presumably secure in the knowledge that not only was he safe from reprimand for this "protest," he was also restating views his commanding general in all likelihood shared. A curious "protest," indeed.[17]

We are thus confronted with at least three divergent interpretations of the identical original source. In my view, the latter interpretation offers the most comprehensive explanation of the evidence, but the point here has to do with the formation of a view of how things really happened, or to answer the question, what did Waldheim actually do by writing this report as he did? The three views of this document, partly overlapping, offered no single answer. The reception of this document in the media, however, favored one interpretation over the others.

The international historians' commission, which had been set up to investigate Waldheim's wartime past, was scheduled to deliver its report on 8 February 1988. There had been conflicting accounts of what it would contain, and how critical of Waldheim it would be, but there seemed little doubt that Waldheim would not escape fully exonerated. On 5 February 1988, the *New York Times* published an article on Herzstein and this 25 May 1944 situation report, which, Ralph Blumenthal reported, was a "new[ly] discovered dispatch found by a U.S. historian."[18] The timing of the report suggests that either Herzstein or Blumenthal or both hoped to pre-empt the historians' commission report with this "new" document.[19] The *Times* report on the document confirmed that Waldheim had faulted the reprisals and quoted Herzstein's view that it was unusual for a younger officer to have done this. Those reading the article could only conclude that Waldheim had, at least on one occasion, protested explicitly against a criminal reprisal policy.

Two days before the historians' commission completed its work, the Austrian daily *Neue Kronen Zeitung* published a banner headline proclaiming "Sensation in USA: War Document Now Exculpates Waldheim!"[20] The rubric over the headline read "He [Waldheim] criticized German atrocities in the Balkans in 1944." The article on page two, the headline of which repeated that Waldheim had criticized the "Balkan atrocities," was derivative of the *New York Times* article from 5 February. The lead, in bold print, spoke of a "surprise in the USA: the *New York Times* published yesterday in a prominent place a wartime document in which Waldheim was exculpated." The document, wrote Kurt Seinitz in the article, was a situation report from 25 May 1944. In this report, Waldheim "criticized the retaliation measures and atrocities against the indigenous resistance fighters and suggested that they were having the opposite effect." The biggest surprise of all, apparently, was the source of the document: "The discoverer and evaluator of this document is Professor Robert Herzstein, until now the head Waldheim hunter of the World Jewish Congress." Herzstein was quoted from the *Times* article as saying that "it is certainly unusual for an officer of this low rank to have criticized Hitler's policies of retaliation." Herzstein's other interpretations were not reported, and the clear message was that Waldheim had been exonerated by a witness whose authority in this question was all the more credible because he had previously been Waldheim's principal critic.

Since this article appeared, the *Neue Kronen Zeitung* has not revised its views, nor has it suggested that other accounts of this document's significance exist. Theoretically, of course, Austrians could obtain all the relevant publications dealing with the document, and even visit the Munich archive where it is located. Barring that, however, the only real basis for forming an opinion about this document would be the disputable interpretation of the document given in the *New York Times* as presented in the *Neue Kronen Zeitung.* And even should interested readers trouble to check the original article against its *Neue Kronen Zeitung* resume, what would lead them to consult Hanspeter Born's book, the historians' commission report or the *Times Literary Supplement*, where these other interpretations are to be found? And if asked about the issue of Waldheim's attitude towards reprisal measures, or, more generally, towards the Hitler regime, most would reply on the basis of the only sources they had seen or consulted, and this would be the only "past" they (and thousands like them) could possibly understand.

There are few individual "facts" which can be so easily followed through their media lifetime as this one. Yet it is possible to speculate as to what the possible effects which similar examples of ostensible historical knowledge might have had on the perception of the criticism of Waldheim and his past, especially when sanctioned by persons recognized as the arbiters of this historical knowledge itself. As we saw in the previous chapter, holders of prestigious chairs in history at the University of Vienna and elsewhere lent their names to a declaration in which they presented as fact an untrue statement about an easily verifiable document. On the assumption that these historians from the Vogelsang Institute acted in good faith, the declaration they wrote would appear to confirm the point about the barriers to credible historical "knowledge" in a striking way. It was to have been expected that Waldheim and his more zealous defenders would do their utmost to discredit Robert Herzstein's interpretation of the documentary material the World Jewish Congress presented on 25 March 1986, and reasonable that they might seek out one or more respected Austrian historians to examine the material and provide an alternative interpretation of the documents. It was not, however, self-evident that these historians would take such liberties with the standards of historical scholarship they themselves—by virtue of their positions in the university—had been instrumental in determining. As a consequence, one of the Waldheim camp's most important assertions—that the World Jewish Congress was making unjustified accusations of Waldheim's complicity in war crimes—could find support in a position falsely attributed to Robert Herzstein but presented by the deans of historical scholarship in Austria as a fact. In the face of such acts, as well as the normal barriers to historical knowledge, it is only through a permanent rigorous and relentlessly honest critical skepticism within the framework given by the conventions of historical scholarship that it is possible to tell a better from a worse, a merely tendentious from a scholarly acceptable historical account. If we exclude the question of forgeries, which present their own difficulties, it is possible to view the task of those who wish to carry through such a criticism as one of remaining in constant debate with the assumptions and conceptions which underlie their own interpretations as well as those they read. Yet some historical accounts are considered superior to others in a way that intimates a closer proximity to the real past, and we also speak conventionally of "the past," a proposition any such evaluation would appear to presume. In the context cited, therefore, a person might be forgiven for thinking that there was something in the Waldheim camp's complaints.

What we recognize as "the past" cannot exist. The selective nature of the documentary sources, historians' personal assumptions and biases and the ever-changing questions which they must pose to their sources, all exclude it. That we assume that it exists can be explained by reference to the version of history which comes to be selected, reinforced and promoted. Not any version will do, but rather the one which survives the institutionalized screening processes which exist in a political culture, which influence not only the quality of the historical profession, but also the broad directions of research. It follows, I have argued, that "the past" is repeatedly "mastered," whenever it serves to explicate and confirm personal or common political goals, sustains a certain geneological account of a given political objective, or simply reinforces the common assumptions of a dominant political culture. This being the case, the task of critical historians, and thinking citizens, is not to "master" "the past," but rigorously to lay bare the biases and prejudices, ideological predilections and normative assumptions which a particular version of "the past" articulates or implies. In other words, constantly to question the purpose of this particular "coming to terms" with the past.

The Waldheim Phenomenon Without Waldheim

Contrary to Waldheim's expectations, interest in the unanswered questions about his past did not disappear after his election. Waldheim received no official invitations from any country in western Europe, and some prominent private individuals, such as the political scientist Ralf Dahrendorf, even boycotted events where Waldheim would have been present. In April 1987, the U.S. Department of Justice announced that it was placing Waldheim on the watch list, further reinforcing his pariah status. Waldheim's diplomatic isolation was broken initially by the Pope, who received Waldheim officially in June 1987, and Waldheim subsequently travelled to a few Arab countries, some of whose papers had defended Waldheim against ostensible Zionist attacks. Though in April 1990 the U.S. Justice Department confirmed its decision to bar Waldheim, an indication of a possible thaw in attitudes towards Waldheim came the following July, when Presidents Richard von Weizsäcker of Germany and Vaclav Havel of Czechoslovakia publicly met Waldheim at the Salzburg Festival, where Havel gave the ceremonial address.

In Austria itself, President Waldheim did not become the kind of integrative figure he had wished. Though he was initially an irritation and embarrassment to many, during the second half of his term Waldheim's treatment in the press suggested that increasing numbers of Austrians had accepted Waldheim as president, even though he would never be accorded the respect and affection his predecessors had enjoyed. Perhaps having personally come to terms with the idea that the burden Austria bore with him in the Hofburg was too great, Waldheim announced in June 1991 that he would not seek a second term in 1992.

Since Waldheim was elected Austrian President, the political face of Europe has undergone enormous change. One of voices heard in the freer political atmosphere after the collapse of Communist regimes in central and eastern Europe, however, has been that of a coarse and angry antisemitism.[21] The more explicit anti-Jewish comments of some of Lech Walesa's supporters in Poland, and the chilling statements by leaders of the antisemitic *Pamyat* movement in Russia evince the potential danger throughout Europe of rising anti-Jewish resentment, even if the threat of officially sanctioned antisemitic violence or discrimination against Jews does not appear acute. What I have termed the Waldheim phenomenon in Austria is the persistence among broad sections of the population of anti-Jewish beliefs, coupled with an actual willingness on the part of some politicians to tap it, encoded in an appropriate post-Auschwitz idiom, for political ends short of discrimination. In my view, it is the presence of this specific (and still relatively low) tolerance threshold against the open profession of anti-Jewish prejudice, as well as the idiom that corresponds to it, which most distinguishes the present situation in Austria from that in Poland and Russia. The political constellation in contemporary Austria suggests, moreover, that most public utterances and acts which trespass the recognized boundaries of post-Auschwitz tolerance will continue to be subject to political censure. Nonetheless, as long as there are political gains to be made in Austria by appealing to anti-Jewish feeling, there will be a politics of antisemitic prejudice, and this long after Waldheim himself has retired from the political stage. In this book I have attempted to decode the vernacular of anti-Jewish prejudice in the public discourse of the Waldheim affair, in the hope that we will be better placed to combat similar instances of the Waldheim phenomenon in the future. It remains to be seen whether the current unwelcome images of Austria's Nazi past will be supplanted by its more prosaic Trapp family pendant, or whether the Waldheim affair becomes the occasion for a more general effort on all sides to "come to terms" with the Waldheim phenomenon in Austria. If so, then Waldheim will indeed be said to have performed a far more important "duty."

Notes

1. But see E. Gehmacher, F. Birk, and G. Orgis, "Die Waldheim-Wahl. Eine erste Analyse," *Journal für Sozialforschung* Vol. 26, No. 3 (1986), pp. 319–331.

2. Under Haider's leadership, the FPÖ has gone from one electoral success to another, and after the most recent provincial elections in Carinthia, Haider was elected governor with the votes of his party and of the Carinthian ÖVP under Christian Zernatto. On 13 June 1991, Haider let slip a remark in a debate in the provincial assembly on employment policy for foreign workers that would lead to his removal from office. Baited by a Socialist Party deputy in the assembly, who compared Haider's proposals on how to deal with "welfare cheats" [*Sozialschmarotzer*] with those in force under the Nazis, Haider retorted, among other things, "In the Third Reich they implemented a proper [*ordentlich*] employment policy, which is something your [i.e., the SPÖ] government in Vienna cannot even manage." Haider's endorsement of the "employment policies" of the Nazis, which, of course, included forced labor as well as the "employment" in the concentration camps, was a transgression of enormous magnitude, because, apart from any intrinsic revulsion at its content, it struck at the heart of the postwar Austrian identity. Haider was condemned by politicians across the political spectrum (including Waldheim), and, although he offered an ambiguous retraction of sorts, he was forced to resign as governor after the Socialist and People's Party fractions in the Carinthian provincial assembly approved a motion of no confidence. Zernatto was elected governor with the support of the SPÖ, even though Zernatto's party was the smallest in the assembly. Haider, in turn, announced the end of the government coalition with the ÖVP. In the Carinthian assembly, however, moral indignation quickly gave way to political realism. According to the Carinthian provincial constitution, seats in the government are assigned on the basis of proportional representation. As the second largest party, the FPÖ was entitled to two posts as well as to nominate one of the lieutenant governors [*stellvertretender Landeshauptmann*]. Its nominee was Jörg Haider. The ÖVP caucus did not oppose Haider's election, and he was elected with the votes of the People's Party (all SPÖ deputies left the assembly during the vote, but the remaining FPÖ and ÖVP deputies constituted a quorum). Afterwards, the Carinthian SPÖ announced that it would not bring in a second motion of no confidence against the duly elected lieutenant provincial governor Haider, since it would be defeated by the combined votes of the People's Party and the Freedom Party. Thus, the political punishment—apparently the Carinthian idea of condign—Haider suffered for his commendation of Nazi policies was his demotion from governor to lieutenant governor. Although there was some evidence from opinion polls soon after the events that Haider's political *faux pas* cost him support nationally, at least temporarily, his party's showing in more recent provincial elections, like that in Vienna in November 1991, showed that any residual negative impact his commendation of the Third Reich's "employment policies" might have had has all but disappeared. The Vienna FPÖ's crude appeals to the fears of and hostility towards foreigners gave it nearly enough votes to deny the socialists a majority of representatives in the Vienna provincial assembly (the Socialists did lose their electoral majority) for the first time since the founding of the Austrian First Republic. See *Wiener Zeitung,* 14 June 1991; *Der Standard,* 15–16 June 1991; *Profil,* 17, 21 and 28 June and 4 and 11 November 1991.

3. Quoted in *Der Standard,* 26–27 May 1990.

4. Other English renderings include "confronting the past" or even "conquering the past."

5. Theodor Adorno, for example, addressed the same issue in 1963, but called it "Aufarbeitung," roughly "dealing with." See Theodor Adorno, "Was bedeutet: Aufarbeitung der Vergangenheit," *Eingriffe: Neue kritischen Modelle* (Frankfurt am Main: Suhrkamp, 1963), p. 125.

6. Something of a minor cottage industry has developed around this issue. A collection of the most important articles which formed the original "Historikerstreit" are collected in *Historikerstreit. Die Dokumentation der Kontroverse um die Einzigartigkeit der nationalsozialistischen Judenvernichtung* 3rd edition (Munich and Zurich: Piper, 1987). See also: Hans-Ulrich Wehler, *Entsorgung der deutschen Vergangenheit? Ein polemischer Essay zum "Historikerstreit"* (Munich: C. H. Beck, 1988); Geoff Eley, "Nazism, Politics and the Image of the Past: Thoughts on the West German *Historikerstreit* 1986-1987," *Past and Present* Number 121 (November 1988), pp. 171–208; Ian Kershaw, *The Nazi Dictatorship. Problems and Perspectives of Interpretation* 2nd edition (London, New York, etc.: Edward Arnold, 1989); Charles S. Maier, *The Unmasterable Past. History, Holocaust and German National Identity* (Cambridge, Mass. and London: Harvard University Press, 1988); Michael R. Marrus, *The Holocaust in History* (New York: Meridian, 1987); Dan Diner, ed., *Ist der Nationalsozialismus Geschichte? Zu Historisierung und Historikerstreit* (Frankfurt: Fischer Taschenbuch Verlag, 1987); and for Austria in particular, F. Parkinson, ed., *Conquering the Past. Austrian Nazism Yesterday and Today* (Detroit: Wayne State University Press, 1989); see also Erika Weinzierl, "Kann Man die Vergangenheit 'bewältigen?'" *Das Jüdische Echo* Number 1, Vol. XXXV (Elul-Tischri 5747/October, 1986), pp. 75–79; and Peter Pulzer, "Vergangenheitsbewältigung," in ibid., pp. 114–117.

7. Richard Rorty, *Philosophy and the Mirror of Nature* (Oxford: Basil Blackwell, 1980).

8. See Quentin Skinner, *The Foundations of Modern Political Thought* 2 Vols. (Cambridge: Cambridge University Press, 1978); see also idem, "Some Problems in the analysis of political thought and action"; idem, "A reply to my critics"; and James Tully, "The Pen is a mighty sword: Quentin Skinner's analysis of politics," in James Tully, ed., *Meaning and Context. Quentin Skinner and his Critics* (Cambridge: Polity Press, 1988). See also John Dunn, "Practicing History and Social Science on 'Realist' Assumptions," in Christopher Kookway and Philip Pettit, eds., *Action and Interpretation: studies in the philosophy of the social sciences* (Cambridge: Cambridge University Press, 1978), pp. 145–175.

9. *Historikerstreit*, p. 36.

10. Kershaw, *Nazi Dictatorship*, p. 181.

11. Ibid., p 170.

12. Richard Evans, "The New Nationalism and the Old History," quoted in ibid, p. 170.

13. Robert E. Herzstein, *Waldheim. The Missing Years* (London: Grafton Books, 1988), p. 121.

14. Ibid., p. 122.

15. Hanspeter Born, *Für die Richtigkeit. Kurt Waldheim* (Munich: Schneekluth, 1987) pp. 117-118.

16. See Hans Kurz, James Collins, Jean Vanwelkenheuzen, Gerald Fleming, Hagen Fleischer, Jehuda Wallach and Manfred Messerschmidt, *Der Bericht der internationalen Historikerkommission*, Manuscript, 202 pp. plus addenda, Vienna, 1988 (printed as supplement in *Profil*, 15 February 1988), pp. 26–27.

17. See Richard Mitten, "L'affaire Waldheim," *Times Literary Supplement*, 7–13 October 1988, p. 1120.

18. *NYT*, 5 February 1988.

19. One must admire Herzstein's public relations acumen even if one must simultaneously lament the gullibility of some journalists. As we have seen, the document in question was discussed and the relevant passage quoted on page 117 of Hanspeter Born's book, *Für die Richtigkeit, Kurt Waldheim,* which had been available since November 1987.

20. *NKZ,* 6 February 1988.

21. See, for example, William Korey, *Glasnost and Soviet Anti-Semitism,* and David A. Jodice, *United Germany and Jewish Concerns. Attitudes Toward Jews, Israel, and the Holocaust,* both in the series "Working Papers on Contemporary Anti-Semitism"(New York: American Jewish Committee, 1991); Soviet Center for Public Opinion and Market Research, Moscow, "Attitudes toward Jews in the Soviet Union: A National Survey," Ms. (Moscow: October, 1990).

About the Book and Author

Ludwig Wittgenstein once remarked, "I think the good in Austria is particularly difficult to understand. In a certain sense it is more subtle than all the rest, and its truth is never on the side of probability." For forty years official Austria, christened by the Allies as Hitler's first "victim," wagered that the sedulously cultivated visions of cherubic choir boys, Lippizaner horses, and Mozartkugels could seduce the world into ignoring another truth about Austria, that of Wehrmacht soldiers, antisemitic slurs, and cheering crowds on Heldenplatz. The debate surrounding Kurt Waldheim dashed such "improbable" illusions permanently.

Richard Mitten seeks to discover the "truth" behind the Waldheim controversy in its historical and political context. Whereas other books have focused on Waldheim's personal biography, Mitten argues that the essential point in the Waldheim affair is not Waldheim himself but the political and cultural climate that made his election possible. Mitten examines Waldheim's 1986 presidential election campaign, which both elicited and profited from profound chauvinistic and antisemitic resentments. *The Politics of Antisemitic Prejudice* is also the first book in English to study the dynamics of the Waldheim affair in the Austrian and American media. The author demonstrates how mistaken perceptions led both Waldheim's supporters and his critics to press their nearly diametrically opposed convictions with an identical moral vocabulary. Finally, Mitten re-examines the debate over Waldheim's criminality and suggests that the former UN Secretary General has come to stand as the symbol of a more general postwar unwillingness or inability to adequately confront the implications of the Nazi abomination.

Richard Mitten is a historian living in Vienna. He holds degrees in history and sociology from Columbia University and the universities of Cambridge and Vienna. He worked as a researcher for the Thames Television–Home Box Office production "Kurt Waldheim: A Commission of Inquiry" and is coauthor of *Wir sind alle unschuldige Täter!: Studien zum Nachkriegsantisemitismus* (1990).

UMASS Dartmouth
3 2922 00356 559 2

0813376300